THE
TERRIBLE
BEAUTY
OF THE
EVIL MAN

THE
TERRIBLE
BEAUTY
OF THE
EVIL MAN

*This
is the
smoke
of the
moon*

the poetry of saudade

FINIS LEAVELL BEAUCHAMP

ISBN: 978-0692237885

Cover design by Emily Mahon
Image credit re_bekka/shutterstock.com

Published & Distributed by
Finis Coronat Opus
www.finisleavellbeauchamp.com

Quotations in this book should not be taken to represent the exact words that emerged from the mouths of the various characters. While the author believes that in many cases he does remember these quotations verbatim, it is important to note that these pages are not the transcribed interviews of a journalist. The author's mind is not a perfect compendium of stenographic recordings of conversations that occurred years in the past. It is possible that one or more characters will remember their words or actions differently than the way they are depicted in this book. Yet the author maintains that the events, conversations, and psychological states of the characters depicted (including his own) do very accurately represent the truth about these events as *he* remembers them. The author has in no way deviated from what he believes to be the true depiction of these events and conversations as they occurred, other than to format them for presentation in a narrative work. No events, conversations, or situations depicted in this book are intended to be gratuitous. The events described are included in this work for the purpose of granting the reader insight into the psychological and philosophical development of the author, as well as to address issues of broader social import, through the medium of prose as a poetic art.

In some cases the names of the characters in this book have been changed. Concerning those cases in which a character's name does not appear to be name of that person in reality, the author recommends that you, in reference to said proper name, consult the *Oxford English Dictionary*.

I extend great thanks to Alec Goldstein for his assistance in copyediting, proofreading, and typesetting the manuscript, as well as for the many other ways he has assisted me in delivering this book to the public.

This book is dedicated to all those evil ones who came before me—those burned at the stake, and those eradicated through other grotesqueries, spirits murdered long before their bodies were destroyed—whose stories were never told, and whose beauty is forgotten. I sing now, in praise of you.

The great epochs of our life come when we gain the courage to rechristen our evil as what is best in us.

— *Beyond Good and Evil*, 116

VOLUME I

Book I

1.

Men call Evil neither more nor less than that which they *fear*.

2.

I would lie awake at night and feel them move inside me. They roiled in my childish body, whispering to me, licking and tickling my virgin soul with their exhilarating blasphemies. They terrified me, though I knew my mother feared them more. She would look into my eyes and see them, see what they were doing to me. She could gaze into my dilated pupils and speak to them.

She spoke to me as well, but I knew when she looked past me, spoke only to them. When she saw through me and spoke they woke and began to dance. My blood quickened and I would inhale and feel as though I were flying. Pure joy shot through me and suffused my boyish brain. She knew when this happened, and would shake my elated body and begin to shout at them, to command them in a name not her own.

And I? I sank away, sank into a dark place where I would not be forced to stand between her and them. But she knew best, as mothers always do. She knew exactly what had happened to me. I was nine, perhaps ten years old, and I was possessed by demons.

3.

I was so young when they took me, a mere boy when they sat me in the chair. I remember sitting in a chair that was far too large, wondering why the room was dim even as the sun shone bright in the Texas morning. The room exuded gloom and men milled and my father stood behind them and watched. I do not remember *Him*, the lines of his face, or the coloring of his skin and hair. But I do remember his smell. He leaned down and put his hands on either side of my face, his mouth an inch from mine, and stared into my eyes. His breath was heavy with rich cinnamon, and his neck and wrists were scented strongly with what I remember as a combination of cedar and musk.

It is as though a man on the battlefield, safely ensconced in his barricaded trench, has been ordered to leap forth, to make the charge that will surely cost him his life. And as he takes that first bound over the wall of his trench, into what will undoubtedly be a fine rain of silvery shrapnel, he smiles, laughs even, as his attention is absurdly thrown away for an overlong eternal instant to a delicate and quite lost butterfly whose lazy pirouettes draw him away from his impending demise and toward the interplay of yellows and reds etched lightly onto its wings.

In just this way my attention was cast far from the demonic activity corroding my soul, from what was about to happen, and I noticed only that this *exorcist*, with his hands swallowing my face, his mouth an inch from my own, had surprisingly strong cinnamon on his breath. And that was when I began to laugh.

4.

The distraction of that man's breath freed my mind for a lone moment from the terror that I felt. My body shrugged, and I suddenly exhaled laughter. In the midst of that morbid room I could think only of how spicy was the cinnamon flooding my nostrils.

I was horrified that I had laughed, and glanced at the men in the room. I tried to choke back any sound rising in my throat. The exorcist grinned.

"It's ok," he said. "They *know* why you're here," he said, pointing to the bellicose demons inhabiting my breast. "And the Devil is a mocker."

He moved his mouth from in front of mine to my ear. His hands migrated to the top of my head, and he began to whisper incoherent gurgling syllables occasionally interspersed with glottal explosions and the name *Jesus*. He was praying in tongues.

Tongues are, according to the Apostle Paul, a spiritual gift given by the Holy Spirit to an elect few. This man, no tyro in this arcane science, began to speak earnestly and eloquently to the dark beings in either their own language or a heavenly tongue that would frighten them. The other men in the room, rustic country squires all, shuffled nervously in their cowboy boots as the work of God began in earnest.

This nonsensical speech, whispered more and more rapidly into my ear, twinned with the spiciness of this man's breath, and flanked by the awkward movements and frightened eyes of the hardened cowboys in the room, caused my timorous chuckling to abruptly become raucous laughter. The man stopped quickly, looked into my eyes, as though he were a doctor noting an unexpected development on the surgical table, and then resumed his holy mumbling with urgency.

His hands came down hard on my head and the mystical logorrhea tumbling from his lips evolved into a ferocity of sound. My whole being contracted until I became little more than a petrified hysterical laugh that strove with his voice for dominance in the room.

And was I wrong to do so? How could I have known what to do? I was only a boy, and was simultaneously struck with both the terror and absurdity of the proceedings. You may read these lines with a simpering smirk and ask how any man, even a boy, can suppose he is possessed by demons. But I ask you, dear friend, how could I have known I was *not*?

5.

Though I was in Texas when this man grappled with the demons manipulating my soul, I am a child of the Deep South, over-hot lands where it is *my* forefathers who, for generations, have manipulated the souls of others. I am the son of an Evangelical pastor, as is my credulous mother.

Her father, Landrum Pinson Leavell II, was so potent a spiritual leader, so melliloquent a sermonizer, both forcefully erudite and intellectually creative, that over his career he was elected president and later president emeritus of one of the largest Christian seminaries in the world, as well as first vice president of the Southern Baptist Convention (the largest Protestant denomination in North America), president of the Southern Baptist Convention's Pastors' Conference, and president of the Baptist General Convention of Texas. From these executive positions, from his fourteen theological works, and through the Leavell College, his metaphysical pronouncements trickled down to many millions of souls.

But even he was not the first in his line to call down on men from hard wooden pulpits. His father too was a pastor, one of nine brothers, eight of whom became full-time pastors or missionaries. They were the nine Leavell brothers of Oxford, Mississippi, the sons of George Washington Leavell, and though they did not found the Southern Baptist Convention, they are largely responsible for building it.

They were friends with Faulkner there, one of them his tutor, though they were stern and hard and abstinent in a way that he never could have been. They were the grandchildren of a slave and plantation owner who was the fifth-generation descendant of John LaVelle, a Huguenot, and the first of that line to reach American shores. Their mother was a descendant of the Balls of Virginia, and through her I am seven generations directly removed, through a line of descendents bearing his name, from Colonel William Ball, of the Millenbeck plantation, great-grandsire of George Washington, father to our nation.

These nine brothers were rigid, driven, puritanical, and merciless towards themselves. They would occupy or found almost every significant position of power within the largest Protestant body in America, and would ruthlessly build the world that my grandfather and men like him would sit astride, the fundamentalist Evangelical world that today serves as such a force in American politics and religious life, and therefore in the essence of the West.

6.

When I was a boy I occasionally travelled with my parents as my father brought revival to far-flung outposts of the Empire. Those were his first tentative steps to establish himself, under his own name, in the world of his father-in-law. On the weekend he pastored a small church in a suburb of Baton Rouge, and during much of the week worked on his doctorate under my grandfather's aegis at the seminary in New Orleans. While in New Orleans I was the eldest grandchild of the premier minister for hundreds of miles. But I was generally shielded from all that, safely tucked away in my grandparents' white-columned mansion as my father went to class. It was on those roving evangelical missions that I first glimpsed, and only gradually understood, how others saw me.

It was not the children, but rather the adults who looked at me with that strange gleam in their eyes. There was something maniacal, or millenarian, in that look, as though all the world around us were collapsing into chaotic debauchery, and we, the Born Again believers, were the last holdouts, the last crumbling wall before the arrival of the Antichrist. And I? I was heir to the great princes of our faith, the one predicted to rise to my grandfather's place. And it was whispered in my ear by my mother, and teachers, and even by strangers on those trips, that no, I would not take his place, I would be far greater than he. I would be the last hero of our faith, one sent by God to gather up the last souls before the judgment. And I was slapped by this Apocalyptic gaze as a boy, and I understood it, for there was something queer about me as a child, something not easily thumbed by the adults around me, something that caused them to exaggerate whatever predications they might have made about me based on Brahmin lineage alone. I was a very *different* child.

7.

"When you were a boy you could solve puzzles," my mother mouthed.

I was in my mid-twenties and had just asked her if she believed that there was something unusual about me as a boy that was *not* related to spirituality.

"What? What does that mean? Everyone solves puzzles."

"Yes, but you were very young."

"How young?"

"Eighteen months."

"There are puzzles made for babies. Why is that unusual?"

"Well you did them all. We had to get you puzzles for the three-year-olds."

"I was a year or two ahead of myself. So what?"

"Well you did those too. I got you the puzzles for the five-year-olds. You only needed to look at them one time to solve them. I had to keep buying them. It wasn't the same with your younger siblings. They had to look at the pieces one at a time and try them in different ways over and over to put the puzzles together. You would see the puzzle complete in your head and put it together on the first attempt."

"So you got me puzzles for seven-year-olds, for adults?"

"No, no."
"Why not?"
"It was just too *strange.*"

8.

Puzzle-solving becomes Evil, the basis for fear, when combined with the will to power, and applied to other humans.

9.

It is not unusual for small boys to tease small girls and vice-versa. But when I was a boy I decided that flinging roly-polys at the girls was simply insufficient. One fine morning in preschool I formed up my male schoolmates on the playground to discuss strategy and tactics. I spent several days drilling them thoroughly. At the end of that time I armed my coevals with the plastic-ware of the play kitchen set in the preschool common room, and then led my militia in a vicious attack on the girls. Carnage ensued. I was four years old.

10.

Demons pervade the New Testament. Jesus and his disciples seemed to find them in others as frequently as we encounter the common cold. And until the development of modern medicine and psychiatry, even the most profound intellectuals of the West were convinced of their existence. How else would *you* have explained a tonic-clonic seizure, schizophrenic delusions, or dissociative identities, prior to the advent of modern medicine?

In the Evangelical world today they do not believe that the sermons and stories in the New Testament constitute mere ethical treatises, or are a grand metaphor, or a *symbol* for anything. To many millions, in the greatest republic of the West, at the height of human civilization, demons truly exist as maleficent metaphysical entities, and are very much involved in the affairs of the material world, as well as in the choices, both major and minor, of its denizens. They are believed to be capable and desirous of literally occupying the soul of a human being, and thereby controlling their behavior and actions.

And this is the world I inhabited, the worldview that suffused the air I breathed. I did not know a single person who did *not* believe this. I would have been shielded from any non-believer, quarantined from any skepticism.

And so when my mother grew more and more concerned by my behavior, at my ability to evade the rules and strictures imposed by the adults in my life using strategies, and puzzle-solving abilities that even they would not have considered, that no child should have formulated, she came to believe that there was no other possible explanation. I was undoubtedly possessed by demons.

11.

There was a deep dualism in my mother's view of me. When my mind, my talents, ran to overturning the rules she, or other adults, had laid down, I was possessed, not myself, acting at the behest or directly under the control of an invidious creature of Hell. But when I waxed creative on behalf of the Lord, in the cause of righteousness, perhaps with a lovely flourish in a prayer over supper, then she began to whisper in my ear, to say those things that scared me in a completely different way. I was chosen of the Lord to lead the last Christians in the End Times, for the coming of the Antichrist was imminent. And others spoke to me in this way, mysterious allusions to this theochristic fate trailing me as wisps of smoke trail a torch. Indeed, for most of my childhood many who knew me were not sure whether I was truly good or truly evil, but I knew they believed it must be one of the two.

12.

There is a majesty inherent in *expectation*. There is an awfulness in *potential*. One never is, one only will be. Their eyes fall over you, and rather than see your form, your shape, your fears and mirthful sighs, they see something else entirely. You are the shifting, ever-changing mass, but your Being, malleable and fluid, is not the thing-in-itself, is only a deception; it is the mercurial reflection of the conglomeration, the agglutination of their fear and will to power as it attaches to you. And so is it you who change, or they? When they sense change in you, perhaps it is not an alteration in you at all, but merely a vibration in the quicksand of their own soul. But they have expectation, and you have potential, and so you are only a catalyst, and therefore not really a person at all.

13.

But was I really possessed by demons? Did this man really look inside me and speak to evil sentient metaphysical entities? His hands pressed down on the mop of brown hair that graced my head, his mouth pressed against my warm earlobe, and his voice called out to *something* in me. In any event, my back immediately arched in that chair, and I shook with shouting laughter. And this was apparently all quite normal, for the man noted the development calmly.

And that was not the first time I had laughed at what was shaking in my breast. Many times as a boy I had lain in bed as the night's dark fingers encircled my little body, and had prayed, with everything in me, to Jesus, my savior.

There was a mantra I knew by heart, which I would chant in those terrible, dark hours. It was a catechism, or an algorithm, of the heart and soul, of the spirit. First, acknowledge Jesus the Christ as lord and savior of your life, including in your admission an acknowledgment of his divine birth, and his place as the only begotten son of God. Second, have faith that he died for you, and took all your sins, indeed, the sins of the whole world, upon his striped back. And in so doing he saved you, and all mankind, not only from the fires of Hell, but from an eternal alienation from God. Third, repent of all your sins, and resolve wholeheartedly never to repeat them.

And I would lie in bed, with trembling lips, and repeat the three steps over and over as weariness wrestled me down to sleep, never certain that I had gotten it quite right. Perhaps I had not meant those three points with perfect purity. Perhaps some disqualifying dross, mingled with my otherwise incontrovertible faith and belief, had tampered with the process, preventing true salvation. How could I be absolutely certain that I had perfectly carried out the acceptance of Christ as my savior, gaining admission to the Elect, joining the ranks of the Born Again? And even if I had truly gained admittance to the body of believers, I was aware, even as a tiny boy, that there was a serious theological dispute about whether one could *lose* salvation, even if once properly gained.

For if I were truly Saved, and not in danger of hellfire, then I could not possibly be possessed, for a Christian soul cannot have two masters. But if I were not possessed then why would I, on occasion, lie in my bed and shake with quiet, uproarious laughter, shivering with giggles at the thought that I was possessed by demons? Why was I so pleased at the feeling of power that gave me? Why did I enjoy the wild consternation that occasionally crossed my mother's face?

And so I lay in bed trembling, repeating my mantra night after night. I was terrified of going down to burn for eternity in Hell, and of what the demons would do once they had me. But sometimes I laughed too.

14.

"Go ahead. Go ahead and laugh them out. Laughing them out is very normal," the exorcist said as he stepped back from me and stood up straight.

He briefly glanced around the room, at the semicircle of cowboys behind him. They abruptly grew still; the creaking of their boots ceased. One of them let out a low, uncomfortable cough, the only sound in the room to match my high-pitched, hysterical laughter. Doubtless they were questioning their qualifications at that moment, wondering what life experience or spiritual trials had prepared them to assist at the exorcism of a small boy—an exorcism, that, at least at the first, did not seem to be going well. My laughter still reverberated from the walls, and the exorcist had stepped back from me.

"I once cast eighteen demons out of a girl. And she laughed out every one of 'em. Don't you doubt it. I've seen 'em laughed out before, though usually they're cried out. I even once had someone *vomit* 'em out. He vomited for hours till they were all gone."

For a moment my laughter stopped, and I gulped down air. I shivered in the chair as I thought about the possibility of vomiting out many demons. But then the man looked at me strangely, and a slight upturn returned to the corner of my mouth.

"Don't you worry. I'll get 'em all out. Don't doubt it."

He leaned back over me, and motioned for the other men to put their hands on my body. Soon I was covered in hands, and all around me tough cowboys moaned and cried out the name *Jesus*. I began to shake under their hands, and they pressed down harder. The name of the son, the carpenter, struck me forcefully, again and again, as though I were reeling under the repeated lashes of a whip. And through all of this I could only laugh and laugh as my terror at what was inside me, and the terror provoked by the possibility of eternal damnation in very literal fire, mingled together with fluid ecstasy in an unholy elixir that filled my breast.

And why did I laugh? How could I have risen on the heights, sat astride the euphoric summit? But that is so easy to know!

I was only a boy, and as I continued to laugh, the men pulled back, looking at me in fear. And what boy can make a room full of hard men, strong men, men of the soil, recoil in fear? But then they could see inside me, and they knew just how evil I was.

15.

"What is your name?" the man called out. "Tell me your name! I command it in the name of *Jesus.*"

I knew with certainty that he was not speaking to me, the child shivering in the chair, but rather to whatever was twisting and turning uncomfortably in my chest.

"I command you, not in my own name, but in the name of our Lord and Savior Jesus Christ. Tell me your name now!"

I began to feel certain that I was going to emulate the man who had vomited out his demonic horde. I made a nauseated retching sound.

"There it is! That is their name!" he shouted, turning excitedly to the men behind him. "Now we can command them."

"*Them?*" a man behind him called.

The man in front of me stepped back, never taking his eyes off me. When he had reached the semicircle of men behind him he spoke.

"Our Lord Jesus once asked a demon its name. 'Legion,' it replied, 'for we are many.' That's what we've got here. Those demons just said their name in that dark language. And let me tell you, brother," he said, as he turned to glance at the man next to him, "we've got to be careful. 'Cause there are a *lot* of demons in that boy."

16.

I was too afraid of the man to disabuse him of the notion that my nausea-induced retching was the demons' actual name. I did not want him to get it wrong, and fail to cast the demons out simply because he had gotten their name wrong, but then, I also thought that perhaps the demons might have used my nausea to force their name through my lips. When concerned that a foreign sentient entity might be in possession of your will, your ability to know if you are responsible for anything you just did diminishes greatly.

I became even more confused about the matter when the man began to make a strange whispering noise, a noise not entirely unlike the sound I had made a moment before.

"Yyyuuuhkhkhk, *in Jesus' name*, you will come out of that boy now!" the man commanded as he stepped toward me. He waved a hand to the cowboys behind him. "Gird yourselves up in the spiritual armor of the Lord, brothers, because when those demons come out of that boy they're going to be looking for a new home. And that means whoever is nearest. If there's a demon of lust in that boy then it will come after someone whose spiritual condition is deteriorated by that same lust. The same goes for theft or anger or bitterness. So if you have any unresolved sins whatsoever that you didn't clear up earlier at our prayer meeting, you better do it now. You're going to need your Shield of Faith today. 'Cause when those demons come out of this boy they're going to be *angry*."

The look of sudden fear that slipped over the faces of the men in the room caused me to laugh so hard that I nearly slipped from the chair. But every moment or so, when I could catch my breath, I cried out with true terror.

"Don't let them get me!" I wailed. But then the reactions this cry provoked, and the unbearably tense emotion in the room, caused me to laugh again, as my little body attempted to expel its fear.

"There is a tremendous level of demonic activity in this room," the man said as he glanced around. He said it as calmly as though he were a meteorologist noting a sudden shift in the barometric pressure. "I've never seen such a concentration of the demonic presence," he said as the men behind him whispered feverish prayers. "You come from a family of great spiritual leaders," he said as he knelt down and looked into my eyes, "and the Devil really *wants* you."

17.

The Southern Baptist Convention, with some sixteen million members, and more than forty thousand congregations, is the largest Protestant denomination in America. Throughout the twentieth century it was the largest single bloc in the Baptist World Alliance, a colossal superstructure of faith with tens of millions of adherents worldwide. The Leavell family, my mother's family, is widely considered to have been the single most influential family in the Convention over the course of the twentieth century.

Leading this movement in the first half of the twentieth century was my great-grandfather, Leonard O. Leavell, and his eight brothers—the half-century when the Convention experienced nearly impossible growth rates. Together the Leavell brothers would hold many of the most powerful positions of executive and theological leadership in both the Convention, and the Baptist World Alliance. Between them they authored dozens of theological books, manuals, and articles which served to equip the many thousands of zealous missionaries who ventured out of the rustic Deep South, bringing Christ's message to the world's heathen masses.

But they were not only scholars and orators, they were gifted administrators and hands-on evangelists as well—a rare combination. The Leavell brothers would engineer, retool, or simply invent many of the sophisticated internal institutions that would allow for the explosive growth in the denomination over the century. Everything from the direction of seminaries to missionary training to childhood education and indoctrination fell under their purlieus.

When the first of the nine Leavell brothers, Landrum Pinson Leavell I, began preaching at the start of the twentieth century, there were perhaps one-and-a-half million Southern Baptists, concentrated almost wholly in the impoverished, rural South. Less than a century later, when his nephew, my grandfather, Landrum Pinson Leavell II, retired as president emeritus of one of the largest seminaries in the world, the Southern Baptist Convention had metastasized into a multinational conglomerate with well over fifteen million members.

When people talk about the rise of the Evangelical world, in truth, they are talking about my family.

18.

My father was raised in tremendous poverty, under horrid circumstances that no person should ever know. But despite this, for some reason known only to him and the angels, he came, as a young adolescent, to believe that the Lord Almighty was calling him to a life of Christian service. He had met my mother's father when my grandfather was the pastor of First Baptist Church, Wichita Falls, Texas, at the time one of the half-dozen largest churches in the nation, and a prototype for the megachurch of today. After my father completed his undergraduate education at Baylor, the Baptist university of Texas, he followed my mother's father to New Orleans, where my grandfather had since assumed the presidency of the New Orleans Baptist Theological Seminary. Despite the profound poverty and misery of his childhood my father went on to earn a doctorate in theology. He also married the president's only daughter.

19.

There is a year I remember, as I sat through junior high school, when my father was serving as the pastor of a large church, in which, despite his official obligations, he found time to personally lead one hundred and twenty individuals to the belief that Jesus is the divine son of God, as well as to the act of baptism, and to membership in our church. I remember him dunking up to a dozen people in the baptistery on any given Sunday that year. No one in the church had ever seen anything like it.

I look back on this today, and am still amazed. Virtually every third day for an entire year he single-handedly convinced a unique person to make a life-altering metaphysical decision, and further, convinced them to make a public declaration of that fact before a congregation of hundreds of strangers. The following year was a disappointment—he procured a mere eighty souls.

But how does one do it? How does one *sell* Jesus so efficiently? How does one pick off discrete souls so rapidly?

To this day I do not know, though I am the product on both sides of some of the finest eternity-salesmen the South has ever produced.

"Afraid of Hell? Call us!"

20.

Did the Devil want me that badly? Was I really so valuable a prize for the enemies of God? One thing that had always confused me, even as a small boy, was that if the Devil had only been able to persuade a third of the angels in Heaven to revolt, then why were Evil and Wickedness everywhere on the ascent? If the demonic hordes were outnumbered two to one, why have Christians always complained that Man is continually sliding toward darkness? And if the Devil's forces really were stretched so thin, how could he afford to stuff an entire legion of his troops into a single man, or in my case, a single boy?

21.

It is quite obvious that a young boy, told repeatedly that he is evil, will in fact come to believe what he is told. We need not delve into such an obvious psychological pattern. It requires no explication. Though perhaps it *is* strange that the boy would grow to love that moniker, that identity. But to relish evil is to reflexively feel a certitude about the permissibility of employing fear to manipulate others. And such an ease and fluidity in the handling of fear, and yes, even an enjoyment of it, can arise only when one *despises* humankind. And there are only a smattering of situations capable of causing a small boy to view others in this way. A deeply pessimistic dichotomy was required.

22.

"You are both a danger to mankind and its last, best hope."

"Why then," I would ask, "should Man be saved? How pitiful a creature, that, throughout the ages, he is bandied about by the choices of a few dynamic individuals. What frailty!"

"It is the will of God. For though we are flawed, He is merciful, and loving. He pours out His Spirit where He will."

"His love is strange."

"His love is perfect. Our perception is distorted."

"Yes," I would say, "our perception is unclear, because it seems that Satan is much stronger."

"He is the Father of Lies."

"His lies are sweet."

"He is *Evil*."

"Then let Evil win!"

23.

He returned to me, as he has returned to me in my dreams these many years. He stepped back to me, and the others followed him noiselessly. Their hands fell onto my body—rough calluses draped over smooth skin. And it was then, as I remember it, that the prayers rose and dipped in an irregular ellipse of sound around me. I closed my eyes, and the sight of the pearl-buttoned western shirts and handlebar mustaches disappeared, replaced in my sensory perception by the smell of leather and aftershave and that intangible smell of the awareness of danger, which is so difficult for us to define, but is so pronounced to the lower mammals.

And all of us, me included, strove forward to our Lord, our sole goal the elimination of the incredible darkness inside me. However my drive to strive for goodness and purity was again corrupted, and the old rebelliousness rumbled within me, compounded and magnified by a recurring awareness of the otherworldliness of the proceedings.

Then I sighed in despair, for I sensed, even as a boy, that the problem I faced was intractable, and that so long as I lived, I would never be free of it. Most are broken by life, and for those that are not, there are myriad ways to break themselves. And I now know, as an adult, of the fasting and ablutions, the flagellations, the incredible and varied forms of extreme abstinence, that many of the highest men have used to break and re-break themselves, to crush whatever terrible excess of spirit God cursed them with. But that is the road to either sainthood or madness, and I knew nothing of that then.

I sat in the hard chair, my eyes tightly pressed shut, and looked into myself. And as the exorcist pressed down hard on my head, as the moaning and muttering, the exclamations and exhortations, grew and then rose, before faltering in a dénouement that was certainly only a prelude to the final crescendo, I felt the frustration inside me grow, and suddenly even the thought of laughter filled me with horror. I grew aware of how deeply disturbing was the perversity of that spiritual pederasty, and my fear of the demonic was suddenly superseded by my fear of the men pressing hands down all over my body. And so I shouted.

"Stop! Now! I want to stop."

The men hesitated, and glanced to their leader. He quickly paused. His mouth twitched as he thought.

"Please," I cried, glancing for the first time to my father, hidden the entire time in the back of the room. "Please make them stop."

The Man of Light, the golden one, the great exorcist, stepped back from his duel with the forces of darkness and stared at my father. He looked around quickly at the men in the room, and then faced me once more. Suddenly, his shoulders slumped and his posture grew lax. He sighed.

"Men, the Devil is strong. We must be stronger. Our Lord, Jesus, was once asked by his disciples why they could not drive out a certain demon, while He was able to send it out with ease. There is more than one kind of demon, He reminded them. There are those who may be sent out with prayer alone, but then there is a far more hideous type of dark creature, one that may only be cast out with both prayer and fasting. That, gentlemen, is what we have here."

And so the siege ended. My father scooped me up, though I could not move for long moments after the supporting cast had departed. The exorcist stayed for some time, speaking to my father and eyeing me warily. They agreed to meet again soon to continue the exorcism, though my father never brought me back.

I, now, pity my father, and so I must believe that he, then, pitied me.

24.

But no, all of this is only impressionism in prose, and I write in riddles. I must tell you more. I will show you the cultivation of the Evil Man.

Book II

25.

I once heard the story of a man who went to hike in the wilderness. He was of middle age, tall, thin, perhaps even gaunt, and with the perpetually unshaven look of a man who has never worked in an office. He drove away from his home in the suburbs on an autumnal Friday morning in his old, frequently repaired light blue pickup truck, and, after several hours, arrived at the edge of the woodlands. He pulled on his sturdy, worn rucksack, grabbed his walking stick from the bed of the truck, and began what he hoped would be a much needed rustic two-day jaunt away from wife, work, daughters, and the repetitiveness of his daily life.

He had not previously been to that reserve, and as he walked he sought the signs, periodically placed, with which reserves are usually marked to guide hikers. However there were no trails in those woods, nor even the occasional litter and bric-a-brac that inevitably accumulate under the weight of repeated visitation. And even the signs, strings, and paint frequently used to mark safe hiking were missing, giving the wood an ancient virginity he found delightful. Regardless, he knew that, with his compass and astronomical knowledge, he would not become easily lost, and so he went to sleep that first night, miles from any semblance of the modern world, and breathed easily for the first time in some months.

The next morning he awoke with an intense headache, and could find neither his pack, nor his compass, nor his walking stick. Assuming that he had been robbed, he wandered off in the direction he thought the most certain way back to his truck. However the wood seemed quite different, and he circled through dense patches of unfamiliar foliage for hours before he sat down to rest. His head still hurting, he determined to wait for nightfall, and to pick his way through the forest by aid of the stars.

He dozed for some hours, awakening in that rare moment which captures the infinitesimal demarcation of night and day. His head hurt less, and he looked up hurriedly, to catch sight of the first stars. However, it seemed the trees had grown as he dozed, and his vision was unable to pierce the tangled crown of foliage as the last of the day's light glanced from its intersecting boughs.

He stood in frustration, determined to find some gap in the treetops, but as he stood he gasped, for he noticed, some thirty meters away, a very old man sitting motionless atop a large rock, staring down at a quickly churning brook that passed under the rock on which he sat.

The wanderer, dizzy from his rapid rise, and jolted by the presence of another person in those empty miles of wilderness, called out loudly in the old man's direction, but the old man did not turn toward him. The wanderer quickly made his way to the brook, standing at the edge of the water directly across from the point where the old man sat atop the rock.

"I say, hello!"

The old man lifted his gaze to the wanderer, who was shocked to see that the older man's eyes were completely white. The older man remained silent, despite having looked toward the young man, so the wanderer tried again.

"Hello! Can you hear me? I am very lost and need assistance!"

"You are lost," the old man repeated quietly. His voiced croaked and was hoarse, as though he had not spoken in a long time.

"Yes, I'm lost. I've been robbed, I believe. I was hiking in the forest and slept here last night. When I awoke I found that my staff, compass, and pack were gone, and my head hurts terribly. Can you help me? Do you know how to get back to the edge of the forest, to a road?"

"I don't know if I can help you," the old man said slowly, as he stroked the wispy hairs of an aged beard. "You are very lost."

"If I could find my compass and other stuff I would be fine. I can't yet go by the stars. They're not fully out. Don't you know the way out of here?"

The old man ignored him for a moment before replying.

"You say that a staff, compass, and pack are lost. But it is not they who are lost. It is *you* who are lost," the old man replied.

It was at this moment, in the deepening twilight, that the wanderer began to feel that the absence of light was playing tricks with his visual perception of the old man. He decided that the old man was senile, but even as he formed that judgment he realized his view of the old man had grown hazy, and noticed that the stranger's clothing was only tattered rags, and that he was staring back at him with large, white, blind eyes which seemed to glow in the fleeing light. Ignoring what he assumed was the disorientation provoked by the strange light, his headache, and the unusual situation, the wanderer quickly replied.

"Yes, of course I'm lost, but with my gear I wouldn't be. Can you please tell me the way to the edge of the forest?"

"How would a staff help you find your way?"

"I don't need the staff, it's just steadies me as I walk. I need the pack and compass!"

"What is in the pack, that it will allow you to discover where you are?"

"Food, water, essentials. How else do you think people trek through the woods for days at a time? And anyway, where are *your* supplies? How did you get this far out?"

"There is nothing you have described that you cannot find in the forest. And anyway, the pack would never help you to find where you are."

"Well!" the wanderer shouted, at that point frustrated, "at least the compass would, and I have to get home! I have a wife and two daughters."

And then, strangely, the old man seemed to shimmer. He grew younger in appearance. His beard grew dark and full. The irises in his eyes slowly and subtly shifted to a deep blue. The wanderer became frightened and backed away.

"What's this? What's going on? Who are you?" he cried in fear.

"You are lost, have no idea where you are or where you are going, and yet right now the only thing that occupies your mind is a concern about my identity—however my identity shifts constantly depending on which moment in time you know me... as does yours," the older man rumbled with amusement, his voice suddenly deep and strong.

"Please, please just help me. I think there's something wrong with me. I have a wife and kids. I need to get back!"

The old man, now young and hale, moved from the rock, and without any discernible motion, appeared next to the shaking wanderer. The wanderer stepped back, startled and frightened.

"Where will you go if you do not already know where you are?" the stranger replied.

"I need to get to my truck. I'm going home, to my wife and kids. I'm lost!"

"Indeed, you are lost. For you believe that you have entered a forest, and are trapped. And, moreover, you believe that you have a wife, and children. Tell me," the old man smiled as he leaned in close to the shivering wanderer, "what is a forest? What is a truck? Are you certain you have a wife and children?" the stranger asked.

"What?" the wanderer nearly screamed, stepping back from the stranger, "Are you mad? Of course I have. I've been married for…." the wanderer said as he shook his head, faltering. "Why I've been married to her for years. And we have children. Daughters!"

"What is your wife's name?" the old man asked calmly. "What are the names of your daughters?"

"What kind of question is that? Who wouldn't know his wife's name? Her name is…."

And then the wanderer grew quiet. All thought ceased and he felt terror. He realized that he did not remember his wife's name, and that the harder he tried to regain the memory of her name, the more quickly all other details about her slipped from his mind.

"What's going on?" yelled the wanderer. "What are you doing to me?"

"You?" the stranger queried with surprise. "I have done nothing to you. *You do not even know who you are.*"

The wanderer panicked, and fell to the ground, as he realized that he could not, at that moment, recall his own name.

"Please help me," he cried to the stranger. "I have a staff, and a pack, and a compass. I know that. If I can just get them back I can go!"

"A staff," replied the stranger, "is nothing but a crutch, and you are physically healthy. You do not need it. In truth, a crutch only weakens. You have a pack," the stranger continued, "but it is unnecessary. Do you think you are in danger of starvation?"

"That's… that's not the point" the wanderer stammered. "Just the compass then. Give me the compass, and I can get out of this forest."

"A compass would do you no good, I'm afraid," replied the stranger.

"What? Yes! Do you have it? Do you have one?"

"A compass only points a direction, and you have no way of knowing which direction you should take."

"I'll go back the way I came!" the wanderer shouted.

"Ah, you poor man, you think you came here," the stranger sighed. "But you didn't. *You have always been here.*"

"What? Are you crazy? I came here in a truck and have a family and I want to go home."

"So you say. But I know of no truck, and you can't remember your family, or even who you are. And as you can see, *there is no forest.*"

The wanderer looked around and realized that there were no trees, rocks, or rivers anywhere in his vicinity. The sound of crickets and the rush of the brook had disappeared and had been replaced by silence. His sensory organs, using the conduit of the synaptic electrical activity in his brain, having just been used to transform raw sensory data into the perceptions and images of trees, wind, and water, were now imbibing nothing whatsoever but an awareness of his own presence and the presence of the man who seemed to glow more intensely with each passing moment. In the absence of all normative sensory input, other than the man across from him, his own Being, and the knowledge that his heart was now beating quickly enough to burst, it was several moments before he could stammer out.

"Please sir, just tell me what this is! Am I alive?"

"Do you feel alive?"

"I can feel myself, if that's what you mean, but this is not Life."

"What is the life you know?"

"I don't know! Stuff! My family! Going to work! All the things I remember."

"Your entire life is reducible to possessions and relationships and memories?"

"Yes! Those things are my things! Those are my life!"

"Perhaps some of them having meaning, insofar as they change *you*, but when you mentioned that which encompassed your life you did not speak of courage or fortitude or faith or compassion or love."

"I have those things too!"

"You have them as a cripple has legs. If you had them you would not feel as you do now. Now you seek nothing more than a return to the courtyard."

"The courtyard?"

"What you call the world. It is only a courtyard, a vestibule, a foyer. In truth, it is a *nothingness*, merely a place to prepare. In the sense of what *does* exist, the courtyard does not exist at all. As you see, your wife, your daughters, even the forest in which you stood, have all easily disappeared."

"Prepare for what? If this isn't real then what is?"

"What is on the *other side*."

"Please! Send me back," the wanderer screamed.

"You wish to return to the nothingness designed only to prepare you for what is real?" the stranger asked.

"Please! More than anything!"

"And that is your Age," the stranger sighed. "If only you had the slightest conception of the true nature of reality, every one of your actions would be different. But you are addicted to illusion."

26.

"This world isn't the real world," my father said, staring at me intently. I was three years old, and my feet dangled from my chair at the kitchen table in our home. We were less than a block from the Mississippi River, just outside Baton Rouge. Upon receipt of this news I looked dubiously over to my brother Andrew, eighteen months my junior, proudly riding his high-chair, baby-food-paste gloriously splattered across his face like a Jackson Pollack.

"Everything you do here is preparation for Heaven. And if you don't do right then you go to Hell. Now tell me, what is Hell?"

"It's where you go if you don't do good here," I replied calmly.

"Wrong!" my father retorted, "Hell is where you go if you don't accept Jesus. You don't get into Heaven for doing good. It's not by actions, but by faith in our Lord Jesus Christ that we're saved."

"So why do I have to do good things?" I responded logically.

"You have to do good things because Jesus wants you to."

"But if I don't do good I still won't go to Hell—if I believe in Jesus?"

My father looked at me curiously, momentarily silenced, undoubtedly pondering why a three-year-old would choose that initial line of questioning as opposed to all others.

"Well if you don't do good things you don't really believe in Jesus, because Jesus wants you to do good things."

"Right, but I still won't go to Hell. I just have to believe in Jesus, then I get to go to Heaven? Because *I already believe in Jesus*. So I'm going to Heaven!"

"You're not understanding what I'm trying to tell you," my father responded slowly. "*This world is not real.* Nothing going on here is real. Everything you think you see and feel is just here to help you understand the beauty and glory of our Lord Jesus. This world is only a test. It's where you prepare for Heaven. Now if you didn't do good, and did bad instead, then that shows that you didn't really believe in Jesus. Then you wouldn't go to Heaven."

As I processed this rebuttal I stared numbly down at the plate before me on the wooden kitchen table.

"Nothing is real? The world isn't real?"

"That's right, son."

"Then tonight I don't want any vegetables."

27.

But did the Christians, and not only the Christians, but the Muslims, Buddhists, Hindus, and every other feverishly convicted legation to revel in certitude beneath the corona *really* come to reject this life, to denigrate it as an ornate but quite deceptive vestibule, because they guilelessly truly in the gulleys of their hearts thought that nothing mattered here except insofar as we were able to prepare for a World beyond this World—one that none of us knew in any way about how to think or feel or imagine or even dream?

But billions today *do* believe that!

28.

An alternate solution: The Christians, and the international complex of mutually exclusive fideist hordes that mimic them, are no more convinced that this world is but a preparation for the next, that indeed this is only a dream before waking life, than are the most arrogant of the Immoralists. Rather, not as preparation in a World-before-a-World do they act, but as a defense against the *World-within-the-World* do they live, and breathe, and move. For in their truest selves, both their tranquil quiet moments and blackest hours, they acknowledge this world as *too* real, and not at all a fit preparation for any unknowable and unproven reality, but rather they fight with every self-deceiving ebullient blood vessel to escape the World-within-the-World, which is the world of inner suffering, a daedalean locus of pain existing in us all, which is multifarious, individualized, terribly real, and found in every sentient animal.

The Christians are not *preparers*; they are anesthetists.

29.

There is, of course, an antidote to the pain of this inescapable carnal reality—to this continual flagrant impact of feet and bodies against the incorporation of insensate soil and metal that form the uncaring earth beneath us. There *is* something more than brute matter flailing endlessly against brute matter, and that is Love.

I will not speak for the fair gender, but for a man-sapling, a boy, particularly a first born, all conception of Love, and what love is, and what it might be, is formed by, and flows out through the mother, who is therefore so rightly known as the Giver of Life.

I had two mothers, and both died when I was a boy, though in very different ways, but if you are to know anything at all about a man, you must know how he loves, and therefore about how he learned to love— and, perhaps even more, you must understand how he first lost love.

30.

My first mother was my birth-mother, and her name was Ann, which means *grace*, though she was anything but graceful. She was pale and (after having me) plump, and had curly long bushy brown hair and eyes so perfectly blue that one could not help but think, after having looked into them, that one had woken from a dream in which all of the light in the dream had been refracted through the rigidly cut lines of a series of sapphires.

She gave me baths in the sink, her long curly hair falling over her shoulders towards me, which I vaguely remember, and told me that I slept upwards of twenty hours a day as an infant, and that I would never, under any circumstances, let her rock me to sleep, which I remember not at all.

I have vivid memories from extremely early ages. I am told this is unusual, but as I have never known any mind other than my own, I can only wonder at the numbness and fog that must surround most humans' early childhoods.

The Terrible Beauty of the Evil Man

My first strong, detailed memory of my mother was of her leaving me. We were still living in Baton Rouge, and she decided to attend a conference of Christian ladies meeting for prayer or some quasi-intellectual Christian venture in Dallas. My father and I drove her to the airport, which I do not remember, but I do remember the ride home, claustrophobic in a child's car seat. I stared at the departing planes for as long as I could, my little neck craned back toward the airport rapidly disappearing behind us, and I kept my face away from my father and the road ahead. But eventually the airport was no longer visible, and even the departing planes became only specks in the sky, and as I sat there, I laid my head into the side of the car seat, and wept, heartbroken.

My mother returned in a couple of days, galvanized and refreshed, but I knew that something had changed. No longer was she the inalienable rock and foundation of my existence. I now knew that she could leave me, and something as minor as that short trip changed me forever.

31.

After my childhood, throughout my youth, and into my early adulthood, I never spoke of my other mother. Neither my father, nor Ann, my birth-mother, nor my siblings, nor any friend ever knew of the relationship I had with her, though several of them knew her quite well. And the reason for that was very simple. My other mother, whose name was Elaine, and who was also very beautiful, and charming, and kind, benevolent, and far more nurturing than my birth-mother (and nurturing is, of course, the most perfect exemplum of just what mothering is), was possessed of one characteristic that made her invisible to everyone who knew her. And that peculiar trait, though such a simple thing, created so complex, though reflexive and unthinking, a reaction in everyone who saw her, that it was only I, a small child, who could see her as she truly was, and who understood that she too, was my mother. For you see, Elaine, my grandmother's maid, was black.

32.

My childhood, my real childhood, was spent between two worlds, two cultures, two mothers, though to those who have never lived in southern Louisiana those worlds may seem superficially identical. During the week I lived in Baton Rouge, the capital of Louisiana, where my father pastored his first small church while completing his doctoral work at the seminary in New Orleans. In Baton Rouge we lived in and among the Cajun bourgeoisie, a small number of whom, through terrible confusion or lapse of judgment, had converted to Protestantism. But though those Cajuns had abandoned Catholicism, they were in every other way thoroughly Cajun—which is to say that they were simultaneously possessed of the arrogance and ignorance that can only occur when one is both a redneck and a Frenchman.

The cuisine was based on the refuse of the swamp, and on rice, and sugar was the cash crop, and the food was very spicy, and everyone drank to such an excess that the Protestant minority, under the influence of my grandfather and his disciples, became rabidly prohibitionist, to the point that he could proudly proclaim to me in his old age that he had "never once touched liquor, beer, or wine!" Indeed, I cannot remember a single time when the larger family was gathered to watch a ball game on television (practically the only television, other than cartoons, that we were allowed) when the channel was not changed due to the profane appearance of a beer commercial.

So I existed in Baton Rouge for half of each week, particularly on the weekends when my father delivered his sermons, and grew up as a member of the Protestant Cajun bourgeoisie. My father presided over their Rotary Club, I played in their little leagues, went to LSU baseball games, got into fights, and climbed trees, and my mother Ann took care of me, cooked dinner every night, did my laundry, and it was all very suburban.

Had it not been for that other world, I might have come to believe that my life in Baton Rouge was the only world, the world of my family from time eternal. But that was decidedly not our world. We were not Cajun, and we certainly were not members of the lower bourgeoisie. But I would not have known any of that but for our weekly treks to our other lives in New Orleans.

33.

It is difficult to depict New Orleans as it breathed and moved when I was a boy. My New Orleans was only a sliver of the larger city. Nevertheless, let me show you what I know of New Orleans as it existed at that time.

First, few of the bourgeoisie remained in the city. There were few middle-class blacks in the Deep South at that time, and the middle-class whites had fled immediately after the Civil Rights Acts, to populate a ring of suburbs surrounding the city. So the vast majority of the people in New Orleans proper during my childhood were either poor and black, or well-to-do and white. But even within these two groupings there were intense divisions. Some of the blacks were Protestant, some Catholic, some devotees of Mama Laveau's voodoo, and far too many were involved in a convoluted syncretism.

The white world was also divided, though I didn't understand that as well as a child. There was a world of ancient (not merely old) white money that had existed in and around the city for centuries—money which had been amassed in finance and land and sugar and slaves and trade on the superhighway of the Mississippi. They gathered to lunch in clubs like the Stratford, the Pickwick, and the Louisiana, and were from the aged Creole and Anglo bloodlines that celebrated Mardi Gras in the racially segregated *krewes* of Comus, Momus, and Proteus.

But my world in New Orleans was rigidly distinct from any of these others, though I was occasionally exposed to gris-gris, Tarot, and King Cake during walks through the French Quarter and French Market. New Orleans, as far as I knew, began and ended with the New Orleans Baptist Theological Seminary, which is possessed of a very large campus on the high ground in the city, is enclosed by tall brick walls, is home to thousands of students, and is guarded by diligent security patrols at all times. Years later, as a student at Ole Miss, one of my classmates, also from New Orleans, once joked that I grew up in what everyone in New Orleans knew as *Mayberry in the Ghetto*. But there was much truth in that statement, for immediately beyond the manicured lawns, lush flowing subtropical vegetation, and high walls of our theological Bastille, there existed a world of tremendous poverty and crime, of which I, as a small boy, was completely unaware.

34.

The city, as I knew it as a boy, was a place of magic, and I mean that as no metaphor. No, I am quite certain that there could not have been any place in America where more magic, necromancy, voodoo, and sorcery were practiced than in the New Orleans of my childhood. The *Li Grand Zombi*, grand serpent deity, was no symbol of evil, but rather a repository of wisdom that worked in conjunction with the voodoo queens for the good of the people.

On rare occasions my mother and grandmother would take me beyond the walls of the fortress of the seminary, and we would take the trolley down the St. Charles line to Camellia's, or go down to either Morning Call or to the French Quarter for beignets at the Café du Monde, where we would sip coffee and listen to street performers of all types, my favorite of which were the tap-dancing boys and the very talented trumpeter who played the Café du Monde every day for years.

But as we walked in the French Quarter, we walked under the shadow of the massive St. Louis Cathedral, and it was a constant reminder, one I noticed even as a small boy, that as soon as we stepped outside the walls of our principality in New Orleans, we were the tiny minority, and the city was really a very different place.

New Orleans was, as I have said, a city of magic and Catholicism, and, as I understood them as a boy, there was little difference. I asked questions, as would any inquisitive child, and was made to understand that Catholics were very misguided and prayed to Saints and dead people, conflated Mary with the Trinity, didn't believe in the Bible, and weren't Born Again. And as the tarot-card readers, psychics, actual practitioners of magic, and perverse of every sort had set up tables in the very sight of the mighty Cathedral, the entirety became jumbled together in my mind, and I understood the city only as dark, magical, mysterious, and impossibly evil. Nevertheless, to me, those things became beautiful.

35.

If, to me, the world outside the seminary was magical and permissive and evil and beautiful, the world inside the red brick walls of the seminary was austere, starkly Protestant, rigid, and frighteningly chiliastic. For the more wicked and debauched was the world outside our walls, the more vital it was not only that our tightly knit theological community was buttressed by prayer and fasting, but greater also was the demand for ideological purity and certainty. For we were living just before the deluge, which is to say, the coming of the Antichrist, and everyone knew this.

Just prior to my birth, internecine warfare had decimated the Southern Baptist Convention, with the rising tide of Secularism, particularly the great evils of Biblical Criticism, Feminism, and Liberalism, provoking a massive backlash against the Convention's moderates, and in the ensuing hieromachy many of the Convention's institutions and seminaries were purged of heretics and those of suspect faith—particularly those who denied the *inerrancy* of the Bible literally read as the word of God. But all of that was very distant to us in New Orleans. For my grandfather, who ruled the seminary with a strong hand, was the purest of the pure, both in ideology and in bloodline, and the fights which devastated the tens of thousands of congregations in the Convention largely bypassed our sacred bastion.

36.

Certainty is the great luxury of the fundamentalist, for with it his mind and body function far more efficiently, and with this additional virility he is freed to pursue ever more ambitious endeavors. But Certainty comes at a cost, because any challenge to it, however slight, is a mortal danger, and must be treated as such. To the fundamentalist, there is no greater threat than Doubt—and therefore, to a particular type of mind, there is nothing that cannot be done, and is not therefore morally justified, to crush Disbelief. An *Inquisition* can take many forms. If there is any speck of gangrene in the body, there are men who will not hesitate to chop off the limb. Because after all, dear reader, you must remember, *this world is not real*, and therefore the limb is not real, but is only the crude corpus encapsulating that which is real.

37.

And *if* this world was not real, then there was an absolute necessity for ideological uniformity and conviction in the face of what was seen as the collapse and demolition and disintegration of all normative values and morality, which undoubtedly was occurring, in the eyes of Evangelical Christianity, in the latter half of the American twentieth century—primarily derived from (though not widely understood to be a result of) the deterioration of *certainty*, due to Descartes and Darwin, and those later philosophers and scientists who further developed their epistemological and scientific questioning, and also to the whittling away of the belief, in the bosoms of Christian laymen, of time *in saecula saeculorum*, in whose inexhaustibility, particularly in the Deep South, there had previously existed an unshakeable faith. The rapid erosion of that formerly ever-existent state of affairs—one based on hierarchy, patriarchy, Christianity, and race—created a situation in which an eschatological war was required to counteract the viable and voracious criticisms of those contumacious heresiarchs suddenly arising from within the Evangelical world itself.

And while any moderate of suspect theology could simply be placed in exile, declared unfit, or removed from authority, there was the rather delicate problem of how to deal with such poison when found in a child, particularly when that child was a scion of the most influential and pure clan in the entirety of the Evangelical world. But again, if this world is not real, then there are no temporal means that do not justify the eternal ends. And Southerners have certainly never been averse to pain.

38.

Soon after I was able to think, I learned to speak. And shortly after having arrived at the glorious conjunction of both thought and speech I was able to question. And questioning soon proved a great talent of mine. My inquiries were primarily directed at my parents, and concerned life, and humanity, and the nature of existence and God, for after all, it was a theologian's home. But frequently the answers provoked more questions, and in many cases one or more of the answers produced confusion, or, as I saw it, a puzzle.

However there were times when my parents did not see their answers as confusing or puzzling, or as riddles requiring solutions. So there were occasions when the solutions at which I arrived, to satisfy the curiosities acquired when padding about as a child, did not meet with the approval of my parents.

Further, there were many times when the answers provided me were not merely puzzling, but were completely unpalatable. And so without compunctions, I felt free to let my parents, particularly my stay-at-home mother, know what I felt about their thoughts and opinions concerning my behavior or beliefs. And all of this questioning and back-talk existed alongside the usual misbehaviors of any normally inquisitive and energetic young boy. And that presented a problem, for I was an extremely willful child.

This sort of childish willfulness did not go over very well in the Southern Evangelical world of that time, where children were *to be seen and not heard*, and physical pain was seen as appropriate, Biblically mandated, and pedagogically useful.

I was just out of infancy when my mother began beating me, and those beatings, which she termed *spankings*, continued several times a day, every day, throughout my childhood and adolescence. And I do not believe, in the beginning, that those beatings were meant to be abusive. I believe my mother really meant those beatings to save me from sin and a possible eternity in Hell.

The Terrible Beauty of the Evil Man

In truth, I doubt my mother believed that it was morally appropriate for a devout Christian parent to employ any form of behavioral correction for their child *other* than corporal punishment. Both she and my father had related to me that she, as both a child and adolescent, had been beaten regularly, and sometimes severely, by her father. Though this psychologically damaged her in ways she would not fully recognize or understand for decades, she did not, or could not, at that time, admit that anything wrong had been done to her.

She was trapped in a web of fundamentalism where her father could do no wrong, and, moreover the Bible itself, in Proverbs 13:24, explicitly states that one who withholds the rod from their child *hates* their child. To condemn her father, to treat me differently than she had been treated, would have required my mother to repudiate the only life and worldview she knew. That, dear friends, was simply not going to happen. My mother, as assured a fundamentalist as her father, interpreted the biblical injunction literally, despite the deeply buried psychological damage it had done her.

In my toddler years her beatings were not too severe, and were carried out using a slim, plastic ruler imprinted with the *Peanuts* characters Snoopy and Charlie Brown. But by the time I was three years old my mother broke that *Peanuts* ruler with one particularly severe smack across my bottom, and she was forced to pick a sturdier implement of discipline.

To this day I still remember the new ruler she used to replace her broken wand. It was wooden, three-quarters of an inch thick, and alternated in color across its surface from green to blue with each successive inch. By the time we moved out of southern Louisiana, when I was eight, the very wood itself was warped where her fingers wrapped around its base.

39.

The white-columned mansion that was my grandparents' home on the campus, where we stayed during our weekly visits to New Orleans, was undoubtedly the worst possible environment for my mother, as one who, having been repeatedly beaten by her domineering father, had, in response, against her father's wishes, married the man who, at least in her youthful naiveté, appeared to be the most yielding, unassuming, and passive male imaginable.

So to throw her back, several days a week, into the purlieus of the father who had terrorized her as a child, only enhanced the likelihood that she would practice on me those same types of corporal discipline for even the most minor of infractions. And it is a great truth about child abuse, that it is often multi-generational, and almost ineradicable, particularly when carried out under the guise of the will of God.

40.

My father was a phlegmatic and weak-willed man when faced with any type of direct confrontation, though he was potently and viciously passive-aggressive after his initial farce of a capitulation. And that dichotomy had developed as a result of a childhood in which he had also grown up in an environment where he was subjected to a variety of forms of child-neglect and abuse.

Nevertheless, one of the only forms of abuse he had not encountered was physical abuse. As he recounted to me, he could not recall having been spanked even a single time during his entire childhood. But when, under the influence and instruction of not only the Imperator, my grandfather, but also my mother, who passionately believed corporal punishment to be the literal will of God Almighty, he felt compelled to spank me, despite the extreme distaste it provoked in him.

Unfortunately, he was so unsure of how to go about the process of thrashing a child, was so much larger and stronger than my mother, and so unlikely to engage in said thrashing unless he was at the height of anger, that whenever he did spank me he left my backside so ravaged that I would often hobble into the bathroom, pull down my pants, and use the mirror to check the severity of the new welts.

I am not unique in having a father who regularly spanked me to the point of welts and bruises, but what is strange, perhaps, is that my father felt so horrible as soon as he had vented his anger through the medium of beating, that he would often force me to hug him until I had done crying, all the while stroking my hair, sobbing onto the top of my head, telling me how much he hated it, that he loved me dearly.

41.

My father, as a pastor married into a lineup of some of the greatest Evangelical orators the South had ever produced, had a heavily vested interest in correcting his natural propensity to stumble and bumble as a martext—an oft-noted, ongoing, and grotesque deficiency in his clerical development. However my father did not choose to improve his elocution and delivery by studying one of Dale Carnegie's manuals, or even the speeches of Demosthenes and Cicero. No, my father favored another famous orator (perhaps one chosen to help counteract his inability to directly confront others) to such an extent that he extensively studied that speaker's native language in order to listen and learn in the vernacular.

When I was small, and we were still in southern Louisiana, I would sometimes awaken late at night, and hear him studying in the living room, in front of the television, from documentaries checked out from the local public library. If I was quite sure my mother was asleep (as I did not wish to risk a spanking for being out after bedtime) I would carefully sneak out of bed, mindful not to wake my brother Andrew snoozing easily in the next bed, and would peer around the corner of the door to the living room, where I would watch my father lying on the floor, a pillow folded beneath him, engrossed in the shouting emanating from the television.

Invariably my father would spot me. If he was in a bad mood he would yell at me to get back into bed before my mother awoke. If he was in a good mood he would place an index finger over his lips, whisper, "shh," and motion me forward slyly with the other hand. Those were the best of nights, for I knew I would get to stay up far too late, and that if my mother knew she would be furious.

And my father and I would lie on the pillows together before the television, and he would offer me a graham cracker, and a sip of milk, which I would accept, and we would both sit in silence, and quietly imbibe and enjoy, and learn from, the stridulous, spittle-spraying locutions of Adolf Hitler.

42.

My father, in a number of ways, simply had no idea how to parent. My paternal grandfather sired him at the impressive (or absurd) age of sixty, and had been heavily inebriated most of the waking hours my father remembered him. My grandmother was a Cuban immigrant who never learned functional English—but yet refused to teach my father Spanish. His entire childhood occurred without any type of oversight or parental guidance. By the time he was twelve he was regularly driving a car, without a license, around a city of one hundred thousand people.

It's incredible that my father not only managed to live until and then graduate high school, but also that he earned a Ph.D. in theology. His high school guidance counselor flatly told him not to bother applying to college, a story he loved to recount in later years, with a well-deserved sense of pride.

Nevertheless, despite the virtues of an indefatigable perseverance and an unshakeable sense of resolution, my father had no understanding of what was meant by the term *parenting*, and as I was his first, and very precocious, child, I became an experiment. When, as a toddler, I cried and screamed, as even the most unassuming children are sometimes wont to do, my father would simply stick my head under the pillow that formed part of the armrest of the couch in the living room, and hold my head under that pillow until I suffocated from lack of air. If I foolishly decided that, upon regaining access to oxygen, I might again wish to cry, back went my head under the pillow. This process was repeated indefinitely until I became too exhausted to cry.

Similarly, if, when made prisoner of the child playpen a great many parents used in those days for holding children, I should decide I wanted out, I was first required to throw my hands into the sky and shout "Hallelujah!" or "Praise the Lord!" in order to secure release. This was considered religious training.

If there was a crowd of guests gathered in my home, simple Cajun parishioners enjoying pecan pie in the home of their spiritual leader, then something rather more dramatic was required prior to release—perhaps a childish homily on the grace of God or the nature of the Trinity.

43.

And in Baton Rouge I was alone and defenseless, at the mercy and whim of my parents. But in New Orleans I was not only at their mercy, but an infraction away from the same treatment by my grandparents—two titans of religious morality, with sixteen published religious works between them, who had no qualms about beating a small child senseless. And so, hardheaded and strong-willed as I was, I was regularly within the reach of four competing personalities wielding instruments of pain. The severity of the infraction would determine the number of *licks*, just where they would fall out, and whether they were pants up or bare-bottom.

And with all of this rampant justice from the Lord, I really had nowhere to turn except to the arms of my other mother, my grandmother's maid Elaine, who would hide me, hold me, take care of me, make me laugh, and love me. And with her I was never afraid, and could be myself, and I felt free and full of joy. Elaine and I loved each other very, very much.

But Elaine died, and I think they told me it was cancer, but I'm not sure, because I was a small boy, and I was heartbroken. All I knew is that one day Elaine was there, and the next she was gone, and there was a replacement named Opal who just wasn't the same.

And that was how my second mother died.

44.

Once, when I was a boy, an old man whispered in my ear at dusk, an old man who, I believe, had also heard similar whisperings from an old man at either a dawn or twilight in his youth. But as to whether these whisperings went back through the concatenation of generations, passing noiselessly and anonymously through seaports and caravans and mundane fields replete with foreign tongues and euphemisms, or perhaps not even through whispers, but communicated through the subtleties and nuances of innuendo and gesture and the plucking of the balalaika of the body, I cannot say, but they seemed to me far older than the man who whispered them.

"Love is real," he whispered. The folds of skin that drooped around his eyes accentuated his seriousness. "Have you forgotten? Don't you remember it?"

"I love God," I answered boyishly, simply.

"No," he said. "Nothing like that. Do you *remember* love?"

"What do you mean?"

"Do you remember giving everything you have and are and were to another, for one thing you couldn't explain, and a thousand details you could, but knew to be found only, singly, in that other person, and which was so powerful, delicious, and unbearable, that you could not think of existing in a You in which any part of yourself was held back from them?"

"I'm a boy. I don't know about any of this!" I said, looking at him in surprise.

"Think! Think!" he exclaimed. "You used to remember."

"I did?"

"Don't you remember who you are?" he asked curiously, and I shivered as he asked.

Something strange happened then, and I felt sure that I should remember *something*, and that it was pressing just beyond the edge of my memory-field, but I blinked stupidly, and it was gone.

"I don't know about love, but I know you can't love people who hurt you. And the people I'm supposed to love hurt me. They hurt me every day," I responded.

"Ah, pain!" he noted. "Nobody ever loved as deeply as you did without first hurting so badly," he said quietly, and then, leaning in and looking at me intently, he queried, "else why would you need to love so powerfully? Did you think love as instinctual as hunger?"

"But I don't want to hurt!"

"You will," he said with certainty, "when you remember how powerful was the love you shared with *her*. It shook the earth."

"Shared with who?"

But he was already gone, disappeared into the gathering darkness, and I had nothing to do but get onto my bicycle and pedal home from that ephemeral rendezvous.

But now I do not remember if I dreamed him, or if he was a dream within a dream, or merely some misremembered fragment of conversation overheard through the fumes of smoke and drink in a long-forgotten pub. But the life of fragmented dream and remembrance is often more real than the events of time and space and matter, and regardless, who can claim that the diktat of memory is not certainly invention and fiction?

Memoir is a reconstruction of *what* exactly?

45.

When I was seven my mother's reproductive capabilities failed after my third sibling, David, a ten-pound boy, was removed from her. She rues that day, because she had sworn that she would never stop having children so long as the Lord allowed it. (We thank the Lord daily he did not.)

When I was eight our parents informed the four of us, beginning with me, the eldest, and then on down to Andrew, Jo Ann, and even the infant David, that we would be leaving the sweet wistaria and jasmine and camellia and Spanish moss and oak of southern Louisiana because my parents had heard from the Lord, through prophetic prayer of some sort, that they were *called to the ministry* in the small cow town of Cameron, TX, pop. 5,000.

We had no say in the matter, and were not consulted. I shrugged. Within weeks we were gone.

46.

Life did not change for me, initially, in the new cow town. I quickly grew accustomed to the odor of manure and chewing tobacco, the subtle scent of mesquite and purple Texas thistle and bluebonnet. My head quickly forgot, though my heart never did, Louisiana's wild subtropical extravagance of lichen-plastered trees, lubriciously dangling their tangled hair of Spanish moss, arrogantly growing from the mud and water of inebriated bayous.

But Louisiana was decadent, and sinking, and always had been, and everyone knew it. And central Texas was nothing if not impossibly plain. And it is not a mistake to realize that the spiritual characteristics of a people are shaped by their physical environs, and whereas it was the French and Africans who had populated southern Louisiana, central Texas was inhabited by the stern and devout descendents of Germans.

"Welcome, young boy, to your new life. We hope you like it!"

47.

Repot the plant, and you will find that you cannot predict the new growth and direction of the shoots. The pot is a restraint. Repot the human, observe the direction of his new growth, and learn his true nature in the sudden absence of old restraints.

The meticulous Japanese have made an art of the artificial manipulation of natural growth. But *bonsai* is not only attempted on small shrubs.

48.

As soon as my father finished his doctorate at the seminary, and we were free to move from southern Louisiana, we did. And as long as was my grandfather's reach within the Evangelical world, we were still, for the first time, beyond the umbra of his direct control. We children had little vested interest in the matter, and my father could only have gained through regular, direct access to one of the most powerful men in the world in which he wished to rise. So the impetus for a movement hundreds of miles away from southern Louisiana, assuming it didn't come directly from God Almighty, came from *whom* exactly?

49.

As soon as my mother was well out of her father's reach for the first time in her life, away from the tyrannical power of his personality, will, influence, and religious instruction, she began to slowly discover something that should not have been in the least surprising—she realized that she did not care for her former life very much at all.

This manifested in a number of ways, which, in our little cow town of endless leather, cowboy hats, handlebar mustaches, and polite, simple, kind, country stupidity, nearly brought about the destruction of our family, and which wrought no small number of ruinous changes in my life.

The first thing my mother realized, through several of the many fuzzy shoots of intuition pushing up erratically from the soil of her subconscious, was that she despised her husband.

My father, as a penniless, young, poorly educated upstart from a sordid background, was the antithesis of her father, and the ultimate statement of rebellion for a young Southern lady of her position and breeding. But once out of range of her father he was obsolete, and quickly became first embarrassing, and then despicable to her.

He was unimaginative, lacked dynamic vigor, was unable to confront and direct large numbers of people, and, perhaps most importantly, he was completely unaware of how to be a father—which to her meant enforcing discipline and sternly beating a child whenever the child looked halfway independent. In short, he was not her daddy, a fact which had been a relief in New Orleans, but which disgusted in Cow Town.

So my mother faced a conundrum of which she was completely unaware. On the one hand, she wanted, *needed*, an escape from the world of her father—the chance to grow and develop in new and free directions for the first time in her life. Yet at the same time she was slowly beginning to understand that every decision she had made until that point was simply a reaction against a world and culture that so dominated her thinking that even when she did finally acquire her release, the vacuum of authority terrified her so greatly that she scrambled in every possible way to reestablish that exact same world under new terms.

And so the first tangible influence her convoluted psychological development produced in my boyish life was that the blue-and-green striped wooden ruler previously used for beating me was exchanged for my father's newly acquired thick leather cowboy belt, a much heavier and more powerful piece of weaponry, and he began to be more regularly excoriated and ridiculed for not using it.

But I too was extremely strong-willed, and my mother was not the only one to notice the sudden bankruptcy of authority and will with which we were all confronted.

50.

There was one other primary, and terrifying, aspect to our new lives in Cow Town, TX, pop. 5,000, and that was that we were suddenly engrossed in a human milieu that made even the lower Cajun bourgeoisie of southern Louisiana seem *sophistiqué* and *à la mode*. And as I have noted, one's environment *is*, to a large extent, one's spirituality.

We had broken out of a spiritual Bastille in which chiliasm, the Antichrist, and the wars of Gog and Magog were bywords, common knowledge—undoubted facts relevant to our immediate future—and had entered a new world, far from even any smaller cities, in which the educational levels were lower, and much of the population more gullible. And to translate all of this for the neophyte, what that meant was that we had escaped the world of the rabid Evangelical Protestantism for the far more frightening universe of *Charismatic* Christianity.

51.

Charismatic Christianity filled my father with unease under the best of circumstances, and, initially, had no part in the workings or theology of the First Baptist Church of Cow Town. But the Charismatic movement, formerly denigrated throughout the Protestant world, and relegated to the lowly Pentecostal denomination, was slowly snaking its way into mainstream Protestant denominations in the years prior to my birth— particularly as a Christian reaction and response to the growth of what were seen as mystical Eastern religious movements, such as Yoga and Buddhism, themselves merely symptoms of Secular America seeking alternative spiritual meaning in the profusion of newfound material abundance that followed the Second World War. And while the hard-line fundamentalist Evangelical denominations such as the Southern Baptists were most resistant to the new, anti-intellectual *charisma*, by the time we reached Cow Town even they were beginning to feel the penetration of the new fervor.

And for my mother, the heady reeling from the sudden oxygen of newfound freedom, the disorientation resulting from the distaste with which she was beginning to view my father (with all the foundational questions *that* provoked at the nebulous corners of her undeveloped critical faculties), the great fear that her children were not receiving a proper upbringing, and her continuing belief that Secular America was really engaging in a moral skydive since at least the late 1960s, all coalesced to produce an intellectual foment in which she came to believe that the Antichrist might really appear at any time—as in possibly tomorrow. She became convinced that a more extreme connection to the *Holy Ghost* was needed, and urgently, even if she could not have consciously expressed those inchoate notions in word or thought. Thus were flung open the gates of our home to one of the most fanatical and philistine movements in contemporary America.

And no, none of this is unique. History is replete with examples of people turning to bizarre religious movements during times of great personal or social upheaval. For example, I am deeply grateful that I did not grow up within range of the knives of the Skoptsy.

52.

I once found myself on a dusty road, weary and thirsty, and remembered wanting nothing more than rest and a glass of cool water. The day was hot, the grass bleached and miserable, and even the wind was on strike. As I reached the limits of my endurance, I noticed, a short distance ahead, around a slight turn in the road, a hamlet beckoning. I entered the village (really not more than a speckle on the road) and saw that it was deserted, except for one man, small in the distance, in what appeared to be the town square.

I approached him quickly, and before I even had the chance to ask he handed me a tall glass of water.

"Rest, brother. You've had a long journey."

"Thank you so much," I said after my first immediate gulp. "Is it that obvious?"

"The road is long, and very difficult, and clearly, you were not prepared," he replied.

"*Prepared?*"

"Let me ask you brother, have you heard the Good News?"

"Good news about what?"

The Terrible Beauty of the Evil Man

"The Good News about our Lord and Savior, Jesus Christ, who died for your sins," the man replied with a kind smile.

"My sins?"

"Yes! Your sins, and my sins, and the sins of everyone who has ever walked that hard road," he said, refilling my glass.

As I sipped from the second glass of water more people began to arrive in that deserted hamlet, wearily stumbling in from the long, difficult road. As each appeared the man produced a fresh glass, but didn't let that slow his conversation in the slightest, for he had a great deal to say about this man Jesus, who had apparently been a carpenter, but was at the same time involved with God in some very complicated way, which the man was trying to explain to me, but which I'm not sure I understood, for he seemed to be indicating that this carpenter *was* God, which was clearly absurd.

By this time a large crowd had gathered around the man, and his explanations and solutions for these bizarre and stupendous claims, which had at first seemed incredible, became so convoluted and recondite that I was no longer certain that I understood him, though I realized that even so, he was certainly making a strong case for why this Jesus character was an outstanding man, or at the very least a decent fellow, and, if nothing else, was a good stand-in for me personally against a chap named Satan, who, the man told me, was an unbelievably perverse deviant, and who, it seemed, was the individual primarily responsible for the difficulty and misery of the road I'd just been on.

Just as I was preparing to accept the implications of what this man was telling me, as difficult as that is to believe (and I wasn't the only one, for there were definitely a few more in the crowd who were finding this tale pretty convincing), we all noticed a man at the other end of the square who had begun yelling. As much as we wished to hear the conclusion of what the first man was saying, to get to the real crux of the matter, his voice began to sound thin next to the shouting coming from the other end of the square, and the difficult but compelling points made only a moment before were now impossible to hear, let alone follow. So I, and many of the others, drifted to the other end of the square to hear just what it was the other man was shouting.

As we got closer we noticed that the shouting man wasn't wearing normal clothing, but only a burlap sack, and that the words coming from his mouth didn't make any sense, but were an outlandish glossolalia, or *speaking in tongues*, which the first man had told us was a rare and extinct spiritual gift from God, and had been, in previous Ages, a mark of the holiest of men. But this man had driblets of spit flying from his mouth as he shouted, and they ran through his beard, though our eyes couldn't focus on that for long because as soon as we drew close his eyes rolled back in his head, and he fell to the ground writhing.

"Demons!" he shouted, and we all wondered what he meant. But as more holy gibberish poured from his mouth we refrained from asking, for even as we caught occasional words, they occurred in no sensible context, and anyway, his writhing both frightened and impressed us.

"Turn to Jesus! Turn from Satan's path!" he screamed, beginning to speak in what was now recognizable language, and in some crude form replicating, far more charismatically, what the man at the other end of the square had been saying. And I noticed that as he continued some of the others who were with me seemed to fall into a trance, and were swaying, arms outraised, in cadence with the words that flew from his lips.

He continued screaming incoherently, disjointedly, and with wild eyes that seemed to focus more and more on me, and so I began to back away in fear. But this provoked him, and he pointed, directing everyone's attention toward me. The others turned and eyed me warily.

"Demon!" he shouted, as I backpedalled.

And then I looked back to the other end of the square, to the polished man with his cool water and his complicated explanations for bizarre claims, and I felt quite certain that I must be in a dream.

And in that moment with which we are all so familiar, that last moment of dream-haze, when one realizes that he is not yet awake, but still has some measure of control over the events within which he is trapped, I chose to run out of the hamlet altogether, back to the road. I chose to run back to the thirst and pain.

53.

My mother's embrace of Charismatic culture, again, was merely a symptom of the inharmonious congeries of fears brought about by the resettling of the sediment of every layer of her life. But this new religious anti-intellectual, hypnotic emotionalism, a powerful opiate against the anxieties of life, both implied and necessitated an increasing loss of touch with reality. And so, when an eldest son, intelligent, precocious, and defiant, reacts strongly against multiple daily beatings by refusing to allow his spirit and soul to be broken to the will of God Almighty, but rather by continuing, and even increasingly engaging in ever more desperate acts of defiance, it becomes apparent to the Charismatic personality that the sequence of disturbing phenomena are not of the material realm.

Ten-year-old boys should not be able to outsmart, outthink, and outmaneuver mature adults who are operating under the divine guidance of the Lord. Clearly the demonic was at work.

And there is no intelligent ten-year-old who will not very quickly begin to experiment with alternative identities, particularly when he has never been exposed to anything other than the metaphysical claims of the inerrant and literal interpretation of the New Testament, with its repetitive passages concerning exorcisms—passages which said boy knew by heart. If the foundation and rock of one's life, that is to say, one's mother, believes that when speaking to you she may not in fact be speaking to you—even while looking directly into your eyes—but rather to one or more maleficent creatures from the netherworld, then you, the precocious, imaginative, ten-year-old, will begin a long process of self-dissociation in which you discover yourself increasingly plagued by the types of epistemological questions that should really not trouble anyone other than tweed-donned and bearded middle-aged professors.

"Am I me?"

"Are there evil beings living inside of me?"

"Did what just happened occur as a result of my actions, or was it the result of an uncontrollable impulse directed by one of the malignant spirits that seem to be hovering all around me?"

"Why did God allow me to become a prime target of these evil beings, simply due to the pedigree of my family, my spiritual potential, and the likelihood that someday I may become a leader of the Christian world? What did I do to deserve that?"

"If it is not me personally who is causing and responsible for these defiant and occasionally uproarious behaviors, then why am I being beaten so thoroughly for them every day?"

And it was this last question that finally occurred to my *spirit-filled* parents, who decided that, as the beatings were proving ineffective, there was, of course, really only one solution left.

54.

"We've got to take him to the exorcist."

"Ann, I'm not sure that's a good idea."

"He's out of control. Nothing's working. We're trying everything, and he's just getting worse. The Devil is working powerfully on him. The Devil knows who he's going to become, and wants to stop it before it can happen!"

"Ann, we've got to focus on prayer and the power of the Lord. There is clearly demonic work at play, but he's *not* possessed."

"I've seen it! I can look into his eyes. Those aren't normal eyes! He sees things. He gets things. Sometimes he thinks like an adult. He *knows* things. That's clearly a sign of the supernatural. And he's using it for evil. He's hanging with the gangs at school. Those Mexicans, the Crips."

"I know. But we took him to a counselor, and we can encourage him in the study of the Word."

"That counselor was a Godly man, but he wasn't prepared to deal with this level of the demonic. We need someone who is *filled with the charisma of the Spirit*. We need someone who has extensive experience in waging real Deliverance and Spiritual Warfare. And Bible study? If they're inside him then *they'll* reject the Word. The soul can't have two masters. I don't understand how you don't see this. He's just a boy and he's already been arrested!"

"Ann, he was stealing baseball cards."

"But it's a gateway. And we found the pornographic note in his backpack he got from that Mexican girl at school."

My father, Finis Pierre Joseph Beauchamp, pastor of the First Baptist Church of Cameron, Texas, pauses heavily on this last point.

"Maybe you're right. We may have to homeschool him again."

"I know I'm right, and of course he should be homeschooled again. That school, O.J. Thomas, is corrupt and immoral, and if I hadn't been out of town I'd never have let you enroll him. Listen, if Satan infiltrates even one member of this family, particularly him, then think about how that will spread. Think about what it will do to the other kids. And it will corrupt your ministry in the church."

My father's eyes narrow. Metaphysical and material concerns mingle as career considerations come into play.

"Well I suppose taking him in for prayer wouldn't hurt."

"Exactly! But it will be prayer directly through the Holy Ghost. And you'll see... he'll become what we know he's meant to be."

"The next great Leavell?"

"No. We're too close to the End Times. The Lord has other plans for him."

55.

And that, dear friends, is how a nine or ten-year-old boy ends up in a chair in a dim room just outside Cow Town, TX, pop. 5,000, with a dozen handlebar-wearing cowpokes nervously shuffling in their snakeskin boots while a charlatan of the first order is given direct access to do the work of God Almighty.

56.

But, and I know this will surprise you, the exorcism did not work, and so the daily beatings resumed. And my behavior continued to degenerate, and the blame for that, in my mother's eyes, rested on my father, who was failing to fulfill his role as Spiritual Head of the Home.

And, I know this too will surprise you, but neither parent, at any point, stopped to question whether my degenerate and defiant behavior was the result of the daily beatings themselves. The idea that spanking might cause deficient childhood behavior would have been, to an Evangelical or Charismatic Christian, akin to suggesting to a Green Party member that primitive coal plants produce cleaner air.

And so my father's congregants began to wonder if there was something wrong with me, and my parents' marriage began to collapse, and eventually my father's relationship with his entire congregation started to dissolve, due not only to the aforementioned reasons, but due also to two others.

First, while there were a number of congregants open to the importation of the charisma my mother had manipulated my father into introducing into the congregation, there was enough resistance to that foolish religious fustian that a serious split developed in the church—and of course I hardly need mention that my mother, and the Charismatic wing behind her, considered the opposing faction to be under the influence of the demonic. But the congregation was largely descended of the Germans, and that race typically brooks little nonsense. And so while some reached out for the new meaning and fervor to be found in Christianity, others dug trenches, and settled in for a long war.

Second, my father was, is, and always has been, unable to confront people directly whenever there is any type of distressing situation that could involve unpleasantness for him. And not only did he suffer from a dearth of this necessary pastoral quality, he excelled in the art of passive-aggressive retaliation. So for instance, a congregant who opposed my father on one front might later find that my father had leaked information about that congregant's personal financial difficulties, troubles that had long before been revealed in confidential pastoral counseling. This sort of thing caused no small degree of fury, and after only a few years in Cow Town, the congregation was in an uproar.

Fortunately, salvation arrived just as we were facing civil war. My father, due perhaps to my grandfather's influence, or perhaps, once again, as my parents claimed, due to the will of God, had suddenly been called to a new and more substantial congregation in a much larger town in Texas.

Again, we children were told *post facto*. I shrugged. Within weeks we were gone.

57.

And when we moved to Wichita Falls, TX, pop. 100,000 (which was on the border of Oklahoma, halfway between Dallas and Amarillo, and hundreds of miles north of Cameron), we were not moving to another mundane location. Rather we were going to the city where my father had grown up, and also to the city where my mother had spent a considerable portion of her youth, as her father, prior to becoming president of the seminary in New Orleans, had pastored the First Baptist Church of Wichita Falls, which had been, under his tenure in the 1960s, the megachurch of its day. And both of my parents sensed that we were vacating a grand conflict to go back home, for they had attended both junior high and high school together in Wichita Falls.

However, Wichita Falls wasn't my home, but a new adventure, and the only hopes I had were that I not be homeschooled again.

58.

Homeschooling was, for my mother, part of her divine duty and prerogative as the guardian and molder of my soul. Initially, in Baton Rouge, I had been enrolled in a normal preschool and then elementary. But one day in the second grade my parents came to visit my school to observe the goings-on and quality of instruction. The particular day and hour they chose to visit the teacher was giving a lesson on the workings of traffic lights. I noticed my parents in the back of the room and beamed with pride. The teacher drew a picture of a green-yellow-red traffic light on the chalkboard, and, anticipating the question, I raised my hand immediately.

"What this do?" she called out, in the patois of southern Louisiana.

"It's a traffic light! It tells you when you can go," I cried out, glowing.

"You is right. Good job!"

My parents slowly recovered from the loss of breath they had suffered on realizing that their child's teacher could not speak grammatically correct Standard English, and the next day I was promptly taken out of the public school system.

59.

Homeschooling, ostensibly due to the poor public schools of southern Louisiana, quickly became the means by which my mother was more carefully able to scrutinize and control my (deviant) behavior. While she swears that without her careful instruction I would to this day be illiterate, the real impetus for homeschooling was to protect me from immorality. I was homeschooled for the second, third, and fourth grades, and was made to repeat the sixth grade in homeschool despite having satisfactorily completed that grade in public school—my behavior having been deemed so immoral that getting me into a grade with kids my age was seen as a dramatic but necessary intervention in the ongoing attempt to achieve my moral rectitude. Until then I had been a year younger than everyone in my classes.

As with beatings, and even an exorcism, homeschooling was one of the most nightmarish experiences I have ever passed through. I was trapped with my mother in the house every day, and had no escape. When I first learned how to do mathematical averages, the first practical use to which I put this new skill was discovering the average number of times per day I was beaten. I kept careful track of each spanking for a week and determined that the average number of times per day weaponry met my backside was three.

But perhaps the horror of homeschool can better be exemplified through an anecdote which I do not remember, but which my mother has recounted to me several times in order to illustrate the severity of my spiritual oppression.

I was sitting at the small wooden desk in the room used as the schoolroom in our house, and I was stuck on a mathematical problem. This was vexing and highly unusual, as I typically required no assistance in order to complete an intellectual task. My mother was surprised, and tried several times to explain the working of the solution, but on that day I was distracted or thick, and could not independently arrive at the answer.

My mother backed away from my side and grabbed my chin, staring down deeply into my eyes. Quickly she realized the problem, and took action.

"Satan, *in Jesus' name*, I command you to come out of him!"

Apparently, according to my mother, I blinked, and immediately shouted the answer to the problem.

Homeschooling was, mildly put, a difficult affair.

60.

When my father was a boy, he regularly came home from school to find his geriatric father in the floor, inebriated, unconscious, and covered in urine. Not that there was much floor to occupy, as the home was completely stuffed, to the ceilings, with the hoarded bric-a-brac and detritus that my grandmother, an emigrant from the chaos of Cuba, saw necessary to accumulate.

I have seen pictures of the home as it was then. The poverty was severe, and traversing the rooms required using trails blazed through the floor-to-ceiling garbage. My father's room, however, was spotless, a pristine line of tennis trophies resting atop his dresser the only decoration.

My father has told me repeatedly of the day when, as a boy, his Sunday School teacher stopped by for a surprise visit to check up on him, in order to encourage him spiritually. The doorbell rang, and my father opened the door a crack. Before he could protest, the teacher pushed through the door and saw what my father had been doing in the living room—mopping up urine and trying get his father off the floor. The teacher hurriedly, awkwardly excused himself and exited.

The next week's lesson, in the boys' Sunday School class at the Lamar Baptist Church of Wichita Falls, Texas, was on the evil of alcohol. My father was mortified, and felt that the teacher was staring at him throughout the entire lesson. My father walked out of Lamar Baptist Church that day and never returned.

He began to attend the First Baptist Church of Wichita Falls, then one of the largest churches in the country, and there fell under the influence of its pastor, my maternal grandfather. There too, as a young teenager, he met my mother, Ann. And finally, it was there, at the First Baptist Church, under the inspiration of the sermons of Landrum Leavell, that he decided to devote his life to the work of God, to become a pastor.

And so he went to Baylor, the Baptist university of Texas. After Baylor he took the unusual step of going out of state for theological training, something rarely done, in order to follow Dr. Leavell, at the time merely his religious mentor, to the seminary in New Orleans, where my grandfather had recently become president. My father had to take the GRE perhaps eight times to attain a score necessary to gain entrance to the seminary, but he had, involuntarily, learned early in life that he would rather be dead than fail to pull himself to that next ledge.

He finally attained his required GRE score, entered the seminary, seduced the President's daughter, and earned his Ph.D.

And when God once again *called* my father to a new church, his third, this time telling him to leave Cow Town, it was to go to a most unusual location, and so I must correct an earlier statement. My father *did* return to Lamar Baptist Church of Wichita Falls, Texas, and did confront that former Sunday School teacher. Only this time he returned as the spiritual master, that is to say, senior pastor.

Rarely, beautifully, there exist, in space and time, points, growing into lines, naturally curving, ending as perfect circles.

61.

In Wichita Falls my parents did allow me entrée to the public school system, though with no small trepidation. I may only have been allowed access due to the fact that those were the same schools that they and their siblings had attended, and perhaps there was a sense that there couldn't be anything too terribly immoral about the schools in a town in the Bible Belt where my family held such tremendous religious sway.

But as I entered Barwise Junior High School, the same school my uncle Roland Quinche Leavell II had attended, I did become exposed to the irreligious—and by irreligious I don't mean merely the members of Protestant denominations not perfectly in line with our pure theology, but also with Catholics and outright heathens.

And at Barwise I grew tall and gangly, and developed exceptionally acute acne, and reveled in the extreme distaste for my personal appearance common to nearly all early adolescents. I also became exposed to the feelings, personalities, joys, and fears of people who were completely unlike me—people who did not think solely within the four walls of the New Testament, literally interpreted.

For the first time in my life I had access to secular information, most importantly non-Evangelical literature. For the first time I began to suspect that other kids, even if they were spanked by their parents, and most Southern children were, weren't beaten regularly, repeatedly, and daily. I began, through trips to the school library (still a heavily censored repository of books in a town like Wichita Falls), to gain some basic awareness of the world beyond the only world I had ever known. But this exposure, this new awareness, led only to death.

In the eighth grade I recall sitting in computer class, listening to several friends from the football team discuss one of the young ladies in our school. At some point the conversation turned ribald, though I did not understand the line of discussion, and the boys began joking that the girl must have a six inch clit. I laughed uproariously, nodded my head, and conceded that there could be no disputing that this was the case—despite the fact that I had no idea what a clit was.

When I got home I made the mistake of asking my mother, quite innocently, what exactly was a *clit*, and whether they could be six inches. Now I had been through years of severe beatings, repeated exorcisms, and the general malignance of a disturbed mother, but that day was the first time I can remember her furiously choking me, screaming, saliva flying from her mouth, demanding to know where I had heard that word.

The question, naturally, came up as to whether I should be removed from the public schools due to this exposure to flagrant immorality. But this time I was not removed. My father had grown to love my football and basketball games too much, and, as I was developing into a stellar athlete, so simple a thing as fanaticism for sports allowed me to stay in the real world.

But the innocent question, asked offhand, of what exactly was a clitoris, proved the catalyst for such a tempestuous madness, that so severe a shock was produced in me, along with the trauma resulting from the choking, that it was exactly that day, that hour, eternally vivid in my mind, that my first mother, my birth mother, Ann, died—though even now she walks and talks and breathes and lives on this Earth.

The Terrible Beauty of the Evil Man

62.

I have just described the day my first mother died to me. At one time I lived inside of her; her essence is eternally embedded in me. It is impossible to remember and write such a thing without tumult, emotional disquiet. Its lack would be inhumane. And so I wait. I cease to write. Days have passed since I wrote the preceding section.

In the intervening time my mother has called. I do not answer. In the voicemail she informs me that she hasn't heard from me—that she would appreciate hearing my voice. I'm due soon for one of the emotionally flat phone check-ups we engage in every two or three months. I attempt to maintain these sporadic fifteen-minute phone conversations, though I have not seen her in years. We will exchange banal pleasantries and chatter superficially about the weather or the health of relatives. I do not know why. There have been times when one of us has seen fit to completely relinquish any attempt to contact the other. But in a day or two I will call her. I do not know why.

As I write this I listen to Satie—the *Gnossiennes*, not the *Gymnopédies*—and I fall away in them, in all of their wistful intimacy and elegance. I close my eyes and breathe deeply, lost momentarily in the notes. What will I read today? Will I overcome this melancholy and finally pick up *Paradise Lost*? It has stared at me accusingly from the shelf since I found it for a quarter in a basement sale. No. I should reread *Anna Karenina*. I've meant to do that for far too long.

More likely I will do neither. Borges can traverse a maze of his own creation and make his point more quickly. Hamsun is haunting, beautiful, damned. Determination is failing and the choices are myriad. Perhaps today I will not make it past the newspapers. Most living writers I find too vulgar. Spiritual rejuvenation is impossibly delicate.

The names of these works, these artists, would be meaningless to her, and she would find the notion of such a use of time incomprehensible. Art itself may be frivolous. I look over at my Bible on the shelf next to my desk. It has been too long since it was opened. I read it now in Hebrew. I read it now having accepted premises she finds heretical. I have rejected beliefs she accepts unblinkingly. As I write this she is probably engaged in prayer in her country house in the wilds of Alabama. She may be praying for me as I type these words.

My mother—my *mother*. A man cannot write about himself without writing about his mother. I had two mothers, and both died when I was a boy, though in very different ways. But to know me you must still learn how I love, how I learned to truly love—but now, at least, you know how I first lost love.

Memoir is not to recount a list of one's grievances against life, or to bask in ultimately vapid glory. There are no miseries or victories I can recount that others, having trod this earth, cannot also document. One biblical writer noted that, "There is nothing new under the sun." That is a truth. There is no single action I will ever take that will be unique.

But there is still a sequence of choices, events, actions and reactions, that only I know, and in that unique knowledge is a story only I can tell. Memoir is *remembering*, slowly tracing the threadwork of the tapestry of one's soul, noting how and where it was torn and sewn and retorn and sewn back again to produce the patterns of beauty and ugliness that coalesce differently in each of us. And I have learned to create Art from Memory. And I have learned that it does not matter whether this world is real.

Book III

63.

Memoir is the solitary confinement of story—my story—and therefore, struggle as I like, I am trapped, for I should like to tell you a great many stories. I should like it very much. But I don't yet know those stories. I am forever snared in the braids of my consciousness.

64.

In Wichita Falls my father acquired a fever—a frenzied determination to convert as many people as possible to Christianity. This madness indubitably stemmed from a desire to prove himself in the church which formed the seat of his childhood humiliation. He was wildly successful. In his first year he converted one hundred and twenty souls. In his second year he converted eighty. Even more, already Christian, began attending. The church doubled in size in two years. Up to eight hundred or nine hundred people, in a town of one hundred thousand, would arrive on Sunday mornings to hear his sermons.

The growth of the church, measured by attendance and new baptisms, was a statistical anomaly in the Southern Baptist Convention, and, even beyond the confines of Wichita Falls, people remarked on the new success of Landrum Leavell's only son-in-law. My father was suddenly a prodigy in the center of the Evangelical world. And with that newfound success, validation in the locus of his boyhood anguish, my mother could no longer claim that the *Spirit* wasn't in him, and my parents' marriage improved dramatically.

But my father's success came at the price of countless hours away from home, and I rarely saw him. However I too was finally able to escape home for the first time as school and sports provided me with inexhaustible alibis.

Though I did return, every evening, to a home shorn of love. My father had little time or attention for me other than a fixation on my sporting endeavors, and my mother was someone who, leading up to and certainly after her death to me in the eighth grade, I spent my best efforts trying to avoid.

My three siblings received this treatment from my mother in degrees of severity that decreased with each successive child. My mother's energy to break us had been focused longest on me, and as I was both the smartest, and strongest-willed, I served as the cynosure of her angst throughout my youth.

I never broke. I merely retreated into a closet—literally. I spent long hours hiding in the closet in my bedroom, sitting atop pillows stacked on shoes, the clothes on their hangers dangling onto my head, with whatever books I could get—by junior high school usually a work of sci-fi, adventure, or historical fiction from the school library. But Church, Family, and Intellect strove unsuccessfully for my focus with the affair that formed the main artery for attention in Wichita Falls.

Wichita Falls is a high school football nirvana—à la *Friday Night Lights*. In 1970 the city was the first in the nation to build an Astroturf football stadium for a high school. It seats seventeen thousand persons. Football was truly the only thing that exceeded Christianity in the affections of the citizenry. And as I was a strong football player, any accolades, sense of worth, or love I ever received throughout junior high or my first year of high school in Wichita Falls were for my achievements on the gridiron.

65.

There was only one other route to distinction among one's coevals for a fourteen-year-old boy in that town, in that town or any other, and that lay in the ability to appeal magnificently to young ladies. But that, unfortunately, was for me an impossibility. Two things prevented girls from paying any heed to my fumbling attentions. The first was that, beginning in the seventh grade, I developed acute acne, and the shyness that naturally accompanies it.

The second reason was that during the last week of the sixth grade, soon after our move to Wichita Falls, I managed to convince my new "girlfriend" to accompany me and several of my new friends and their girlfriends for a make-out party in a tunnel in the local park. Unfortunately I was unprepared for what was meant by *make-out*, did not realize that my tongue or the girl's would be involved in the kiss, and therefore had not taken appropriate precautions. My breath that day appears to have been rather fetid, a fact which cost me that girlfriend, and quickly became known throughout the world of girlish adolescence, causing me no small shame. I became the bad breath boy from that single encounter.

And so for the following two years, at Barwise Junior High School, even though I excelled at football in a world where that sport was paramount (and where I was therefore privy to all the parties and connections and friends that entailed), I was still unable to attract a girlfriend, or anything remotely resembling female affection.

66.

Due to my family's moves, and to reasons still unbraided, I was in twelve different educational institutions, including homeschool, from the time I began preschool until I received a high school diploma. Barwise was the only school I ever attended from start to finish. Unfortunately Barwise was the only junior high school in the city to split its students between different high schools. So as I progressed to Wichita Falls High School, the high school both of my parents attended, one of the three large high schools in the city, and referred to simply as Old High, I lost half my friends, had just lost my mother, and was suffering from incredibly low self-esteem that was in no way ameliorated by any love or support at home. My only sustenance was football and the intellectual palace I was building in the closet at home. But no football stud could also be an intellect. The two were incompatible. To the world around me I was a crass, cynical jock who goofed around in class, and who cared little if women didn't go for me, as after all, I had my mates. That intellectual world was hidden, shameful, concealed, even from my family, in a cramped closet. It had nothing to do with God, Football, or Women. And it would be many years before I would emerge from that closet.

67.

Homeschooling had spoiled me in at least one major way, and the ramifications would affect me for many years. In homeschool the day lasts only as long as is required to learn and complete the material. If students are intelligent and motivated, it is not unusual for them to graduate high school at the age of fourteen or fifteen. But my mother would not let me do multiple days of schooling at once, as she specifically did not want me, due to fears for my soul, out of my appropriate age group. Later my father would refuse to let me skip grades because it would have destroyed my football career.

So in homeschool my school day lasted as long as it took for me to learn how to solve the required problems, which is to say, not very long at all, and much of the rest of my day during those years was spent on chores in the home, playing ball in the yard, or cruising the neighborhood on my bicycle.

This left me completely unprepared for traditional American schooling, which is comprised of significantly longer and set hours, and is also targeted at the human cognitive mean. Grading in my classes was typically determined as follows: forty percent to homework, twenty-five percent to examinations, ten percent to attendance, and another quarter masquerading under the nebulous title of *classroom participation*—which apparently meant that one needed to show up with a pulse, occasionally raise one's hand, and not cause the teacher any trouble.

Obviously such a grading system is specifically, intentionally designed to eliminate advantages based on either fluid or crystallized g, giving a massive advantage to students (typically girls, the more mature adolescent gender) who needn't be exceptionally bright, but who excel in attending class, *appearing* quietly attentive and interested, and who studiously complete rote homework. Rowdy, highly intelligent boys are disproportionately penalized in these grading schemas.

The homework, particularly in math classes, was usually copying out, each night, fifty examples (long-hand) of the exact same type of problem, showing all the steps—a task which could swallow no small chunk of my evening free time. In English it might be the same, with sentence-diagramming or repetitive discussions and written reports concerning the simple meaning of patently obvious texts the preferred mode of persecution.

And this really hurt, quite a lot. It greatly amplified the emotional pain I was already bearing at home. I simply could not understand why I should be forced to sit in a classroom for slow-ticking hours repetitively copying out the problems I understood before the teacher got to them.

I was a caught in a lie, as I was far ahead of the other students, but struggled mightily to prove that I was not, as I did not wish to be seen as the nerd. I arrived at a poor, immature unraveling of this knot, which was to loudly answer a difficult question with the crass aplomb of an asshole, thereby demonstrating to the teachers that I didn't need them, and simultaneously showing my friends that I was the rebel, not the nerd. I began to spend much of my time in class trying to get thrown out of class. My grades suffered accordingly.

68.

My parents dropped me off in each new school (in Wichita Falls alone there were three), enrolled me, and left, never making inquiries about educational options—to them the schools were ubiquitously distasteful, and the curriculum was, at best, a peripheral concern. It was up to my teachers, after the first six weeks or semester, to demand that I be removed from their classes and placed in the Gifted programs. But allow me a brief divagation to debate an educational truism derived from an *argumentum ad populum*, namely that Gifted programs serve the *gifted*.

Many of the students in Gifted programs throughout this country are not gifted (whatever that means), but are rather the sons and daughters of high-functioning and often wealthy parents who have ruthlessly pushed their children to emulate them. Private tutors and a multitude of amenities grant these privileged but often mediocre minds the ability to keep up. Enrollment in those exclusive classes, inevitably following the end of my first grading period at each new school, placed me in an environment with kids who might be closer to me cognitively, but who were, without exception, far more hardworking and devoted to their academic lives.

While the Gifted programs did make a point of largely eliminating busywork, I do not recall the work itself as more difficult. Significantly more powerful and complex challenges were not presented. *Tristram Shandy* and Schopenhauer did not replace *Animal Farm* when one ascended into the exalted ranks of the gifted. Mathematics courses still focused on the completion of large numbers of problems, rather than permitting the flexibility of allowing students movement through the textbook at the pace at which they demonstrated competence—for that degree of individualism in education would demolish the notion of the *class*.

69.

Even the novitiate psychometrician is keenly aware that chronological and mental ages are not synonymous. Dumping children into a milieu in which their mental age radically differs from the mental age of their chronological peers is child abuse.

How would *you* react (possessed, as you are, of all the emotional composure, maturity, and life-experience necessarily lacking in even a very bright youth) if forced by law, under the threat of corporal punishment, to sit in a room for the majority of each day, required to pay diligent attention to the delivery of a seventh-grade curriculum? Would you not find this torturous? How would you cope? Your personal mental age, dear reader, might or might not correspond closely to your chronological age, but if you can understand the volume you now hold in your hands, your mental-age is certainly not thirteen. When I was thirteen years old, neither was mine.

Deviations from the mean, in *either* direction, provoke powerful psychological and educational needs. The farther from the mean, the greater the need.

70.

This tedious mandatory educational paradigm represented another complex of ipsedixitisms, another fundamentalism, a secular Christianity, and I revolted. Clever, very bored in class, and with emotional problems at home, you may quickly guess the nightmare I presented to teachers unequipped and untrained to deal with the student they would, in all likelihood, encounter only once or twice in their pedagogical careers. At Old High, I recall being permanently kicked out of my freshman geography class for loudly pointing out to the other students, with the embellishment of a vociferous sneeze, whenever Coach Simpleton confidently, falsely asserted the location or habits of a particular country or people.

After a few weeks of this I was taken to the principal's office for a good thrashing, and was then assigned to a new geography class. The vice principal and new teacher stood with me outside the new class, before ever letting me step foot inside, and informed me, with iron authority, that in the new geography class I would pass, if and only if, I showed up every day, and never asked a question or opened my mouth to comment on the material in any way. That was it. That was American schooling as I knew it from the seventh to eleventh grades.

"You show up and you keep your mouth shut. Nobody cares if you know the answers to every goddamn question in the book. *This is a school.* Being smart doesn't give you a right to act different."

It was a warning I was to receive many times and in many ways throughout life. It was my mother's credo of Christian conformity rehashed. But it is a doctrine, today almost universally unquestioned, I have never been able to accept.

The lesson underlying the doctrine is simple: brilliance, unorthodox thought, newness, creates fear in others. Men call Evil that which they fear. To do Good, to be Good, is to *follow rules* well. In another Age, under a different regime, they would have permanently silenced me. Servetus and Galileo understood this well, as did many brilliants whose names have not come down to us.

71.

The South was just beginning to come under pressure to end corporal punishment during my years of schooling in the mid-1990s. I remember the first time I had to have a parental permission slip signed before the principals were allowed to smack me. The slip, depending on the school district, usually noted that the principals must refrain from giving more than three licks. My mother would write an addendum on those slips saying that they waived their or my rights to that clause. Some of my principals were not displeased.

72.

The reports from my teachers that I was a horror to deal with only reinforced my mother's certainty that the schools themselves were proving a morally degenerate environment for me. And so I felt my mother begin to pull away, as though she had failed with me, though after she died to me, I had to pretend that it didn't matter that I was a moral failure.

And this formed the crux of the next conflict between my parents. My mother's only concern was that I be placed in a holy environment, while my father's primary interest was in my sporting achievements. The question of what would prove the best *intellectual* environment never came up at all.

73.

How long can a man-sapling grow in poisoned soil before he begins to wither and die? Certainly I, a mere freshman in high school, though resilient, could not forever withstand the myriad horrors that seemed structurally integral to my every waking hour.

By my freshman year at Old High even my father was again in trouble. The rapid doubling of the population of the church (a largely geriatric congregation that didn't particularly desire precipitate growth), combined with my father's continued failure to directly confront others, as well as his ineradicable passive-aggressiveness, soon led a cabal of powerful elders to begin ousting his supporting staff one by one. Eventually he too was asked to leave, given a year's severance, and we were forced to move to our other spiritual bastion in town, the First Baptist Church of Wichita Falls, my grandfather's old pulpit. There my father was offered the temporary position of staff evangelist as he looked for new work.

My father's success, achieved so quickly, and lost so unexpectedly, brought him home each day forlorn, particularly as he felt himself twice a failure in the location in which his subconscious most desperately begged success. And this failure, with the resulting deterioration in the emotional climate of our home, restarted the slow collapse of my parents' marriage.

It was at this time that my father came under renewed pressure to become the *Spiritual Head of the Home*—by which my mother meant that he must reassert his masculine, Godly authority by bringing me under restraint. Theology aside, in practice this meant that the tough cowboy belt that had been used to beat me since Cow Town was now exchanged for a large, thick wooden board, not dissimilar to the fraternity paddle used in *Animal House*. My father, with his new preponderance of free time, took up the hobby of calligraphy, and with that newfound skill graced one side of the hardy weapon with the motto: *The Fear of the Lord*.

Today, when I reflect on those times, I feel cheapened by the fact that he had not retained enough of his Greek or Hebrew to pen the slogan for a classical punishment in a classical tongue. Regardless, by the end of the eighth grade my parents were no longer beating me with a leather cowboy belt. They were assaulting me, several times a day, with a heavy wooden board on which was inscribed a message from God Almighty.

My misery seemed unavoidable, unassailable, and constant. My home roiled with violence, shouting, and misery. My father's work throughout the latter half of junior high, at the church where I was forced to attend services every Sunday morning and evening and Wednesday night, was a beaker cracking under pressure. At school I was trapped in hour upon hour of terrifying anesthetization in classrooms that left me desperate and angry. My only outlet for that silent fury was on the sports field.

But no outlet for anger can ever replace a complete vacuum of love. For at home I received no love or affection, and at school I was (or believed myself) hopelessly unattractive to girls. And young, brawny football players in Texas do not express any more affection toward each other than a hearty chest bump and a "Hell Yes!" when one has done well on a play. The only hugs, or affectionate touches I ever received were the forced hugs that came after my father's beatings, as he tried to assuage his guilt.

Gradually, subconsciously, I realized that I did not want to be alive. I became fixated on a passage in the first chapter of Philippians, penned by the Apostle Paul, who wrote that, "For me to live is Christ, but to die is gain. But if I live in the flesh, this is the fruit of my labor: yet what I choose I wot not. For I am in a strait betwixt the two, having a desire to depart, and to be with Christ; which is far better: Nevertheless to abide in the flesh is more needful for you."

It seemed clear to me that for Paul too this life was nothing but anguish and torture, and, were it not for the Christian service he was obliged to perform, he would much rather be dead—however else a pastor might choose to spin that passage. So I began to pray daily that God would kill me, that I might join him in Heaven.

However God did not choose to kill me, and I, almost imperceptibly, grew aware that I had but one alternative. The absence of any Love in my life had desiccated my young heart. I was the dead oak, proud on the outside, hollow within. After some time, nearing the end of my first freshman semester at Old High, shortly after my fifteenth birthday, I finally accepted that there was only one solution.

I had to kill myself.

74.

Slow drops from the sweet deadly honeycomb of despair drip daily onto the brain, washing away anything or anyone, including God, that will alleviate the eternity of misery which can be compacted into each black overlong instant of temporal existence. And when each flickering, flitting, infinitesimal sliver of effervescent life squeezes and hurts and nauseates, the thought of going through another day without Love appears worse than an eternity of literal hellfire and brimstone, and it is then, and only then, my dear reader, that you are ready to shed that crude corpus grossly encapsulating your eternal soul. You would rather burn eternally. You are truly ready to die.

75.

I had decided to kill myself. And yet I had to reach out to God one last time, from *this* world, before I went before the heavenly tribunal a suicide. I could not kill myself, a fifteen-year-old freshman in high school, without a last sincere prayer for mercy, help, or the alleviation of my suffering. And so I went to my bedroom, closed and locked the door, and I prayed, with the last of my will to live, shedding the tears of a youth prepared to die. And as I prayed, my problems, which had seemed, in my adolescent imagination, so intractable and multifarious, coalesced in my mind into a single problem—that for the last long years of my life I had not even a sprinkling of real, true Love.

To me this lack of love achieved its greatest symbolism in the very real fact that it had been *years* since I had received even a simple kiss. And with that sudden intuition—that the lack of a single kiss perfectly symbolized the dearth of years of love—I realized that for just one taste of that single token of love, I would gladly trade my entire life.

The Terrible Beauty of the Evil Man

As soon as I reached that understanding, in what I thought would be the last prayer of my life, I had a second, Faustian flash of insight. I swore to God, strenuously, dearly, that if he would show me, through the simple token of a kiss, that I was loved, then I would not kill myself, and further, that I would devote my life to his service. I promised God that if he would grant me that kiss within three days I would not kill myself.

I figured I had the same right to test God, particularly when my very life was in the balance, as had Gideon in the Bible. I assumed that the chances that I would be kissed within three days due to natural causes astronomically slim, and that I was therefore asking God for a miracle. It had been almost three years since I had last been kissed, since the debacle of my infamous make-out session in the sixth grade, and there was not a single girl in Old High who had shown even the slightest interest in me. I therefore assumed that I would die in three days, and began to prepare accordingly.

76.

Despite my pessimism, I went through the morning of the first of those three days looking longingly into the eyes of the hundreds of girls that passed me in the labyrinthine hallways of Old High. But as the afternoon waned my eyes darkened, and I realized that God was going to let me die. By the second day I was sure of it, and planned the logistics of how I would kill myself. I thought there might be some degree of leniency the following evening in the afterlife, as I had given God the chance to remove my hopelessness with only a single, simple token.

I awoke on the third day with the dire, acute awareness that I would die that very night. I possessed not a granule of doubt. I had clarity, determination, and the *how* of it posed no problem at all. We lived one block from a major thoroughfare in the city, and I needed only to dress in dark clothing, wait for a large commercial truck moving at high speed, and then step out onto the road. My death would be instantaneous.

I was as sick of life as any man can be, and wanted nothing more than for the day to pass quickly, that my mortal suffering might end. I truly *believed*, and the severity of that awareness should not be understated. I knew that on that very evening I would begin to burn eternally in hellfire, but knew also that before I did, I would exist in one glorious moment before my creator. It would be a grand encounter, where he would sit in judgment, but where, in that precious twinkle in time, I would point the finger back at him, to declare him exactly what I knew him to be—the omnipotent torturer of the powerless, the sadistic jailor of anyone unwilling to be his slave. And then, do with me as he liked, I would have the amaranthine consolation of having spoken the truth, for even one instant, to the Lord God Almighty.

And these morbid reflections coursed relentlessly through my mind as I took a hall pass in one of my afternoon classes to use the restroom. I strolled about the school for several moments, taking what I knew would be my last look at its brick and mortar, and as I walked toward one of the hidden stairwells that slash and cross Old High in its mysterious architectural plan, as the third day's mid-afternoon sunbeams broke the windows and splashed down along the mop of brown hair atop my head, I turned a sharp corner to ascend the secluded stairs. And there she was.

77.

She was sitting on the first few steps, her knees together, her arms around them. As I turned the corner we both looked at each other, startled. Her name was Melissa, and I knew her, though only vaguely, for she was a year older, impossibly, intimidatingly beautiful and cool, even for the sophomore class, and I had previously met her only due to my football connections.

She must have seen in me the ferocity that only appears in a man who knows he will soon die, or perhaps the turns and tricks the light played in my eyes in the shadows of that cloistered stairwell electrified her in some ethereal way I do not understand, for her eyes, which had been staring down blankly at the steps beneath her, met mine, and the lethargy which had been paramount in her beautiful irises disappeared, and suddenly her eyes began to glow, pupils dilated.

"Hello," I said.

"Hi," she replied, and, as she did her arms fell from where they had wrapped around her knees, and she used her elbows to lean back on the step behind her. Her knees, still propped up on the lower steps, opened. Her legs, clothed in tight jeans, spread, and as they did her body fell open to me in a sensuality both languorous and virile, an intoxicating and paradoxical elixir of femininity crystallized perfectly in the rococo rondure of memory, but rendered nearly ineffable due to the impoverishment of

English as a language for matters of love and the heart. I knew in that moment, as one animal senses it in another, that the sudden lassitude of her body was no mid-afternoon apathy, but an invitation to possess her, and even had I not known it from her body I would have known it from her glowing eyes. No thought propelled me. Instinct enveloped me. I stepped between her spread legs and leaned over her, my hands on either side of her body, my mouth inches from hers.

"What are you doing out of class?"

"I don't know," she whispered.

But almost before the last syllable had slipped between her lips my arms were around her. She scrambled up a step and bit her lower lip. I pressed forward again and she placed a hand on my chest.

"What do you want from me?" she asked.

But there was no answer when the answer was known. She was on her feet, and my arms were around her, and my mouth was on hers, and her lips were sweet and beautiful, and my tongue danced with hers in a frenetic waltz that mimicked her half-hearted attempts to climb the stairs away from me. We slowly climbed the stairs, one at a time, my body pressing her against the wall, locked together, our kisses frenzied, then slow and passionate, then alternating back to that ecstatic rhythm, and I tasted her, inhaled her, felt the smoothness of her cheek.

We reached the top of the stairs with my arms around her. I pulled back, taking her saliva with me, feverish, but wanting to look into her eyes, to know if she too, wanted this. She did.

I looked down and saw that my right leg was shaking uncontrollably. Mortified, I tried my best to still it, but that was impossible. She looked down, saw my shaking leg, looked back up at me, wrapped her hand around the back of my neck, and pulled me to her. And once again we were bound together in a kiss that forced every dream, memory, act, or thought I had ever experienced to appear as silly and fruitless digressions from the beautiful delicious heat flooding through a heart that had perished slowly over long years without the sustenance of even the lightest drops of love. And in that moment, that perfect inexhaustible moment of magic and miracle and bliss, I, who had been so close to death, returned to life.

Even the most cynical of us knows that there are things that can give us life or kill us, things that we cannot explain or define, phenomena whose walls Science has not begun to breach—the blood of our Spirit.

And whatever it is in a man that gives him life, and which had atrophied so terribly in me, sprang back suddenly into being, and in her arms and through her lips I awoke.

As soon as it began it was over. Someone came up the stairwell behind us, and she bolted from my arms. But I stayed at that spot for long moments, eyes closed, tasting her, smelling her, dissolving in the memory of her touch. Living.

78.

I saw her occasionally, in the days and weeks that followed, but she would not look at me. What had happened had happened, and in her mind, I presume, there was simply no explanation for it. Certainly the young men who surrounded her with attention were in a league far beyond mine. And I was to remain in Wichita Falls only one more semester, as was she, though neither of us knew that at the time. She moved West, to Amarillo I think, and I, I went much further in the other direction, due East. After that year I never saw her again.

79.

But before I take leave of Wichita Falls I should tell you that my life did radically change before I left, as my father intentionally milked his severance to the last week before taking a new job. The kiss that saved my life reinvigorated my life, but did so in conjunction with one other important alteration in me.

By the middle of my freshman year, around the time I was ready to die, my parents decided that my acne, which had spread all over my upper body, was so severe that I needed to see a doctor. So I was taken to Dr. Garbacz, a dermatologist, the father of a boy in my class at school. My skin did not respond to several rounds of different medications, and so finally Dr. Garbacz had no choice. He placed me on Accutane, a very powerful drug.

Accutane was an unpleasant option, as it came with a number of side effects, one of which I discovered that winter, during basketball season, when Coach Simpleton (who, aside from his geographical and pedagogical acumen, doubled as the boy's freshman basketball coach) took me aside and asked if there was something wrong with me. Strangely, I could no longer run and dribble simultaneously. I, who had never faltered in even the most demanding athletic feats, and who would, in my freshman track-and-field season later that spring, run a fifty-four-second quarter-mile, could no longer make a simple layup. That winter I had to quit the basketball team.

But that mattered to me not in the least, for as the spring semester began my acne disappeared, and it was discovered that underneath that blanket of redness and pustules there existed a bone structure shapely enough that I, a lowly, ugly freshman, gradually noticed that girls were stealing glances at me in class.

What began as light flurries of attention by winter's end soon became a blizzard of commotion. Within weeks I was talking, laughing, and flirting with girls throughout the school, and not only those in my class. Even several older girls approached me. I particularly remember a ride home from a distant varsity basketball game with two of the most beautiful sisters in the school, their father driving. The younger, a ravishing junior, chatted with me amiably for hours. Her older sister, a senior cheerleader, and one of the most popular girls in a school with hundreds of students per class, actually pouted when her father refused to let her drive me home alone that night after our return to Wichita Falls. An avalanche had occurred in my life.

I was born Finis Leavell Beauchamp, but from my infancy it had been decided that I would be given a nickname, so as not to be confused with my father, Finis Pierre Joseph Beauchamp, when our names were called. The name, chosen near that great river of southern Louisiana, is Beau, which in the French patois spoken there means *beautiful*.

For the first time in my life I believed the nickname now fit. In two or three brief months I came to abandon my general disgust with my appearance. I felt that I had finally, unbelievably, become beautiful.

80.

It was as my life had turned sharply for the better, and I found myself desirable, sought after, and with a rare slot open, the following autumn, for me to advance, with an elite group of my fellow freshmen, to the varsity football squad, bypassing the junior varsity, that my parents informed me that we were moving. But in the continuing absence of any healthy home life, football and the newfound attention from girls had become the totality of my existence. I screamed. I raged. I threatened. I cajoled. Nothing worked.

In my final plea I appealed to my father's love of sport, for my football squad, specifically the members of my class, would prove to be the most talented group to pass through Old High (the school possessed of one of the most celebrated football programs in the history of Texas high school football) since the team of my uncle, Landrum Pinson Leavell III, a generation before. Numerous teammates, some, children of the members of that old, storied team, would in later years play for Division I college programs, as I likely would have, had I stayed.

For a brief moment my father wavered, considering the possibility of letting me live with his spinster sister in Wichita Falls for my last three years of high school. But my mother would hear nothing of it. Her father had ripped her out of Old High, despite the rage it provoked, in the last semester of her senior year, so that he might take control of the seminary in New Orleans. Though you might think her personal experience would have granted her a measure of empathy, she showed me no pity.

And so with great rage, but without further ado, we packed our bags, and moved East, to the 1950s.

81.

There is a block of land within the United States known to the rest of America as *The South*. And while this cognomen can refer to a geographical region, many Americans primarily think of the South as a culture—one noticeably distinct from the rest of the nation. But non-Southerners, in my experience, are typically unaware that the cultural South is not monolithic, but is populated with a variety of sub-cultures and dialect or accent regions, and that it is arranged in irregular concentric ellipses that grow more intensely Southern the farther one penetrates.

There are Southern states, like Virginia, which may seem foreign to the denizen of Manhattan or San Francisco. However, layered within the South lies the much more exotic Deep South—an arc of land beginning roughly with Louisiana, proceeding through Mississippi, Alabama, Georgia, and curving up to include South Carolina. And the Deep South today may appear as strange to the contemporary Virginian as Virginia does to the San Franciscan. Movement deeper into the South today means movement between decades, or even centuries, in ideology and mannerisms.

It is true that inside the Deep South there are Northern bubbles, like Atlanta, but there are also three pockets left within the Deep South that are un-Reconstructed, that are essentially antebellum, that differ as greatly from the rest of the Deep South as the Deep South does from Manhattan's Greenwich Village, and where modernity, where it has no specific practical or financial application, has been fought with ruthless vehemence. The first of these, southern Louisiana, I have shown you. When I was a child, in the 1990s, the Grand Wizard of the Ku Klux Klan ran a strong campaign to become governor of the state, and, though he lost, he did receive the majority of the white vote.

Lanterns on the Levee, the memoir of William Alexander Percy, particularly in its latter half, is an elegant literary exposition of the universe that is the second of these last remaining truly Southern locations, the Mississippi Delta, an alluvial plain that is one of the most agriculturally fertile regions in the world—yet is simultaneously one of the most economically destitute areas in America.

But when my parents tore me from Wichita Falls, it was to go to the last of these three bastions of pre-modernity. They took me to the Black Belt of Alabama, and not to its periphery, but into its very core.

Dear friends, when I awoke that first morning, I was staring out of a window at the cotton field that bordered my new home, in the countryside several miles outside Selma, Alabama, the most Southern place left in the world.

82.

I walked outside of our new home that summer, that first week we lived in the 1950s, the summer before my sophomore year of high school, and breathed in an air that reeked of the thick, sweet perfume produced from the endless and varied vegetation that grows from every inch of the loam from which the Black Belt derives its name. The land is so fertile that there are a number of plants that exist and thrive solely through their ability to feed on other plants, particularly the blankets of the kudzu vine, which are so widespread, thick, green, and leafy, that when we drove from our country house into Selma it appeared to me that we were lost in a tropical Arcadia. The Alabama River snaked through the area, and the humidity was overpowering after our abandonment of the oil-rich, but very dry, windy plains that gave rise to Wichita Falls. I hadn't been back in the Deep South, not to live, since I was eight years old, and I had forgotten how much I had forgotten.

I had stepped through a warp in time. The men were gentlemen, the women belles. The earth was as fertile as any to be found on the globe. The people were so polite that you, on first impression, were certain they were either senile or sociopathic. The demographics and politics were simple. Selma was roughly eighty percent African-American and twenty percent pure, undiluted Anglo-Saxon, yet the mayor was still the same white mayor involved in the attack on the Civil Rights marchers more than three decades before—the infamous Bloody Sunday of March 7, 1965.

Selma, iconic catalyst of the Civil Rights movement, was, at the turn of the twenty-first century, if not *de jure*, at least *de facto* racially segregated, from schools to churches to restaurants. The elite prep school I would attend, John T. Morgan Academy, founded only three months after Bloody Sunday, had never admitted a black student. The public high school, Selma High, had no white students other than those sent from the orphanage. The middle class was endangered. It was a tower of aristocratic and patriarchal sentiment. Whole areas of the region, certainly after dark, were off-limits to members of the other race. Crime, illiteracy, and poverty were pandemic. Anything and everything of real value in the area that could be owned was owned by a tiny fragment of the population—a small oligarchy of purebred WASPs who had nothing to do with the poor whites.

It was lush and exotic and possessed of an overpowering physical beauty and fragrance that existed in tandem with a potent voracious commitment to every social dynamic you can't imagine possibly existing in twenty-first century America. And it was my new home.

83.

The abandonment of my friends, my athletic and newfound social success in Wichita Falls, my entire world, to move back to the Deep South, sent me into shock. Even though, quite strangely, moving to Selma felt, inexplicably, like moving back home, as I am a Deep Southerner, not a Texan, my body and mind resisted the transition, and I slowly shut down over the summer. I lost my appetite, my desire to emerge from my bed, my will to live. And for the first time my parents, surprisingly, did not try an irrational Evangelical cure or an exorcism. They took me to a normal medical doctor, who diagnosed me with a simple case of depression, and prescribed a common anti-depressant.

The Terrible Beauty of the Evil Man

The medication took effect within a few weeks, just as two-a-days began with my new football team. Or perhaps it did nothing, but the strenuous physical exercise that came with the start of the football season, getting out of the house daily, meeting and bonding with new teammates, as well as the slowdown in the physical beatings during the depression, all worked together to reignite a correspondence with the world, and I emerged from that lifeless enervation.

However, affecting me perhaps as much as any of these other things was the fact that I had, through good fortune, landed on the most talented varsity football squad in the entire prep school system in Alabama. They had won the state championship the year before, and would go on to win it the next three years, the years of my graduating class, setting a record for consecutive championships in the state. The training was not nearly as rigorous, or intense, as what I had known in Texas, but then my new prep school was much smaller, and they, of course refused to play with non-whites. However, considering the uncontrollable situation into which I had been thrust, I could not have found, in the segregated Black Belt, a more gifted group of athletes with which to play the game that, until then, had probably saved my life.

And it was from Jerusalem that we learned guilt, which saved our souls, but from Athens we learned play, which saved our lives.

84.

I began school at John T. Morgan Academy, a fortress of wealth and exclusivity and unblemished whiteness in a town that was impoverished, overwhelmingly black, and mired in gross ignorance. I believe, based on my observations in Selma, that a full quarter of the population, both white and black, would have been incapable of reading and understanding a basic news article in *The Wall Street Journal* or any other serious adult publication. Access to education, like access to capital, is a potent form of social control—though the denial of access to a quality liberal education can be, and has been, used from both ends of the political spectrum, as Václav Havel discovered under the Communists in Czechoslovakia.

Selma is a potpourri of paradoxical social dynamics. It is a third world village in the first world, a disconnected amalgamation of nouveau plantations, *Junker* manors in no danger of *bodenreform*, a delicately balanced world adamantly refusing to fall off the precipice of time. But the refusal to move with time makes it timeless—and though you may find it uniquely grotesque, unjust, it is impossible to deny the beauty of anything, or any place left in this vulgar world which maintains a powerful sense of timelessness in our shallow, crass, fractured Age, where news is no longer news twelve hours after it is Twittered. Selma, quite simply, means to cease to move. Selma is terrifying. Selma is beautiful.

85.

I blinked slowly, uncertain if I was being teased, when warned by a school administrator at summer's end that, starting with the new school year, students would no longer be allowed to store firearms in their automobiles in the school parking lot. Incredibly, she was not joking. That first week in my new school I listened to the grumbling from the adolescent student body about the great annoyance of no longer being able to keep a high-powered rifle or shotgun in their trucks at all times.

However, I did attempt to start at Morgan Academy with an open mind, and as I began it without the furuncles and craters that had plagued me throughout junior high, I was the new, attractive face in the intimate, unchanging world of the young, bored, and wealthy, and so became a source of fascination. And as I was able, as a sophomore, to not only make varsity on the football team, but to start several games as Morgan won its second consecutive state championship, I was granted a degree of immediate social prestige few in my class could command.

The development of that social power outside the home, contrasted with my powerlessness in the home, resulting from the wooden board beatings that were slowly, post-depression, picking back up in both frequency and brutality, had a complex, and very destructive effect on me. My anger, misery, and bitterness had not gotten better with the move to Selma, or even with what I saw as that miraculous kiss. That kiss and my newfound attractiveness had only deepened the misery, forcing an inescapable awareness of the painful contrast of my home-life with my social life. I do not think it strange that only then did I come to gradually compare my home to the outer world. It had still not been so very long that I had acquired significant exposure to the world outside the home.

However, pain is only pain, and I had been inured to physical pain since I was a toddler. One of the primary reasons I was able to deliver powerful hits on the football field was that I had no fear of pain or injury, allowing me to accelerate through the moment of impact. Most players, fearful of injury, will, just before the moment of contact, imperceptibly slow—and that subconscious fear is ineradicable for anyone who has not learned to delink pain and fear through repeated exposure to powerful bouts of physical pain.

But if pain caused me no more fear than it did ancient Spartan youths, I was psychically far less healthy than they, for it was the lacerations of the heart and psyche, quite naturally, which turned me into the demon my mother had so dreaded all along. I have never found it bothersome that my parents repeatedly subjected me to physical pain, no more than did a harsh upbringing disturb Xenophon in his examination of the *agoge* attended by his sons—but *how* they did it, and *why* they did it, and the combination of coldness, irrationality, and unpredictability that surrounded it left scars on my soul that took many years to heal.

Perhaps the most intractable of those psychic wounds, the one that, during those years in Selma, led me to doubt my very sanity, was my initial awareness and acceptance of the overarching principle that it was not me who was ill, or possessed by demons, but rather my parents who were irrational, unhealthy, and unstable. That meant the upending of my entire worldview and value system, though that new comprehension developed with the most ponderous locomotion, for it implied the overthrow of dozens of beliefs peripheral to and dependent on the formerly coherent dynamic that had given reality shape.

Were demons real? Were my parents morally good? If demons were real, were they influencing me or my parents? If demons were both real and influencing me rather than my parents then were demons good rather than evil?

It was at that point that I began to question the veracity of the claims of the New Testament. But as I had no knowledge of an alternate system capable of explaining the nature of existence and reality, I did not look to replace the New Testament, but to reinterpret it. As far as I knew, it was the good guys who had been cast from heaven. Viewed through the epistemological lens of Quine, I was suffering from the rapid disintegration of some of the most central strands in my belief-web.

The possibility of a radically new worldview had never existed in my mind, and the inability for an otherwise bright person to consider such a simple solution is difficult to explain. However, consider a possible world in which you had never, even a single time, met someone with a sophisticated worldview different from your own—in my case the viewpoint of a liberal Christian, or a Muslim, Jew, Buddhist, Agnostic, or Atheist—nor had any exposure whatsoever to their literature or ideology. How could you possibly be so bold as to assume that every intelligent person you have ever known is completely wrong concerning the totality of what constitutes existence? How could a sophisticated Frenchman of the early fifteenth century have posited that the world was round, that millions of persons existed on undiscovered continents, or that the universe did not revolve around the Earth?

Every human I knew viewed my father as a spiritual master, a moral paradigm, son-in-law to one of the great leaders of the generation. And I? I was the disrespectful, sarcastic, aggressive, rebellious jackass sent by God to test my holy parents. I was the one who had spurned an outsized pouring out of God's natural gifts, along with the chance to become a future leader of the Christian world. I became the object of prayer for many, that I might repent and return to the pure path, in order to take up my proper position.

So I too thought, for long years. If I had attempted to hint (as I would have been far too frightened to explicitly say) to an adult in my life, perhaps a teacher in school or in the church, what was going on in my home, by fumblingly describing the daily beatings, or the religious and psychological terror, I would have been reminded quite clearly that what my parents were doing was an inescapable and just mandate from God, and was for my own good. Specific verses, especially Proverbs 13:24, as well as biblical stories of demoniacs, which of course I knew by heart, would have been used as justifications for my parents' actions, as indelible proofs, replete throughout the New Testament, of regular demonic intervention in the mundane.

To completely invert everything you think you know about the metaphysics of reality, as a sixteen-year-old, is to traverse an impassable maze in the dark, your only guide the echoes of doubt and fear, trial and error, that reverberate from undefined and shifting walls. Understanding that it was my parents and society who were deluded, and that I was reacting terribly, albeit naturally, to horrific conditions, required passing through the Cretan Labyrinth of the poisoned mind, where to become lost means insanity, and if and when one does regain his way, it is only to find that he has not been obviated from the responsibility of slaying the Minotaur—which is the irrational Guilt of all who have ever been forced to revalue all values.

87.

If *you*, today, were locked in an asylum, and left for years, or worse, were born in one, how would you learn to distinguish yourself from all others? How would you come to certainly *know* you were the one who was sane?

88.

The physical law of the conservation of energy has a spiritual equivalent in the conservation of pain. Hell introduced into my parents as children found its way into me, and once in me could not remain indefinitely stopped up. Pain, as a type of energy, requires either a release or conversion. It is the wise and blessed who are capable of converting pain into Art or reinvigorated Life. As a scared, hurt, confused adolescent I simply lacked that capacity.

There are those who externalize their pain, harming others, and there are those who internalize, reserving the greatest atrocities for themselves. My pain was too great, my will too strong, for either. I needed both.

89.

It was at the afterparties following Morgan football victories that I learned to drink. I would tell my parents that I was spending the night with a friend, and would travel to whichever schoolmate's rural hunting cabin housed the party that weekend. The uninhabited miles of woodlands exulted on those autumn evenings, nude but for a gossamer slip of starlight, full with the chaotic symphony of a bacchanalia that erupted into the night's blackness from the throats of the inebriated.

I had been raised with the notion that the consumption of alcohol, of any kind, in any amount, was grossly immoral. And so, without any adult guidance as to moderate or responsible drinking, I assumed that as I was sinning by drinking a single beer, I might as well have twenty.

By the time I reached the final months of my junior year I had, at least twice, discovered a new concoction derived from the admixture of a half-gallon of vodka with a gallon of orange juice. I would empty half of the gallon of orange juice onto the ground, and pour the half-gallon of vodka into the orange juice jug. I would then finish Paul Bunyan's libation over the course of an all night party in the woods—with a joint. God had seen fit to curse me with a tolerance for amounts of alcohol that would have killed a ruddy Viking.

90.

A predilection for consuming copious amounts of alcohol, when one is cycling through the routine throes of adolescent hormonal flux, and is burning with an inner angst resulting from regular physical abuse, produces a predictable proclivity for rash behavior that inevitably brings deleterious consequences. I got into fights. Or rather, I got into one fight, for after that none at Morgan wished to further engage me in that way.

It was the fall semester of my sophomore year, and I had spent my entire history class one Friday before a football game flirting with a girl who, as I well knew, had a boyfriend in the senior class. However, this young lady was responding very well to my attentions, and promised to fellate me at the afterparty that night once her boyfriend was too drunk to note her absence. I was pleased.

At the afterparty that night, flush with our victory on the field and the eighteen beers I had consumed over the course of four hours, I stumbled over to the girl, who was sitting next to her boyfriend on a log bench around the bonfire that was traditional for those autumnal parties in the countryside.

"Are you ready to give me that blowjob now?" I whispered.

But then she was blushing furiously, and there was a sudden scattering of dozens of young men, and I found myself shoved some yards away, into the center of a tightly packed circle of dozens of onlookers, stark across from the livid boyfriend who was two years older than me. I have reflected deeply on this matter, and in time have come to realize that after consuming eighteen beers, one's whisper is not as inaudible as one might wish.

At this point a great deal of whooping and hollering occurred from the gathered onlookers, primarily to the effect that he (the frighteningly angry senior trembling with adrenaline two feet away) should really whip my ass. I did not take well to this line of conversation, but made no move toward my antagonist in the makeshift, ever-shifting human boxing ring. And as he seemed to hesitate as well, a gross breach of his honor in the Black Belt, the massed onlookers shoved him into me. It was on perhaps the third of those careening bounces off me that he aimed and landed his one blow—a shot that glanced lightly from the top right of my forehead.

I reached back instinctively, and delivered a punch to the center of his face. He leaned back, stumbled, but kept his feet. The mob urged him on to another effort. He drunkenly fumbled toward me and swung, missing wildly. This time I stepped forward and punched him so hard that the skin of his face split. He began to bleed. I told him that if he knew what was good for him he would quit.

It was clear that he had discovered a new recalcitrance in his earlier desire to defend the honor of his beloved. He looked around uncertainly, mopping the blood from his eyes with his sleeves, seemingly shocked by the ravenous screams of the mob demanding that he recoup his honor. Clearly he could not be allowed to walk away the loser in a fight with a boy two years his junior, even though that young man was acquitting himself with a defense he would have deemed impossible only moments before. The crowd would not part for his escape. I looked around, and was shocked to hear the most vociferous screaming coming from his girlfriend. Fickle girl. Only that morning she had promised me her most intimate attentions.

He reached back, and I stepped aside before he even began the forward thrust of his last clumsy punch. And this time I had no choice. I hit someone, for the first time in my life, in the face, with the full power I could mass. I did not miss, and it looked as though his face exploded. What was left of his visage was a bloody mess.

His girlfriend helped him hobble from the field, and drove him to the hospital. I saw him the next Monday in school, his face bandaged. I asked his forgiveness for shaming his girlfriend, and he granted it. He told me that when he was in the emergency room he had refused the sheriff's request to press charges. He also told me that the doctors did not initially believe he had been in a fist fight. It had appeared to them as though his face had been shredded with glass. I had hit him three times, but as I came to learn, and as boxers know well, a punch well thrown can, rather than bruising, simply split the skin, as though it were a ripe plum.

For the remainder of that Friday night I sat on the log bench freshly vacated by the departed couple and reveled in the glorification of my fighting prowess that descended on all sides from the young men of the Black Belt's gentry. Fighting there is no crime, but sport, as it was in Rome, and personal honor is paramount above most other considerations—and in that sense the culture is not dissimilar from that of the Arabs or Japanese. The Black Belt is a wild and aggressive region, and the Anglo-Saxons are a historically warlike people. What had happened that night reflected well on me in their eyes. I remember passing my hand repeatedly through that bonfire, seeing if it could burn me. It did not. I felt invincible.

91.

My inner turmoil, churning so roughly within me each day, could not be expelled solely through collisions on the field of play or even through fisticuffs in midnight's wood. My personal pain, hidden from the world, was too great to eliminate solely through its distribution to others. In order to quench the conflagration within me, it was necessary to learn how to visit punishment upon myself as well, just as a man, miserable from the itch of a slow-healing burn, may yell at those nearest him, and then, finding that unsatisfactory, the wound insatiate, will scratch his scabs until they bleed.

I do not remember consciously learning to cut myself, or hearing someone discuss the fact that there were those who did. Nor do I recall the first time it happened. I imagine that it was unintended, that one day I must have accidentally ripped open the skin of my arm or leg, perhaps brushing past an old barb projecting from a country fence. Then, the blood flowing freely, the sharp bite of pain sudden and searing on my flesh, I found relief in an agony that came with a clear and comprehensible reason, unlike the nebulous impenetrable heartache within.

The vermilion drops, gathering in the puncture, riding momentum in a stream down my limb, dripping softly, steadily to the ground in an inaudible patter, would have kept rhythm with the exultation of my heart as it reveled in the surprising jolt of adrenaline. And in that outer hurt I would have discovered that for a moment, perhaps a few hours, my inner, incommunicable hurt would dissipate, dissolve in my consciousness, as my focus was flung toward the flow and coagulation and encrustation of blood on my body.

I found that, in a moment of dire necessity, there was a specific spot on each wrist that needed only a touch of the blade to spout a few dark drops before healing almost instantly, leaving no mark. Occasionally I cut deeply, considering again the relief of suicide, but, though my left wrist still bears the visible scar of one particularly thorough adventure with a dagger, that was a relief I did not dare claim. I was unable to summon the unflinching will to die I had possessed the day I demanded a kiss from God. You see, I believed he had granted my request of a single, pure kiss, and in so doing he had gained not my gratitude, but my fear. And without the removal of my structural circumstantial pain he had also gained my hatred.

I was sixteen years old, six foot two, well over two hundred pounds, and was being beaten daily with a heavy wooden board by persons my society considered paradigms of moral virtue—persons who had, under the law, every right to afflict me in a way that, had they performed the same act toward an adult, would have resulted in felony assault charges.

Do you realize how hard you have to hit a youth of that size and muscle, one who was almost immune to physical pain, in order to elicit cries?

92.

Years before, as a teenager at Barwise, I had threatened my mother by telling her that I was going to call the police, to report that she was physically abusing me. I threatened to take pictures of my backside and bottom after several beatings and use that as proof against her in court.

Her response was to make me read an article she had dredged up, a horrendous tale of egregious physical and sexual abuse in which some poor young girl had been chained for years in a small closet, nude, starved, at the merciless whim of deranged parents, beaten daily to the point of actual physical deformity. By the time the police discovered her, removed her from the closet, and got her back to a healthy body weight, her spine was permanently disfigured, and there were numerous scars she would carry for life.

"*That's* abuse," my mom informed me. "You're just getting spankings. Call the police if you want. They won't do anything. *Everyone* gets spankings."

Only many years later did I learn that this is a trick of child-abusers. Simply expose the child to stories of far more grotesque forms of abuse, convince the gullible kid that that is what is meant by *child abuse*, and then the more moderate abuse will appear normative parental discipline. And indeed, virtually every child I knew in the Southern Evangelical world had confirmed, when asked, that they were spanked by their parents. So I had no way of knowing, until several more years had passed, and I asked the same questions in greater detail, that others' spankings differed radically in both frequency and severity.

However by my sophomore year I had come to believe that, even granting the existence of far more horrific cases of abuse, what my parents were doing was illegal. In Selma I again threatened my mother with the police, particularly as the beatings with the board grew more severe. I remember clearly her response to my threat. She calmly ordered my father and me to get into the car, and we drove into Selma. I did not know where we were going. We eventually stopped in front of a building.

"Do you know this place, Beau?"

"No," I responded blankly.

"This is Selma's orphanage. You ever call the police, pull some stupidity like reporting child abuse, and guess what? This is exactly where you'll be living the next day. This is where you go when they take you away from your parents. And guess what else? You won't be going to Morgan anymore. You'll be at Selma High. And how many other white kids you think are going to be there with you?"

This threat terrified me, because I knew she was right. If I reported my parents there was only one place for me (and perhaps also my siblings), and that was the orphanage. I also knew my mother was earnest in her threat, as my father had told me that on multiple occasions her father had threatened her in the same way.

93.

I remember the day the beatings came to an end. My father was out of the house, and I had come home from school. I do not remember if my siblings were present in the home, nor do I remember the triviality that infuriated my mother that day, but at that time in her life, due to certain hormonal medical issues, she did not require a significant provocation to tell me to fetch the board.

I went to retrieve it, and prepared for my daily dose of corporal medicine. I too was furious that day, revolted by the thought of my mother forcing me to touch my toes or bend over the kitchen table so that she could aim blows at buttocks already sore from the squats I had done that day or the day before in the school gym.

I brought the board and handed it to her, stared down into the pools of blue ice that were her irises, shivered with disgust and humiliation at what was about to happen.

"Bend over and put your hands flat on the table."

I stood sullen, eyeing her.

"Did you hear me, punk kid? I said turn around and put your hands flat on the table and bend over or I'm going to add on licks."

It was in that moment that I simply lost the ability to compose rational thoughts. A memory flashed through my mind. I remembered once reading of Hitler relating that after suffering the trauma of years of his father's beatings, he had conquered the violence in a single day by taking dozens of physical blows without crying out. His father never beat him again. By demonstrating immunity to pain and fear he had ended his suffering. That thought flickered in and through the door of my mind in a trice and I didn't hesitate. I simply cried out, almost incoherent.

"Do you think you can hurt me?"

"*What* did you say to me, you little punk?"

"Do you think you can hurt me with that board?"

My mother's flushed face suddenly blanched, and I stepped toward her, staring down, true madness pouring from me. She trembled. I had never brazenly refused a beating, and I could see her quickly trying to determine whether I had broken completely with reason, whether I would take her to the ground and strangle her in the kitchen floor. But my mother, at that time in her life, was not gentle, but was possessed of an indomitable tenacity and cunning. She quickly regained her composure and struck out at me with the board, slicing at my torso, poking me repeatedly in the chest, taunting me.

"Do you think that hurts?" I cried. "Do you think anything you can do with that board can hurt me? There is nothing you can ever, ever do with that piece of wood that will be worse than what I can do to myself!"

I reached back and slapped the right side of my face with my right hand as hard as I could. The reverberation rang out in the kitchen, and through the open doorway of the dining room behind me.

"Can you hit me harder than that?" I whispered, breathing hard.

I then struck the left side of my face. The clap rang out. Blood rushed to my face, beginning to discolor it, the first incarnadine symptom of the bruises to come. My mom stepped back, trembling, holding the board with both hands like a broadsword.

"Stop it!" she barked.

"Stop it? I don't have to stop it!" I said, my voice sick with anger. "You want to hurt me. But you *can't* hurt me. I can't even hurt myself!"

I began slapping myself, harder and harder, repeatedly, alternating hands, snarling like a dog. With each blow I visited upon my face I cried out: "Can you hit me harder than *this*?"

"Stop it, stop it, stop it!" she demanded.

I continued to beat myself until I was exhausted, losing vision, and nearly unconscious. The blows slowed and then ceased. I stepped forward, and leaned down over her. She was trembling and terrified. My face was battered, my eyes bloodshot, my breathing ragged.

"No matter what you ever try to do me, no matter how hard you or dad hit me, you'll never, ever be able to hurt or hit me harder than what I can do to myself. Don't even try. *You cannot hurt me.*" And with that I walked away from her and went upstairs to recover in the closet in my bedroom.

And finally, at the age of sixteen, a lesson was learned, and neither of my parents ever tried to beat or hit me again.

94.

With the cessation of physical assault, combined with my ability to disappear from home due to the acquisition of a driver's license, my parents were at a loss as to how they might police and rehabilitate me. They settled, grudgingly, on the idea of therapy, though they were opposed in principle to therapy or psychoanalysis, which they saw as derivative of a materialistic, atheistic worldview that eliminated or ignored the spiritual component of emotional disturbances—in their minds the root of nearly all chronic emotional pain. In order to eradicate the possibility of the nefarious ambuscades of heresy likely to arise in normative therapy my parents arranged for me to meet with a special *Christian* therapist they had contacted and interrogated.

I met with this man a couple of times, and found him so amusingly bizarre that in school each day after an appointment I would form the center of attention over break by regaling my classmates with tales of his eccentricities. After one such recounting, my friend Palter privately admitted that he was seeing the same therapist. With this serendipitous discovery I struck upon the idea of having a bit of fun with our very unusual therapist. Palter, ever ready for a good prank, eagerly enlisted as my partner in a caper.

Palter and I had regular appointments on different days of the week, so we arranged and scripted a story that we would tell him, from divergent points of view, on alternate weekdays. Palter was, and remains, the most natural and convincing liar I have ever met in my life, so I anticipated little difficulty in implementing our prank.

We both began hinting to the therapist that "something big" was destroying our lives, but which we weren't yet comfortable discussing. Of course he was eager to discover the source of our angst. Eventually, in session, I grudgingly disclosed that Palter was pressuring me to engage in magical occult rituals, and that I had reluctantly agreed to participate. During his sessions Palter hesitantly admitted that I was encouraging him to participate in the same behaviors, and that these rituals involved lying down nude in the center of magical pentagrams, reading from Satanic books, chanting incantations, and interacting with the demons physically manifesting before us in the room. This therapist, who had blithely dismissed the notion that my parents had ever abused me, particularly once I related that the beatings had come to an end, was now truly convinced that, conversely, it was the practice of magic that had put me in immediate peril.

Palter and I soon began to entertain a large crowd at break each week in Morgan's quadrangle, as we recounted, with every possible flourish, the latest supernatural tales we had spun to tease and toy with our amadan of a therapist.

Eventually the therapist communicated with my parents. I finally, after many years, had an explanation for my inexplicable ungodly behavior. My parents were saddened, but not shocked, by the prognosis. I found, when looking into their sad and serious eyes, that I could not hold back my rollicking laughter, and confessed to the entire multi-week scheme.

Dear friends, it seems that the fountainhead of my psychiatric disturbance and misery was due not to a chemical imbalance, physical abuse, or to deleterious environmental stimuli, but rather to repeated cases of demonic sexual assault. No, I do not jest. He told my parents that he believed that I had literally been sexually abused by demons.

95.

This subject matter is admittedly so fabulous that I could scarce think it strange if you, the reader, weren't skeptical concerning the veracity of this episode. Perhaps you are certain that there couldn't possibly be licensed therapists, much less serious, legitimately credentialed medical doctors who would assent to such primitive and bizarre notions.

However, a surprising number of works on the subject have been written by men with mainstream academic degrees. Others are for popular consumption. There are more than a million printed copies of *Pigs in the Parlor*, a manual which provides instruction on how to use spiritual judo to fight off these demonic infestations. America recently discovered that its military was not immune, when one naval chaplain (and Air Force Academy graduate) soberly claimed, on syndicated radio, that he was able to cure a sailor of homosexuality through the use of an exorcism.

Moreover, belief in the malignant activity of demons is not restricted to Evangelical Protestants. In 1998 the Catholic Church issued an updated manual (their first since the early seventeenth century) on how to perform exorcisms. The Vatican also maintains an active International Association of Exorcists. One of the association's founders, from the diocese of Rome, publicly claimed to have personally performed some one hundred and sixty thousand exorcisms, often up to twenty a day.

Yes, gullible fundamentalists exist. However, there are also elite contemporary medical doctors, authentic psychiatrists, who have publicly espoused a belief in the proposition that literal demons negatively impact mental health. An associate professor of clinical psychiatry at the New York Medical College, who is also a faculty member at the Columbia University Center for Psychoanalytic Training and Research, has published an article documenting what he believed was an authentic case of literal demonic possession. Another medical doctor, the director of residency training and medical education in the psychiatric department at the University of California, Irvine, edited and updated *True or False Possession: How to Distinguish the Demonic from the Demented*, a book which purports to assist mental health professionals in distinguishing whether people are mentally ill, or are possessed by demons.

Tens of millions of people in the West today, including some sophisticated mental health professionals, do not consider demonic possession and assault an absurd or fringe belief.

96.

In my personal experience those unfamiliar with fundamentalist Christianity will assume, when confronted with a person professing belief in a literal devil or demons, that said person must be mentally deficient, grossly uneducated, or lying. However, not all who believe in the existence of evil sentient metaphysical entities are unsophisticated fideists.

For example, a person accepting but a single proposition, namely that *the New Testament is the divinely inspired, literal, and inerrant word of God*, must then accept the existence of these malevolent beings. This is a simple truth. Since tens of millions of people living today in the West assent to that initial proposition, it follows that they must accept the existence of demons. Assent to the first proposition, but not the second, implies a severe cognitive dissonance.

I digress merely to note one subset of a larger complex of attitudes toward fundamentalists today. In my travels I have frequently encountered the urbane scoffer who believes that all Christian fundamentalists are necessarily unintelligent or uninformed. These skeptical philosophasters are typically oblivious to the advances in logic, set theory, and probability that have revolutionized the study of metaphysics in the latter half of the twentieth century. A number of the world's most eminent philosophers, men such as Alvin Plantinga or Richard Swinburne, espouse a strident Christianity. At these rarified heights, many of the arguments in support of fundamental Christian claims are so erudite and rigorous that one cannot hope to understand them without a strong foundation in the sentential, predicate, and modal logics. Though it is very strange, even bizarre, it is unfortunately not the case that all those who believe in the existence and malignant activities of demons are either lying, uneducated, or unintelligent.

97.

The indelible imprint left on my mind by the atonal aria of demonic abuse (grotesquely poetic and reminiscent of all the horror encapsulated in the *terza rima* of Dante's *Inferno*), conceptualized by that exotic and fabulous psychological detective, provided fodder for the fertile fields of my imagination—a creative, immature mind truly desperate for a serious alternate metaphysical explanation of nature and reality.

Throughout my childhood and adolescence I had heard too many arguments against the theory of evolution, as well as against the seductions of secular philosophy and competing religions, to completely break with what I believed was the sole coherent explanation for reality and existence. So I was stuck. I was sixteen, in a great deal of pain, and did not know what to do.

Yet it is from our denigrations and demoralizations that we often arise reinvigorated, and the humiliation, amusing though it was, of sitting before a psychologist who truly believed that demons were mounting me, resulted not in further frustration and anger, but in the germination of an idea that was perhaps long overdue.

In the theological world that served as both my bastion and penitentiary, there was only one alternate belief system acknowledged by Evangelicals as coherent, grounded in some true statements, but yet not Christian. This system also purported to adequately explain the nature of reality, existence, and moral valuations. The problem was that the alternate system was regarded as the quintessence of Evil.

I came to believe that there was only one course of action available, and that belief came, ironically, from inspiration provided by the credulity of that pseudo-therapist. The very idea of demons provoked fear in everyone I knew, and Christianity had provided only pain. I came to believe that nothing could be lost in the repudiation of all I had ever believed, for all prior piety and devotion had resulted only in suffering. I decided to join the Heavenly rebellion. I renounced Christ. I decided I would become a Satanist.

98.

Satanism was unknown to me. I had no notion of what might comprise its tenets or rituals. My attempts to contact, through ritual or prayer, the demons and dark prince himself came to naught and quickly convinced me that the supposed saturation of reality with these maleficent beings was likely as much a myth as were the catechisms of my youth. I soon repaired to a bookstore in nearby Montgomery, where I acquired a copy of Anton LaVey's *Satanic Bible*. However, I found the book laughable. I quickly decided that Satanism, too, was derived from fable.

In the absence of guides, knowledge, or anything resembling Satanic spiritual truth (whatever that might be), I decided that my practice of "Satanism" would consist of nothing more than the day-to-day application of the opposite of everything I had deemed revolting in Christianity. The first tenet, then, of my new religious doctrine was the renunciation of guilt, and with that renunciation I saw much depression evaporate. The second doctrine of the new faith was to aid and abet others in the recognition of religious falsehood wherever needed.

Given enough time, my Satanism would probably have evolved into a Randian psychological egoism or the utterly free immoralism of de Sade. But alas, that was not to be. For there is no way a young man can so completely repudiate the foundational beliefs of his host culture, or promote those beliefs in the surrounding mob, without creating a furor. But that furor is nothing to the fear which compels it. Men call Evil that which they fear. And Evil must be eradicated. I did not realize it at the time, but a number of the burghers were already prepared to permanently remove me.

99.

The good people of Selma, and good Evangelicals everywhere, are usually quite convinced that it is impossible to be either truly happy or joyful without a *personal* relationship with Jesus Christ. That is a matter of doctrine, a necessary truth. For them, the appearance of any manifestation of joy in unbelievers is a temporary and illusory mirage. This gives rise to any number of buttressing doctrines and outreach movements, particularly for those they see as victims or perpetrators of whichever sin is currently at the forefront of the culture war.

However, those sins are only temporary afflictions that can be overcome with prayer, repentance, and counseling. In me they confronted a youth possessed of an intransigence so deeply rooted that I could be safely classified an apostate. I was not possessed of a temporary sickness, nor overcome by a single, albeit severe, temptation; I was consumed by pure evil, and therefore represented a malignant tumor imbedded in the larger society.

In order to combat this perception it was necessary for me to learn to hide, to the extent that I was able, my double life. Apostasy in a region like Selma was no different than apostasy in Medieval Europe. I wasn't in danger of being burned at a stake, but I was certainly in danger of being removed from society, through a variety of means. I was forced to adopt a Janus-face. To those who demanded a pure, holy, authentic child of God I resembled exactly what they desired. Later, when tales of my heresy spread, the general sentiment in the community, particularly among the elders, was unanimous. "Surely this can't be. He couldn't be that bad, couldn't believe *that*!"

100.

Perhaps due to the ever-present sense of powerlessness lurking in my father's psyche, both as a result of his traumatic childhood, and as a result of his professional failures, he was strongly determined that I *become a man*, no matter the cost. Though he had previously made attempts to promote my development in this way, in Selma those efforts became troubling.

The day after I finished my sophomore year at Morgan, I anticipated a summer of pleasure, relaxation, swimming in the river, and perhaps some part-time work mowing lawns for extra cash. My father disagreed. That first summer morning I was awakened at 5:30 a.m. and told to get dressed in work clothes. I did not know what he wanted, but his tone brooked no disagreement. By six o'clock we were out the door and he was driving me even farther out into the country than we already lived. When we were some twenty miles outside Selma, after navigating a bumpy dirt road off a bumpy dirt road, we pulled onto the land of a pristine farm. My father told me to get out, and we walked over to an old white man I vaguely recognized from the church. He was the owner of the farm before us, a turf farm that stretched to the horizon or tree line in every direction.

My father told me that I would work on the turf farm that summer, that he would be back to get me that evening, and that I was to do a good job and make him proud. The owner sent me to the foreman, who quickly assigned me to a tractor which chopped the turf into blocks of sod that I, standing on the back of the moving tractor with the other workers, was meant to stack onto pallets for the next eight hours.

After two hours stacking the muddy squares of sod under the sweltering Southern sun I was at the point of collapse. The foreman took pity, seeing that, though I was in excellent shape for a three or four-hour football practice, I was unequipped to repetitively stack heavy, wet sod slabs for eight hours. The muscles and the pacing required in the two activities were wholly different. He allowed me the mercy of spending the rest of the day washing tractors. I returned home that night exhausted, broken in body and spirit. I couldn't imagine continuing on in that way for two more months.

The Terrible Beauty of the Evil Man

The work that my father had deemed so toughening, and therefore necessary for my education, had placed me in the new Southern slavery. Most of my coworkers had prior felony convictions, and would never be hired for anything but hard manual labor. They worked at the farm solely to avoid starvation. Only one of my coworkers could read, and therefore, as the only one who could pass the state driver's examination, was the only one who could legally drive. The other field-hands, incapable of otherwise legally getting to work, and unwilling to risk a parole violation for driving without a license, each day gave him one hour's salary (minimum wage) as gas money in order to secure transport to and from work. The others paid the white foreman for their ride.

The second day I again collapsed on the back of the tractor. The foreman once more took pity, and I was given a pole-axe and sent with another laborer to a remote road several miles away, to clear overhanging branches that obstructed the way. Though I was tall and strong, my new companion dwarfed me. After a year of living in Selma, and having heard several vivid stories of racially motivated murder, I was miles from the nearest human on a deserted country lane with a large black man armed with a pole-axe. I breathed deeply and attempted to engage him in conversation.

"Hi," I timidly proffered.

He stared at me as though I were an imbecile.

"So how did you start working here?" I continued.

"P.O. got me this shit job," he muttered.

"P.O.?"

"Parole officer," he replied, eyeing me darkly.

"So you were in prison," I mumbled. "If you don't mind, may I ask what you were in for?"

My companion stopped slicing at the branches overhead and hefted his pole-axe with both hands, gazing at me severely.

"You don't want to know, white boy."

And truly, I realized at that moment that he was correct, and that I had absolutely no interest in any of his prior offenses. I hefted my pole-axe and braced myself, waiting for the attack I thought might follow my impertinence. I felt that I would be able to acquit myself passably if attacked. Nevertheless, I was sure he would be able to decapitate me, hack me into bits, and, as we were deep in the woods, I didn't suppose it would be too difficult for him to dispose of my body. My adolescent imagination was drunk on adrenaline.

But in all of that I was mistaken. He read my thoughts, smiled at my youth, and began to converse. He told me about his life, about the culture of the turf farm. I learned that he was a good man who had fallen in a hard, harsh world, and that the other workers, all black except the foreman, were struggling in a condition arguably worse than the old slavery. They were paid minimum wage, were not compensated for overtime, and had no healthcare. Their vices and joys were malt liquor and hand-rolled cigarettes. They were living out their lives in dilapidated shacks and brute ignorance. They could not have left even had they wished. I realized that they were truly slaves, though that institution had ostensibly been abolished more than a century before.

After the third day in that time-capsule I informed my father that I would not return. He threatened me repeatedly, but I remained firm, and he eventually acquiesced on the condition that I immediately find a new job. I found work with the local YMCA, and was sent out to ready the rural YMCA summer camp for the campers who would arrive in a mere week. The camp had been abandoned to the weather since the previous summer, and I despaired as soon as I arrived. That despair was alleviated within the hour. A van soon pulled up, and a guard unloaded a bus of trustee-prisoners from the local jail. I, a white teenager, was placed in charge of a dozen black adults, and told to direct them in the repair of the neglected campground.

Slavery was, in Selma, inescapable.

101.

My father sending me into indentured servitude on a rural farm stirred no small interest at Morgan when I returned that fall for my junior year. Many of my classmates had done heavy work in the summer fields, but they had done so on their own lands. They were incredulous at the idea that I had been sent to work with paroled convicts.

However, that fiasco was not the end of my father's plans for making me a real man. In the spring semester of my junior year my father told me to put on athletic clothing, and ordered me into the car. I assumed he wanted me to train for the track-and-field season, as the basketball season had recently ended. We headed into Selma, and drove into a black neighborhood. This was not a part of town I had entered. We soon pulled up in front of a ramshackle building. My father ordered me out of the car. I hesitated, but got out.

The Terrible Beauty of the Evil Man

I entered the building, and found a boxing gym full of several dozen perspiring pugilists, all of whom went silent on our entry. My father called out loudly for Frank Hardy, and a man approached from the far side of the room. He greeted my father with a handshake and a warm smile.

"So this is your boy," Frank surmised with a pleased look.

"He's an excellent athlete. Won state with Morgan the last two years," my father replied.

"Well the ring is different. We'll see what he can do here," Frank responded.

My father grunted his approval and left, promising to return in a few hours. I stood stupidly for some moments, abandoned, as the buzz and bustle of boxing slowly resumed. Several eternal moments later Frank ordered me, along with a dozen other youths, into the back of a waiting cargo van. The van started, and we drove away. I noticed, from the windows, that we were passing far out into the country. The other youths in the van were completely mute. I did not know why we were leaving Selma. We stopped on a dirt road in the woods ten miles out of town. We were all ordered out of the van. The van drove away, back towards Selma. The youths began jogging after it. I started running with the pack and asked the guy next to me what the hell was going on.

"We got to get our warm-up jog before we start practice. When we get back we'll train."

"But the gym must be ten miles away!"

"Yep. That's the warm-up jog."

Ninety minutes later I pulled up to the gym. I was then introduced to true suffering as I was forced to do two hundred push-ups, then two hundred sit-ups, followed by twenty minutes of jump rope, twenty minutes on the speed bag, and twenty minutes on the heavy bag. Some three hours after I arrived at the gym I was finally allowed entrée to the ring.

I was large, muscled, and heavy. Most boxers are not. However, there was one boxer on that team (which I would discover was one of the better amateur boxing teams in the Deep South) who was larger and more powerful than me. He had, I was told, competed in the semi-finals of a national boxing competition the year before in the super-heavyweight division. As I got into the ring across from him the entire gym ceased work and gathered around, curious to watch the first white person they had ever seen in that ring.

This young man and I danced around each other for some time, neither of us attempting or landing any blows. Truthfully, I was so exhausted I could barely shuffle, and was doubtful that I could properly respond when he did begin the inevitable attack. He glanced repeatedly to the side of the ring, smirking, winking, and laughing toward his friends. He apparently saw me as a joke. I heard laughter beyond the ropes.

I, unaccustomed to being seen as anything but the toughest youth in any room I entered, did not find the situation amusing. Further, I was exhausted by the workout I had endured, and impatient to end the charade, even if it meant I was soon to occupy a bed in the emergency room. I knew that I had little energy remaining, and didn't care to form the butt of amusement for strangers. Anger partially ameliorated my exhaustion. I determined to use my remaining strength to immediately knock my antagonist unconscious. I reached back and smote that young man in the face so hard I do not know how he remained standing.

The chattering buzz in the gym instantly ceased. There was an audible intake of breath around the ring. I continued to dance around the young man, waiting for him to totter, feeling that in the interest of sportsmanship I could not hit him again while he was on the brink of collapse. I greatly underestimated my opponent. His fists were so fast that I did not see his blow coming.

I remember only green. All I could see was green. He had hit me so hard that I lost vision for several seconds. And this time it was he who resumed a slow dance, waiting for me to collapse to the canvas. But my vision cleared after only a few seconds, and that was when pandemonium broke.

I looked at this man who had just delivered the most powerful blow with a fist I had ever received. I didn't think at all. Madness suffused my brain. My inner caveman emerged and primal evolutionary instincts abrogated all higher executive functioning. I let out a hoarse, animalistic scream and leapt, determined to tackle and pummel him.

But as soon as I leapt, the observers, gathered at the ropes around the ring, instantly entered and dragged us apart.

"You aight, white boy. You aight!" they exclaimed with broad smiles.

The entire bout had been a test. They had needed to know whether I could, after the exhaustion of a grueling multi-hour workout, take a crushing blow to the face and still summon the will to fight. I had met and exceeded their expectations. I became the first white member of a boxing team known throughout Selma. My father was pleased.

The Terrible Beauty of the Evil Man

102.

I returned to Morgan the next day, my eye swollen and discolored, a spectacle that created instantaneous chatter. Everyone wanted to know who had dared punch me. I initially refused to answer questions, but then the head football coach, Coach Nub, demanded to know where I had gotten the black eye. I had to tell the truth.

The story spread rapidly. My schoolmates were astounded that I had entered that part of town to join the mythical boxing team. The concerns they had possessed regarding my martial abilities were magnified, and the growing fear already inspired by my apostasy was greatly increased. Exacerbating this fear was the knowledge that I had, for my own pleasure, and concurrent to my training in boxing, persuaded a local gymnastics instructor to take me as his sole student in the study of *wing chun*, convincing him that I could assist in his long-term project of creating a hybrid martial art synthesized from his expertise in *wing chun* and *aikido*.

Children told their parents. Parents spoke to each other. Several contacted my father, who resented the attempt at direct confrontation. I finished my junior year at Morgan the most decorated student in my class. I was seriously dating the girl who would, the following year, be head cheerleader. I had started both ways for a state championship football team, and started many games for a basketball team that made the state quarter-finals. In track-and-field I placed second in the state in the shot-put, third in the discus, and fifth in the one-hundred-and-ten-meter high hurdles. I was the only junior to make the state-championship winning scholars' bowl team, and I won other coveted academic awards.

But none of this mattered a whit to the frightened parents of my classmates, or to the members of my father's congregation. They were beginning to recognize me as a talented, angry apostate. Moreover, they came to believe that I posed a significant physical danger even to any full-bodied adult male who might wish to confront me.

The deluge would soon be upon me.

103.

There is often a quiet before a storm, and so it was for me. In those last months of hell and oblivion in Selma I found solace in the hours I spent in Frank Hardy's gym. There, as the only white, I found more peace and camaraderie than I had ever known in Morgan's coteries. In that gym I was not the only one from a dysfunctional home. There I was not the only abused child. There I found friends who cared not at all what kind of car I drove, what clothes I wore, or for any other ephemeral detail.

In that gym I found friends who knew what it meant to suffer—but yet did not allow that suffering to stifle the music in their souls. These were not the coddled, pasty classmates I found at lunch break in school. I needn't hear what fraternity they were planning to pledge at Auburn or Alabama, what deer they planned to bag that weekend, or what freshman they would seduce at the next party. In that gym I, and several others, found the closest thing we had to family. In Frank I found a model. I didn't learn much about *how to be a man*, as my father had hoped, but for a brief moment I could breathe freely. In that world where *nigger* was the only recognized appellation for African-Americans, I had found some small peace, not with the white landowners, but with the incandescent blacks.

104.

The New Testament, in 1 Timothy 3:5, says, "For if a man know not how to rule his own house, how shall he take care of the church of God?" And this verse, interpreted literally, formed the first and best ammunition of my father's enemies in Selma as he, once again, in less than two years, found himself at the epicenter of a spiritual civil war. With his eldest son an apostate, both spiritually and physically terrifying to the communal elites, and his marriage once again in an open and public shambles, the congregation he was meant to lead rapidly disintegrated. Dozens of members either left the church or threatened to, and an outside mediator was called in to arbitrate before the congregation completely collapsed.

As this was the third consecutive church my father had polarized to the point of disintegration his career as a pastor was now in jeopardy. Some church members, realizing that there were traits in his personality indicative of deeply rooted psychological disturbances, began an in-depth investigation of his work in previous pastoral positions, and soon realized that these problems were neither new nor unpredictable. They quickly discovered that, when hiring him, they had moved without adequate information, mesmerized by his name-brand academic credentials and his father-in-law's glamorous reputation.

But my father was cunning and is a survivor. He managed to prolong the process of arbitration. Had it not been for *my* destruction, he might have managed to salvage enough of the congregation to continue as the pastor of Shiloh Baptist Church. For, aside from two or three crippling personality deficiencies, he was still possessed of an indefatigable work ethic, as well as the effluence of magnetism that had allowed him to convince so many individuals to give their souls to Jesus.

However others in the area, unrelated to our church, and quite outside my father's spiritual authority, had decided that *I* no longer had a place in Selma. The Black Belt is a merciless and unforgiving region. Once I had crossed the wrong people, even unintentionally, provided that the bulk of the elites were against me, all that was needed was a pretext, any pretext, for my removal. Though I did not know it, my time in Selma had ended.

105.

My final demise came from an unexpected location, as grand collapses frequently do. It was through the family of my best friend, Palter, that I was eventually destroyed and removed from Selma. Palter was that same accomplice who had assisted me in the long-running burlesque that had so mortified and confounded our demon-obsessed psychotherapist. That extended prank served to spark what became my closest friendship in Selma.

Palter was in my class in Morgan, a member of the football team, and came from a family that was influential, wealthy, and possibly even more dysfunctional than mine. We were acquaintances from football, became bound together through the escapade with the therapist, and grew into bosom buddies through the shared understanding that comes when two teenagers can commiserate in confidence about traumatic home lives. I found him the perfect alibi and escape from home, as I was able to persuade my parents to frequently let me spend the night at his house on the weekends during my junior year of high school.

He had two homes, one his mother's, the other his father's, and the beauty of both environments, from my adolescent perspective, was that neither of his parents cared in the slightest about what he was doing in his free time. It was he who introduced me to binge drinking and cannabis at the woodland parties, and I proved a studious pupil.

And as I have noted, he was the most talented and natural liar I have ever met, so even on those rare occasions when his parents did wish to police his delinquent behavior, he was always ready with a duplicitous and convincing retort.

He was a grossly spoiled young man, most notably evidenced in the exorbitant presents his father made him. By his junior year of high school he was possessed of two gleaming SUVs and a new Jet Ski. In the nicer automobile he invested several thousand dollars in a premium speaker system, while the other was used primarily for mud-riding, or joyrides around town where he frequently found his weekend's amusement by driving, drunken and high, over traffic and street signs. But his father wielded great influence in Selma and the Black Belt, and there was no way, short of being caught directly in the act of vehicular manslaughter, that his actions would have had any serious legal repercussions.

His father was distant, viciously angry, and willing to pay his son and daughter extravagant allowances rather than spend time with them. His mother was an emotional wreck, struggling to cope with her divorce from the father by taking up both binge drinking and smoking in the dissolution of her middle age. Both parents, at both residences, allowed us free access to their liquor cabinets, required no curfew when we traveled to the all-night parties in the countryside, and were intentionally oblivious to the rampant sexual activity of their two children.

Despite the malfeasance of their son, it was through their daughter that my destruction arrived. Palter's sister, Drazel, two years younger than me, a freshman during my junior year of high school, developed an infatuation with me during my repeated visits and sleepovers at their homes. What had begun as a simple crush soon developed into dangerous obsession. Finding that simple flirtation had no effect, she began explicitly offering herself to me sexually, but as I had a serious girlfriend, a popular cheerleader in the school, I repeatedly declined her advances. Compounding her difficulty in the attempted seduction was her inability to separate me from her brother when I spent the night, and her brother, with all the patriarchal sentiment of the typical Southern male, had no interest in his sister becoming sexually involved with anyone at all.

But this young lady, much like her brother, was unused to being denied anything she might wish, and, also like her brother, was cunning in the pursuit of her desires. She developed a clever plan to acquire my affection. She began inviting one or two of her most promiscuous friends over for slumber parties on the nights that her brother and I traveled out to those weekend parties in the woods. When her brother and I returned, heavily inebriated and stoned, she sent those friends into her brother's room to have sex with him, leaving me kicked out of his room and alone on the couch for the night. She was then free to make her move.

Drunk, stoned, and in little position to give consent, Drazel made light of my protestations and proceeded to fellate me with a gusto I found incredible. I felt terribly guilty about cheating on my girlfriend, as well as betraying the confidence of my best friend, but felt trapped, and kept the matter to myself. My friend emerged from his room the next morning, smiling broadly, reveling in the glory of the new day, glowing from his sexual escapade of the previous evening. Similar weekends followed, and Palter quickly learned of Drazel's sedulous attempts to corral my affections. However, as they brought a steady stream of young vixens into his room, he chose to overlook her maneuvers.

Further corroding this already sordid environment was the fact that Palter's mother, in the throes of her mid-life crisis, was regularly sneaking up on me at times when I was in varied stages of undress. She was physically unattractive, and her efforts to engage me in solitary conversation with intense, prolonged eye contact left me distinctly uncomfortable. She always managed to catch me with a question or request at the exact moment I would traverse the hallway, clad in naught but a towel, between the shower and her son's bedroom.

106.

This series of dysfunctional, substance-abusing, orgiastic weekend trysts came to an end at the beginning of the summer following my junior year. Aside from any intense infatuation with me, Drazel was not the most psychiatrically stable young woman. She had confessed to me that in the previous year she had once been hospitalized after a suicide attempt (though her brother implied that there had been multiple attempts or pseudo-attempts), and I can only surmise, with the hindsight of years, that my repeated rejection of her advances invoked and mirrored the deeply rooted pain she felt following her father's rejection of her mother.

As summer began, Drazel began to eruct with frantic angry tantrums concerning my failure to break up with my girlfriend, declare undying love for her, and make her my crown and glory in time for her sophomore, and my senior, year. She was also aware that her brother was growing bored with the same brood of girls with which she had, for the preceding months, repetitively supplied him.

I blithely brushed aside her unpredictable outbursts, thinking them normative for a girl, particularly one who was frequently suicidal. Drazel, conversely, was unwilling to concede defeat in her multi-month effort. She determined to end the game by bringing in new girls, and by drinking enough to quiet her anxiety sufficiently to demand, via ultimatum, that I reciprocate her previously unrequited love. Disaster quickly ensued.

The two new girls she recruited to satisfy her brother were a year younger, entering the ninth grade rather than the tenth, only fourteen years to our seventeen, but they were excited by the appeal of partying with varsity football players, with two young men who would both be seniors and two-way starters on the upcoming Morgan football team—a team everyone was certain would win its fourth consecutive state championship.

That night the three girls became heavily inebriated at Palter and Drazel's mother's house while Palter and I partied in the countryside. Before we returned Drazel became so intoxicated that she passed out on her bed. The two young girls designated to satisfy Palter migrated to the living room, drinking, listening to music, impatiently awaiting our return.

When we arrived one of the two girls followed Palter into his bedroom, but the other, an ambitious freshman-to-be named Jade, seeing me as a paradigm of southern football masculinity, and noting that her hostess was still safely passed out in her bedroom, followed me to the living room couch, rather than going with Palter as she had been directed. There she jumped on top of me, and told me that she had desired me since I had first moved to Selma.

Straddling me in the living room, Jade slobbered on my face, and attempted to unbuckle my pants. I was too inebriated to do more than fall back on the couch, and when she got on her knees to fellate me I was unable to attain an erection. She got back on top of me, grinding and moaning, running her hands through her hair, doing her teenage best to look like a movie star. Finding me still flaccid, she slipped off her mini-shorts and panties and flipped upside down on my supine body. I wasn't going to let her smother my face with her furry, sopping mound, so I slipped a finger into her, hoping to maintain distance rather than to pleasure her, praying for the room to stop spinning. It was just as she managed to coax my insensate member to attention that Drazel recovered from her drunken stupor and stumbled into the living room.

The caterwaul that ensued between these two girls should have summoned the police, but not only did Palter and the third girl not emerge from his bedroom, neither did their mother emerge from hers. Drazel and Jade shortly resolved their difference by demanding that I immediately choose between them. That presented some difficulty, as I was seeing four girls rather than two, and was in some danger of urinating on myself. However I did have the presence of mind to point out to both girls that I was in a relationship with a girl they both knew, and that I would continue to see that other girl for the foreseeable future. Neither girl cared for my response, and they stormed from the room, shouting curses as they left.

Several days later Drazel and Jade invited me out to dinner with them at the Tally-Ho restaurant in Selma. Drazel's maternal grandmother chaperoned the meal and ate with us. At that dinner the two girls reiterated, very clearly, out of the hearing of Drazel's elderly grandmother, that they were giving me one more chance to break up with my girlfriend and choose between them, or I was going to pay dearly for leading them on.

I laughed out loud. I saw the entire matter as silliness that had lasted far too long. I had some idea of how spoiled Drazel was, but certainly didn't think she would be able to drag her younger friend along in any type of sinister revenge plot, nor did I think that two teenage girls were capable of devising a nefarious plan that could seriously harm me. I have never been more wrong about anything in this life.

Several days later my father told me that the police had called and that they wanted me to drive down to the station in Selma to answer a few questions. I drove away, through the lush summer woods, on the county road snaking its way from my house to the trap I didn't see coming. I didn't know it at the time, but I would never see my home again.

Book IV

107.

The man slowly opened his eyes. His vision was hazy. He blinked
several times. He was seated on a faded beige leather couch in his living
room, staring at the cracked mud coating the work boots that lay near
the screen door which led to the backyard. He yawned, and as he did so
the blood rushed back to his brain and he had a brief, terrifying flash of
the dream he had passed through. The memory faded almost as quickly
as it arose, but left a strong sense of disquiet. He looked around the
room, then settled back into the couch as his wife emerged from the
kitchen on his right.

"Everything ok, hon? You had a strange look on your face."

"No, no, everything's fine," he replied. But then he looked at her
closely. "Are you ok? Are the girls ok?"

"What?" she asked, a bemused expression on her face. "Don't I look
ok?"

"Yeah, sure you do. It's just…. Oh never mind. Funny dreams, I
guess."

"You must've been really tired not to have gotten that early start you
wanted for your camping trip. It's eight o'clock. I was sure you'd be
gone by at least five."

"Well I...." the man stuttered. He paused. "I was...." Suddenly his face blanched, leaving a motley organization of freckles to struggle against the new pallor smeared across his cheeks, nose, and forehead. "I was in the woods," he finally gasped. "I remember!"

"You remember getting to the woods on fairy dust?" his wife chuckled. "Honey, I felt you get out of bed around four, and you haven't been anywhere but snoring on that couch ever since."

The man felt a constriction in his throat, as though all of the air in the world was being sucked out into space. With every passing moment he felt it more difficult to breathe, to say anything. He looked at his wife, and for an instant she blazed in a palette of color. Her eyes were so blue they appeared violet, and they looked at him over high, prominent cheekbones. They looked at him through tresses of hair that flickered across her face with the breeze from the backyard. It was hair once golden, now merely blond and shot with streaks of white, hair that hid the crow's feet etched by long years into the skin around those violet irises. Her eyes suddenly widened, full of terror, the pupils shrunk to nothing.

"What's happening?" she cried.

"I was... I was in... the woods," he replied, straining to find the air to speak. He looked down at his hand, his hand on his knee, his knee attached to his leg, his leg resting on the couch, and saw that in all of them the color was fading to nothingness. He looked back up, fear throttling his mind, fear and love, for even as terror enveloped him he could still see his wife, a riot of color in a room that had otherwise passed from vision.

Time slowed and he noted her hair, no longer blond and white but once again golden and soft, the skin, tanned and smooth and freckled, the time-weary wrinkles suddenly absent, and through all of that her eyes, two orbs of deep blue flame shivering amidst the other colors. A rush of sound crashed all around them, though even in the chaos the man could hear his wife scream out a phrase repeatedly. The man could not distinguish the words through the noise, and even the collage of color that was his wife began to fade away until there was nothing left but those two violet orbs pleading with him. And then he understood what she had been screaming.

"Just remember my name!"

Then the man opened his eyes. Everything that had passed through his mind slipped away from him like the seeds of a dandelion on the wind. He had been asleep. He was still breathing heavily from the dream through which he had fallen, from the noise which had seemed to burst his eardrums. He lay quietly on the rock, listening to the water as it slapped the rock a dozen feet below, where it broke from the ocean.

"I remember now," the man mouthed as he sat up. But it was not his wife's name he remembered; indeed, he had already forgotten that part of the dream. He was remembering that all that had drifted through the canals of his slumbering subconscious was not real, was an illusion brought on by hunger. The dreams were growing worse. He had been on the rock for three days, and he was ravenous. The hunger was making the dreams worse, he was sure. He did not know if he could survive another nightmare without going mad. He shivered as the lingering remnants of terror oozed out from his brain to his muscles.

He stood on the projection of rock and looked longingly once more into the distance. He could see the faint line of the shore to the east. In every other direction there was naught but cold grey water. He stepped carefully over the irregular surface of the large rock, slick with lichen and painful on his bare feet.

He had been trapped on that rock for three days, though he could not remember how he had come to be there. He supposed that was a result of the crack his head had taken when the waves had first flung him at the rock. He remembered only grasping out at the rock in the dark, as the storm whipped around him. He had grasped at its base, found a hand-hold, and struggled mightily to retain it. Slowly he had pulled himself into a crevice in the side of the rock, and there had curled up until the storm passed.

After the storm he slept, and had the first of the nightmares. When he awoke he gingerly washed the caked salt and blood from his hair with ocean water, and then carefully scaled the dozen feet to the top of the rock to look around. And atop that rock he had stayed for three days of hunger, thirst, and nightmares. He stood again, wondering, not for the first time, if he could possibly swim the ten miles that he estimated lay between him and the shoreline in the distance.

"If I don't go now I'll never make it," he thought. "No," he reasoned, "I'm already too weak from hunger and thirst to make it. I'll drown long before I get there."

He put a hand to the side of his head where it was cut. He realized that it hurt much less, no longer throbbed with every waking moment. That realization, along with the hunger and thirst slicing through him, gave him the courage or desperation needed to descend the rock. He had decided that it would be better to die swimming than to perish slowly of hunger and thirst on an isolated rock. Anyway, he didn't know if he could endure another nightmare.

He slipped into the water and began paddling. He felt hale and determined in the first mile, certain that the adrenaline coursing through him would carry him to the shore. Midway through the second mile the adrenaline was gone. All that remained was a slow, steady splashing toward a shore that never grew closer.

His arms no longer ached. He could no longer feel anything at all except the chill wetness in which he was immersed. He made a great effort to rise in the water, to look out and gauge his distance from the shore. He looked back to the rock. He was nearly halfway to the shore, too far to make it and too far to turn back. He realized that he was going to die. He settled back into a slow, steady, emotionless stroke, and closed his eyes.

A face appeared in his mind's eye, startling him. He opened his eyes, and picked up the pace of his swim. He had seen that face, he was sure, though from where he did not know. That strange face had a thick, black beard, tangled and wild, with vivid blue eyes, the skin around them crinkled in amusement. The man kept swimming, closed his eyes, and tried to forget the face. Yet as soon as he closed his eyes it appeared again, stronger and more vibrant, inescapable in his mind's eye.

The man opened his eyes, and began paddling furiously, not to reach the shoreline, but as though the movement of his writhing arms and legs would steer him away from the unavoidable smile he saw whenever his eyes were closed. But no matter how he kicked and paddled, he could not move quickly enough to escape that face. And soon it was before him even when his eyes were open.

"What do you want?" the man shouted. But the face only looked at him, the half-smile implacable. And it was then that the man recalled how he knew that face. It was the old stranger from the woods. But that could not be, the man knew, for that had been a dream, or a dream within a dream. He could not remember.

"I'm hallucinating," the man said to himself. "I'm starving and thirsty, and I'm hallucinating," he declared to the face before him. The stranger looked back reprovingly, and the man felt certain that the stranger could hear him. "You don't scare me, you know! I know this is only a nightmare," the man shouted, and then floundered as he swallowed a mouthful of saltwater and began to choke. He began to tread water, shaking as he coughed. He finally expelled the water, his body limp as the last of his energy went out with the mouthful of water he spit up. He drifted for a moment, trying to float as waves crashed over him, ignoring the stranger's rude stare.

"You're not real," he declared between waves. "You're not real and never were. I was never in those woods!"

The stranger shimmered, his body coming into focus. He stood over the man floundering in the water between rock and shore.

"I'm going to die, aren't I?" the man asked. "Answer me, damn it!" he shouted at the mute face. But then he inhaled another mouthful of water, and began to choke once more. And this time he knew that he would not be able to expel the water from his throat and lungs, and knew that he would die, and though he wanted to shout at the stranger that accompanied him down through the water, his mouth was full of water and he could only retch. He wanted to tell the stranger that he knew that none of it was real, and that he wasn't afraid, but he couldn't, because he was choking to death, and consciousness was fading as rapidly as will.

Some time later the man opened his eyes, but could see nothing. His eyes were open but they detected absolutely no light. Moreover, his body seemed to rest on nothing, yet he was not falling. The man stood and spread his arms out in all directions, searching for a wall that did not exist. He put his hands down, to feel the ground beneath him, and touched nothing but air. The man grew quite frightened at this and stood on one foot, trying to reach down and touch the ground on which his other foot had rested. His hand touched nothing, and yet when he placed his foot back down it came to rest on something.

"I'm dead," he thought soberly. "This is Death."

He put a hand down to steady himself in order to sit, and this time his hand connected with something solid, and he was able to sit down. However, once he was seated, anywhere he placed his hands about himself, including the area that should have been the ground directly around where he was sitting, he felt nothing but air. He closed his eyes and opened them. He repeated the process slowly several times. Nothing. There was no difference, not even the slightest hint of light.

"Can I be certain I'm dead?" he wondered. "How do I know this body is real?"

He pinched himself, found that it hurt, and then ripped out several hairs from his forearm to be certain.

"Perhaps I'm not dead. I wouldn't hurt if I didn't have a body, and I wouldn't have a body if I were dead," he mused.

Once the man realized that he was not dead, but alive and trapped in a void of nothingness, he grew frightened. He closed his eyes, finding it reassuring to avoid the fact that there was nothing for his eyes to see. Indeed, there was nothing to hear or smell either. Even the tactile impressions that should have been given by the surface on which he was sitting were mute. He didn't feel as if he were flying or falling. He might have been floating, though even that provided not the slightest tactile sensation.

With his eyes closed the man began to see strange things, patterns of color and shape rotating through his mind in a strange whirl. The patterns and shapes frightened him greatly, for he had forgotten, in that minute or century he had been seated, what colors and shapes were. But then the patterns coalesced, and he saw a conjunction of lines, color, and texture, and remembered that this was called a face, and moreover, that he had previously seen the face.

It was a face both familiar and strange. He could not recall where he had seen this stranger with his thick black beard that separated lips and chin from Roman nose and blue eyes. The face was both beautiful and stern, terrifying. The man opened his eyes. The face was still there, staring at him. He turned away from the stranger and noticed a glow, far off in the distance. Eagerly he blinked several times.

"Yes, it's definite. The glow is only there when I open my eyes," he said, though when he spoke aloud he very nearly could not hear himself. The sound was swallowed up in the darkness and void.

He set off eagerly toward the source of the glow, and soon broke into a run. After several moments he drew close, and saw that the source of the light was a flickering candle in a silver candlestick, though the light was not sufficient to reveal the surface on which the candlestick rested.

He picked up the candle and waved it about to find some end or beginning to the void. But though the candle had emitted a glow bright enough to be visible at several moments run, he found that once he held it the light emitted was so weak he could not illuminate any space that was not immediately around the flame. He singed several of his arm hairs trying to see his forearm. He held the light down to his feet, attempting to see the ground, but the lower he held the candlestick the more the light waned, and his eyes registered nothing but darkness where his feet should have been. Still, the candle, though providing no illumination, granted him immense comfort. He sat down softly and gripped the candlestick tightly with both hands.

The Terrible Beauty of the Evil Man

Suddenly there was a great burst of light behind him, and he twisted, shielding his eyes, looking for the source of the light. It was the stranger. The man quickly stood and turned toward the stranger, bright and glowing in manifold colors that radiated out from him in streams of warm iridescence. The man took a step back and looked down, noticing that his own arm still appeared only weakly, and only when he held the candle quite close.

"Who are you?" the man called out, his voice tremulous in the void. The stranger stared back at him sternly. "I don't... I don't know who you are. I don't know where I am. I don't even know who I am," the man admitted.

"Don't you?" the stranger replied in a rumbling, booming voice that filled the void and seemed to reverberate from dozens of surfaces. "You were so confident when last we spoke."

"I don't remember speaking to you," the man called out. "I don't know what's happened. I'm sorry. I don't want to be here. Can you help me?"

"I wished to help you," the stranger replied solemnly, "but you wanted to return here. You *asked* to come here."

"I never asked to come here. This is nowhere. This is *nothing.*"

"You are correct. This is a nothingness."

"There is nothing here but this candle, and it doesn't burn very brightly."

"That is no candle."

That man looked down at the object in his hands, and then back up uncertainly at the man glowing bright in a riot of iridescent light.

"Please sir, I don't know then, exactly what this is. I thought it was a candle."

"That is your soul, son of earth."

The man wondered briefly whether the stranger was mad, but then glanced around, his eyes meeting only blackness, and he shivered, humbled in the center of his being.

"Please sir, I want to leave. I want to go very much, but this light is not enough for me to find a way from this place."

"Can you not see me?"

"Why yes sir, I can. You are much brighter than this light."

"You see me only due to the presence of that light. Without that light I would not be visible."

"But sir, I can barely see myself, and certainly not anything else."

"You are very faint, almost not there," the stranger intoned, looking deeply into the man's eyes.

The man looked down at his arm again, at his two hands tightly gripping the candlestick, and he felt the truth of the stranger's words. A tear trickled down his cheek. He wept softly, his head down, destitute in the knowledge that he was nearly swallowed up by the nothingness.

"Please," the man said, his voice breaking, "I know that I'm not like you. I know that I'm almost nothing. But please, please, can't you take me from this place?"

"I can take you nowhere. You can leave here whenever you wish, but we both know that you do not wish to leave. Do you not remember what you said to me in the wood?"

Then the man gasped, for he remembered the wood, and not only the wood, but what it was to camp, build a fire, strap on a pack, and slog through mud. He remembered his wife, remembered his two daughters, and his heart yearned for them, and as it did the stranger before him gradually melted into the very iridescence he radiated. As the stranger transmuted from line and angle, form and shape, into a cornucopia of colored light that was collapsing and reforming in endless waves, the man's vision waned, until he lost all sight, until he was consumed in the nothingness and even all thought ceased.

The man then slowly opened his eyes. He was lying in the woods, just where he had stopped to sleep on that first night of his camping trip in the woods. He glanced around, and realized that he had been dreaming.

"Dreams dissolving relentlessly into more horrible dreams," he thought with a shudder. "What a nightmare!"

He stood unsteadily. The world around him wobbled and only slowly came back into focus, wobbled again thrice more before becoming steady. As he pulled on his pack and stumbled away he felt sick, for the world would not seem to hold together, and the colors around him had run amok.

He put a hand on the tree next to him and watched the bark melt down its side and run over his hand in a flow of molten brown. He snatched his hand back. He looked around wildly, and then up, seeing the treetops and foliage with perfect clarity, noting that it was twilight. He kept glancing up, afraid to look down at the melting bark on the trunks of the trees. After a moment he noticed that the leaves above were slowly falling to the ground. As each leaf detached from its tree it dissolved, falling to the ground in a green liquid drop, hissing and steaming as it hit the forest floor.

The Terrible Beauty of the Evil Man

The man slapped himself in the face and began running. He ran and ran, pushing through the spray of colors and opening his eyes only long enough to avoid the blobs of brown that signaled trees. When he was exhausted and could run no further, he simply fell to the ground, and lay panting, eyes closed.

After some time his breathing slowed, and he noticed the nearby sound of a bird chirping cheerfully in the early dusk. He cautiously opened his eyes, keeping his body and both hands on the ground to avoid the sickening sway of the woods he had navigated. But when he opened his eyes the forest appeared normal, and the man sat up slowly and breathed. He rubbed his eyes. The forest remained stationary and mundane.

He sat in that spot for some hours, trying to process all he had seen and dreamed. He still wasn't sure that he was awake. He felt that the earth might still conspire beneath him, ready to tremble deliriously, to gallivant the next time he tried to walk. He might have remained sitting until he returned to sleep but for the fact that he spied movement several meters away, down a lane of trees. He squinted, and realized that there was a woman in the distance. He rose unsteadily and made his way toward her. As he drew closer he saw that it was his wife.

"Come," she called, smiling and waving him toward her. As she called out and waved she stepped back and waved him to her right, where she disappeared behind a hedgerow formed from a pristine line of bushes.

The man wanted to stop, knew he should stop, but his legs kept moving despite the knowledge that this too must be an illusion. He turned near the bushes where he had seen his wife disappear, and as he turned he found that the forest behind the tangle of bushes resembled a garden. With every step he took toward his pointing wife the trees and bushes grew more orderly. He trotted after her, dropping his pack as he went. He could not understand why she kept beckoning to him, waiting just long enough for him to catch sight of her before moving farther into the garden.

But then he stopped, slowed to a halt, and looked around. He was in a perfectly manicured garden with immaculate hedgerows forming three-meter walls on either side of him. Tall marble columns topped with burning baskets of fuel, resembling a row of torches evenly spaced, marched down both sides of the wide path on which he stood. He saw his wife before him in the distance, at a place where the garden path diverged in two. She was urging him to follow her to the left.

"I know that this is all a lie!" he called to her.

To prove his point he quickly walked to the divergence in the path, letting her disappear before him down the left-hand side. He walked directly into the right-hand path, following it aimlessly. He wandered for several moments before he saw another divergence ahead in the distance. It was then that he first realized that he was in a maze.

He turned around, to get back to the first fork, and then to the forest, when he heard a call in the distance behind him. He knew that it wasn't his wife's voice. He turned back once more to that second fork in the path. His elder daughter stood at the left-hand divergence, auburn hair moving gently in the night breeze.

"Come, father!" she waved to him, walking slowly away down the curving left-hand path.

The man walked forward a dozen paces and stopped. He sighed deeply and began to turn back to the first fork, but stopped mid-turn.

"There is no point!" he cried. He saw a marble bench several paces away alongside the right hedgerow. He walked to it and sat. Some moments later he heard a voice and looked up. It was his younger daughter calling to him, beckoning him to follow her down the right-hand fork in the path. The man looked at her longingly for a moment before dropping his head and staring down between his feet. However, this daughter did not move away after calling him. She stood at the entrance to the second fork in the maze, calling to him incessantly, begging him to come to her. The man put his fingers in his ears to block out the sound of her voice. After some time her voice died away, and he put his fingers down. He sat like that for some time before noticing bare feet quietly step into the line of his downward gaze. The man looked up. The stranger stood before him.

"I know what you're doing," the man said bitterly.

"Oh?"

"You're playing games with me. You're sick. You know that? Sick!"

"I have done nothing. Everything you have seen is in you."

"Well it's rotten. All of it. It's a terrible thing to do to a man."

"I asked if you wanted to leave. You wanted to return to the nothingness."

"*This* isn't what I wanted. I wanted my life back. Not this parade of feverish illusions."

"What do you think your life was?" the stranger asked, his blue eyes burning into the man. "Your reality was fragile and illusory because there was nothing in you. What you see is all that you had—wisps of feeling for three people that vanished in the night's air as soon as they became tedious. That was the sum of your thoughts and feelings and consciousness."

"They weren't real. I know what's real," the man responded sullenly.

"*Do you?*" the stranger asked, searching the man with his eyes. "So much in this vestibule is a construct of the mind. But you can leave all of this. Take what's real and go beyond, move to the *other side.*"

"I'm sitting right here. I'm not going anywhere. Give me back my old life or leave me alone. I know what you mean by the other side. You want me to die. Well I won't."

"After all you have seen, still the fool," the stranger said sadly. "You cannot begin to live until you let go of these illusions. Choose to begin the *true* life. You cannot be taken. You must choose to go. There you will continue to be, but you will *be* without lies, illusions. Don't you understand? There is no escape from consciousness," the stranger declared.

"There is no escape from anything."

"There *is* an escape from nothingness. True freedom is just beyond this."

"No," the man shook his head sadly. He looked up at the stranger. "You don't understand. I will always be a prisoner."

108.

I woke up trembling, blinked, and sat up on the metal sheet that projected directly from the wall, forming the cot on the right side of my cell. I was seventeen years old, and in solitary confinement. I was a prisoner.

I sat up and swung my legs over the side of the cot. I ran my hands through my hair and then touched the corner of my eye to wipe away a tear. I lay back down on my cot and gave in to a quiet flurry of tears. I wished to get up and begin my day, but there was nowhere to go.

When I had finished crying I sat back up and eyed the toilet with distaste. Finally I stood and took the one step that separated my cot from the rimless toilet projecting from the other side of the cell. I undid the fly on my ill-fitting one-piece orange jumpsuit, and directed a stream of urine into the toilet, trying not to splatter. I would have to sit on that same rimless toilet later in the day, and there were no cleaning supplies.

When I finished urinating I turned to the small sink next to the toilet and ran water over my hands. I dried my hands on the neon orange jumpsuit. There was no towel. I took three steps to the far wall of the cell. There was a window on that wall. The window was perhaps a handbreadth wide and three feet high. It was a narrow slit that broke the uniform grid of sky-blue cement blocks that formed the cell's four walls. The window allowed me to see a sliver of rural farmland that included one tree and part of one small catfish pond. I was in Hale County, Alabama, two counties over from Selma and Dallas County, and I was locked in solitary confinement in the West Alabama Youth Services, or WAYS, a detention facility for delinquent juveniles. I had been there a week.

I slid into my shower flip-flops, my only shoes, and stretched. I went to my cell door and looked out the window. I stood almost parallel to the window, straining to see the clock in the main room. It wasn't time for breakfast. I didn't know what to do. I had nowhere to go. I went back to my cot, sat down, slid out of my shower shoes, and lay back down on my bunk. I had to think. I needed to stop the onslaught of thought, but I had nothing else to do, and could not dam the flood of memory.

109.

I had driven from the countryside to the police station in Selma a week before. When I arrived at the station I was made to wait. Eventually a detective called for me and I was escorted into a small room. There were two chairs and a typewriter on a small table. We were alone in the room. He closed the door.

"Beau Beauchamp?"

"Yes sir."

"Have a seat. Do you know why you're here?"

I paused. The previous day Palter had told me his parents had said he was no longer to see me, though he had not wanted to talk about why, and had ended the phone conversation abruptly. I assumed that his sister had told her parents we fooled around.

"No, not really," I responded.

"Do you know a girl named Drazel, or a girl named Jade?"

"Yes, I do," I answered, my suspicions confirmed.

"I'd like to ask you a few questions about these two girls."

I sat numbly for a moment.

"What kind of questions?"

"I just need to ask you a few basic questions about how you know them, and if you've ever done anything to harm them."

"Well I definitely never did anything to harm them!"

"Fine, but I need to ask you a few details."

"Well," I said slowly, "if I'm in trouble I should probably talk to a lawyer."

"You don't need to," the detective mouthed slowly. "You haven't been charged with anything, you see. I'm only going to ask you some basic questions. If you didn't do anything wrong you don't have anything to hide."

"I'm not sure," I said warily. "I think I should have a lawyer."

"Look," the detective said, with a touch of impatience, "you can wait for a lawyer, but if you do it's going to take some time to arrange. The judge will probably hold you in the detention center out in Hale County until we get your statement."

"Lock me up you mean?"

"Yes sir."

"That's crazy! I didn't do anything illegal!"

"Well that's exactly what I want to ask you about."

"But you could ask me about anything. I don't know what this is about. Really, I would feel better if I have a lawyer. My dad would probably want me to have one."

"Look," he said, this time his impatience clearly visible, "like I said... you're more than welcome to wait for a lawyer. But it wouldn't make a bit of difference, because I'm only going to ask you very basic questions. Also, you really ought to think about your image here. The judge will likely ask me to give my impressions about how you appeared when confronted with these questions. And right now you seem suspicious. If you don't have anything to hide it makes no sense to delay answering a few simple questions. That won't look good to the judge, and in the meantime we'll probably have to send you to the detention facility."

"I guess that makes sense."

"Good. Glad to hear you're cooperative. The point here is to do the right thing," he said, leaning in and giving me a warm smile. "Telling the truth about things is important, and your father's a preacher, so I know you understand that. We just want the truth to come out. I only need you to sign this sheet."

"What is it?" I asked, taking the paper.

"Says you're agreeing to let me ask you a few questions."

I looked down at the paper. It said that I was waiving my right to remain silent or have a lawyer present. I initialed and signed.

"Ok, let's get started. First, how do you know Drazel and Jade?"

"Drazel is my best friend's sister. Jade is her friend."

"Are they older or younger than you?"

"Younger. I'm seventeen. Drazel is fifteen and Jade is fourteen."

"Have you had sexual contact with these girls?"

"What do you mean by that?"

"Have you had vaginal intercourse with either of these two girls?"

"No, definitely not."

"Have you had oral or anal intercourse with either of these girls?"

"Well they both gave me blowjobs. They both have a crush on me. Drazel has been after me for months. I only hooked up with Jade once, but she told me she's liked me for a while too."

"What do you mean, you hooked up with Jade?"

"We made out and she gave me a blowjob."

"So you received oral sex from both of these girls. I see. Did you force them to do it?"

"No! Absolutely not."

"I see. Have you penetrated either girl's vagina?"

"No. I told you—no sex. Well... actually... I guess there was technically penetration of the vagina. I fingered them."

"You fingered the girls before or after the oral intercourse?"

"Well during. They were upside down on top of me."

The detective quickly suppressed a grin.

"Did you provide oral intercourse to the girls?"

"No. I just kinda, you know, rubbed around down there."

"I see. Did you threaten to kill the girls if they told anyone about this?"

"What? No! That's crazy. No way. They're into me. Why would I threaten them?"

"Did you force the girls to provide you with oral intercourse?"

"You already asked me that. I told you no. That's crazy. Look at me. I'm *really* good looking. I don't have to force anyone to do anything. I have a hot girlfriend."

"Have you ever threatened either of the girls or their families with violence? Threatened to kill them all? Massacre them? Wipe out their families?"

"What? Are you serious? I'm not a psycho. How would it even be possible for me to do something like that? Look, detective... these two girls like me a lot. Drazel's kinda obsessed with me. She's been after me to go out with her for a while. And I fooled around with Jade the other night after me and Palter got back from a party. I was drunk and had smoked a bit of pot. Otherwise it wouldn't have happened. Drazel saw me and Jade, and they got in a fight about it. They said I had to choose between them or they were going to get me in trouble. I said I wouldn't because I have a girlfriend and because I'm not into either of them. That's really all that happened. And I definitely didn't ever say I was going to kill people or massacre their families. Seriously. Like, that doesn't even make sense. We're talking about my best friend's family here! I probably spend more time with them than with my own family! Palter was in his bedroom having sex with one of Drazel's other friends while I was fooling around with Jade. He can tell you all about it."

"Look, Beau. I don't think these girls like you or are obsessed with you. If they did you wouldn't be here, see? Are you sure this is the story you want to go with?"

"But I didn't do anything! I fooled around with a couple of girls. I didn't start it. They both made a move on me! You have to understand. Drazel is seriously crazy. She tried to kill herself last year. She swallowed an entire bottle of Pamprin!"

"Beau, I'm gonna shoot straight with you here. Your story doesn't add up. If you're not interested in these girls sexually, and you have a girlfriend, why did you allow oral intercourse?"

"Detective, have you ever had a girl climb onto your lap while you were drunk and tell you she wanted to blow you?"

"Fine," the detective responded, a smile playing at the corners of his mouth, "I'm going to type this up. If you want, you can tell the judge the whole bit about the girls' mental health and liking you and this being a conspiracy against you. I'm only going to write up the facts. You say you had oral sex with these girls. No vaginal intercourse, though you did manually penetrate them vaginally. You claim you never threatened anyone with violence. When I finish typing up your statement you can sign it."

"Well what are the charges?" I asked.

"No charges yet," he responded. "We only wanted to know what happened. No big deal."

I left the office and was introduced to my new probation officer. He asked me to come outside. We walked out to the front steps of the police station.

"What are we doing here?" I asked him.

"We're waiting on the police unit to come by for you."

"Come by for me?"

"You're going to have to go to detention until the judge can give you a detention hearing."

"You're telling me I'm going to be locked up?"

"Locked up pending the judge's decision about whether you have to remain incarcerated until your trial."

"What am I being locked up for? I thought I wasn't charged with anything!"

"Detective says you admitted to receiving oral sex from those girls."

"Ok, well that's not against the law!"

"It is if you made 'em do it. Plus, they say you want to kill them and their families."

"That's total crap!"

"Well until a judge rules on that you've got to be detained in the interest of public safety."

"Well when will that be? He said I wasn't going to be locked up if I gave a statement!"

"Detention hearing should be within a day," he said as he looked me over. "I can't tell you anything about whether your statement will help you or hurt you, but I can tell you that telling the truth is always the right thing to do. Now, you're not planning on trying to run on me are you?"

"Is that a joke?" I asked, laughing incredulously. "Yeah, I'm totally going to run away," I chuckled, wondering where exactly he thought I was planning to run on foot.

"Beau, I'm going to need you to turn around and put your hands behind your back."

"Are you joking?"

"Does it look like I'm joking?"

"Look, *I* was joking. I'm not really going to run. Where would I go?"

"Turn around now and put your hands behind your back or I'm going to put you on the ground."

And that, dear friends, is how I ended up sitting on the ground out front of the Selma Police Station with my hands cuffed behind me.

111.

The police car came and took me to Greensboro, Alabama, home to WAYS, the juvenile detention center. I got out of the car and passed through a series of steel doors that clicked and buzzed shut with electronic locks as the police officer and new, flanking guards brought me through each one. The escorting police officer released me into the custody of two prison guards who then directed me past additional doors, into a small locked room somewhere nearer the center of the prison. I was told to completely strip. I did so, worried both about strangers seeing me naked, and also about whatever fungus might be on the bare floor of the room. I could not believe that I was really there. It might have been a dream. My state of shock ran so deep that nothing seemed real, not even the adult hands that then gave the once-over frisk to my nude teenage body.

"Son, I'm gonna to need to see buh-neeth yer tester-kulz."

When they had satisfied themselves that I had secreted neither projectile weapons nor cocaine anywhere on my bare body I was handed a one-piece neon-orange jumpsuit and a pair of shower flip-flops. They took my clothes, wallet, whatever rubbish I had in my pockets, and the summer flip-flops I had been wearing. I was taken past a row of inmates en route to another part of the prison, past their jeering exclamations about the new white boy, and to my new cell. Other than my fancy rimless toilet, glossy metal sink, stainless steel desk and cot, and a backless steel stool bursting up from the floor like a metal mushroom, the room was bare. Everything had been painted an extremely bright sky-blue. I could not turn off or dim the light in the cell. After some time my door was opened and dinner was handed in. The tray was retrieved shortly. They turned out my lights at 8:30 p.m. Night one as an outlaw.

112.

I was awakened the next morning by the lights automatically coming on. There was an intercom in my room, and someone yelled through it for me to wake up. The guards came down the row of cells beneath me, then came down my row of cells upstairs, banging on doors and yelling at the inmates to wake up. I was on the upstairs row, in the cell at the very end. I woke up, stood, and realized I didn't need to change clothes. I had only the orange jumpsuit. I sat on the thin mattress coating the cot. I waited.

After some time all of the cells but mine opened. The inmates emerged from their cells and lined up against the wall. I looked through the slit-window in my door down to the main room. The guards showed up and the outer door of the main room opened and the guards began to take everyone away. I banged on my door and shouted. One of the guards looked up at my door and cursed.

"Hey! Stop that shit!"

"But my door didn't open!"

"It ain't supposed to open. You in cool-down."

"Cooling down from what?"

"You just got here. Sit tight. We gon' bring you breakfast later."

Some time later the massed inmates returned and reentered their cells. My door opened, and a guard slid in a formerly warm breakfast. The door buzzed and clicked shut. I ate greedily. It was a small breakfast. I sat in my cell.

Then I sat a while longer.

This continued on indefinitely.

After some time my door opened. I was led through the main room and a hallway or two, doors buzzing and clicking open and closed every few yards. I reentered the room where I had been stripped, and my regular clothes were handed to me. I changed. I was led through several more doors and handed over to a policeman from Selma. It was time to go to the Courthouse. It was time for my detention hearing. It was time to decide whether or not I posed a threat to Society.

113.

I got to the courthouse and met the lawyer appointed to defend me.

"Hello, Mr. Beauchamp, let's take a look at your case."

My lawyer perused several papers in a brief.

"You've given a statement?"

"I spoke to a detective yesterday."

"Hmmm…" he frowned.

"Well… can you get me out?"

"Seems the families have asserted that you pose a significant danger should you be released. Hmmm…."

"Sir, I can't go back there. It's terrible!"

"We're about to step in to see the judge. I'll ask him to freely release you to your parents' custody. It's your word against theirs, so he's likely to err on the side of safety until we can arrange a trial. But perhaps he'll release you on house arrest."

"But sir, I haven't done anything!"

My lawyer smiled condescendingly and we went, with the police officer, into the courtroom. Palter, Drazel, Jade, and all their parents were gathered. The judge was raised, seated several feet above us at the imposing bench.

The judge asked if the prosecutor would like to begin.

"Your honor, the victims have provided statements that Mr. Beauchamp has threatened to kill them and their families if they attempted to press charges concerning the alleged crimes. We ask that he be held in detention until we can arrange for a trial."

The judge turned and looked at my lawyer.

"Your honor, my client absolutely denies these accusations. There is no evidence that he ever made any such threat. He has never previously been arrested. He has never even had a speeding ticket. He is a teenage boy. The notion that he is capable of mass murder is ludicrous. We request that he be freely released into the custody of his parents to await trial. Barring that, we ask that he be granted house arrest under the custody of his parents."

"Denied. I have reason to believe the defendant poses a significant danger to these families."

The judge looked at me.

"I'll tell you something off the record, young man. I've received phone calls about you from a number of prominent members of the community. You get into fights, you're a trained fighter, and you've even put someone into the hospital in a violent altercation."

"Your honor, that guy who went to the hospital, he was two years older than me! And he threw the first punch!"

"So you admit to assaulting someone to the point that hospitalization was required," the judge noted as he looked sternly at my lawyer. "I see no reason to deliberate further. We will arrange a trial as speedily as possible. We will remand the juvenile into the custody of the West Alabama Youth Services until that time."

And throughout, as I stood and endured that farce of a proceeding, I watched Palter, tried to catch his eye, to catch either of the girls' eyes, to signal to them that it was ok, that the joke had gone on long enough, that they could tell the truth. I was especially hoping that Palter would rise up to defend me. I did not know why he wasn't speaking on my behalf. I didn't realize it at the time, but those girls could never have turned back from their grand deception. The matter had proceeded too far. I searched their faces. I knew them well. I could clearly see that they had never thought their lie would end up in court. Perhaps they had thought that their fathers would, in proper Southern tradition, threaten to shoot me, and that would be the sum and total. But even in the courtroom the parents of those girls were glaring at me, barely concealing their rage.

The three young people were staring straight down at their feet, shifting uncomfortably. Glancing only at each other. Blushing.

114.

I was back in WAYS. I had been there for several days. Gradually they began to let me out of the cell for more of the day. First I got out for showers. Then I got out for meals. Finally I was let out with the other inmates in the main room while they played cards. Then I got to go out with them to the concrete cage, roughly fifteen meters square, known as the basketball court. I couldn't play ball though. Throughout my first week I didn't have any shoes. After my first week I got a pair of shoes, but one of them had a hole in it, so playing ball, though possible, hurt.

There were about two dozen prisoners, all but one of whom were black, and several of them let me know that they were interested in assaulting me if they caught me away from the guards. But I was a big guy, and I casually mentioned that I was the only white member of the Selma boxing team, and that slowed the threats a bit.

I still didn't have anything in my cell, and most days I was in there at least twenty hours a day. All of the cells were sole-occupancy. On the bad days, if any of the other inmates were rioting or fighting, or if the guards were simply in a foul mood, we were locked down twenty-three or even twenty-four straight hours. It wasn't at all like the solitary confinement depicted on television specials, where the inmate has a mini-TV, a radio, a small personal library, letters and pictures from home. I truly didn't have anything in the cell—not pen and paper, not a book, not a magazine, nothing but a few pieces of torn-off toilet paper.

I was no longer Finis Leavell Beauchamp. I was Wing B, Cell no. 214.

A few days into my captivity my lawyer showed up at WAYS, and I was led into the visitation room. That was the first time I had been given the chance to speak privately to a lawyer for more than five minutes.

"Hello, Beau. I'm sorry your detention hearing didn't go as you had wished. How are you?"

"Are you serious?"

"Hey, I know you don't want to be here, but considering the situation, it could be worse. Some people have to wait months for a trial. But juveniles go to the front of the line. Yours is in a couple of weeks. That's not too far off. So let's get ready. Let's talk about what happened."

I told my lawyer the story. He listened carefully and took notes.

"So, what can be done?" I asked slowly, glad to be done with my long tale.

"Beau, I hate to tell you, but you have a serious problem here."

"Well what is it? I certainly didn't threaten anyone, and I know they can't prove I did. And I didn't do anything illegal. I know there's no evidence I did, because I didn't. I know the law. I'm innocent until proven guilty!"

"Hmmm, first they are charging you with having forcibly demanded oral sex."

"How could you *forcibly* demand oral sex? That's impossible. The girl could just bite, couldn't she? You'd be in the hospital immediately."

"Drazel claims you threatened to kill them unless they did it."

"That's just not true! She had a crush on me. A lot of people know about it!"

"We have confirmed that she invited you and Jade out to dinner at a local restaurant with her grandmother after this allegedly happened— but before they first claimed that you wanted to kill them. Obviously if they thought you were going to kill them it seems unlikely that they would have invited you out to eat. No one denies that there are deeply problematic elements in their testimony, and it is, after all, their word against yours as to whether you forced them. But it still won't help you."

"Why not?"

"Beau, do you know what a statutory crime is?"

"No, sir."

"It's like this… in the state of Alabama it is illegal to have any sexual contact with a girl if you are older than sixteen and she is younger than sixteen and you are separated by more than twenty-four months in age. You're seventeen. Jade is fourteen. You're just over the statutory limit. You've already admitted to what is considered deviant illegal sexual behavior whether what you did was consensual or not. Legally it does not matter if Jade wanted to do it—even if she initiated the activity. In short, you have already admitted to committing a felony."

"I'm less than three years older than her!"

"It is an extreme case, yes, but it is technically statutory sexual assault in Alabama. The statement you gave the detective has seriously undermined your case."

"But I didn't know that! I thought you could do something with a girl if you were both minors. *I'm a minor.* It's not like these girls are small kids. We all go to the exact same school. I didn't know I was admitting something illegal. That detective said if I didn't answer basic questions I was going to look suspicious."

"Beau, I'm sorry to tell you, but ignorance of the law doesn't excuse violations of the law. The judge is not going to accept that you should go free because you were ignorant of the statute."

"But I only got a blowjob! *Lots* of people in our school have gotten blowjobs from girls more than two years younger than them! I doubt anyone in my entire school has ever heard of this law. You know how many seniors are dating sophomores *right now*? I'm not even a senior in high school yet."

"Well that may be, Beau, but in those cases the father of the girl isn't furious or doesn't know about the sexual activity. These girls' families feel... frankly, as though you've made their daughters look like sluts. That doesn't go down well in Selma, even in normal situations. And this is not a normal situation. You know I don't have to tell you this, but Drazel's father is a very powerful and wealthy man."

"True," I reflected glumly. "But Palter is my best friend. I'm sure he'll back me up."

"Beau, I don't think you understand the gravity of this situation. I've got Palter's official statement right here. He's not backing you up at all. Palter claims you told him that you *raped* Jade. Now Jade has said that isn't true, and that there was no vaginal intercourse, so his statement is in conflict with both yours and hers. That is one of the bigger conflicts in their statements. Still, based on Palter's testimony you have been charged with attempted rape. To resolve the question Jade's parents are taking her to a gynecologist this week where she will be inspected for signs of virginity. If she is not found to be a virgin that charge will be upgraded to rape. And like I said, it doesn't matter if you forced her or not. The sex could have been consensual. You are seventeen and she is fourteen, so this is a statutory crime. Since you've already admitted to a detective that you've had sexual contact with Jade, the burden of proof will be on you to show that you didn't have sex with her if she turns out not to be a virgin. Now tell me the truth… have you had sex with that girl? Because if they discover that she's not a virgin this is going to become a rape trial."

"No, no, no! I *never* had sex with her," I said frantically, nearly losing vision in my sudden panic. "But she's pretty wild, has a reputation," I babbled, nearly incoherent, "she could have had sex with anyone before me! I had my fingers in her. Who knows what a doctor will find? She *wanted* to have sex with me, so she definitely could have had sex with someone before. That wouldn't mean *I* did it!"

"Well Beau, I hate to tell you this, but you better pray to God she hasn't, because if she has the judge is almost certainly going to certify you as an adult. At that point you'll be transferred to the county jail and incarcerated with adults. You'll be charged as an adult with the rape of a minor. And then that girl's parents are going to try to make sure you spend the rest of your life in prison."

116.

Shortly after my arrest, but well before my trial, the local paper ran a descriptive front page headline. "YOUTH RAPES TWO," jumped out at the citizenry in big, bold letters. Never mind that neither girl claimed to have had intercourse with me, the local news was not to be outdone in getting to the front of a breaking story. (In truth, the paper was in no danger of losing the story, as nearly every other major media outlet in the area was owned by Drazel's father.)

That a Morgan Academy student, scion of a powerful ecclesiastical family, a white person, had been publicly declared a serial rapist shook sleepy Selma to its foundation. My name was destroyed in a single day.

As my parents were fundamentalist Christians, it never occurred to them to sue the newspaper for libel. 1 Corinthians 6 made it clear that lawsuits were wicked (provided the person you intended to sue was a Christian). Unwilling to take legal action to defend me from libel, my father was confronted by other fundamentalists with 1 Timothy 3:5, which states that if a man cannot rule his own house he cannot lead a church. My father promptly resigned as pastor of Shiloh Baptist Church.

I went back into my cell, and life went back to a long succession of hours with nothing to do. On days when there hadn't been a fight in the showers or at a meal (or if the staff were bored) we would be taken out of our room for ninety minutes and allowed to watch a movie. But movies didn't come every day, and the threat of impromptu violence was ever present.

Try, dear friends, to imagine a dozen consecutive hours in a small, bare room with nothing to read or watch—and then a dozen more to follow that, nothing breaking the molasses-flow of time. You urinate and defecate one foot from where you sleep. Meals slid into your room achieve the status of major life events. Getting up to look at the lonely tree through your slit-window is a major indulgence you grant yourself after the passage of a terrible hour.

Imagine that, despite this paralyzing inactivity, you cannot definitely wish to enter the main room (nothing more than a small pod with three sky-blue tables located directly beneath the cells) during free time due to the fact that you might be spontaneously assaulted simply because another inmate is frustrated or bored. You know that you will wake up the next day and it will be exactly the same as this day. Your mind wanders endlessly with no direction other than to wonder why your best friend betrayed you, why he wanted you to spend the rest of your life in jail, if the whole thing was nothing more than an attempt to alleviate the tedium of his privileged life.

When not agonizing over betrayal your mind jumps to the permanent destruction of your reputation, or the loss of your father's job and career. To moderate this misery you work on regulating your breathing, particularly during the panic attacks that arise whenever you remember that if a certain young slattern doesn't turn out to be a virgin you will be transferred to an adult facility where you will, in all probability, be assaulted and gang-raped. Of course you, the reader, conduct this thought experiment from the security and nuance of detached, sophisticated adulthood. I struggled through this congeries of terror with all the drunken horror of a teenager who has never lived outside the home.

To escape the anxiety of the panic attacks, in the complete absence of any meaningful stimulation, many of the inmates practiced counting the cement blocks forming the walls of their cell over and over—hundreds of times per day. As I reflect back on that now I realize that the practice must have functioned as a type of focused meditation, not dissimilar from many practices in Buddhism and Hinduism.

Counting cement blocks didn't work for me. During the time we were let out into the main room of the prison, during which most of the inmates played cards (spades the only game played) I was sometimes able to persuade the guards to give me pencil and paper so that I could write down my feelings. But it didn't help. The guards read anything I wrote, whether journal entry or letter. They also opened and glanced through every letter I received. I had to be extremely careful about what I wrote. My lawyer had given me specific instructions on how to appear a model citizen during the time I awaited trial. It must not appear that I was blaming anyone else for my actions. Most importantly, I needed to be a good *Christian*.

After a week in solitary confinement I was upgraded from red level to yellow level, which meant that I was allowed a second five-minute phone call during the second week, and my lights were turned out at 9 p.m. rather than 8:30.

WAYS was designed to hold dangerous juvenile prisoners in solitary confinement for *no more* than two weeks. By the time my trial arrived I had already been there for three.

118.

I was delivered to the courthouse an hour early in order to have time to consult with my lawyer. He was in a meeting with the prosecutor. I was deposited in a room to wait, but stood as soon as he entered. There was a second lawyer with him.

"Beau, I'm glad you're here. I have great news. The results from the gynecologist came in, and Jade is in fact a virgin! You won't be charged with rape!"

I sat down immediately, afraid I might faint. Several seconds later I realized that Jade's intact hymen seriously undermined Palter's statement. I wondered if that would affect the case. Pondering this, I looked up and remembered that there was another lawyer in the room.

"Hello, Beau, I'm Mr. Jeofail."

"Mr. Jeofail, will you represent me today with my lawyer?"

"No, Beau. I'm here because I know your father, and he's asked me to help craft a deal with the prosecutor so that we can avoid a trial."

"Did you make a deal? If they let me go back to Texas for my senior year I'll leave this town tomorrow!"

"Beau, I don't think that's going to happen. This is a very unusual case. The prosecutor has said he does not want to prosecute it. It's clear the girls were not coerced into this behavior. But the parents are still very angry, and their pride is not going to allow them to back off charges already filed. Now I'm not going to be able to go into the court with you. I ran against your judge, a two-time incumbent, in the last election for district judge, and came extremely close to unseating him. He's still not very happy with me, even though he won, so it would hurt you if I went in. I'm only here as a favor to your father to help with the prosecutor."

"So it'll just be me and my lawyer?"

"Yes, but I know the prosecutor well, and we have worked out a deal. Your father is friends with clergymen throughout Selma, and one of them has told us about a Christian rehabilitation facility in Florida where you can get sound, Godly, Christian treatment for six months. Then, when you've engaged in serious repentance for what you did, and gotten your walk right with the Lord, you'll be able to get your GED and go on to college. The prosecutor thinks this is a fair deal. So if you plead guilty to the charges you'll go to Florida for six months, and the entire thing will remain a sealed juvenile case. You won't have an adult record at all. The facility in Florida will not be locked-down like the detention facility in Greensboro. You won't be in a cell. It will be a therapeutic environment. However, if you plead innocent, and force a trial, the whole thing is going to get very sticky since you've already admitted to a statutory felony."

"Well I didn't know that whole bit about a girl can't be more than two years younger. I thought everything was ok if you were both minors!"

"Beau, do *not* say that to the judge," Mr. Jeofail emphatically replied. "Even if it wasn't a statutory crime, what happened between you and those girls was morally despicable, whether consensual or not. The whole situation—drugs, alcohol, sexual activity with multiple girls—Beau, have you even thought about how severely your walk with the Lord must've deteriorated for you to get to a point where you thought this was normal behavior?"

"Beau, this is important," my lawyer interjected more calmly. "The crucial issue here is making sure you are not certified as an adult. If you contest this case the judge will almost certainly certify you. You probably can't be convicted on all charges, but even if you're convicted of only the statutory sexual activity to which you've already admitted you will serve time as a felon in an adult prison. When you get out you'll have a public record as sex offender, and that felony will be on your record for life. Trust me, Beau, you do not want that. It makes six months in Florida look like a quick time-out."

"When would I go?"

"You'd go within a day or two. Just as soon as we could arrange the paperwork. Plus, your parents will be allowed to drive you down. Just think, this time next year you'll be in college and this will all be a bad dream."

"And this year you can work on your walk with the Lord," Mr. Jeofail added.

"But I'm going to lose my senior year of football!" I said, squirming in my chair, trying not to cry. "I start both ways, and we've won the state championship three years in a row! I was going to play college football. Coach Nub said so."

"Beau, you can never go back to Morgan again," Mr. Jeofail said firmly. "Even if you got off completely the school would never let you back in. There would be a riot. The judge has gotten a lot of calls about you from concerned parents, parents who are worried that you've allowed Satan to build a stronghold in your life. And to be honest, getting right with the Lord really is the most important thing in all of this—*not* going free. You should praise Jesus that he's given you this opportunity before you allowed Satan to gain complete power over your life. I'm truly sorry that you're not going to have a senior year, but the Lord knows that getting right with Him is worth far, far more than football."

"Do you know the judge is going to accept this?" I asked, blinking back tears. "Do you know he's going to let me go to Florida? It *would* be good to get out of WAYS."

"I wouldn't say we *know*, per se," my lawyer replied. "We're going to plead guilty to the charges and throw ourselves on the mercy of the court. The judge will then ask for the recommendation of the prosecutor. At that point the prosecutor will present our plea bargain."

"So this is going to work?" I asked, looking at Mr. Jeofail.

"You just have to trust in God, Beau. All things work together for those that love Him."

119.

We went into the court. The judge was staring down at me from his bench. The opposition was on their side of the court. The teams lined up to play. The judge began.

"Young man, I am looking at these charges and they are very disturbing," he said, looking at me over a loosely held sheaf of papers. The judge solemnly read out the charges. I noted that attempted rape was still on the list.

"I feel as though I must give some thought to certifying you as an adult with this array of charges. Son, do you know the penalty for these charges if I convict you as an adult?"

"No, sir."

"No, your honor."

"No, your honor," I squeaked.

"It's more than forty years, son! I can sentence you to more than forty years should you be found guilty of these charges. That's most of your life! Do you understand the severity of this situation?" he asked, his eyes burning into me.

I slowly nodded my head, unsure if it was a good idea to throw myself at the mercy of this judicial Attila.

"We also have a report from your former psychologist. He believes you stand in need of serious and intensive psychological treatment. He has taken time to evaluate you and has apparently met with little success in helping you. Nevertheless, his opinion is informed."

"Informed enough to think demons are having their way with me," I thought to myself.

"Yes, your honor," I meekly mouthed.

"Your honor, if it's alright I'd like to consult briefly with my client," my lawyer interjected.

"Can he sentence me to more than forty years?" I whispered madly.

"Technically, yes. But only if you were convicted on every charge and weren't allowed to serve time for those charges concurrently. Attempted rape has still not been stricken from the charges, and in addition, the penalty for forcing someone to provide you with fellatio in the State of Alabama is the same as the penalty for holding someone down and forcibly sodomizing them. But look, none of this is pertinent. His tone is unusually menacing, but I believe he is only warning you to take the plea bargain. He has been in communication with the parents. I'm sure the last thing they want is a trial in which their daughters will be forced to submit to a thorough cross-examination on the details of their sexual behavior."

"I don't want to plead guilty though. I heard him reading those charges and I just... feel like this is *wrong*. I never made anyone do anything sexual in my life. Those charges say that I forced them to give me a blowjob. That's just not true. This isn't right!"

"Beau, it does not matter if you forced them or not. The penalty will be the same. You are already guilty according to your statement to the detective. You need to understand this. I don't think this is right either, but if you gamble with this you will probably throw away your entire life."

I sighed and we turned back to the judge. My lawyer entered my plea of guilty. The judge looked to the prosecutor who then reminded the judge that a plea bargain had been discussed. The judge looked keenly at Palter and Drazel's father, who ever so slightly shook his head, signifying displeasure. The judge leaned back in his chair and sighed. Then he sat up and looked at me.

"Young man, you've confessed to charges of tremendous gravity. I'm told that you have done very well in school, and that you have never been arrested. Based on that, I'm inclined to show you great mercy. But as to the plan presented by the prosecutor... that I cannot do. This is no simple case of juvenile delinquency. I'm declaring you a Serious Juvenile Offender and mandating a year's sentence at the Mt. Meigs Juvenile Correctional Facility. There you will enroll in anger management and sexual abuse counseling. The year's sentence will begin once you reach Mt. Meigs. I wish you good luck, and hope that you can make the changes necessary to turn your life around."

I felt dizzy and nearly collapsed. The *Serious Juvenile Offender* designation was only given to one to two percent of juvenile convicts, and was reserved for only the most heinous juvenile criminals in the state. Only a few dozen received the designation each year.

I had heard of Mt. Meigs from the other inmates at WAYS. It had a terrible reputation. Almost no one was sent there for a first offense, unless that offense was a serious assault or outright murder. The other inmates spoke of it with anxiety, even though most of them would never commit a crime serious enough to be sent there. Mt. Meigs, the Mountain, located just outside Montgomery, Alabama, was the central prison compound for the worst of the worst, the two hundred and fifty most lethally dangerous young felons in Alabama.

After the hearing my lawyer followed the prosecutor and the judge into a backroom, and I was led away to a holding room to await a police unit to escort me back to WAYS. Twenty minutes later my lawyer entered the room. He looked almost as broken as I felt.

"I'm so sorry, Beau. I really thought he would accept the deal."

"What the heck happened?"

"Don't you know?" my lawyer sighed, as he pulled up a chair and sat down.

"No. I'm supposed to go to Florida!"

"Beau, what color was the judge?"

"Black. So?"

"Beau, he's *elected*. How do all elections in Selma work?"

"What do you mean?"

"What is the dynamic of every election in Selma?"

"A black person runs against a white. The blacks have more people but the whites have more money."

"Correct. In the last election your judge ran against Mr. Jeofail, who represented the whites. The vast majority of Selma is black, but the election between them came down to less than one hundred votes. Do you know what that means, Beau?"

"The blacks don't vote?"

"No. It means he's a terrible judge. It means he's not popular. It means he'll need help to win another election."

My lawyer stood and trudged to the door. He looked back at me sadly and shook his head.

"Now do you understand?"

"*No*. I don't get it. We had a deal!"

"Beau, Palter and Drazel's father had been informed of that deal by the prosecutor long before we got into the courtroom. But he took one look at you in that courthouse today and rethought the deal—decided he doesn't want you running around free in Selma in just six months."

"Still… it was a *deal*. What does this have to do with the judge's reelection?"

"It's not often that in Selma a black judge decides a sensitive case between two important factions of whites. Your father is a Southern Baptist pastor, and in Selma that is not to be despised. But when he resigned his church, he lost his base of power. Palter and Drazel's dad is the biggest media owner for several counties. That provides enormous influence in Selma. The next election isn't for several years, but who knows, your judge is likely betting that this decision will ensure that there won't be a united white vote in the next election, or that he may get a deal for campaign advertising. Do you think Drazel's dad will forget this? Now do you see?" my lawyer asked as he turned his face away from me. "That decision today may have won your judge's next election."

121.

I was back in WAYS, back in a cell, waiting on a transfer to Mt. Meigs. The other white guy who had been incarcerated was gone, and I was affectionately known, to the inmates who didn't want to assault me, as *white bread.* I was lost in a dream from which all the color had faded.

A little over a week after my hearing the new school year started— my long-awaited senior year. We were herded into a large one-room classroom with two teachers. The head teacher, the first white staff-person I'd met since my incarceration, took me aside to converse. She said that she'd reviewed my transcripts from Morgan, and wanted me to know that she would do her best to challenge me. She did feel sure, however, that I would enjoy using God's gifts to give back to others— which meant tutoring the other inmates when I finished the day's work.

The schoolwork was self-paced; finishing a school day took me less than an hour. I began doing multiple days' work in a single day, but that didn't help. The work was exceedingly boring, and I had little to do when I had finished, though it was an immense relief to spend those brief hours around other human beings, even if the work was done in strict silence. I began to spend most of my class time tutoring the other students, effectively serving as the third teacher. But then this provoked complaints of racial paternalism from some of the guards, so the teacher had to think of other things to do with me during school hours.

"Beau, Mr. Vick needs help."

I didn't know who Mr. Vick was, but I was taken out of the classroom and through a series of locked doors to the kitchens. In the back of the kitchens, in an area where no prisoner was allowed, was an office where a very fat, pale, bald, middle-aged man sat snacking in front of several books of spreadsheets.

Mr. David T. Vick III was one of the jolliest men I have ever known, fond of conversation and snacking, but not over-fond of the mundane bookkeeping necessitated by the supervision of the prison's kitchens. He was from an old-money Southern family of the planter class, and, due to disability, he was only able to work part-time. He explained the mechanism of accounting, told me that in private I was to call him Big Dave, and then set me to work while he kept up a stream of cheerful chatter. Each day when I finished cleaning up the mess of paperwork he gave me a piece of cornbread, or a plate of biscuits and honey. This was exceedingly well-received, as the state's caloric allotment was certainly not calculated with a muscular two-hundred-and-forty-pound juvenile in mind. Since my imprisonment I had felt that I was slowly starving each day.

Within a week my senior year of high school had become extremely practical. I was organizing the books and accounting for all foodstuffs entering the prison.

122.

"I've met your new judge, Beau."

"You have?" I asked, stealing a side glance at Big Dave as I added columns for the next week's food order. He was referring to the circuit judge appointed to the legal appeal arranged by Mr. Jeofail. Even Mr. Jeofail, with his excruciatingly Evangelical worldview, believed that my sentence had been out of proportion to the charges, despite my spiritual *degeneration*.

"Yep. He's the circuit judge for several counties. But he's from right here in Hale County. This is his home base."

"Do you think he'll go easy on me? Will he give me the plea bargain I was supposed to originally get?" I asked, wondering if perhaps the appeal was a good idea, or would make things worse.

"You know, Beau, I've told you several times that I knew there was something different about you—when I first saw you in the line with the other inmates," Big Dave mused, smacking his lips as he munched on a snack. "You didn't strike me as the typical guy who comes into a place like this. But the same reason you're here now will hurt you with this judge."

"What do you mean?"

"You're here because of money and politics, and this judge is as crooked as they come. He's a conspirator. He's only been in office a year, but he's damn crooked. You may not see any improvement with your appeal."

"I sure hope you're wrong. How could he be so crooked if he's only been in office a year?"

"The voting here is extremely corrupt. There's a tremendous amount of voter fraud. And he's an elected judge. Though that's not really the main reason."

"No?"

"No. He's a scam artist."

"A what?"

"Last year in Greensboro a woman and her parents sued a big corporation because they had both been overcharged six hundred bucks while financing the purchase of a satellite dish."

"So?"

"So he awarded them a million dollars in compensation for mental anguish. The whole thing was a scam arranged right here in Greensboro."

"Wow. A million bucks for getting overcharged six hundred dollars? I should get overcharged more."

"Beau, that was just the compensation. He awarded an additional three hundred million dollars in punitive damages. First year in office. The state legislature is going to have to rewrite the tort laws. If they don't we won't see another large corporation ever come into this state."

"What does that mean for me?" I asked, wondering what kind of mercenary was going to decide the rest of my life.

"It means that if the other side has more money, and it sounds like they have a lot more, you could be in for one hell of a time."

123.

Big Dave was not entirely wrong about voter fraud in Greensboro, or my judge, though that truth would not be discovered until long after my case had been decided. Several years after I passed through that judge's office he was suspended without pay by the State of Alabama. He was not convicted of engaging in voter fraud, but rather was found to have used his office to impede the investigations of three of his relatives who were, including his brother-in-law, a state senator. He was convicted of numerous ethics violations, though his worst offense was actively using his position as judge to derail an investigation of his sister, who would eventually be indicted on thirteen felony counts of voter fraud. Strangely, the State of Alabama chose not to permanently remove him from the bench.

124.

Frequently, the initial subterranean emotion one feels when beset by adversity is guilt. Perhaps that is illogical, but it is to certain whimsies of our inaccessible selves that our consciousness appears eternally abject.

In that time, alone and condemned in a small, sky-blue cell, I was harassed and harangued by the incessant murmuring of that inscrutable hidden self. My consciousness was isolated, trembling and starved on the lonely rock that shook in the waves of a grey sea. Everyone I had ever known had condemned me. Even the most well-meaning letters I received in that cell were naught more than pages of quoted Bible verses, urging me to use my afflictions to turn my life around, to cast aside sin… to embrace *Jesus*.

125.

What do the hoi polloi mean when they claim to have *embraced* Jesus? One does not physically grasp a long-dead Jew. Is this just lazy speech?

Perhaps they refer to a conversational commonplace. One says, "I have *embraced* a truth." But this does not mean that one has chosen to believe something. One cannot choose to believe a thing. You may choose to *say* that you believe that our sun exists in the shape of a cube rather than a sphere, but you may not choose to believe it. Rather one believes something involuntarily, as an amalgamation of new information coalesces in the subconscious, rises to awareness as realization, crystallizes as belief. I have *embraced* a truth, ergo, I have, through the mechanism of one or more of my sensory organs, received information previously unknown to me, resulting in the formation of a new belief. But this cannot be what they mean when they say they have *embraced* Jesus, for they already claim to have knowledge of Jesus.

Can they have such knowledge? Surely even the rudest epistemological foray should dispel this notion. They *believe* certainly. But what is the justification for this belief? On the basis of *what* do they assert the truth of a proposition which states that they have definite knowledge of the identity of a Being both metaphysical and corporeal?

Perhaps we should not ask what they mean when they say they *embrace* Jesus. A more foundational question would ascertain how they claim to have any *knowledge* of Jesus at all. Nay, I must step back even farther. To what, exactly, are they referring when they say the name? I see now that it is essential to determine what is meant by the syllables *gee-zus*.

However, they cannot mean, when stating that they embrace Jesus, that they have somehow chosen to enter a state of blissful emotional attachment toward their man-god. The man is long dead; the god, by definition, unknowable. Such an attachment would be an impossibility.

The more I seek to understand the rabble when they state that they embrace Jesus, the less sure I am of what they mean either by *embrace* or by *Jesus*.

126.

My old lawyer was gone. My new lawyer, Mr. Jeofail, author of the bargain, the imbroglio, the failed agreement in my first legal escapade, was to take the lead in my defense before the corrupt circuit judge. I met very little with Mr. Jeofail. It seemed that all of the proceedings for this appeal were to take place between serious Southern men in closed rooms. When I did speak to him he repeatedly emphasized that the main thing was to get my life right with Jesus. He made it clear that there would be very little he could say to the appellate judge if I didn't have my life right with the Lord. I pondered this for some time in my cell.

I wanted out of jail. I began a religious fast.

127.

Sitting in my cell, slowly starving after a second day without food, I once more turned over the problems that beset me. The judge was set to rule on my case. But then his wife got sick so he couldn't. The administrator of WAYS had told me that loving Jesus was well and good, but if I didn't eat the police would take me to the hospital where I would be cuffed to a hospital bed and fed intravenously. If that happened, she guaranteed, it would look very bad for my case.

But sitting in my cell, I wasn't sure if I was engaging in a religious fast in order to demonstrate to the lawyers, judge, and parents that I was a good Christian teenage boy, or if I was merely on a hunger-strike. I told them that I wasn't eating in order to demonstrate my commitment to Jesus. But what was I really doing? Truthfully, I wasn't sure.

Less than a year before I had abandoned Jesus for the egoism of an inchoate Satanism. But that theological emancipation held little metaphysical content. I had no knowledge of any dark deity, incantations, or obscene rituals. Certainly the notion that I might be involved in direct blasphemy caused the good burghers of Selma to shiver in their manure-encrusted boots, but when they demanded that I return to Jesus it was unclear whether they were asking me to accept certain theological premises or simply to admit that I was a bad person.

I had reached that place where the pangs of hunger stop, where the brain ceases to scream for glucose. Everything had become numb. I was growing faint. I suddenly realized, against the backdrop of my weakening life-force, that since my incarceration, since the shock, the trauma imposed by the unexpected loss of everything that composed my world, I no longer had any desire to harm myself.

Every terrible thing that had happened served to rip me away from myself, and in so doing had torn me from a desire to ravage my own flesh, for, after all, self-harm was no more than an attempt to feel when nothing could be felt. Self-harm is a result of the desire to relearn *feeling* when one's pain has become so ecstatic that in order to survive one has involuntarily become permanently numb. But in the unending silence of the cell there was no avoidance of sensation. Pain could not be turned off, avoided, submerged in alcohol or drugs, cut away. Pain was ever-present.

Yet one thing remained constant. I was, as ever, completely disallowed from telling the truth about why I was in pain. When in Society there had been no one to tell what my parents were doing to me. There was no one who would have thought them wrong or immoral. Again, in prison, there was no one who cared if I thought that I was innocent. Indeed, saying openly, even to my parents or lawyer, that I had done nothing wrong, was a definite way to ensure that my appeal would go nowhere, that I would serve a full year in Mt. Meigs—a year which would not begin until the appeal had ended, and I was actually sent to Mt. Meigs. And I did desperately wish to be free, to have an appeal overturn my conviction and send me away to the fairy-land of rehabilitation in Florida.

But wrong had been done, whether I was free to express that or not. I had not had Miranda Rights read to me. I had been questioned, as a minor, without a lawyer present or my parents' consent. I had been questioned without witnesses present. It had been strongly and repeatedly asserted that if I did not sign away my right to remain silent, or to retain counsel, then I would be presumed guilty and locked up until I did give a statement. I was slyly questioned, as a minor, about something that I was unaware was a crime. I was told that I might either plead guilty to actions I did not commit or spend the next four decades in jail. I acknowledged the ultimatum and pled guilty, but then was not given the agreed upon plea bargain. I was placed in a cell designed to hold a teenager for no more than two weeks while for more than a month a new judged angled away, trying to determine which line held the bigger fish.

Surely you see what I slowly realized. *Not even my own lawyer and parents wanted me to go free.* Neither my Evangelical lawyer nor my God-drunk parents thought me innocent. They were of the informed opinion that it did not matter if the laws of mankind were broken. Far more important was the violation of God's law. I was a teenage boy, and I had received fellatio from multiple young women. That was enough. That was illegal, no matter how old the girls were, no matter if it was consensual. I wasn't supposed to go free; I was supposed to repent, and embrace Jesus. My supporters did not support me, they supported an abstraction of an ideal me.

I realized that nothing would help. I was completely alone. My fast or hunger protest would do nothing. I buzzed the intercom, and called for the guard to bring me food.

128.

There are days when we awaken to find that our past has become a noose. What then is the memoir but rope? A man writes. He writes more and fills pages. In search of the present he succeeds only in dangling from memory. Oh, how carefully he tied that knot!

129.

I have missed my brothers, in those years that I have been gone, in those years since they took me from home and locked me away. When I left I had a family. It was no good family to be sure, but, I had a family. I have missed my brothers.

While I was gone my father lost his work. He had no other training, no other skills. He quickly became impoverished. I felt that I was to blame. Our family lived in a parsonage. They had to leave. I was not there. I was locked away. And I have missed my brothers.

My mother did not want me to come back. My father and mother fought. No one thought to look after the children. I was locked away. For this too, I felt blame. Years have passed. That life is gone. The past will never change; on this everyone agrees. I was gone, and could not return. I have missed my brothers.

130.

That judge, that infamous circuit judge, incorrigible in his endless procrastinations, did time and again find ways to postpone a decision on my appeal. My lawyer pressed tirelessly, seeking to eradicate the Serious Juvenile Offender status, as well as the extant charge of the attempted rape, which even Jade readily admitted had never occurred.

Day bled into day, and I continued to wait. I quickly finished all of the schoolwork that was available. I was started on an assigned program of literature, designed to take so long in the reading and testing that no inmate could ever possibly run out of work. I finished the course in a couple of weeks. The teacher began to bring me scientific works and novels from the local library. An exception was made in my case, as I had been there far beyond the maximum time the facility was designed to hold a youth, and I was allowed to keep a book in my cell.

The administration was unsure what to do with me. I had been there far too long. I believe they felt that the situation must in time appear abusive. The summer passed. In the fall I turned eighteen. On my birthday Big Dave secretly gave me a candy bar, a coke, and a five-minute phone call. It was the best birthday present I have ever had. I did his work for him. I discovered that he had dated my ex-girlfriend's mom three decades before. We became fast friends.

I asked my sister, on one of my family's visits, to smuggle in some blades of fresh-cut grass. I wanted to touch something green. It had been months since I had stepped foot on grass. The loose green blades were discovered a week later, on a routine room inspection. There was nowhere to hide anything. I had no possessions. I was punished.

A barber was brought in. This was an anomaly, but they did not know what else to do. My hair had grown shaggy, and there was no word on when I might be transferred. A mentor was brought in. His name was Justin Kelly, a former Division I college football player, and an artist. We spoke of theology. He was the first educated non-Christian I can recall having ever met. I liked him very much.

One of the part-time guards, a podiatry student, would take me aside during the rare free period that was neither school nor solitary confinement. He began to teach me organic chemistry. I learned to draw variations of carbon molecules using a pencil and napkins in the main room pod.

Every guard was African-American. Some began to resent me. Two factions formed. In one I found protectors. Mrs. Jones, Mr. Skipper, and

Mr. Ross strove to guard me, in that truer sense of the word. Their peers, however, were certain that I was a prime example of the white privilege that had thoroughly corroded the entirety of the Black Belt. They did not understand why I was awarded *Student of the Week* each week. They questioned the one black teacher, informally questioned the other students, trying to determine how I was cheating in my schoolwork. They complained to the facility administrator both that I was cheating in school and that I was being taken out of school. Big Dave stopped coming for me, and I was made to return to the classroom. I would have been willing to resume my tutorial work, but that had been deemed racially patronizing, and so even for class time I was in a cell, reading a library book. My time in solitary confinement increased, and I was let out my cell for, at most, two hours per day.

Some of the guards, more virulently opposed to what they saw as my special treatment or white privilege, determined to take aggressive action to bring me low. One shift-leader threatened several times to violently assault me. He would taunt me daily in an attempt to get me to punch him, that we might fight without him losing his job. Another guard began frisking me during line-ups. No one else got those intimate searches. The others in line were allowed to look on and laugh as he used the pretence of those frisks to fondle my genitalia. He bounced my cock up and down in his hand and asked me if I was eyeballing him, if I had a problem.

I did indeed have a problem. I complained to Aaron Ross, the righteous African-American guard who believed in truly guarding me, and he alerted the administration. Complaints were lodged against those two over-zealous guards, and their actions were more carefully scrutinized. They determined to use different methods.

131.

A decision came down in my case. After numerous delays, the judge ruled that I would go to Mt. Meigs until the end of February, at which point I would be transferred to the rehabilitation program in Florida for the duration of my year of incarceration. My Serious Juvenile Offender status was to remain in place, as that status mandated a minimum incarceration of one year. My attempted rape charge was amended to simple sexual assault. I surmised that the sexual assault was for inserting a finger into Jade when she tried to mount my face.

I was told that if I got in even the slightest trouble during my year of incarceration I would be certified as an adult, and would serve out the longer adult sentence the judge assured me was still possible. I did not know if that was possible, though my lawyer said that it could be done. He called it a suspended sentence.

Given that everything I had seen of the legal system resembled the lawless Wild West, I assumed it was true. I had been told too many times that the judge would let me out, that I would be home that night. Over and over I felt hope that the new judge would realize how asinine was my sentencing, that he would give me probation or community service and send me home. Each time he had the opportunity to make a decision in my case, and did not, left me feeling as though I was running through a world that was melting beneath me. I was so sick of the uncertainty of what would happen that when the decision finally came down I wept. I did not care that I would not get out for many months, that I would not get my plea bargain, that I would have to go to Mt. Meigs. All that mattered was knowing *when* I would get out.

Yet the knowledge that I would get out in a year was tempered by the condition that my release would take place only if I stayed completely clear of trouble throughout that entire year. At each of the three facilities my release would be determined by the good report of the administration. I immediately realized that I had a problem. My two aggressive guards were actively urging the other inmates to attack me. I knew I would soon have to choose.

I could not be sure if I would defend myself and go to an adult prison, or take the inevitable beating in order to get to Mt. Meigs.

132.

He had three children who lived with their mother in a trailer in the countryside outside of Selma. He was big and strong and had coal black skin and a face pitted from acne. His hair was a couple of inches long, neither shaved nor afro, and it was unkempt. He came into WAYS raging and fighting. He was completely locked down more days that not. The guards who saw me as their nemesis had found their man. He was seventeen years old.

I was bigger than him, stronger than him, and white. He did not need a great deal of encouragement to see me as the Devil. He began trying to trip me in the line to meals, to elbow me on the way to our recreation time. I had previously been threatened, but never attacked. I was too sizeable for anyone to take on the project lightly. It needed a rabid wolf, and he had finally arrived. The other inmates, with the instincts of pack animals, sensed weakness, smelled blood on the air.

I knew that I had only a day or two before he threw an outright punch. Every day that went by in which I did not respond to his taunts and blows, that the guards encouraged him and got everyone to laugh, was a day I drew closer to a group beating. But I could not fight him. A single serious fight would get me certified as an adult and sent to an adult prison. Incarceration was ripping me apart, and I did not want to spend several years locked up. I became desperate, and formed a plan.

The next day we went out to the basketball court. The air was tense. The inmates expected to finally see me fight. The guards were amenable. The young wolf and I were on different sides in the game. I chose my moment carefully.

We went up together for a rebound, and I came down with it. Gripping the ball, I swung my arms side to side, ostensibly to prevent anyone from ripping the ball away. At least that is what I would have argued in court. What I actually did was drive my elbow ferociously into his jaw while coming down with the rebound. I expected his mandible to shatter. It did not, but a loud pop resounded in the cement cage, and he stumbled away. The game immediately ceased.

Everyone waited for him to shake it off. The guards intentionally stayed back. He shook his head and approached me. I knew that if I did not meet his eyes, if I trembled, if I in any way showed weakness, that I would be lost and alone in a mêlée.

He was shivering with rage, breathing hard, flecks of saliva shooting from his lips. He was staring at me and gauging his prospects and letting the anger course through him and I had nothing before me but the will of the Fates.

His breathing slowed. His chest relaxed. The inmates clucked. A guard stepped forward and said that it was alright, that they could go in. When that guard put a hand on the wolf's shoulder pandemonium broke. The wolf screamed and lunged for me. However once the guard had extended his hand he had committed himself, and when the wolf began to struggle and scream, the guards tackled him and took him to the ground. Reinforcements were called via walkie-talkie, and a team of guards carried him to his cell and threw him in. I remained in the cement cage, standing on the court, alone with the other inmates, momentarily unguarded. They had their chance to rush me. They did not. The mob had lost its fervor.

133.

I waited in my cell. Days passed. Weeks passed. I knew that I was to go to Mt. Meigs. The guards knew it. The administration knew it. I was not sent.

I sat in the back of the kitchens with Big Dave. After the groping and threats and completion of my schooling the vigilantes had declared an armistice. Big Dave had been allowed to call for me again. I resumed the organization of the facility's paperwork. I waited. I then continued to wait. I learned to sleep very well. I generally spent between twenty-one and twenty-four hours a day alone in my cell, and developed an ability to sleep for approximately sixteen of those hours each day. Twenty-four straight hours of lockdown were not normative, but the guards did impose complete lockdown when inmate tensions were high. Sometimes they didn't let us out, brought our meals to the cells, and never told us why.

Months passed. Winter came. The nights were very cold in the cells. The guards kept moving me from cell to cell. The movements were incredibly disorienting. My lonely tree next to the catfish pond kept changing position in slight ways that massively disrupted my worldview. They didn't realize, couldn't know. They went home every day. But WAYS had become my home.

My personality, formerly powerful and cool, became introverted and timid. I was so terrified of getting in trouble, specifically due to the high probability of assault, that I began to request to stay in my cell even during those hours that I might have been allowed out. I was willing to do anything to make it to the next stage safely, to get to Mt. Meigs. My personality began to warp in ways that at that time I did not fully understand.

I did, however, get to know a steady succession of fellow inmates. Many were in and out several times during the months that I was incarcerated there. I learned that of all the Black Belt counties, the guards generally considered the inmates from Selma the most racist and prone to violence. I learned that there are in fact a goodly number of young men in the world who are fourteen or fifteen years of age and are already possessed of multiple progeny. I learned that young men were willing to gamble their lives and futures in order to engage in fisticuffs for the dubious honor of representing Selma vs. Tuscaloosa and vice versa, that is to say, they were freely willing to fight, risking indefinite lockdown, for the honor of the municipalities that had condemned them.

The guards once rewarded us for several days of good behavior. They let us listen to the radio while we cleaned the main room. I nearly broke down. I couldn't be seen crying in front of the other inmates, but I could barely keep my feet and hold back the tears. It had been so long since I had heard music. No man should ever know that feeling. I realized that my soul was dying.

134.

No one had been able to give a satisfactory answer as to why I had been held in WAYS for so long after my case had been decided. Big Dave had used his old-boy network to learn what was going on. He had come back howling. I sat in the kitchen and listened to him.

"They told me that I better high-tail it on this case."

"Why? Did you learn why it took so long for them to decide? Why they're keeping me here?"

"Beau, there are folks in Montgomery apoplectic on this one. Told me not to get mixed up in it. A lot of people have heard about your case. This thing has stirred the waters. This family you pissed off… the way they see it, once everyone in Selma and at your school heard about the case, well… you've made their daughter look like a public whore. Guess some folks don't believe she was *forced* to do anything. The family wants their pound of flesh, and they won't leave off until they've had it."

"Well they still have to let me go to Mt. Meigs at some point."

"Maybe. But I can't get involved. If I push on this I'll lose any pull I have. This goes way up. Your lawyer has to lay his cards on the table delicate."

I went back to my cell. Time passed and a pound of flesh was carved from my body. But the day did come. I was buzzed out of my cell and given the clothes in which I had arrived. I went to Mt. Meigs in January wearing the clothes I had worn in July. It was a chilly trip.

A decade later, Juan Mendez, the United Nations' Special Rapporteur on Torture, would determine that the incarceration of a juvenile in solitary confinement, for even a single day, constitutes a form of torture, violating international conventions on political rights, civil rights, and torture. By the time I was sent to Mt. Meigs I had been locked down in a sole-occupancy cell for six months—frequently for twenty-four hours or more at a time—in a facility designed to hold youths for a maximum of two weeks.

135.

Today I walked a Manhattan sidewalk. I stepped off the sidewalk, onto a small square of soil round a schizoid tree lonely in that concrete collusion of humanity. I had a need, a compulsion, for my foot to touch something green. Years had passed since I went six months without my foot touching a blade of grass—more than a decade. But trauma like that never dies.

136.

The one benefit of my long incarceration in WAYS was that whatever terrors awaited me in Mt. Meigs would only take place for six weeks, at which point I was to have my next hearing, and then, given satisfactory progress, I would be sent on to the mythical rehabilitation in Florida. I asked the escorting officer about the sexual offender program I would attend once I arrived at Mt. Meigs.

"Don't know what you're talking about, son. I don't have any orders to take you to the sexual offender program."

"What? I've been ordered to sexual offender programming at Mt. Meigs. I'm also supposed to be in anger management counseling. Those were the judge's orders."

"Not that I'm aware. My orders are you're headed to general intake. You'll go into boot camp with everyone else. When you finish they'll put you in population."

"General population? I'm classified as a sexual offender. If anyone finds out I'll be targeted!"

"Can't help you there, son. These are my orders. In an hour you'll be in boot camp. You got one heck of a month coming up."

I looked back down the road behind me. I felt strange. WAYS was hell, but hell had been the only home I had known for the last six months.

137.

When I got to Mt. Meigs I was unloaded, uncuffed, and stripped naked. Once again my testicles and buttocks were inspected for concealed firearms and cocaine. When it had been determined that I concealed no weaponry or narcotics on my visible body, they sat me in a chair and shaved my head.

I got up and was given a uniform. I was in a line, before some and after others. It was intake day for the week at Mt. Meigs, and there were boys from all over the state. We shuffled nervously as older inmates marched through the halls with their uniforms and precision and shaved heads.

In time I was called into the command room where guards milled around a small, wiry, middle-aged black man who looked up at me and scowled.

"Finn-us Beauchamp?"

"It's *Fine*-iss."

"Sir!"

"Yes, sir."

"Get down and give me twenty. Next time you say, 'Sir, yes sir.'"

I got down and did pushups while this small man flipped through a sheaf of documents.

"Says here you're a Serious Juvenile Offender."

"Sir, well, yes sir. But I was never arrested before."

"Well I know you did something. Nobody gets SJO for nothing. Take off your uniform. Strip down to your boxers."

I stripped down, and this man, Mr. Besteder, looked over my body carefully, lifting up my arms and inspecting me like a bull before an auction.

"No tatts," he said to one of the guards, who made a notation in a book. "You in any kind of gang?" he asked me.

"Sir, no sir. No gangs for me."

"No white power? No Ku Klux Klan? You a skinhead?"

"Sir, no sir. I have black friends. I was on the all-black boxing team in Selma."

"A boxer, huh? You planning to fight here?"

"Sir, no sir."

"Well I have my eyes on you, Finis. Serious Juvenile Offender status is serious."

Thus passed my first meeting with Mr. Besteder, a man I would know a mere twenty-eight days, but who will forever flow easily in the fistula of memory.

138.

We were seated at tables in the main room of the boot camp barracks, enduring an orientation from Mr. Besteder. He was making the boys stand one at a time, quizzing them on various types of academic questions, and running through a routine in which he demonstrated that he possessed far more gangsta knowledge than anyone in the room.

"You! Stand up!" he called out to a young boy, who stood sullenly. "What does *eloquence* mean?"

"I ain't got nair."

"You *ain't* got *nair?*"

"I mean I don' know."

"I don't know, *sir!* Now get down and give me thirty. Eloquence means you speak well. Clearly you are not eloquent, as you believe that *ain't* and *nair* are words in the English language. When you're eloquent you have an education. When you're possessed of eloquence you don't have to wear a Raiders jacket to tell people that Right After I Die Everybody Run Scared."

The collected eyebrows in the room rose as if jerked by a puppeteer dosed on amphetamines. Testosterone and adrenaline surged through the room at Mr. Besteder's proclamation, rising palpably as the young man began his pushups, and then was forced to restart the sequence repeatedly after he failed to properly count them out. The guards lining the wall smirked. Mr. Besteder turned to another helpless inmate.

"What does *intrepid* mean?"

"Sir, I don't know, sir."

"It means you're brave. You didn't know that so get down and give me twenty. It's important to know what it is to be intrepid, to be brave. When you're intrepid you don't have to wear a Bulls hat just to let people know that Bloods Usually Live Longer. You don't have to wear Calvin Klein to let people know you're a Crip Killer."

Several mandibles were visibly hanging as Mr. Besteder called another boy.

"What does *venerate* mean?"

"Sir, I don't know, sir."

"Down and give me twenty. When you venerate someone it means you show them respect. Everyone here thinks they want respect, but none of you know what it means to venerate. When you're worthy of veneration you don't have to disrespect someone with your clothes, your set, your signs. You don't have to wear Adidas to let everyone know that All Day I Disrespect All Slobs."

As Mr. Besteder went on to describe the difference between the Folk Nation and the People Nation, between Crip and Blood, between a five-point star and a six-point star, the inmates entered a visible state of shock. Those teenage boys had never met an adult with this level of gangsta knowledge, particularly not this intricate knowledge of sets, hand signs, colors, and codes. Mr. Besteder walked around the room, openly displaying the gang signs of every set represented. The boys, who would, without hesitation, have assaulted anyone who dared to sign their gang in the outside world, could only stare dumbly. A few of them looked as though they were thinking about leaping from their seats to attack the small, wiry man moving about the room. But Mr. Besteder seemed to have extrasensory perception for this subterranean agitation. Pacing the room rapidly, he would immediately move to the boy who showed even the slightest visible tension, query him, trap him, force him to the floor for pushups. If the boy showed any hesitation the number of pushups would go up, and the row of guards lining the wall would move into position.

"Don't think for a second we can't take you to the ground," he told us. "You belong to me for the next month. And it's a month only if you do well. I can and will keep you here for as long as it takes you to learn to follow directions."

Mr. Besteder continued to walk the room, performing his rehearsed routine, qualifying the boys, causing them to feel self-doubt, flippantly exposing the *sanctum sanctorum* of their fragile gangster cabala. When he began to describe, in detail, the incarceration and seedy lives of Stan Tookie Williams or Larry Hoover several of the boys began to exhibit downright panic. It seemed that many of them were unaware that King Hoover was alive and in a supermax facility rather than divinely ascended and ruling with Jesus from heaven. I had learned a bit of this frivolous lore while at WAYS. I looked around the room and tried not to giggle.

"I know what 88 means he said," turning suddenly to me. The rest of the overwhelmingly African-American population of the room turned in unison. "H is the eighth letter in the alphabet. 88 represents HH, which Neo-Nazis use to say Heil Hitler without anyone knowing. But that doesn't fool me, does it Beauchamp?"

"Sir, I don't know anything about Neo-Nazis, sir."

"Beauchamp, do you know what *disingenuous* means?"

"Sir, it means that someone is insincere or putting up a false front, sir."

"Are you disingenuous, Beauchamp?" Mr. Besteder asked, his eyes narrowing. I was the first person to correctly define a word in his series of verbal traps.

"No, sir. I try not to be."

"Perhaps you think prevarication will help you here, Mr. Beauchamp. Do you know what *prevaricate* means?"

"Sir, it means to lie or be dishonest, sir."

"Do you know *indefatigable* means?"

"It means you don't tire easily or at all."

"You'll need to be indefatigable to make it through my boot camp," he said. I could see that he was hurrying to think of a new word. I was upsetting the momentum of his domination of the room.

"Do you know what *deplorable* means?"

"It means a bad state of affairs. A very negative thing."

"Correct," he noted, his eyes narrowed to slits. "I find it deplorable that so many fine young men have chosen to act in a way that causes them to end up at Mt. Meigs," he said, buying time, thinking, reaching down to the bottom of the verbal vault. I began to feel angry at this staccato barrage of questions that no other inmate was facing. It seemed, from the piqued interest of the guards, that nothing like this had ever happened before.

"Do you know what *circumlocution* means?"

"Circumlocution is exactly what we're doing right now. We're talking around something, not about something." And then, in the rush of invulnerability that seizes the man who has already taken one irrational step from the cliff, I spread my wings and jumped.

"Do you know what a *dolt* is?" I asked. The blood immediately rushed to my head. I certainly expected him to know what it meant, and to have the guards take me away to a back room where I would be flayed alive. But to my surprise he did not know. He was intrigued. He walked to the bookshelf against the wall and pulled down a dictionary. He looked up the word and his eyes narrowed. Then he smiled, ever, ever so slightly. He looked up at me. His eyes twinkled. I could see that we were going to be friends.

139.

The security in boot camp was incredibly tight—far more so than at WAYS. Every detail of our lives was monitored and controlled. But concerning this I should explicate further. I do not mean that we were carefully watched as we were herded from activity to activity, and that at those times we were not carefully watched we were locked down. No, I mean that absolutely every physical movement of our bodies was studied and logged.

The Terrible Beauty of the Evil Man

If we, sitting in the main room of the barracks, felt a dust mote land on our nose, precipitating a compulsive need to scratch our face, we were first required to ask permission to do so. Failure to ask permission to scratch one's face, to spontaneously do what any human would unthinkingly do if they felt a slight itch on their face, would result in a regimen of pushups before the collective, counted aloud, and repeated if not done correctly.

When we sat to defecate we did so in doorless stalls, with a guard smugly watching. There was no roll of toilet paper. The guard held the toilet paper roll as he or she watched us, and would rip off several pieces only on request.

"Sir, may I have some more toilet paper?"

"Do you require more paper to complete your defecation?"

"Yes sir, I do."

Then, depending on the guard, and how sadistic they felt that day, an either small or sufficient amount of toilet paper was ripped off, allowing us either to wipe completely, or be forced to ask once more for sufficient toilet paper.

When it was time for our nightly shower we were made to line up nude. If requested, a small amount of shampoo was squeezed into our hands and we were told to lather up and apply it to our hair before entering the group shower. We would not have time to lather up and apply shampoo once we were in the showers. The showers were only ninety seconds long and were strictly clocked using a stopwatch. Guards watched us shower. We were advised, that in order to avoid body odor and rashes, and given the ninety-second time limit, we should "hit the pits, feet, and groin, and forget about the rest."

There was a portly female guard who often showed up in time to watch us leave the showers, marching in line. I get the feeling that she was not supposed to be there, but then there was no way I could have questioned her or protested. She wore a slight smirk, and I can't imagine that it wasn't perversely enjoyable for her to watch a line of teenage penises bounce from thigh to thigh as the boys marched, wet and in unison, from their group shower.

At mealtimes we received a tray of food. Conversation was completely prohibited during the meal. The amount of food given was insufficient to replace the calories lost during the many hours of rigorous exercise we performed each day. When we sat to the meal we were prohibited from touching the food until permission had been granted. Once allowed to eat we were prohibited from reaching for the salt, pepper, or extra napkins without permission. Failure to comply resulted in a series of pushups, and being given a *no*.

If a person received three *no's* then they *lost their day*. If one lost too many days in a single week then they would *repeat their level*. There were four levels in boot camp, and it was intended that juvenile convicts would complete one level per week, thereby graduating the boot camp in a month. I received my first *no* for foolishly forgetting myself during the first week, taking a sip of my breakfast juice before the guards said to begin.

Some of the boys were sneaky. We were all starving, rapidly losing weight, so the boys kept a close watch on the guards. If the guard turned for even one second, a boy might risk a fight, a guard take-down, and even a repetition of his level, just to snatch a piece of cornbread from another boy's tray. He might be caught, and he might not. He would lose his day or even his level, depending on the degree of violence that resulted from the theft. Such incidents were frequent and kept many boys in boot camp far longer than a month, but men will do almost anything when they are truly hungry.

I had learned the rule at WAYS, but it was permanently reinforced at Mt. Meigs. You eat with your arms around your tray. But your arms are only a moat. It's with your eyes that you silently shout your unconditional willingness to kill rather than lose that piece of cornbread. Discipline and punish.

140.

We were losing weight. At least I was. I had been locked down in a tiny cell for six months. Before that I had been used to vigorous work and exercise for many hours a day. That had all gone away, and I felt physically sick most of the time I was in WAYS. However at Mt. Meigs I was suddenly, with no preparation, forced to do hundreds of pushups and sit-ups each day for every minor infraction of body movement. We completed up to a dozen miles per run, and often ran multiple times a day. Mr. Besteder personally led the runs, and we kept up or got in trouble.

Running until you knew that you would vomit had never bothered me. Football, basketball, and track-and-field prepared me for that. I cannot forget following Mr. Besteder on those runs. He was like a small, tireless, black jackrabbit. We were forced to sing military-style marching tunes as we ran.

The Terrible Beauty of the Evil Man

We ran in the freezing cold of winter. My boot camp was from mid-January to mid-February. On days when it was truly frigid we ran in sweats. When not running we were forced to do long PT sessions, where we did exercises of various sorts, such as standing in a squatting position, and holding that position until one's quadriceps screamed. Discipline and punish.

141.

We attended religious services, where we were given the opportunity to *embrace Jesus*, and turn from our wickedness. Theoretically the religious services at Mt. Meigs were optional, as those at WAYS had been. But in truth the services, in either location, were not optional for two reasons. The alternative to a religious service was either to remain locked down, or to take part in a more unpleasant activity, and second, I knew that notations were made every time we chose to go to or avoid religious services, and that my attendance would be included in the report to the judge on my conduct.

In Mt. Meigs that scrutiny of my moral character was very close indeed. We were made to keep a daily journal. Each evening we turned in our journals to the guards, who would carefully read our entry.

"How do you feel today? What did you think about? What are you unhappy about?" they wanted to know. If they thought we weren't taking the journal seriously, or that we were lying, we got in trouble, and were labeled non-cooperative.

Each inmate found that it was nearly impossible to avoid all of the many things that could get you in trouble, since almost anything, even a thoughtless wipe of the sweat from one's brow, would get you punitive exercise. The punitive exercise was in addition to the mandated runs and PT sessions. The average inmate was doing fifty to three hundred pushups per day in punitive exercise alone. When you aggregate the persistent hunger, mandatory interrogation of your inner thoughts and feelings, unavoidable religious services, non-existence of physical privacy, and regular fear of serious violence against your person, I imagine life in the Mt. Meigs boot camp to be existentially similar to daily life in contemporary North Korea. Discipline and punish.

142.

Mr. Besteder began to single me out each day during our group meetings in the barracks. I suspected that during most months the boot camp convicts would be more equally treated to a selection of his rehearsed routines, routines designed to achieve psychological power over the group. But I was upsetting those plans. The other inmates, at the beginning of the rehearsed questioning sequences, would begin to glance at me, and Mr. Besteder's instincts were incredibly sharp concerning subtle shifts in the group's attention.

Mr. Besteder was highly intelligent, and possessed of one of the most powerful *intuitive* faculties I have ever seen in a human—undoubtedly a necessity in work as dangerous as his. He had an almost telepathic ability to quickly determine the nexus of psychological pressure in a room of dangerous, violent, unstable young men, and then to quickly turn to those human fulcra and achieve mental domination, inducing group submission. Those who resisted were violently taken to the ground by the guards.

Invariably he turned the questioning to me, and there it ended each day. In time he began to skip the other inmates, and focus on questioning me as a means of demonstrating group control. He would pick an arcane area of academic work in which he had some knowledge, and then shoot at me with a burst of rapid-fire questions. The other inmates looked on open-mouthed, uncertain whether to hate me or see me as their champion. I generally knew the answers to his questions (we were not discussing Lie Theory or Tang poetry), though the questions were sufficiently recondite for even a bright teenager.

Since I knew that he was aware, as a result of the first day's questioning and display, that I was not stupid, I developed a strategy to deal with his acute focus. I would answer his questions politely, though with the maximum amount of disinterest I could safely project without risking punitive exercise. I was in a tough position every time I endured those lengthy question-games (which, indeed, were but games within games). I absolutely needed Mr. Besteder to form a positive opinion of me, as his would be the single most influential voice in the official Mt. Meigs report sent to my corrupt circuit judge. On the other hand, being seen as the teacher's pet in a place like Meigs was almost certain to lead to an assault, even one of which, assuming I defended myself, would likely disbar me from being sent to Florida.

There would be a two-week gap between the end of boot camp and the court hearing to determine if I would go to Florida, and during those two weeks I would be released with the graduates of my boot camp class into the general population of Mt. Meigs. And general population in Meigs is an extremely dangerous place to be too smart and too white. Discipline and punish.

143.

Mr. Besteder's questions were not the only questions to which I was subject at Mt. Meigs. All of the other inmates convicted of sexual crimes were isolated in a separate program. For some reason I was not, nor was I ever told why I was not placed in the regular sexual offender program. But because I was listed as a sexual offender, I was occasionally pulled from regular activities in order to engage in a series of tests which would help the State of Alabama determine if I was a pedophile or otherwise a permanent menace to Society.

"Are you sexually attracted to children?"

"No," I responded, my eyebrows rising at this bizarre initial question.

"Are you sexually attracted to small boys?"

"Are you serious?" I asked the faceless social worker across from me.

"Yes, Beau, I'm very serious."

"No. I don't like little boys."

"Are you sexually attracted to small girls?"

"No!"

"Are you sexually attracted to teenage girls?"

"I *am* a teenager! What's that supposed to mean?"

"Let me rephrase that. Do you find attractive teenage girls who are not sexually mature, that have not yet hit puberty?"

"No. I like girls my age, or if they are a bit younger, then girls that have hit puberty. I *know* you know what I'm in here for. I'm sure it's in that file you're holding. When I was seventeen I hooked up with one girl who was fourteen and one who was fifteen. It was completely consensual, and both girls were physically developed, sexually mature, and had sexual experiences before me. If *you* fooled around with someone three years younger do think you'd be locked up? That has nothing at all to do with getting turned on by small kids!"

"Beau, I'm mandated by law to ask you these questions. This is standard procedure for anyone who has been convicted of sexual activity with someone under the age of sixteen. You need to take this very seriously. Now, do you enjoy sexual activity in which giving or receiving physical pain plays a part?"

"*What?* No!"

"Have you ever had sex with an animal?"

"Oh my God. No!"

"Have you had sexual relations with someone in your family?"

"No!"

"Do you find men sexually attractive?"

"No."

"Do you enjoy sexual activity in which urine or feces play a role?"

"*What the hell?* No."

"Do you use sexual toys during your sexual activity?"

"No."

"Do you receive oral sex during your sexual activity?"

"Yes. That's in the report. You already know the answer."

"Do you enjoy this type of behavior?"

"Who doesn't?"

"Have you ever engaged in sexual relations with a man?"

"No."

"Do you practice anal sex with women?"

"Is that considered weird sexual behavior?" I asked.

"Some people think it is. This is Alabama," he said with a hint of a smile.

"Um, yeah. Well I guess I've had anal sex with women. I didn't know that was weird. It's pretty popular in high school these days."

My interlocutor smiled at this, and continued to question me, asking me many, many variations of every question about bizarre (and not so bizarre) sexual practice you can imagine. He asked me the same questions so many different ways that I began to panic and fear that I wouldn't be able to convince him that I wasn't a child molester. By the end I was dizzy and had learned things about perverse sexuality that no teenager should ever know. Discipline and punish.

144.

But the questioning continued. Eventually I was called in to meet my new Mt. Meigs psychologist. This was the first psychological *treatment* I had received since my incarceration began more than six months earlier. However, I assumed that the real reason I was being sent to a psychologist had nothing to do with treating me, but was rather so that they could better study me, in order determine if I was going to rape and kill children upon release.

In order to combat this potential perception I made a point of emphasizing to my psychologist that I was not sexually interested in younger girls, but in fact had always been attracted to older women, developing, as my defense of this thesis, the notion that my cognitive abilities left me cerebrally frustrated and unfulfilled by girls my own age.

Unfortunately my psychologist took this repeated insistence of my attraction to older women as a sign that I was sexually propositioning her, a woman well more than twice my age. I was then forced to try to explain that no, I was not attracted to her, but rather that by older women I had meant young ladies in their twenties.

I began to feel, during my time at Mt. Meigs, that no matter how I tried to explain my sexual feelings I was going to end up in trouble, that I would never be free again. Adolescent sexuality is enormously confusing even under the best of circumstances. It does not assist if, in the transition to adulthood, a teenage boy is made to endure repeated batteries of such perverse questioning. And again, it is obvious that a boy, told repeatedly that he is Evil, will come to believe what he is told. To question repeatedly is to *tell* repeatedly. Discipline and punish.

145.

"You know," said my new case worker, leaning in conspiratorially, "you are probably the smartest person that has ever been incarcerated in Mt. Meigs."

I sat in silence, wondering what exactly I was supposed to say to that. He looked at me closely with a knowing smile.

"So what do you think about that?"

"I'm the most Evil," I replied.

"No, 'the *smartest*,' I said. We've run some diagnostics on you. It's really very interesting," he said, leaning back in his chair and staring at me with all the attention due an exotic lizard.

"The smartest is the most dangerous. And the most dangerous is the most Evil, whether he's done something very wrong or not. That's really why I'm here. That's what being the smartest gets you. That's why a guy who gets a consensual blowjob is locked up with the most violent repeat offenders in the state."

"Hmm..." he said. And then he sat for several moments, playing with his hands, staring at me quietly. "That is... an interesting theory."

"Being smart doesn't get you anything good. It's gets a target painted on your back," I replied.

"Well most smart young men don't end up incarcerated. They end up getting asked to help with their classmates' homework. They get scholarships to elite universities."

"Those are the nerds. Everyone knows that kind of kid. That was never me. I'm big and strong. I play ball. I would only do those kinds of things... Scholar's Bowl and all that, if it could get me out of classes."

"Why can't you be both? Why do you feel you must conceal one side of yourself in favor of the other?"

"I always hid. I had to."

"*Why* do you hide, Beau?"

I sat very still, because there was no way I could answer his question. There was no way to explain why I had traveled life so alone, and likely always would. I could not tell him that it was ok to be smart, but not too smart. You could be strong, but not too strong. You could be attractive, but not too charming. There was an invisible line, and I didn't understand it, but I knew there was a demarcation between where adults thought that you were cute and lovable and where they were threatened, and felt the need to discipline and punish. The entire field was a mystery to me, incredibly vague, and I felt sure there was no way to define the boundaries of the problem.

A tear welled up in my eye, but I did not want it to fall. I had to conceal my feelings.

"You don't have to hide, Beau," he said, placing a hand gently on my arm.

I blinked, and that tear fell down my cheek, and time slowed, and I felt ill with the strain of holding back my accumulated pain. I wanted to tell him that people will love you as long as you want what they want, that they will cherish you unless you've taken something they believe is inalienably theirs, that what others desire of you is no more than to exist only as a subset of their Being, to lose yourself in them to the exact extent that they wish you to do so—and that all of that exists to the exclusion of true *loving*, which is giving, sacrificing one's will to power, and even one's fear, for another, granting them grace and kindness even if it causes pain.

I could not tell him that because that is not what he wanted to hear.

146.

The night before I graduated boot camp I lay on my thin cot in the barracks with dozens of other young men on their cots while the guards sat around in chairs and watched us try to fall asleep. They had given us the option of staying in boot camp a while longer if we wanted. Some took that unbelievable option. The rumors were that people who were small or suspected of being gay were quick targets once in general population. There were fairly horrible stories that circulated about the violence that could break without warning once you were released into the wild.

I chose to enter population. I couldn't take another two weeks in boot camp, forbidden from scratching my own face and having to ask for toilet paper. Mr. Besteder's daily grilling was in some ways amusing, and I personally admired the man, but the pressure was wearing me down. And ninety-second showers were simply not for me. I needed a proper five-minute shower like any other convict. I decided to accept the higher risk of assault that came with the greater personal freedom of life in population.

I requested to go to Phifer B, a unit where I would once again be locked down in a cell alone. I figured that if I was locked down alone in a cell much of the day, I could minimize the chance of trouble or assault over the following two weeks. However they told me that, as there would be school and job training, I would be out of my cell much more than I had been at WAYS.

It was imperative that I avoid any trouble during those two weeks in population. My court hearing was due, and Mr. Jeofail had let me know that the judge (or rather Palter's father, through the medium of the judge) was suddenly reticent about the agreement to the appeal arrangement releasing me to Florida. If I wasn't perfectly behaved in the world of general population, where the most vicious ruled, then I would be taken out of Meigs, certified as an adult, and sent to an adult lock-up for the next few years. I did not sleep well that last night in boot camp.

147.

I got to Phifer B, and the first thing the guards wanted to know was how long I was going to be there. When I told them that I was getting out in two weeks they began to laugh.

"Nobody gets out of Meigs in less than a year, white boy." I suddenly felt queasy.

We were let out into the main room of the Unit on most days for an hour, and I got to play cards, for the first time in my life, with young men distinguished by their capacity for murder—as well as by the fact that they had committed those murders as children. That was interesting.

There were a number of guys on Phifer I had known from boot camp, and even one from WAYS, so I did not feel totally disoriented by my third incarceration venue. I was allowed to listen to a radio, and I was shocked to discover how many new songs had come out in the previous seven months. Listening to music, and the rapid sense of liberation that came with being able to scratch my face whenever I wanted, made me feel, even when locked in a room with dangerous criminals, that I was almost a free man.

I have no doubt that general population was more socially segregated by race than any Jim Crow town in Alabama had ever been. I resisted all calls to join the white posse on the grounds (who incidentally, and I presume due to their smaller numbers, struck me as far more vicious than the blacks when violence erupted). I kept to myself whenever moving between units over the prison grounds, when traveling to class, or to my work program. The only convicts I spoke to (all black) were those I had known in either WAYS or in boot camp.

A violent attack from a single individual didn't frighten me. I knew how to avoid those who looked most unstable, ready to explode. And no single individual, so far as I knew, had any motive or vendetta that would prompt a personal assault. I wouldn't need protection from anything other than a group attack by a gang. But a coordinated multi-person attack within a prison (that is not the result of a spontaneous riot) takes planning, and I knew that, and didn't intend to be there long enough to provoke one.

The first week went by without a problem, and the second started well. I only witnessed one multi-person spontaneous violent combustion—an intra-black attack on one of the very few (I knew of only two) openly gay inmates, who, incidentally, was truly impressive in hand-to-hand combat. I believe he got the better of three opponents. A larger riot nearly occurred, as the sight of fighting arouses inmates, but was averted by a sudden massive influx of guards.

A couple of days away from my hearing I could think of nothing other than the rumors from my father and Mr. Jeofail of the judge's new hesitation to send me to Florida. However, I was certain that at Mt. Meigs I had nothing left to fear. I could not have been more wrong.

148.

It was my second to last day and I was sitting in my work program, horticulture, doing absolutely nothing, because our work program instructor maintained that there was no such thing as horticulture in February. A guy I had known and befriended back at WAYS was sitting next to me, filling my ear with a recitation of the endless gangsta knowledge he possessed.

Once more I was treated to a story that included Crips and the Folk Nation, King Hoover, the biblical King David (who may or may not have also been reincarnated as an OG named David Barksdale), Magic, Growth and Development, and some type ascension to heaven that I didn't quite follow. The entire recitation took place in a sing-song freestyle of quasi-rap that included the visual aids of the tattoos decorating his arms and torso. I attempted to look interested. Time passed slowly.

He asked me if I wanted to go out behind the horticulture building and smoke a hand-rolled cigarette he had secreted somewhere on his person. I didn't smoke, but said yes, hoping it might end the monotony of the eternal monologue on the apotheosis of Original Gangstas. We asked our instructor for permission to go outside and stretch our legs. He nodded us out and then reburied his head in a newspaper. My homeboy and I smoked a piece of paper that may have contained tobacco. He went back inside. I decided to wait outside until I stopped hacking up paper fumes.

I was standing, letting my lungs fill with winter air, wondering how much warmer it would be in Florida, reflecting with pride on the fact that I had finally made it through an environment so tough each day had seemed a month.

I heard a noise and quickly turned. There were two inmates behind me, standing ten yards away, at the opposite end of the rear of the horticulture building. It was clear that they had not casually strolled behind the building for a breath of fresh air. They weren't even members of the horticulture work group. They were staring at me with the intense grimace of men who have arrived to fight. One of them held a crowbar.

My radial iris dilators played with my pupils until they were dimes. I could not imagine where they had found such a deadly weapon. A crudely fashioned shank was like a paper-clip compared to the explosive power of a crowbar. I stared. The crowbar was covered in grime and rust. Undoubtedly they had found it by dumb luck, almost completely buried in some isolated area of the campus, lost and forgotten.

"How you like to die today, bitch-ass white boy?" one of them called. The other smiled and slapped the crowbar up and down in his empty palm. I had seen these two before, and while I assumed that they did not feel any special love for me, neither did I think that they held me any special hostility. I was wrong.

The two boys stepped towards me, and it was then that I faced the single most terrible decision I have ever faced in this life.

The nearest guard was my instructor in the horticulture building. By the time he could get to me, I would potentially have taken several blows, though with such a powerful weapon only a single accurate, forceful strike would have been needed to kill or give permanent brain damage. No other guards were close. They would have to be called in by walkie-talkie. Even if I did scream, my cry would be sure to bring far more inmates than guards, and there was nothing that inflamed inmates like the sight of violence. It was likely, even if I called, that I would bring far more attackers than defenders. In any event, I'd seen enough fights at WAYS and Mt. Meigs to know that single guards never attempted to break up fights until back-up had arrived. All of this passed through my mind in a trice, and I knew that I had only one instant to make a decision.

I knew they were not bluffing about killing me, or at least minimally doing such damage that I would rather have been dead, for we were in an isolated area of the campus. For all I knew, they might have been incarcerated for murder or aggravated assault. They were almost certainly, as inmates in Mt. Meigs, no strangers to serious violence. They had initiated contact with me by asking if I wanted to die, and by referencing my race. I knew that even though they didn't have any personal vendetta against me, white skin alone was reason enough to kill. Whites had likely arrested them. Whites had likely judged them. Whites would likely decide when they got out. Whites owned everything. Whites had ruined their lives. Whites had destroyed their culture. Here was a white person, alone and unguarded. Here's a crowbar we just found. Let's do something about it.

But for all that I knew they weren't certain they wanted to kill me. I knew it instantaneously and instinctively, as an awareness surged through me, alerting me that I had one chance to avoid death, or worse, permanent brain damage. If they had been certain they never would have paused for the verbal taunt. I probably wouldn't have heard them coming, and you would not be reading this sentence.

The Terrible Beauty of the Evil Man

I had to make them believe, though they were two and I one, though they were armed and I was not, that I was just as likely to kill them as they were to kill me. The psychological wars of the prison yard are the important wars of the prison yard.

However, most of that horrible instant was not spent thinking about guards or determining how best to engage their offensive threat. The real choice that had to be made that very instant was whether I would let them kill me, or whether I would kill them (and I never doubted in the slightest that, with a crowbar involved, the fight would end in either their or my death), and in so doing guarantee that I would be ripped out of Meigs, and sent to an adult prison for what would likely be the majority of my adult life. It was the single most terrible instant and decision of my entire life. I had to choose to be killed, or to kill and live out the rest of my life in prison. So I chose to live. I did not hesitate. I chose to kill them.

"Hey!" I yelled, stepping forward and raising a pointed finger eye level with my antagonists. "You can come at me, but you sure as hell better make sure you kill me 'cause if you don't I'm 'a kill you with that thing!"

And then they paused. They ceased to move forward. We were perhaps five yards apart. They faced their own eternal instant in the prison yard. My eyes were glaring straight through theirs and they looked down to my body. When they looked down I looked down. I realized that my body was strongly, visibly shaking. I immediately understood that I had only a single second before they assumed that the trembling was due to fear and not the flood of adrenaline coursing through my body.

"I swear to God either of you come at me I'm 'a kill you. You gon' get one swing, but thet it. Then I'm 'a kill you. Bet it," I said as slowly and coldly as I could manage, lapsing into their prison patois.

I stood to my full height and bowed out my chest. I looked straight at them and used my eyes to tell them to come, to fight with me to the death. I tried to project certainty, to let them know that I was supremely confident of ending their lives in the next few moments.

They realized that I was as ready to kill as they claimed to be, and that I had the desperation of a man who doesn't intend to die easily. They glanced at each other. They were gauging each other's level of resolve. But I knew as soon as they paused to look at each other that I had won. True killers don't pause to check their resolve. There would be no fight that day. I had won the important war, the psychological war.

"Don' worry, white boy," said the one with the crowbar, pointing it at me, letting it gyrate on his palm, tracing an invisible circle meant to represent my head. "We ain't got you today, but they gon' come a day— maybe in a week, maybe in a month—and you ain't gon' be lookin'. Then we got you. This gon' be in the back 'a yo head. You good as dead."

They walked away with wide smirks, laughing and snorting about the white boy they had just punked. The entire incident had certainly lasted under ninety seconds. Once they were out of sight I put my hands on my knees and tried to get air into my lungs. As soon as I could breathe there was a thunderclap in my brain, and I was first able to feel the heavy pulse of adrenaline that had my entire body trembling uncontrollably. It was so powerful that when I first felt it I nearly blacked out. I have been in a number of car accidents, in two of which I ought to have been killed, and can tell you that, while both types of situations provoked the sensation that events were unfolding in slow-motion, the adrenaline-clap of a near-death car accident comes nowhere near what I experienced in that moment.

I slowly stood. I kicked the hard winter soil, and then kicked it again, waiting for the storm in my veins to calm. They would look for me in a week, but I would be gone. I knew that had I shown the slightest hesitation or fear, had they in any way suspected I was not serious when I threatened to kill them, I would have either died, been hospitalized, or been on my way to serve a multi-year sentence in an adult prison. I walked back into horticulture and sat down. The instructor didn't even look up. I closed my eyes and breathed, suddenly glad to listen to any amount of gangsta lore.

149.

That's how fast a potentially lethal prison yard altercation can begin and end. That one moment could have forever altered or ended my life, and it was over that quickly—in an instant.

The typical felon, contrary to popular imagination, is not willing to kill another human being. Incarceration quickly separates the majority, not hardwired for deadly violence, those who readily acknowledge a need for protection, from the lethal minority. Prison forces virtually everyone, at some point, to fight. But prison will, given enough time, also reveal that small minority with the authentic capacity to unhesitatingly kill.

The Terrible Beauty of the Evil Man

Possession of lethal capacity and will is categorically *not* something one can fake, particularly in a prison. Prison is not a poker table. It is psychologically impossible to maintain a cool bluff against hardened violent convicts when the consequences of having that bluff called are likely to involve serious injury, rape, or death. There is an evolutionary, mammalian sense-perception-instinct that I readily admit I can neither explain nor define, but which I know from repeated experience exists, giving hardened criminals the ability to identify with near certainty who is unconditional and serious when making an immediate lethal threat.

I believe there is no way one can know in advance whether they possess the psychic aptitude that will allow them to take human life. The only people who truly know are those who have personally needed to end someone's life in a violent confrontation, mentally accepted that fact, and physically acted on it. One need only look at the universally dismal accuracy statistics of police officers who have fired their weapon in the line of duty (even at very close range) to recognize that this characteristic does not obtain in most men—even in men who have self-selected to enter a profession where they are aware they may need to take human life, and who have received extensive training in how to do so. As with football, the overwhelming majority of humans seem hardwired to hesitate at the moment of collision.

Men aware they possess this lethal capability are precisely those who do not speak of it—for that first time, that first unconditional decision to kill or be killed, permanently sears the psyche in irreversible ways. It is haunting not because of the specific act you have chosen to commit (almost universally an act of self-preservation), but due to a brute abrupt collision with the realization that you are capable of killing without hesitation. That ineradicable awareness is burned into your newly expanded consciousness, is self-knowledge that will forever separate you from the vast bulk of humanity, which leaves you *inhumane*, so that even if you wished to, you could not speak of it freely and easily, and certainly not to boast.

My immediate, instinctive decision to kill two young men was not glorious or heroic. I was not standing at Thermopylae. This is no more than a recounting of the most petrifying, terrible moment of my entire life.

150.

A couple of days later the police jitney came and took me back to Greensboro. The circuit judge was indeed reticent about following through on the plea bargain. He listened, seemingly skeptical, to a full recounting from Mr. Jeofail as to the nature of the Christian rehabilitation program in Florida, and the spiritual recovery God would provide me there. It seemed, for several moments, as though I was going to be sent back to Mt. Meigs.

Nevertheless, my judge did sign the order, telling me he would see me again in four months, and that I better have an amazing report from the preachers in Florida. I left the courthouse and immediately began the trip to Florida. The next day I was delivered to my new home, a large religious compound in the countryside outside Orlando, Florida.

151.

I snuck out to the screened-in patio at the back of the cabin where I would be staying on the compound. It was a three-story log cabin, and I would share it with at least a dozen other men. I had been surrounded by these other residents—they didn't consider themselves inmates—and by the priests, for the entire first day. I needed a moment alone, away from their probing, sticky questions.

That I could have a moment truly *alone*, watched neither by person nor closed-circuit camera, came as a shock. I sat quietly for a moment and listened to the bugs, exulted in the warm, thick air. When I had left Alabama it had been freezing. In Orlando the temperature was in the sixties, even in the February dusk which enveloped me.

It is very difficult to explain, to anyone who has not been incarcerated, what the mundane process of breathing is like once you are no longer locked down. Obviously one can inhale air while incarcerated, but, no matter how many lungfuls you imbibe, it never feels as though you have breathed deeply. It is a slow torment that goes unnoticed because it is an integral facet of the world that has become your reality. You cannot breathe naturally when you know that people are watching you on cameras, when one wrong look could embroil you in violent conflict. You never, ever relax. In Orlando, on that first day, I was assimilating a massively different paradigm, set of expectations, and troupe of actors. But what I really remember, during those first few moments alone, was how the simple act of breathing provided a release so profound that it physically hurt.

152.

I looked around cautiously at breakfast on the second day. Some of the other residents noticed that I kept my arms around my food at all times. They smirked. I stared back warily.

They wanted to know everything about me, and though I had tried to give them a general summary the previous day, it seemed they were stuck on one particular point. They kept circling back to the drugs I had done.

"No, seriously, what did you do? Crack, smack, meth?"

"No, I told you. I've smoked pot maybe a dozen times. That's it."

"Let me see your arms," one demanded.

"When did you do the pot?" the first interrogator resumed.

"Junior year of high school. That's it."

"You never tried crack? Never did some pot with hash? No pills?"

"What? No! I never even knew anyone who had done that stuff before I went to jail. It was unheard of."

"Trust me, man, everyone has done crack. Everyone has tried a little blow at some point."

I stared back at my interlocutor, a small, dilapidated sack of skin and bone. He was probably in his forties, but looked sixty. Most of his hair was gone, but what was left was long and greasy.

It would take a few weeks, but I would learn this man's story, as well as the stories of the other men in the rehab. All of them had been in and out of various rehabs for years, if not decades. Their environments had warped their perceptions of reality. They really could not conceive of someone ending up, by court order, in a place like Renaissance Gardens, without having done many types of drugs, much less not having even been exposed to these substances. It had been years or decades since most of them had closely known anyone like that. The immediate group consensus was that I was still in *denial*, and also that I would make a quality mascot. I was barely eighteen years old. The next youngest resident was in his mid-thirties.

153.

I had to meet the priest in charge. He was a large man, even taller than me, with broad shoulders, spindly legs, and dark blond hair. He sat down at his desk and put his hand on my forearm.

"I want you to know that I love you, Beau."

"Excuse me?"

"I love you with the love of Jesus Christ."

"Er, thanks. I love you that way too."

The priest smiled at this and leaned back in his chair, withdrawing his hand and contemplating me with a warm smile.

"Beau, what brings you to Renaissance Gardens?"

"My appellate judge sent me. It was part of my plea bargain. I'm supposed to be here four months. If I do well and you give me a good report then I'm going to be free, and I can go home."

"No, no, no. Goodness! Let me stop you right there, Beau. That's *man's* view of things. *Jesus* sent you here, Beau. Not a judge. Now tell me again, why are you here?"

"Because Jesus sent me?"

"Right!" the priest said, his face lighting up. We sat in silence for some moments after this pronouncement. I squirmed.

"You know, Father, my dad is a pastor. My mother's dad is as well. He used to be vice president of the Southern Baptist Convention."

The priest frowned at this and drummed his fingers together.

"Yes, Father. I'm very concerned with growing spiritually and theologically during the time that I'm here. I'm really looking to grow in my walk with Christ."

"Beau… I don't know quite how to put this. The Southern Baptist Convention is very focused on matters of theology. But this is the Society of St. Dismas. We're a religious order of the Charismatic Episcopalian Church. Here I don't want you to focus on your family's religious positions, or on theological disputation. That isn't really what we do here."

"No?"

"No, Beau," he said, leaning forward and putting his hand on my forearm again. "We're not here to focus on *theological* Christianity. Here we're interested in developing *relational* Christianity."

The priest leaned back once more, his eyes wide, and he became very solemn. I understood that he believed he had just said something terribly profound.

"I see," I said, though I did not know what he was talking about. "Well I'm really looking forward to developing in relational Christianity."

"Are you, Beau?" he asked, seemingly attempting a pathetic fumble through my soul.

"Um, yes. Very much. Whatever I can do to grow in my love for Jesus."

"I'm very glad to hear you say that, Beau," he said, but his eyes were narrowed. "Here, why don't we stand up and you can go out with the others. But let's hug before you go. Hugs are a part of relational Christianity."

"Ok, well I like hugs."

I was then treated to a very long full-frontal hug from a large priest clad all in black. Jesus smiled.

154.

The regimen at the compound was simple. This religious compound, which was also a tropical flower nursery, was a capitalist venture. That meant that we, the drug addicts, were to spend half of each day working in the flower nursery. The other half of the day was spent in Bible study and telling the priests any deeply held secret they wanted to know.

I found some solace during the slow hours in the fields of the flower nursery. My job was to sit on a bucket and gradually work my way down rows of tropical flowers the length of football fields, weeding the plants in their little black buckets. There were acres of these long rows, and so by the time you finished weeding all the plants in the nursery weeks had passed, and it was time to begin again. I therefore spent hours a day in solitude, awash in greenery, caring for little plants and flowers. Weeding the entire nursery, every plant, was a process without beginning or end. Those were some of the first quiet, meditative moments I had had since early childhood. It was essentially *zazen*.

155.

It was during the religious programming that I realized I would have trouble. I had never been exposed to crackheads before. I was suddenly, as an eighteen-year-old, living in a house full of them. I do not wish to impugn all crackheads (some, I have discovered, are quite good at chess, a quality I greatly admire), but it would be inaccurate if I did not point out that a great number of persons who have done crack, heroin, or meth for many years are not terribly stable people with whom to live. It is not just that they will lie, cheat, steal, manipulate, and fight for the most innocuous of reasons; it is the sheer level of desperation you can see in the eyes of someone who has suffered serious structural decay to their brain matter. They are misshapen humans.

I was made to sit in a circle each day, with men who were between twenty and forty years older than me, while we talked incessantly about how Jesus would help us get clean. I wasn't sure what to say when my turn came. I, like millions of high school students in the country, had smoked pot a few times and done some heavy binge drinking at a few weekend parties after football games. I did not know how to respond when the guy before me in the circle admitted that he lost his wife and kids because he got gonorrhea of the throat while doing what needed to be done to pay for his crack habit.

I was only eighteen. I was still a boy.

156.

I was terrified that one of the crackheads would snap, forcing me into a situation where I would have to defend myself. I was terrified that I too might snap, as the slow grating frustration of showing patience to men who have no compunctions about lying, cheating, and manipulating took its toll. The judge had made it clear. One strike and I was out. Four months remained.

157.

As difficult as were the residents, the priests were far more frightening. The report of the head priest, that advocate of hugs and relational Christianity, would be the primary document which would determine whether the judge set me free. And he, with all of the savvy that comes from dealing with manipulative drug addicts on a daily basis, would not believe that I was taking my Christian growth seriously.

"Beau, did you know that I used to be a drug addict?"

"No, Father, I didn't."

"I did."

"Well…" I said, not sure how I was supposed to respond, "what was it like?"

"I had the world in front of me. But I blew it. Literally. Up my nose. I used to get high and then go running in the night. I would run twenty miles at a time."

"Man! You must have been in really good shape."

"No. I wasn't. It's the drugs. Those runs destroyed my knees. Now I can't run at all."

"That sounds terrible, Father... but, if I may, I'm having a bit of trouble relating. I never did anything like that. I'm here because I got a blowjob."

"Beau, sexual purity is far more serious than cocaine."

"Oh."

"Beau, Jesus cares very much about how you sanctify your sexuality. You didn't *just get a blowjob*. You destroyed the purity of the covenant that God intends to exist between you and your future wife. You destroyed the purity of the covenant between that young woman and her future husband."

"I see."

"No, Beau, I don't think you do see. I believe you think this is a game. Perhaps you look at the other residents here, see their problems, look down on them, and don't think that's you. But you don't realize that *man* didn't put you here. Jesus put you here. And He's not laughing about this. He's giving you a chance to turn your life around and get serious about Love."

"I want to be serious about... Love."

"Then you have to get serious about sexual purity. That's an addiction too—probably the most serious addiction of all. If you can't be serious about sexual purity then you can't be serious about Love. Sexual purity is a lifelong pursuit. It even applies when one is married. It applies with one's wife."

"You have to be sexually pure with your wife?"

"Absolutely, Beau! I pray in the Spirit every time I'm with my wife. If Jesus is not there with us in the bedroom during the sexual act then the act is not sanctified."

"*Wow*," I responded. I was so stunned by this bizarre assertion that I couldn't mouth anything more than those three letters.

"It's serious, Beau. Before I allowed Jesus to take control of my heart my sexual life with my wife was very impure. When it's impure you aren't focused on holiness. Things that have nothing to do with Jesus take control of your sexual relations. Things like *positions* become very important."

"Wow," I said, again unable to respond to this gross excess of information.

"Wow is right. You need to take sexual purity as seriously as any addict takes their preferred substance."

"I want to do my best. I want to grow here and then go home and make a positive impact in my community."

"It's not about getting out, Beau. It's about surrendering everything to Jesus. If you can't surrender everything to Jesus then it won't matter if you're here or free or in prison. Any life in which you haven't surrendered everything to Jesus *is* a prison."

"Well just tell me what I have to do. I'm here to learn. I really want to surrender everything so I can be free."

"I hope so, Beau. For your sake, I do hope so."

158.

It quickly became clear to me that if I was going to get out, if I was ever going to be a free man, I would need a good report from this emotive priest. And, as a former cokehead who dealt with addicts each day, he simply wasn't going to be taken in by vigorous protestations of faith or religious verve. His bullshit-detector was extremely keen. If I was going to get out I would have to force myself to feel what he wanted me to feel. I was going to have to *want* to hug crackheads, to genuinely care about their destroyed lives. I was going to have to pray and mean it. I was going to have to engage in the endless Bible studies with authentic enthusiasm and curiosity. In order to become free, I was going to have to become a prisoner. I was going to have to surrender everything to Jesus.

159.

You cannot live the lie, submerge yourself in the lie, for any indefinite period of time without coming to believe. Reality becomes unclear. Hallucination is real. Perception falters. What begins as subterfuge grows undefined. At some point you will espouse even manifest falsehood with all the zealotry of an Inquisitor. Yet there are times when we must submerge in the waters of falsehood in order to live. This is a most delicate matter.

Today there was a blizzard. "Ah!" I say, "God made it snow so that I should not go out to work, but rather that I might have the opportunity to engage in the study of the Word, which I have neglected."

Today I missed my bus, and was late to work. I was fired. "Ah!" I say, "God has punished me for the affair I've had with my neighbor's wife."

Today I lied to my wife, and I could see that she knew, and that she was hurt. "Ah!" I say, "I have not been selfless, have not loved my wife as Christ loved the Church. From this now, I must learn and repent."

The Terrible Beauty of the Evil Man

But is that really it? Everything which transpires under the sun can be reinterpreted using this method. There is no concatenation of physical or emotional phenomena that a comprehensive religion cannot redefine in this way. In time, the devotee's ability to perceive anything outside this methodology atrophies.

There is no action or inaction which cannot be deemed a sign, an omen, a manifestation of God. Yet nothing can be said about God, as the theologians claim he is unknowable. Our minds have been trained since early childhood to attribute every minutiae of existence, the wilting petal of the rose, to an entity completely beyond our perceptive capacity.

In our depths, the most impenetrable crevices of our subconscious, we suspect that this is not a serious explanation, that perhaps there is no more to the wilting of the petal than a lack of rain or nutrients.

In the modern world we exist in a state of explanatory schizophrenia. The progression of scientific discovery has made it impossible to deny the mechanical explanations for physical phenomena formerly attributed to any number of spirits, supernatural forces, and gods. However the biologists and chemists have not yet mapped the human brain. Because of this one uncharted interior galaxy we have room still for the ineffable deity. We have some place to allow him to soothe the terrors we cannot understand. Neuroscientists and computers will soon eliminate even this last gap.

Our minds recoil in horror from the thought that there is no higher meaning in *our* suffering. Moreover we must have clear parameters, divine instruction, for how to purge the guilt that inevitably arises when we have not done as we should. Repentance is a drug. Atonement is a tranquilizer. Confession is cathartic. There could not possibly be something more anesthetizing to the human psyche than the belief that every pain and terror you will ever suffer is the result of a higher purpose.

But now, my dear friends, do you really believe that you exist to form a piece in a galactic, ineffable jigsaw puzzle? Could it not be that when you hurt you simply hurt? Perhaps that hurts your ego. Many of you have a deep emotional need to feel close to Divinity.

We seem to know that we talk and move and breathe in a grand lie, and yet we cannot stop, we are fully compelled—and that is true addiction. The lie then *is* reality. The mere thought of living in truth provokes terror.

160.

Even with his liver gone, Kierkegaard composed odes to the bottle.

161.

These priests speak in endless cliché. I should like to know why it is necessary to spread a religious patina over puerile psychology. Is the patina needed, or is it but mandated custom? They tell me that I must engage in *pulling down strongholds*. They say that I can accomplish this by *taking thoughts into captivity*. If I do this then I will be *more than a conqueror*. At that point I will have conducted *spiritual warfare*. At the apex of said warfare I will be able to combat *wickedness in high places*. I will then be *married to Christ*, and able to function as an *ambassador of Christ*.

Ah, yes, dear Priest, you tell me that I will *know* all of this, that I will have certainty, because of the *fruit* that is borne in my life. I will be led by the Holy Spirit, as was Jesus. But what does that mean? If the Holy Spirit and Jesus are one, does the deity lead himself? If Jesus was omniscient, did he require leadership?

I have never once heard a coherent, plausible explanation of how one may have certainty that he has received a message from the deity.

162.

I toiled in the garden day after day. I potted plants and removed weeds. I cultivated and nurtured seedlings. I helped life flourish.

But that was half a day. During the remainder of the day I helped to end life—my own. I sacrificed my *self* so that I might go free. I had to be everything they needed me to be, and so, in order to become a proper Christian, it was most necessary to destroy the self. At various times I was told that God wished me to be an unformed piece of clay, an empty bowl, a bleating lamb, and number of other metaphors designed to help me learn to think of myself as a non-entity.

Apparently drug rehabilitation is similar to Marine boot camp. They break you down in order to build you up. Most of the residents arrived fully broken. But after the drugs were out of their system, and they had a week of regular sleep, exercise, and meals, they became incredibly arrogant. That was where religion came in. Evangelical and Charismatic

Christianity excel at helping you realize that you are valueless without Jesus. Those priests possessed a superlative ability to psychologically raze a man so that they could rebuild him in what they believed to be the image of Christ.

The priests made us keep journals, which they carefully read each week. I filled my journal with as much piety as I could muster. It did seem, however, that no matter how eloquently I debased myself, or praised the miraculous nature of Jesus, my very relational priest did not think that I was truly opening up to the Spirit of Christ.

He called my lawyer back in Alabama and told him that I was out in Florida playing games. I began to have panic attacks. I wasn't sure what more I needed to do to prove myself a devout Christian. I began to seriously consider another lengthy fast, or perhaps flagellations.

163.

Shortly after I arrived in Florida another young man arrived. I was quite glad about this—for perhaps an hour. However, soon after his arrival everyone in the residence realized that he was insane. He did not seem to know where he was. He appeared to be hallucinating regularly, and he was prone to violent outbursts. The priests blamed it on demonic oppression and drugs and told us to be patient and to pray for him.

I became extremely afraid that he would attack me. I was in a prolonged state of toxic hypertension resulting from the possibility that I would be sent to an adult prison for several years for even a single mistake. With this young man in the house I felt that I might have to defend myself at any moment. My nervous system simply could not handle the strain. I had a convulsive seizure in the floor.

The priests told me that I was experiencing demonic affliction due to the demonic emanations from the new guy, who, it appeared, was possessed. Weak, confused, and somewhat delirious after my seizure, I nodded and wrote down in my priest-reviewed journal that I had been writhing and shaking in the floor due to demonic activity.

The young man ran away from the facility after only a few days, but I continued to feel quite ill. About ten days after my seizure they finally sent me to a hospital where I had a CT scan and an EKG. The tests showed nothing unusual, and I was sent back to work in the gardens.

164.

The day I was finally sent to the hospital was the day I learned that my parents were separating. During the entirety of the time I was incarcerated I kept hearing innuendos, hints, slivers of meaning that led me to believe that my family, free on the outside, was undergoing terrible suffering. My father had resigned his pastorate, and though there was already a civil war in the congregation concerning his performance before I was arrested, it seemed my family still blamed the loss of his job on me. With his resignation my family was asked to leave the parsonage. My father found a much less appealing residence in the countryside and managed to secure a few hours substitute teaching in some of the local schools. My family soon reached a dire point as their savings were depleted.

My mother, from at least my junior year of high school on, had been having explosive bursts of irrational fury that did not resemble the corporal punishment-inducing tempestuousness of my earlier youth. Those earlier fits were still bounded by a perverse rationale, a fusion of inner anger and religious belief which were compatible with her Charismatic-supernatural worldview.

The new explosions of rage were more like truly inexplicable breaks with reality, and were due to medical causes. They were eventually diagnosed as the result of hormonal issues which would necessitate a hysterectomy. There was an unpredictable day or two each month where my mother would simply have to lie on her bed alone, door closed, undisturbed. On those days, during my sophomore and junior years of high school, I could not approach her without provoking streams of fury and vitriol.

With my incarceration, my father's unemployment, and the state of my mother's mental health, the complete breakdown of our family unit was inevitable. No one in the history of my family, on either side, had ever separated or divorced. But pressures like this had never been faced.

165.

With my parents' decision to separate, the sticky question arose as to what would be done with me once I was set free in July. Palter and Drazel's father had demanded that the circuit judge prohibit me from going free without a lifetime ban from the demesne of Selma and Dallas County, Alabama.

The Terrible Beauty of the Evil Man

According to my father, it was at this time that my mother began to pressure Mr. Jeofail to have the judge keep me in Florida for an additional year—so that the work of Christ could take root in my life. The truth was twofold. My mother probably did think that I was still in need of Christian treatment to ameliorate the powers of Satan. But she also intended to continue living in Dallas County, near her best friend, and undoubtedly preferred continuing to live near her best friend to a forced move that would have allowed me to move back in with her and my siblings.

I was destroyed when I learned this news. It was all I could do to make it through even a single day at the cult-like rehab that was my home. With slick oiliness my mother pointed out that I should really want to stay in Florida, so that Jesus could gain dynamic control in my life.

I floated the idea to my parents of possibly living with my grandparents, by then in retirement, back in Wichita Falls, Texas. I assumed that I could live with them, and go back to Old High, my former high school, where I could complete my senior year and get a diploma. My grandparents told my parents they did not want me. I then questioned my father's sister, and her new husband, who also lived in Wichita Falls, as to whether I could come live with them. They discussed it with my grandparents at the First Baptist Church the next Sunday, and my grandparents instructed them not to let me return to Wichita Falls. My grandmother was furious with my new uncle when he displayed a lack of tact by revealing the details of that backroom demand.

Shortly after this fiasco I received the first communication I had received from my grandfather during the entirety of my incarceration. He scrawled a mere four or five lines on the back of a stock email (general family updates my grandmother periodically sent to all family members) telling me that he knew exactly what I was going through— he had recently spent a few days in a hospital bed with pneumonia. This apparently gave him insight into my condition.

That, dear friends, was the Christianity of one of the great Evangelical leaders of the twentieth century. Jesus was actively involved with the sick, the criminal, the whore. Landrum Pinson Leavell II did not contact his eldest grandchild for more than eight months while that boy was in prison. He had enormous influence and a number of prominent connections throughout the South. He almost certainly could have telephoned a Senator or Congressman from Alabama to pressure the courts to get me out of solitary confinement. He had a number of extra bedrooms in his luxury condominium. He could have given me a place to live when I got out. He didn't want me near him. He might simply have refrained from blocking me from being able to live in the same town as him. He actively worked to keep me out of Wichita Falls. Perhaps he believed I would tarnish his reputation. He spent the time that I was locked up in quasi-retirement, traveling the country, leading revivals, winning souls to Christ, delivering sermons on the love of Jesus.

166.

As time went on I became aware of a disturbing pattern. All of the religious teaching, all of the heavy work with the sledgehammer of Salvation, was not having much effect on the lives of the crackheads with whom I lived. Unlike me, they had all volunteered to come. I was not free to leave the grounds. They were not free to leave the grounds unless they left the program, but they were free to leave the program at any time. And many of them did.

I remember the first time I saw the failure of the program in high resolution. One of our most outstanding recovered addicts was to graduate the program and go out into the world. He was a beautiful man, with blond hair, light eyes, strong jaw, chiseled muscles—really what one would imagine as a successful product of the *Lebensborn eingetragener Verein*. He had been in the compound when I got there, and was capable of leading the Bible studies and delivering impassioned diatribes on the restorative powers of the love of Christ. He was kind and thoughtful, and often helped to make peace between the different factions of warring addicts. He graduated the program and left one weekend. I assumed that, other than on our weekly trips into Orlando for Sunday services at the Bishop's congregation, I would never see him again.

He returned in a week. It is difficult to describe the shock I felt when I saw him. He appeared to have lost twenty pounds. His skin was a slightly different color. He was very sick. Even the shape of his face seemed to have changed. It was as though his muscle had melted away. I was a teenage boy, and I had never seen someone blown up after a week's crack binge.

Some days later I asked him what happened. He described a week of non-stop drugs of every kind, a variety of whores, and becoming the kind of man who can, in dark alleys, make the quick money necessary to pay for more drugs and whores. I felt sick. It was a trauma for me.

But as my four months drew to an end I saw that his was not an isolated case. Most of the men left and returned, and the primary distinguishing characteristic was not between those who went on a hard drug binge and those who didn't. No, the defining characteristic was whether they attempted suicide at the end of the binge. I began to have trouble sleeping, began to feel continuously ill. I was too young to be exposed to that kind of thing.

167.

The Charismatic Episcopal Church in Orlando was led by Bishop Frank Constantino, a man the other residents told me was a former Mafioso that had at one point served several years in prison for stealing millions of dollars in an armed robbery. He found Jesus in prison, which was convenient, as it helped him get a reduced sentence. Upon release he went on to recruit a bevy of former criminals and drug addicts that would serve as priests in his new religious order, the Society of St. Dismas.

Generally either the Bishop or one of the ex-addict priests were the only ones allowed to give the sermons at the society's church in Orlando. However one weeknight we travelled to Orlando to hear a guest pastor who was not a member of the Charismatic Episcopalian Church, but was rather involved with a movement with which I was unfamiliar, the Foursquare denomination.

The new preacher was a fiery fundamentalist, ranting against the evils of this world, while promoting the absolute authority of the Word of God, and the need for complete submission of every area of one's life to Christ. Hell was mentioned frequently. He must have been in at least his late forties, but was so animated that he jumped and bounced around the stage, simply ecstatic with message of God.

My attempts to restrain my giggles at his gyrations were nearly thwarted when he related a tale from his early ministry. Apparently this man, in his youth, and freshly convinced of the call of God, had acted on the commandment to take the Word of God to the lowest and most unclean. To him that meant walking into a strip club with a Bible, and preaching to unclad young ladies otherwise engaged in pole-Pilates. When I heard this I put my hand over my mouth and drew my head down to my knees, hoping that my shaking laughter appeared to be a *movement of the Spirit.*

However, with my recovery from mirth came an idea. I realized that this pastor was clearly unusual, and, though he was a raving fundamentalist, he was disconnected from my religious compound, and therefore might be someone to whom I could pose a serious religious question without fear of the judicial reprisal I would face if the St. Dismas priests thought that I wasn't completely *sold out for Christ*.

The exorbitant amount of time I had been given to study the Bible during my incarceration had, rather than convincing me of the truth of the Scriptures, only reinforced my belief in the fallaciousness of the doctrine of inerrancy, as well as my intuition that the Bible could not possibly be literally true. I determined to approach him with some minor but obvious biblical contradictions, in truth hoping there was some obvious rejoinder I had overlooked.

"Hello, Pastor. I really enjoyed your sermon tonight. I was inspired by the lengths you've gone to share the Gospel to those in need."

"Thank you. I hope the Lord was able to move in your life tonight."

"Oh, he was. Definitely. I really feel a recommitment in my walk. But that does lead me to something that's been troubling me. I've had a couple of questions about the Scripture that have been weighing on me during my quiet time studies this last week. They are causing me to have concerns about the inerrancy of the Holy Scriptures."

"Please, son, share your heart with me."

"Well, it's like this. In Matthew 27 it says that Judas, the betrayer of Jesus, full of remorse, tried to return to the priests the money he had received for the betrayal of Christ. They didn't want it back, so he threw the money into the temple, and then, consumed by regret, committed suicide by hanging. The priests then took that money and used it to buy a field which became known as the Field of Blood. However, in Acts 1 it says that Judas himself used that money to buy the Field of Blood, and in that field he fell down and his guts burst out, resulting in his death. So there is a contradiction both about who bought the field, and also about how Judas died. Do you see why I am troubled?"

"I think I see where you're going," the strip club evangelist replied with a frown.

"My other question is similar. In Matthew 27 it says that Simon of Cyrene was compelled to carry the cross of Christ. It says the same thing in Mark 15 and Luke 23. However in John 19 it says something completely different. Simon of Cyrene isn't even mentioned. In the Gospel of John it says Jesus was forced to carry his own cross. So who really carried the cross of Christ?"

For a moment he stepped back from me, his expression nonplussed, but then followed one of the strangest experiences of my life. Slowly a warm, very intent look passed over his features. He stepped close, brought his face very near to mine, and placed his palm flat on my chest.

"*You,*" he said, pressing down on my chest, "see this. And *I,*" he continued, placing that same hand on his own chest, "see this. But *they,*" he said, pointing to the motley groupings of addicts huddled in conversation, "will *never* see this."

And then he looked at me with an expression of finality that was both serious and knowing. His eyes seemed to paradoxically radiate both warmth and impenetrability, and I felt as though I had been initiated into the Illuminati. I did not know what to do as he slowly backed away from me, enveloped in an aura of mystery, nodding kindly.

168.

My time in the compound was drawing to a close. I had seen wave after wave of addicts voluntarily leave or graduate the program, only to collapse within weeks of returning to the world. They would return to the compound shards of their former selves, and I began to wonder how any program could possibly continue to receive funding with such an abysmal success rate.

However, I had maintained a perfect, if disingenuous, record of compliance with all the minutiae of the program, and had high hopes that the priests would give a solid recommendation to the circuit judge when I went back to Alabama for what I hoped would be my final hearing. Yet the hug-friendly priest in charge of Renaissance Gardens, with his nearly supernatural radar for feigned religious zeal, seemed disinclined to give a positive recommendation on my release.

Despite my best efforts, I had continued to fail to impress him with my love for Jesus, and therefore he did not seem to feel that I should be readmitted to Society. He simply would not give me a direct answer when I repeatedly asked him if he would report that I had complied with the requirements of the program. But I was the only resident there under court order, and so he had an unparalleled degree of personal power over me. In short, he owned me.

169.

In addition to my corrosive anxiety concerning whether I would get the recommendation needed to go free, I faced deep uncertainty as to whether I would have a place to live if released. My mother was determined to stay in Selma with her best friend, and it appeared that I would be legally banned from ever entering that county again. My grandparents didn't want me to live with them, nor did they want me to be able to live with other relatives in the same town. The consensus among my mother, lawyer, and the priests was that, despite the agreement, it would be best for me to remain incarcerated in Florida. Nobody seemed to want me, except for the priests, who had an interest in my labor in the gardens, and in the money the program received per resident. The only person who seemed to want me out and was willing to let me live with him was my father.

However, my father was in a state of severe depression resulting from the simultaneous collapse of his marriage, family, and career. Moreover, he didn't have anywhere to go outside of Selma where he could hope to find work. He decided that if he had to separate from his wife, who was determined to keep custody of the other three children, then he wanted to be back in Texas, his home state, in that culture which was so much more comfortable for him than the noblesse oblige of the reactionary Black Belt.

He applied for teaching jobs, essentially the only non-religious career his theological credentials would allow him to access. He was soon accepted for a position, at a fraction of his former salary, teaching history at a middle school in a suburb of Dallas. It seemed, therefore, that if I was released at the beginning of July, I would go to an unfamiliar location in Texas, accompanied only by my father, a man suffering from severe depression.

I felt very ill. I didn't know if, in a month, I would be in Dallas, back in Orlando, or at an adult prison in Alabama. Eighteen-year-olds are simply not equipped to deal with this level of emotional uncertainty. I was near collapse.

170.

For my final month in Orlando the Society of St. Dismas had a treat for me. It seemed that we were going to be allowed to forego most of our half-day Bible lessons in order to work full days under central Florida's June sun—laying sod at the Bishop's new multi-million dollar lakefront mansion.

It was unclear to me how a man who had served hard time for armed robbery, having spent most of the years since functioning as the bishop of a tiny religious society, had amassed the fortune necessary to purchase and ornately decorate a multi-million dollar luxury lakefront property. The plants, trees, and sod for the landscaping alone cost more than most of the homes in the Black Belt. We would install many thousands of dollars of sod—which would stretch from the house down to the lake—as well as a variety of expensive tropical bushes and palm trees. Some of the palm trees, which were sold out of our tropical flower nursery, cost thousands of dollars each.

I looked on the labor as an opportunity to escape the tedium of the endless religious indoctrination, and figured that the hard labor would keep the crackheads too tired to fight each other at the end of the day. However they were terrified by the prospect of full days of heavy manual labor under the blazing Florida summer sun. Most of their bodies were wrecked by years of hard drug use, and I had no doubt that their concerns about potentially collapsing in the field were legitimate.

That June I took the largest share of the labor, and worked every day until I was sore and exhausted, as did the others. A couple of the residents, realizing that we were doing slave labor for no pay, took this as their cue to abandon the process of drug recovery. The Bishop occasionally strolled the grounds, watching us labor in true plantation-owner style.

However after a few weeks of this even my body began to fail. The priests were using me as unpaid labor and were continuing to refuse to tell me whether they would recommend my release. I felt I was being ground into nothing. I was an emotional wreck and my body was exhausted. And it was time to go back to Alabama. It was time for my hearing.

171.

I walked into the judge's office. Palter and Drazel's father was there. I had not seen him in many months. The sight of me seemed to unnerve him. He shifted nervously in his chair. Jade's parents were absent. My incarceration had never been about her or them. I sat down. My lawyer handed a letter to the circuit judge from Bishop Constantino. The judge looked at my former friend's father before speaking.

"It seems that Mr. Beauchamp has complied with the requirements of the treatment program in Orlando."

I breathed a deep sigh of relief. My lawyer cleared his throat.

"Your honor, at this point we understand that Beau is to be set free."

The judge looked at the media baron of the Black Belt for further instructions.

"He can never come back here again. We don't want to ever hear from him or have him contact us again. Zero contact of any kind. Ever."

"You heard him," the judge said, motioning to my nemesis. "You are hereby trespassed from ever entering Selma or Dallas County for the rest of your life. And you are trespassed from having any contact whatsoever with the victims or their families. You may never return to Dallas County. Do you understand?"

"Your honor," my father interjected. "I have, since this case began, separated from Beau's mother, and I intend to take up a new position in Dallas, Texas, where Beau will live with me. However we need a night to pack his possessions, and we were hoping to have one meal together as a family. Would you object to allowing us to leave tomorrow morning rather than tonight?"

The judge looked at my grand adversary, who nodded that he found this acceptable.

"You may return to Dallas County for this one evening. However you must be gone by the early morning. You can never return. You are permanently trespassed from Dallas County forevermore. Do you understand?"

I nodded meekly, squeezing the fists on which I was sitting, hardly able to believe that I might, in moments, be a free man. My lawyer and the judge asked me to apologize once more to the man who had demanded a pound of flesh, but had instead taken my entire soul. I apologized with the most docile expression I could command, stood up, and walked out of the courthouse.

The youth that had walked into the police station a year before was not set free. I emerged from that courthouse a corpse. Whoever I was in that life before had certainly perished. A teenage boy died in those dark cells, alone and abandoned.

What was lost can never return. On this everyone agrees.

172.

I sat down to dinner that night with my family. They were in a new home, a house that was strange to me. My mother was cold and distant. My parents spoke only in short, clipped sentences. My siblings seemed to view me as a stranger. They had divided my possessions in my absence, and so, other than clothes, I had little to pack for the trip in the morning.

I had been banned from entering Dallas County for life, and so the very location where most of my family intended to remain was prohibited to me forever. I stared at my siblings silently over the meal, wondering when, in how many months or years, I would see them again. I went to sleep that night in a strange bed, in a strange home. I left with my father early the next morning.

That was the last time the six members of my family ate a meal together.

Book V

173.

I have discussed heartbreak at length. A man's reprieve is in the delectable memories which meander blithely through the labyrinths of his mind. Lachrymose layers of sound unfold unceasingly until we slow, stop, demand a dissipation of that eternal dissonance, to hear, emerging from the intricate maze of the fugue, the soft pleasure of the cadenza *tranquillo.* These soothing sounds of memory coalesce as no plangent claque, but resonate delicately through the maelstrom of the present awaiting a future.

It is solely through our past, our memories, that we have any ability to order our present, and so much of our present is but an attempt to pivot toward a future which has not arrived. Our present seems an illusion, an erratic bombardment of sensory impressions decipherable only through the lessons of memory.

Memory is a stern instructor. It guides us through the deluge of detail in which, each instant, our consciousness is sublimated. Movements, impressions, the fragrance of time past—these are but cornices and columns in the architecture of an ever-crumbling present. As soon as we build a present it has collapsed into memory.

Some then, perhaps the poets of *saudade*, pivot toward a future in which they may search for lost time—memory as a future—using the present to create a future where they become liberally lost in the past. Shall we call this person the *historian of the personal*, the *archaeologist of the psyche*?

Proust showed that psychological archaeology may become perfection in Art, though he did it by night, alone, shut away from the very world that had provided the blueprints for his Cathedral. To document the games, boredoms, loves, frustrated ambitions of the living, to recreate those dozens of individual worlds (which were so many personalities encapsulated in the overflow of *his* soul), did he not abandon Life? Perhaps not. It may be that anyone who would compose the sonata, paint the image that does not leave the mind, capture, in whatever medium, the fleeting moment in which we recognize the intertwined tragedy and beauty of Being, inducing the intake of breath and concomitant paralysis that recognition brings, must retreat to a solitude so profound as to constitute an abandonment of all that lives. It requires no semiologist to find symbolism in that life born from death, the death that makes a man god-like. We men have known many dying gods.

Is there an antidote to this inevitable loss of present to past? Would you choose to escape the inundation of memory, step from the river of consciousness? It is so difficult—for many an impossibility. The present is persistent, powerful, pervasive. The gossamer strands of memory form webs interwoven through the latticework of our minds. Monks on mountainsides in China spend years attempting to control the flow of past and present, though that is a nullification of true existence. But what is possible? Can one escape, at least temporarily, both past and present, and still remain deeply rooted in *Life*?

Close your eyes. Breathe. Do you recall your last period of reflection, consideration of what freedom would be for you? How would you live if released from *your* prison of past and present and present-made-past? Ah, there... perhaps you had it. For a moment you may have glimpsed, and had it. Memory was only a perfume, the future a dream, the present irrelevant. This is the world of imagination. It is in imagination that we may look beyond our prisons, let go of memory. Pure imagination is the domain of creation. It is the most elusive of all modes of consciousness.

The Terrible Beauty of the Evil Man

174.

You leave a prison. You leave a series of nightmares that have bled into each other for so long that you can no longer be sure what wakefulness should feel like. You delight now in this air. Have you ever inhaled such air? It is so pungent you taste it!

You drive, and as the car moves the miles fall behind and you stare, hypnotized by country and land and entire worlds that open to you in your newfound wakefulness. All-that-might-be lies before you, and that set of all possible futures seems infinite.

But how long does this euphoria last? How long will you maintain that castle of imagination against the brutal onslaught of the present?

Who is this man in the car next to you? A year ago he was your father, a pastor, the head of a home, the communal purveyor of moral authority. Now he is a stranger. Look at him. Do you know him? Do you know this broken man?

This stranger tells you he will find you a high school, that you will play football again, live a normal life, graduate high school, finally have your senior year. Is he lying? You cannot know. He can barely keep from weeping as he drives. How can he possibly create a new world for you?

But you have spent an entire year learning how to hide your thoughts and feelings. To reveal what you think, to tell the truth, to breathe freely, is to risk pain immeasurable. And so you shut your mouth, turn from your present, retreat to your crumbling castle of imagination. You survive.

175.

Imagination is the domain of creation. But who is the creator? Man, of course. But who is the creator of the creator?

How similar are the creation tales of Jerusalem and Athens! In Eden God creates man—yet it is the serpent that grants man enlightenment. Woman inadvertently proves a terrible scourge to man, upsetting God's blissful paradise of gross ignorance. God is wroth. Severe punishment ensues for all.

Let us examine a different version. Zeus, master of the Olympian gods, tasks the Titan Prometheus with the creation of man. Prometheus, in serpentine fashion, grants man the gift of fire—or shall we say *awareness*. Zeus, furious that Prometheus has dared to enlighten man, curses the old Titan with a punishment so horrific the Semitic serpent seems lucky in comparison.

Further, Zeus, unsatisfied with punishing the author of the crime, determines to vent his fury on an unsuspecting mankind. What punishment could satisfy so ferocious a deity? Zeus determines to scourge man by commanding the—you guessed it—creation of *Woman*. How awful! But horror is multiplied. Pandora, the first woman, is not tricked into eating a fruit, but rather unwittingly opens a box containing all manner of Evil, thereby giving us a second creation tale in which God despises enlightenment and Woman ruins the world.

The parallels do not require explication. Let me return. Imagination is the domain of creation. Creation is the antithesis of submission. *Submission is to follow a rule.* Creation is the formation of new awareness and existence beyond all extant rules.

In imagination the future is unshaped, and in that time yet-to-be exists the fluid potential for creation. But to create is to do what has not been done. To create is to see what has not been seen, and then to act. To create is to solve a puzzle that has no rules and is missing pieces. I do not speak of the Randian creation of money-making motors. John Galt is not the creator. I refer to the creation of new awareness. That was the sin of the serpent. That was the iniquity of Prometheus.

Imagination is the domain of creation. The creation of unorthodox awareness is Evil. And it is through such Evil that humanity has always risen.

176.

We arrived in Garland, Texas, a suburb of Dallas, and disembarked at a church property. My father was friends with another pastor who, having previously been through a divorce, sympathized with him. Until my father could locate permanent housing we would stay in a residence for visiting clergy on the church property.

This is perhaps not as small a detail as it might first seem. The Southern Baptist Convention takes a stringent line against pastors who have divorced. Generally, divorcees are disbarred from the pulpit. While my father was not yet divorced, he was considered unfit to head a congregation. He was fortunate to have a friend who understood his predicament.

The immediate effect in my life was to move from a fundamentalist religious compound in Florida to a fundamentalist religious compound in Texas within two days.

177.

When I got to the church where we would temporarily live the collected clergy's first interest in me was taxonomical. I had not graduated high school. Did I belong in the Youth Group? But I was already eighteen. Perhaps I should be placed with the College Group. But no, I was not enrolled in a college, and, since I was no longer technically a minor, there was some talk of placing me with the Young Adults.

I had been ripped out of Society a boy, and thrown back in limbo. "Are you a boy, or a man?" they demanded.

In truth, I did not know.

178.

My father's only spark of life at that time came from the attempt to ascertain where I would restart my football career with a senior year that would doubtless lead to gridiron glory and the promise of a college football scholarship. The Dallas area was possessed of a number of excellent high school football programs, and this, as well as his new poverty, seemed the only considerations in his determination of where in the Dallas metro we would live.

It was only after we visited several schools and spoke to several coaches that one of them thought to ask where I had played my junior year *the year before*. When I responded that I had played my junior year at Morgan Academy in Selma, Alabama, but that it had been the year before last, the coach frowned and said that he needed to make a call. He left us in the school's weight room and returned with a somber expression. It seemed that I was ineligible to play football in the State of Texas, as I would be playing my four allotted seasons in non-consecutive years. There were a small number of contingencies that would allow a person to skip a year and then resume their athletic career, but incarceration, sadly, was not on the list. That phone call ended my football career forever.

With this devastating news my father quickly took the cheapest housing he could find in Garland, home to his new teaching position. We woke up that first morning in our unpleasant new apartment complex, and my father told me to walk down the road and enroll myself in Garland High. He no longer cared where I went to school, or, for that matter, anything about my education, but I did still need a diploma.

I walked into the guidance office of Garland High School and was ushered into the office of a matronly woman eager to help me achieve academic success.

"Well, young man, what can I do for you?"

"Hello. My name is Beau Beauchamp. I need to transfer to Garland High."

"I see. And from where are you transferring?"

"From Morgan Academy, in Selma, Alabama. My parents separated, and my dad got a job out here, so… this will be my senior year."

"I understand. Do you have your transcripts with you? What courses did you take last year?"

"Um, last year I took a few classes here and there, but I don't think I got any credit for them."

Her eyebrows rose and I realized I would have to reveal the shameful truth.

"I was incarcerated in Alabama last year. I got out of prison a few weeks ago. It was all juvenile, so I don't have a criminal record, but I don't think I got credit for the class work."

"*You* were incarcerated last year?" she asked, leaning back in her chair and staring. "For what?"

"For numerous felonies. I was a serious juvenile offender. I'm banned from Dallas County, Alabama, for life."

She grew quiet and settled into her chair. Her eyes moved over me, again and again, as though searching for a puzzle piece she could not locate. Finally she smiled, leaned as far forward in her chair as she could, and placed her palm down on the edge of the desk near me, as though she wanted to take my hand.

"Look, Beau, I've done this a long time. Decades actually. I've seen all types—even the very worst. You're put-together, you're well-spoken, you just don't fit the type. I *know* criminal young men. I know dangerous young men. I've worked with them for years. That's not you," she said, her all-knowing eyes staring into mine. "I don't know what happened in Alabama, but we can help you complete your education here."

"Ma'am," I said, smiling softly, leaning forward in my chair, returning her deep eye contact, placing my smooth palm over her wrinkled hand, "I'm quite certain that I'm the most dangerous person that has ever walked into your office."

"Well, how did it go?" my dad asked. We were trolling through the grocery store, and he was filling the cart with meats and cheeses and vegetables of every sort.

"Hmmm, I don't believe they think I'll be a good fit for their regular high school. They want to enroll me in their night high school. It's for people on the fringes—pregnant girls, gangsters, people who have previously dropped out and want to try again. Criminals."

"Gotcha," my father replied, though I could see that he was staring down into the cart, not listening, trying to determine if he had forgotten anything.

"So I think they want me to go by night, and graduate in a year."

"Yep," he replied absently.

"Don't you think we'll need some bread?" I asked.

"Sure. You can get bread. I was going to ask what you wanted."

"I'll eat this stuff. But I think we should also have bread. Don't you?"

"Beau, the stuff in the cart's for me. We'll get you some bread, cereal, peanut butter, stuff like that."

"What?"

"The food in the cart's for me. It's part of my new diet. I can eat anything but carbs. But you're in great shape. You can eat whatever."

"What if I want some of that food? I don't get meat or vegetables?"

"We can't afford it right now. I need it. You don't. Just get whatever's cheap. You need filler."

A tremor of revulsion passed over my face. I recognized his strategy. He realized that if he ever wished to get laid again he would have to lose the slovenly lard that had accumulated around his midsection during a quarter-century of marriage. Money was limited. I was going to eat bagged cereal and instant noodles while he ate steaks and salads.

"You know this is total crap, right? You can't treat me like this! I'm your oldest child. Your children should come first. You want to feed me non-nutritious garbage while you eat like a king every night and claim that you don't have money for better?"

"Listen, you little punk," he said, leaning in close, his tone suddenly quiet, fierce. "It's because of you I'm here. Sounds like you're going to be in night school now. So guess what? You want better food? Pay for it yourself! You're eighteen now, a man. Get a job."

And that, dear friends, is how I ended up taking two buses each way to neighboring Richardson, Texas, where I was able to secure daily employment as a waiter in a Mexican cantina.

181.

Thus began an isolated existence in which I lived as neither boy nor man. By night I was a high school student, sitting in classes with pregnant girls and gangsters. Little or no instruction took place. The unmotivated instructors were there for paycheck supplementation and nothing more. The students possessed only dubious interest in learning, but attended in order to acquire a credential. My opportunities for meaningful human interaction were limited.

By day I took two buses each way to work lunch shifts serving quesadillas and fajitas to the copiously obese bourgeoisie who left the tips that bought the essentials I needed to stay alive. My father gave me free rent, and subsidized basic essentials such as cereal, toilet paper, and toothpaste. I paid for everything else.

The Youth Group at church (for that was the genus to which I had been assigned) was proving difficult, as the youth director did not understand why Faith was insufficient to allay my concerns about the inerrancy of the Bible, and moreover, why I felt it important to ask riddles about the contradictions in the Gospels during group Bible studies.

In addition, it was becoming apparent that most of the young ladies of the youth group were interested in getting to know me with an intensity of spiritual passion that might best be characterized as the physical love of Christ.

This alarmed me greatly. I was, like any teenage boy, and particularly any teenager who has been kept away from girls for a year, a raging mass of hormonal instinct. But I was also aware that I was eighteen, and the girls in the youth group, even if also high school students, were mostly still minors. After what I had been through for a simple blowjob, even a prolonged hug was terrifying.

182.

I woke up in the mornings and went into the bathroom of our shitty apartment and stared into the mirror. I had just gotten out of prison, but it was my father who had capsized. He was unable to directly acknowledge his emotional problems, and so his emotional processing took the form of passive-aggressive maneuvers against me or unprovoked flurries of tears at random moments. He was in dire need of a caretaker, but I was a boy-man, and was too embroiled in my own trauma.

I would take a washcloth and rub the mirror, vainly attempting to buff the scratched glass, that I might see myself clearly. Every morning I looked into that mirror, and the only thing clearly reflected was that I was lost.

I had spent so long looking forward to being free. I did not know that when I finally got out I wouldn't slip right back into life. I had gone into prison a popular, intelligent, athletic student at a top prep school. I had emerged into impoverished chaos.

You would think, wouldn't you, dear friends, that it would be simple. One day you are locked away. You spend weeks, months, perhaps years, thinking about the error of your ways in a restricted environment. When Society deems fit, you are released, and life goes on, undoubtedly with some stigma, but otherwise just as it always had, excepting only the uncommon *penitential* knowledge gained.

But no. It is nothing like that. Nothing like that at all.

183.

I didn't know how to walk into a room. Obviously I had not forgotten how to pass under a doorway. I simply couldn't do it. For so long I had been *ordered* from room to room. You didn't walk into or out of a room of your own volition. Even in Orlando, with its greater degree of freedom, the course of the day and the movements of the population were heavily regimented.

And even if not in a subconscious state of trepidation about *whether* I should move on my own I was struck with conscious fear when confronted by the *act* of entering a new domain. In prison, or in a den of crackheads, you do not quickly approach others. Persons do not suddenly walk up to you—and certainly not from behind. The eighteen inches of personal space we generally require in polite society are minimally doubled. In prison you advance towards others slowly, cautiously, and make sure they see you coming. Failure to do so is potentially life-threatening.

When I reemerged into the world in Garland I did not know how to handle people walking up behind me and giving me a friendly slap on the back, a banality among the Spirit-filled evangelicals in our new church. The chaotic environment of a fast-paced restaurant made waiting tables excruciating. My fight-or-flight reflex kicked in every time. On a number of occasions I felt myself on the verge of rapidly, involuntarily, turning and pushing the bones of anonymous nares up to an anonymous brain. I wouldn't, but then would have to fake a smile and chuckle, and would try to breathe and avoid a myocardial rupture.

I discovered that I could never stand or sit anywhere in a room unless my back was against a wall. Once in the room, I was, at all times, keenly aware of the location of every other occupant. I found that if I consciously forced myself to eat without my arms around my food, the moment my thoughts drifted my arms immediately went back around the food. The situation felt most akin to the commoner who walks unendingly through a dark and dangerous nighttime alley. There was no off-switch for the hypervigilance.

I would wake up, several times a week, sweating after a dream in which I had again been found guilty, where I was back in prison. In my dreams I was in jail, a deviant, though in the dreams it was usually for a crime far worse—one in which I could never hope for release, and in which I was locked in the highest security section, with the prison gangs out to kill me. In some of those dreams I started a prison gang. In some of the dreams I killed myself. Yes—it is possible to die in a dream. You just wake up.

As years have passed the nightmares have gradually diminished. But several times a year I still have them, and it has been more than a decade. And, like those dreams where I find myself writhing from hordes of demons within, I doubt they will ever completely go away.

Crowds were, and still are, uncomfortable for me—though strangely this does not apply at parties, where everyone pretends to be happy. I continue to find it distinctly unpleasant to sit next to someone in a darkened movie theater unless I have been romantically involved with that person for some time. I can now sit in a room without my back to a wall, but I often reflexively glance behind me at regular intervals without being aware that I do so.

Dear friends, you go into prison, then you go out of prison, but prison never goes out of you.

184.

The only close acquaintance I had in life at that time was an old South American-Native American (he preferred *Indio*) who lived in my run-down apartment complex, and who was a shaman. I found him interesting for his numerous idiosyncratic characteristics, for instance that he was a shaman, which was exotic, and for the fact that though it was in Spanish that he possessed his greatest linguistic fluency, he resolutely detested the notion that he might be considered Hispanic. He had a strong hatred of what he called *the Spanish*, by which he meant all Hispanic persons, as he believed them responsible for the destruction of his native culture and people.

As a corollary to the principle of hating *the Spanish*, he strongly detested Catholicism, and by extension, all forms of Christianity. In this unusual Indio I found, for only the second time in my life (my assigned mentor in WAYS was the first), a chance to converse with a person of at least moderate intelligence who did not believe that the Bible was the word of God.

Our conversations inevitably led from problems with the inerrancy of the Bible to the fact that I was experiencing trauma following release from prison, as well as my difficulty in relating to my deeply depressed father. He attempted a shamanistic Indian cure, which was meant to release the "bad energy." I lay down, and he placed stones on my torso which were apparently possessed of salubrious mystical properties. He mumbled nonsense for several moments. I got up and put on my shirt. I felt no different, but told him that I did.

I remember this man both because he was my only close acquaintance and quasi-confidant during that dark time, but also for one additional idiosyncrasy that made little sense to me. He greatly detested *the Spanish* and also Catholicism, but far more than either of these he told me that he hated Jews. I was struck by the inexplicable nature of this fanatical hatred because, following further probing, he revealed to me that he had never met a Jew. I had never met a Jew either, and was frustrated by my inability to get a coherent answer from him that would allow me to understand why they should be hated. He seemed to view Jews as the literal source of all evil in the world, much as the Christians I knew viewed the Devil. This unusual man stands out in my mind, years later, as the first anti-Semite I can remember having met.

185.

Eventually both my father and I realized that our living situation was untenable. Neither of us was able to heal in the presence of the other. The poverty was acute. He needed me to leave.

A number of options were discussed. His first notion was that I should live with his sister and her new husband in Wichita Falls, Texas, my former home, as they had two unoccupied bedrooms, and I could finish my degree at my former school, Old High. I reminded him that my grandparents, still his in-laws, had explicitly told his sister and her husband that they did not want me in Wichita Falls after my release. Not feeling particularly amiable toward his in-laws at that time, he promised to speak to his sister.

My father's sister, my Aunt Ann, who we referred to by the pet name Nena (rhymes with henna), agreed to speak to her new husband about the matter. My new uncle, anxious perhaps to curry favor with my grandfather, one of the most influential men in Wichita Falls, or perhaps desirous of remaining the only man in his new household, did not wish for me to live with them. However my Aunt Nena is a tenacious woman, and, as she had been a spinster into her forties, and was sole owner of the house, she possessed a greater degree of independence than most Evangelical Southern wives. Additionally, it was my paternal grandmother, Isabel, who had initially purchased the home in which they lived, and so I had something of a multi-generational claim to an empty bedroom.

Eventually my father and aunt won out, and the ambitions of my uncle and maternal grandparents to keep me at a distance were frustrated. I was loaded into a car and driven two and a half hours west, to Wichita Falls. I had very little to take with me.

186.

I went to the guidance office at Old High that first week I was in Wichita Falls. This time there was no quickly retracted condescending liberality. I was told that I would not be well served by attending my former high school for an entire senior year. Instead I would go to the Harrell Accelerated Learning Center, where I would, again with pregnant young ladies and gangsters, have the opportunity to study for my high school diploma. The difference at this location was that I would be able to study for and pass classes at my own pace. I was told that students generally spent between several months and several years there, depending on their motivation and capacity. I would only need to pass final examinations in each of the required courses of what would have been my senior year at Old High. I was told that, if I was very intelligent and motivated, I might graduate high school with a diploma in just three months.

I needed far less time.

187.

My aunt was soft and fat and kind. My new uncle, who I barely knew, was a roughly six foot four, three hundred and seventy-five pound, former US Army drill sergeant with the booming voice to prove it. He had a penchant for bloody Vietnam movies and an IQ of (if I am generous) ninety-five. He saw me as one of his former boot camp soldiers—young, dumb, and in serious need of discipline. Excepting the absence of youth, I felt the situation was mutual.

As soon as I graduated he demanded that I get a job. Once again I found myself serving tacos and fajitas to the corpulent bourgeoisie of Northern Texas.

188.

My aunt and uncle attended the same church as my grandparents—the almighty First Baptist Church of Wichita Falls, at that time pastored by Robert Jeffress (a man I have always strongly suspected is a closeted atheist). It was expected that I join on the first Sunday—my grandfather, though retired, was the pastor emeritus. I complied, and my grandmother requested, with an icy smile, that I sit with them on Sunday mornings.

In fact I was able to fill an unusual but useful niche for them. My grandfather, who had ignored me so thoroughly when I was alone in a cell, found that I made an excellent prodigal grandson—an Evangelical accessory.

189.

It was at this time that my thoughts turned towards university, and what I intended to do with the rest of my life. It was a time of excitement for me. I thought I might finally resume a normal path. Throughout my earlier youth I had assumed, as had those around me, that I would join the lineup of powerful Leavell pastors. With my attachment to Christianity literally contingent upon the fact that if I did not attend church my uncle would throw me out of the house, that career possibility seemed unfruitful.

I gave some thought to the matter, and decided that it was the human brain, as that organ that had most greatly aided and alienated me in the world, that was the object most worthy of my study. I wasn't sure if I was more interested in the brain as a type of hardware or in terms of its output, and therefore was uncertain if I wanted to work as a neurosurgeon or a psychiatrist. I realized that either path lay through medical school. I figured that both options would provide prestige, financial security, and interesting work. I promptly took the SAT, and applied to the local university, Midwestern State, which reputedly had an excellent pre-med program. My test scores allowed me a full academic scholarship, and, as I was living rent-free, I was making money by choosing to stay in Wichita Falls for college.

Even with no lack of funds, my uncle demanded that I remain employed. As I detested the ineradicable smell of nachos, I ceased working at the local Mexican cantina in favor of new, and far more interesting work. With my decision to become a doctor came the awareness that I would need either volunteer or work hours in the medical field. Volunteering did not hold a great deal of appeal for me, but paid medical work did. Wichita Falls is home to the largest hospital for mental illness in Texas. I applied for work as an orderly at the North Texas State Hospital, and was accepted. Thus I began both university, and the most interesting job of my life.

190.

The training for an orderly in a mental hospital is lengthier than the training for a taco-dispenser, and involved long weeks of all-day classes. Fortunately I was able to finish during the summer prior to my first fall semester at Midwestern State. Because I was tall and muscular, I was assigned to the intake unit, where large persons are needed to tackle (correctly: non-violently restrain) individuals who have been brought in off the streets (jacked up on meth and convinced they are Napoleon), and pin them to the ground long enough for the nurse to plunge a needle into their buttocks. This unit, obviously, was a locked-down affair. A year after I had been an animal in a cage *I* had become the guard.

Since I would attend college in the daytime, I requested the overnight shift on the intake unit, which is generally the most dangerous shift. Intake patients are more likely to be high or inebriated late at night, and are therefore more difficult to restrain. I had done brief rotations on each unit as part of my training, but even so, I, like the other new orderlies, did not know what to expect. I was looking forward to the experience.

The late nights were less exciting than I imagined they would be, although I did get to see a number of experimental Pollack-like works in fluid-art by several disgruntled patients. Generally, the patients I had the most interaction with were those to whom I was assigned for the duration of the shift, that is, those persons who were on twenty-four-hour suicide watch. Otherwise I spent time with the large numbers of insomniacs who roamed the unit throughout the night, waiting for their medications to take effect and tell them that they didn't really want to end this mortal life.

I had a number of interesting conversations with many of these individuals, and had an intimate knowledge of the details of their lives, as I had access to their files, which included their private charts, medical histories, and doctor reports. One of the most important things I learned in the hospital is that poor mental health, though I tend to treat it with persiflage (as otherwise I speak of it far too morbidly), is more common than most realize. This point was solidified early in my tenure at the hospital, when one of my coworkers on the intake unit tried to kill herself on her off-night, and had to be brought in as a patient on the very unit where she was employed. This was a bizarre and awkward situation for all involved, particularly her boyfriend, who also worked in intake, and who had to be transferred to another unit for the duration of her inpatient experience.

I spent my nights conversing with the patients, many of whom you would never, had you met them on the street, have guessed were in need of mental health care of any kind. When not conversing with the patients or making rounds I was memorizing the Devised Statistical Manual or studying for the classes I went to each morning at the end of my shift.

In studying the patients the most personal realization I came to was that much of what I was now helping to treat was either varied types of acute disease or psychological reactions to divers past experiences of trauma and abuse.

The fundamentalist Christians I had known would have rushed to label these same illnesses demonic oppression, and perhaps called for a group prayer meeting. I could see, for the first time, that schizophrenia, or epilepsy, were biological phenomena, without mystical roots. I had read about such things, but to see is to learn, and those nightly lessons had a powerful effect in nullifying much of my lingering belief in sentient evil metaphysical entities—a belief that is more difficult to eradicate than you would think.

191.

One night a young, blonde, not unattractive woman was brought on the unit and dosed by the nurse. We watched her, waiting for the drugs to kick in, as she wandered the unit, babbling incoherently and occasionally speaking with intense clarity of meaning to chairs and doorposts.

On the first floor of the two-floor intake unit there was a women's side, and a men's side, and they met in the middle in a large common area that possessed a television and a number of magazines. That night one of the perpetual insomniacs was sitting next to me, relaxing in gentle, unsleeping silence. He was an amiable, mostly bald man of late middle-age, with thick glasses, and he had come to the hospital after a poorly executed and probably unserious suicide attempt brought on by low self-esteem, a large belly, and the fact that he had not accomplished anything of import during his decades under the sun.

I enjoyed speaking with him, as he was never disagreeable, and was always glad to engage in conversation on any topic that might interest me. That night our eyes followed the woman wandering the floors of the common room. I casually thought that there, in that woman, existed a prime example of someone who would, in the world of my childhood, or in decades and centuries past, have been thought possessed by demons, or worse, condemned as a witch. Just as I had this thought, and perhaps to prove the point, she came over and knelt down in front of the man sitting next to me. I immediately stood, and moved to the side, preparing to intervene if she should become violent.

But no. Rather she knelt down before him and her babbling became once more comprehensible as she directed her fervor to the startled man before her. He looked up at me, unsure of what to do. I looked back at him with a half-smile and an uncertain shrug. Dear friends, the woman kneeling before him had begun to pray with all the intensity of a medieval stigmatic—and she was directing those prayers directly at him.

I tensed, looked around the room to locate the on-duty female staff, and waited, almost certain that something dramatic would follow, as she continued to direct devotions to this man who had, for the moment, become God omnipotent. The man looked at me once more, but then settled in with deep focus on the woman, apparently as interested in her prayer as she was. Then, suddenly, he leaned forward and placed his right hand atop her head.

"Bless you, my child," he said with a gentle, sacerdotal authority.

At that, the woman, to my shock, and to the surprise of the female orderly, lay down at his feet and began to breathe with quiet serenity. Perhaps it was for just that moment that the man had attempted to take his life. These are the whimsies of fate.

I looked up at the ceiling and let out a long breath. In the world of mental health, I was sure I had arrived.

192.

I have known fearful humans. I have known liars. I have seen misshapen humans. I have looked on broken people. I perceived each of them in turn, as I learned to see progressively deeper into whatever is meant by the word *soul*.

The fearful are the simple. Hellfire is terrifying; I will go to church. Divorce is painful; I will not cheat. Obesity is unattractive; I will diet. The fearful are terrified of the external, of the unknown. These were the first human minds I recognized as unhealthy, and I learned to do so as a small boy. These are the gentle laymen of the church. Their Bibles smell of old leather, and are stained with years of tears and clenching. These are the pious.

The liar is the commoner. The liar is fat. The liar is bourgeois. The liar lives for comfort. I recognize that there are discrepancies in Christianity; Jesus soothes me. My wife is terribly unattractive; a divorce would be unpleasant. I have put on a few pounds; that is the luxury of middle-age. These are the men and women fabulously incapable of zealotry, unless that be zeal in pursuit of a good meal. These people teach

Sunday School. They are deacons. They join the Rotary Club. I learned to recognize this species of corpulent humanity early in adolescence. Their Bibles are sleek, with perhaps some conspicuous underlining at key verses, and likely have their names embossed in faux-gold lettering on the covers. These are not intentional hypocrites—their lies do manifest to others, but are intended for themselves alone. The liars are the fearful whose fear is internal; they are most afraid of themselves. Self-deception is the condom that protects them from the consequences of *Being*.

The misshapen are ugly. We do not look at them. We turn away. The misshapen live to take, and this predacity warps their spirit so strongly that it manifests in their very appearance. The face is not easily transmogrified. It may take years of unchecked hunger to produce the glazed eyes and lubricious pallor recognizable even to the unperceptive. The pie tastes good; I will have a third piece. My mother doesn't give me enough pocket money; I will take twenty dollars from her purse. My boyfriend isn't paying me attention; I will have sex with his friend. I haven't any more money for crystal meth; I will suck a stranger for cash. *I want* becomes *I need* becomes *I will have at any cost*, for I am ravenous. I can and will do anything to take what I must have.

I saw my first concentrations of the misshapen in prison. I first saw the *grotesquely* misshapen in Orlando. That was no high-priced rehab for the woman sidetracked by pain-pills, or the man who has drunk too heavily following a divorce. No, Orlando was for men who had sold themselves repeatedly, and for long decades, to feed their avarice. The misshapen are liars taken to an extreme. Every malefic movement of their eyes unmarked by simple laziness is a glance meant to determine what can be had. Their movements are a feline reticulation of contortions in the service of guile. They have Bibles, and those Bibles are excellent *props*. They will lie, and cheat, and steal, until they no longer know anything else—for reality has become neither more nor less than *what they need*. Thus they are misshapen.

No joy can exist in such a state. The misshapen are never happy, even when submerged in the object of their desire. You might think, at first, that the esurient are unhappy because they do not know how to *give*. But no, my friends. Their misery exists because they have lost the ability to *experience beyond need*.

But, ah! None of this chills as does the *broken* human. I did not see a broken human, not a truly broken human, until I went to work as an orderly at the North Texas State Hospital.

193.

The fearful, the liar, the misshapen are wholly unlike the broken. The former are twisted by varied deceptions. The broken are fractured by Truth.

I have picked fruit from the Tree of Truth. Those fruits are always filling, though you never know how they will taste. Some are sweet. Some fragrant. Some are delicious, yet act as a poison, leaving you ill for days, weeks, perhaps for life. Some paralyze from the very first taste.

I have walked into my home outside my usual routine; I find that my wife has a lover. I open my mail at work today; my rival has received the promotion I desired. I go for my routine mammogram; I learn that I have breast cancer.

But what of those truths that become lies? I am in love with my secretary; my love was infatuation; in truth I love my lost wife. I believe in radical equality; I am a Communist; the Communists have confiscated *my* property.

The truth is oblique. Many wrong paths narrow the way.

194.

Then we are broken. Who will be broken *of his own volition*? Who will pluck the fruit, not knowing how it will affect him? Who will pluck again and again until he is either dead or a god? Who would rather be dead than human?

195.

I would talk to him in the nights. He could not sleep. He was Israeli. Let us say that his name was Dorit. Dorit was young, thin, short, with a perpetually whiskered face, and had, as far as I knew, arrived due to an unsuccessful suicide attempt. I hadn't had time to read his chart. I had been busy with other patients the first week he was on the unit.

I was fascinated by Dorit, during those first nights I had a few moments to snatch conversation with him. I repeatedly asked him questions about the Israeli military—essentially the only facet of modern Israel that interests contemporary Southern males. I knew that all Israeli males went into the military, and that Israel never lost wars, and I kept trying to elicit information from Dorit, though he was frustratingly reticent about his military experience. I couldn't understand why he wouldn't share what I found so interesting. I had never met anyone from the Middle East, and an Israeli seemed particularly exotic. I assumed that he was traumatized by some ferocious military engagement, and that the trauma had led to his suicide attempt.

Then one night, not long into, or shortly after, his first week, I walked into the men's restroom, doing normative rounds. Someone was sitting on the toilet, and I heard the sound of irregular urination. However, there was no smell to indicate defecation by the time the toilet flushed and the patient emerged. It was Dorit.

"Couldn't get it out tonight?" I asked amiably.

He grunted, washed his hands, and hurried from the restroom. His manner seemed strange, and I decided that it was past time I read his chart. When I sat down with his chart I suffered a greater shock than from that of any other patient's case I would encounter during my time in the hospital.

Dorit, it seemed, was not exactly a man. That is to say that she wasn't yet. She had testicle implants, hormonal therapy, and had taken other steps towards manhood, but had not yet had a surgery to provide a penis. Dorit looked like a man, had a male voice, grew some facial hair, and did not have breasts. But Dorit needed to pee sitting down. And apparently Dorit was not entirely sure that she did in fact want to become a male.

Hence the suicide attempt.

The next time I saw Dorit was after a couple of days off work. I looked at her, into her eyes, then glanced away. Gathering my courage, I looked back up, into her eyes—and when I looked into her eyes I saw inside her, and she saw into me. And that was a curious, terrible moment. A tear gathered in my eye, slowly trickling down my cheek. When she saw my tear she realized that I knew, and that I knew not only about the numerous operations and the hormonal transfigurations, but that I knew, as did she, that she was a broken flower, lost on the wrong side of the world. A tear gathered in her eye, and we both quickly turned and walked in different directions. I shivered then, and wiped away the tear, though inwardly I continued to weep. For the remainder of the time that I worked with Dorit I treated her with all the gentleness I possessed. More than any of the others who had tried to kill themselves, I seemed to instinctively identify with this person who had attempted to die, not due to depression, but due to an uncertainty as to their identity—to die in what might have been a failed attempt to find their true self.

I would not realize it for many months, as I, perhaps naively, did not think a Hebrew-speaking Israeli (a nationality) was synonymous with a Jew (which I had been taught was a race), but Dorit, that broken flower, somewhere between man and woman, between life and death, was the first Jew I am aware of ever having met.

The truth is oblique. Many wrong paths narrow the way.

196.

I was going to First Baptist. I was going, and I was getting fat on the Jesus and donuts they served the college kids in Sunday School before the main service. We had a praise *jam* band. We were meant to sing along with the band.

I would stare at the closed-eyed hippie-like swaying about me as the others sang. I would try to join in with them, but the attempt to reach a spiritual high by singing intimate lyrics towards an unknowable deity left me inanimate.

I felt as though something were wrong with me. I didn't understand why the clapping and swaying and throbbing drumbeat didn't help me connect to the divine. Only slowly did I come to understand. Those college students, those kids, used the music as a weekly cathartic in an attempt to allow their troubles to ooze out. They didn't think they were singing to an unknowable deity. They believed that they literally knew Jesus, and that they could have a two-way casual conversation with him at any time. With those songs they were channeling the presence of the carpenter. This was their weekly attempt to *feel*.

With that realization the depression resulting from my insensate response to the jam band vanished. I didn't need an intense emotional reaction through weekly peer singing in order to turn off my brain and feel something warm and fuzzy. I didn't require religion to function as a liver-friendly drug. Singing *at* Jesus wasn't going to jerk me into a higher spiritual awareness.

I did not need what the others needed. I was already very much alive.

197.

First Baptist had a carnival. Everyone knows the type—rides for small children, dunking booths, rings thrown at bottles. Tickets were won. Little trinkets were bought at the end of the night with the tickets.

I went to the carnival with a couple of friends, and paid for several tokens in order to play the games. I enjoyed myself for an hour, and then went with my friends to redeem my tickets for a wristband or a pair of dice or some other form of cheap plastic.

I was waiting in the line, perhaps two from the front, when I suffered a great humiliation. An associate minister of that massive corporation of a church walked by. As he did he stopped by the booth where the tickets were redeemed for trinkets. He saw me and his eyes went down to my handful of tickets. His eyes narrowed.

"Did you steal those tickets?" he called out loudly, in the hearing of all those massed around the ticket booth.

"I cannot believe you would ask me that," was all I could mumble. The crowd turned and stared. My friends backed away.

"Did you steal them?" he repeated.

"Sir, I paid money for the tokens I played with, and did not steal these tickets," I replied. I then placed the tickets on the counter and walked away, blushing furiously, and without my cheap plastic trinket.

It seems my grandparents had spread the story of my incarceration. Within my first month back at First Baptist Church, Wichita Falls, the hierarchy already had me marked as a dangerous criminal. The story was spreading.

198.

That incident so humiliated me that I considered never returning. But my drill sergeant uncle had promised that if I stopped going he would kick me out. I would be homeless. I told Landrum and Jo Ann Leavell what had happened (though doubtless they had been informed before I told them), and they reminded me that there were consequences to sin, and that a good name was worth more than gold. And that Jesus saves.

I thought on the problem for some time. I realized that perhaps I might have better feelings about the church, and possibly also rehabilitate my image, if I were to do something selfless for the church. I decided to get involved. I decided to volunteer.

The church had, every summer, a large program called Vacation Bible School that lasted for roughly a week, and which served as a mix of recreational outlet and religious indoctrination for the hundreds of children in the church. I have always found small children adorable, so I volunteered to work with the kindergarteners for the week.

For the first few days of that week I had an amazing time. The little children were delightful, and I enjoyed holding their hands as we walked in line from activity to activity, serving them fruit punch and cookies, and swinging them around until they giggled uncontrollably. The adult staff in charge of the program smiled when he saw the children mob me.

"They really love you!" he said approvingly.

I felt, for the first time in a long time, like a truly good person, no longer the Evil Man. But then the night before the last day of VBS the phone rang in my aunt and uncle's home. My uncle answered the phone, and then bellowed for me to come.

"Is this Beau? Beau Beauchamp?"

"Yes. Who is this?"

"This is Associate Minister Roorback. I need to let you know that we won't need your help at Vacation Bible School tomorrow."

"What's the issue?" I asked, astonished at the panic in his voice.

"Many of the parents in the church have become aware that you have been convicted of child molestation. I had no idea you were working with children! I'm sorry, but this should never have happened."

"But I never molested children! I received consensual fellatio from two girls within three years of my age! These are *kindergarteners*! You're accusing me of being some kind of psycho!"

"I'm sorry, Beau, but you cannot show up tomorrow. If you come we will have you removed from the premises."

And with that, the holy minister of God Almighty slammed down the phone. I slowly placed the phone back in the cradle, went into my room, turned up the music so my uncle wouldn't hear me, and then cried for hours.

199.

I did go back to First Baptist, Wichita Falls, one last time. The next Sunday I went, mumbling through the music of the jam band, blankly turning pages as the couple who led my Bible study group talked about the grace and forgiving power of our Lord Jesus, thinking about the fact that a lowly associate minister could not possibly have made that call without first speaking to Robert Jeffress and my grandfather, the pastor emeritus.

At the end of the scriptural deluge I asked the couple who led our group if I could speak to them privately before the start of the main service. He was a slightly pudgy economist at the local university with a penchant for cycling, she a gentle woman who served as his tranquil, cheerful ornament. They were sweet people, and part of the reason I had been able to muster any enthusiasm for attending at all.

"What can we do for you, Beau?"

"I was thrown out of VBS last week. There was only one day to go!"

"Yeah, we heard about that."

"Well it's crazy, right? They can't do that? I'm not a danger to toddlers! I got in trouble in Alabama—true, but it was for doing consensual acts with girls who were very near my age. This is an attempt to paint me as a pedophile!"

My teacher's little trophy wife sighed, looked at me with compassion, and then turned to her husband, placing a hand on his shoulder. He looked at me with the love of Jesus Christ.

"Beau, you have to understand, people aren't going to feel comfortable with those behaviors. Who wants to risk their child with someone who has been in trouble for anything like that at all?"

"But you both recognize the difference, right? You have to! An eleventh grader fooling around with a ninth grader is not the same thing as an eleventh grader molesting a kindergartener! It's just not!"

"Beau," he said gently, "Jesus preached the power of forgiveness, so we forgive you for whatever wrongs you've done. We forgive you with all our hearts," he said, looking at his wife, who stared at me, nodding intensely in subservient agreement. "But Jesus also preached wisdom. No wise man can afford to take chances with their child, even if what you're saying makes sense. We have small children," he said, nodding to his wife, "and I can tell you, with all the love of Jesus, that we would not feel comfortable with you working with them."

His wife looked at him and nodded vigorously. I looked at him. I looked at her. I looked back at him. I blinked back tears. I got up without a word, and I never entered that church again. I was nineteen years old.

200.

To this day I find small children lovely, magical creatures. I think they are beautiful and a blessing. But I simply cannot be alone with them. I will not. For years this manifested as outright panic—though with the passage of a decade it has deteriorated to mere anxiety. Even accepting an insistent mother's caterwauling infant for a momentary hug has been an act performed with fear and trembling. For years after that incident at First Baptist I avoided being anywhere near a small child... and that is a travesty, for to lovingly hug a small child is one of the most cathartic acts a human can perform.

201.

I knew that I could never go back. I would never go back. I wept before my aunt, and she pleaded with my uncle. We worked out a compromise that, despite his shouting and threats, kept me from being thrown from the home.

I knew that I did not believe in Evangelical Christianity, did not believe that Jesus was either divine or the son of God. And yet, I hypothesized, perhaps everyone I had ever known had simply gotten it all wrong. Perhaps God had never intended the Bible to be interpreted literally. Perhaps the other denominations (the ones I had been told were wicked) had gotten it right after all. Perhaps the Bible was meant to be a symbolic document, designed to provide us with ethical guidelines rather than stringent schematics of inerrancy that corralled us away from hellfire. Our compromise was that I could stay in the home if I went to the local Episcopalian Church.

202.

Certainly, my dear friends, I have given more than enough reason to allow you to believe that when I finally left Evangelical Christianity it was due to the repeated emotional trauma I suffered at the hands of the fundamentalists. That is partly true. I did suffer terribly at their hands. But I did not lose my faith because of the actions of humans, as hurtful as those actions were. It would be disingenuous to suggest otherwise.

I lost faith because I did not believe the Christian Bible was the divinely inspired, inerrant, literal word of God. I had an interminable amount of time on my hands in solitary confinement, and during most of that time I was allowed nothing in my cell but a Bible. I became aware of many things I had never previously noticed—though others, such as Voltaire, or the Baron d'Holbach (or even Christian saints) had noted them, in some cases centuries before. So, for the sake of honesty, I will list a few of the salient points that demonstrated to me that the New Testament was not divinely inspired by God, but was composed by exceptionally mediocre men who possessed nothing of the divine afflatus.

I needn't list arguments from evolution or cosmology or epistemology, though those would suffice. No more than the New Testament itself is needed to convincingly demonstrate the fallaciousness of Christianity.

But of course nothing I write will matter to a Christian. I know them too well. They do not care if the New Testament is *true*—they need it like a drug—just as it does not matter if the addict knows that it is *true* that mainlining heroin will eventually kill them. They will always need the drug. It comforts.

203.

The first thing, perhaps a frivolous matter, that caused me to believe that the Holy Bible was written by a few uneducated fishermen, and not the divine movement of the Holy Spirit, was a topic which now serves to make me chuckle.

I wanted to know *where* the Bible says you can't have sex before marriage. I am not the first teenager to hunt through the Bible for the source of this prohibition, and I won't be the last, but it deeply mattered to me as an adolescent. The Sunday School teachers and pastors found some way of working the prohibition against pre-marital sex into almost every lesson they gave us, so I was sure it must be in there somewhere. But guess what? It's not!

There are clear prohibitions on adultery, incest, bestiality, homosexuality, coitus during menstruation, and an entire host of tangentially related sexual acts, but there is no prohibition, in either the New Testament or the Old, that prevents two unrelated, heterosexual, unmarried young people from making the most of each other's genitalia.

Pastors will cough and slurp and burp and tell you that it is covered under the prohibition against fornication, but that is very unlikely from the context of those verses, and, anyway, who is to definitively say what was meant by fornicating two thousand years ago, particularly in translation from ancient Greek? In any event, teenagers everywhere can rejoice. God never explicitly said you can't take a roll before marriage. Anyone who tells you different is lying.

204.

I was bothered by the realization that I could not imagine a perfect, omniscient, omnipotent deity requiring *two* tries to get his message across to mankind. He gave over the Torah to Moses, and the Christians claimed it was unlivable, because the *Covenant was broken*, and therefore an additional testament was needed.

I thought that absurd. An omniscient, omnipotent deity would not give mankind a testament, or Torah, for some thirteen hundred years that then required supplementation because he gave it to people who just couldn't cut it. What nonsense! Even if that was the case, why would he wait thirteen hundred years for the Torah 2.0?

The Evangelical logodaedalist will tell you that it wasn't that God got it wrong—it was *our* fault. The Torah was just too much for our impure, naturally corrupt human nature. Nonsense! If God is omniscient, why would he initially send a legal code he knew was doomed to fail? That would be sadistic.

Further, if God really did need two takes to get it right, then who is to say he didn't need three, or four, or as many as you like? Certainly the Koran, or the Book of Mormon, or the adherents of Bahá'í would like you to think along those lines.

If God is *perfect*, he can get it right the first time.

205.

The deity who inspired the Old Testament seemed to have a radically different *ethical* worldview than did Jesus. Consider Jesus' teachings from the Sermon on the Mount in Matthew 5.

"Blessed are the poor in Spirit, for theirs is the Kingdom of Heaven."

"Blessed are the meek, for they shall inherit the Earth."

"Blessed are the merciful, for they shall obtain mercy."

Jesus is advocating a distinct ethical worldview. We might say that Jesus had a concern for the *Other*. Let me reinforce the point with additional pacifistic moral teachings found later in Matthew 5.

"But I say unto you, that ye resist not evil, but whosoever shall smite thee on thy right cheek, turn to him the other also. And if any man will sue thee at the law, and take away thy coat, let him have thy cloak also."

"But I say unto you, love your enemies, bless them that curse you, do good to them that hate you, and pray for them which despitefully use you, and persecute you."

These were revolutionary ethical notions in the Semitic and Roman worlds at that time. They fabulously contradict the ethical positions advanced by the deity of the Old Testament (who, incidentally, fundamentalist Christians believe *is* Jesus). Consider the divinely inspired prayer to God in Psalms 137:8-9.

"Fair Babylon, you predator, a blessing on him who repays you in kind what you have inflicted on us; a blessing on him who seizes your babies and dashes them against the rocks!"

Or consider instead God's view of Saul, who fails to fully carry out the heavenly command to perform the act of genocide and ethnic cleansing against the men, women, children, and even livestock of the Amalekite nation in 1 Samuel 15. Samuel, the divinely inspired prophet of God, instructs Saul, King of all the Jews.

"Thus says the Lord of Hosts: I am exacting the penalty for what Amalek did to Israel, for the assault he made upon them on the road, on their way up from Egypt. Now go, attack Amalek, and proscribe all that belongs to him. Spare no one, but kill alike men and women, infants and sucklings, oxen and sheep, camels and asses!"

You might think, if Saul knew what was good for him, he would obey the Lord of Hosts, and slay some asses, but no, he did not. Perhaps he was looking forward to God in the form of Jesus, who would advocate mercy and turning the other cheek, but for whatever reason, Saul failed to obliterate both the livestock and the king of the Amalekites—Agag (though in all fairness, Saul was successful in murdering every one of the women and children). This oversight seriously pissed off the Lord of Hosts, who, when he tells you he wants some asses slain, expects those asses to be slain. Later in the chapter Samuel lets Saul know how the Lord of Hosts feels about the situation.

"Rebellion is like the sin of divination, and defiance, like the sin of idolatry. Because you rejected the Lord's command, He has rejected you as King."

"I did wrong to transgress the Lord's command and your instructions," Saul admits sheepishly, *"but I was afraid of the troops and I yielded to them. Please, forgive my offense and come back with me, and I will bow low to the Lord. But Samuel said to Saul, I will not go back with you, for you have rejected the Lord's command, and the Lord has rejected you as King over Israel."*

At this point, Samuel, the divinely inspired prophet of God, pulls the lone surviving Amalekite, King Agag, out from where he is shivering among the shit of the unslain asses, and says to him, *"As your sword has bereaved woman, so shall your mother be bereaved among women."* Samuel, under the inspiration of the Heavenly Father, then hacks Agag into pieces with a sword.

Can anyone look in a mirror and say with a straight face that the same deity is inspiring these two *ethical* systems?

206.

The sermon *par excellence* of the traditional Southern Baptist pastor, before he tucks into a lunch replete with copious amounts of mashed potatoes and greasy poultry, is a description of how bad Hell is going to be for the people who fail to become Born Again Christians.

You would not believe how many ways I heard hellfire vividly described as a child. Seriously. You wouldn't believe me.

Moreover, these often morbidly obese purveyors of morality will not be satisfied unless you know that this very literal fire will burn you eternally without ever causing you to become consumed in the flames. They love to emphasize that the first several million years of brimstone are only the first *second* of eternity. Oh my!

The problem is that this doesn't line up with the Old Testament, which doesn't contain a single mention of an afterlife that involves either eternal punishment or hellfire. Once again, these two books seem clearly inspired by different deities.

The best the porcine pastors can respond to this obvious divergence between the testaments is that the Old Testament occasionally mentions an afterlife referred to as *Sheol*. However it is clear from context that *Sheol* simply means afterlife, or at best, the resting place of the dead. It can *in no way* be semantically stretched to mean a place of eternal torment and literal fire. Some of the more disingenuous pastors might reference *Gehinnom*, which was a garbage dump outside Jerusalem. But even with an attempt to stretch biblical mention of that garbage dump into a place of punishment (and indeed, being stuck in a garbage dump would be horrific) there is not a single source in the Old Testament for the notion that there exists a location, either literal or metaphorical, constructed of eternally burning fire, where the wicked go when they die.

It is, however, a very effective innovation for keeping the commoners in line.

207.

The Evangelicals are fond of discussing this terribly frightening fellow who goes about dressed in red, and who seems to have a penchant for roaring like a lion. He may have horns and a pointed tail—I'm not sure. They call him Satan, or the Devil, and attribute to him every form of malevolence imaginable. He is all over the New Testament, getting into people's minds and causing pain and chaos. He thrice tempts Jesus—which is interesting if you ever stop to consider how it would be possible to tempt an *omniscient* being. He controls hordes of evil minions and lackeys. He is a seriously bad dude. Watch out.

The problem is that he is not mentioned in the Pentateuch at all. (Nowhere in the Old Testament does it state that the serpent in the Garden of Eden is Satan.) The Hebrew word *satan*, virtually everywhere it is used in the Old Testament, means nothing more than *accuser* or *adversary*. It is regularly used in reference to literal, human, male characters throughout the Old Testament.

It is used in only two locations in the entirety of the Old Testament to refer to a non-human metaphysical entity—in the book of Job, and in Zechariah 3—and in both of those locations Satan is portrayed as a prosecutor (an allegorical personification of *accusation*) before the divine court of God. He is certainly not portrayed in any way as the Prince of Darkness, leader of a Heavenly rebellion, captain of a third of all the angels ever created, or even as a necessarily evil entity. These attributes are creative inventions of New Testament authors.

Even the name Lucifer, a Latinized form of the euphemism *heylel-ben-shachar*, or, *shining son of the morning*, found in Isaiah 14, is, in the context of the chapter, clearly referring to a man, as Isaiah calls the subject under discussion *ha-ish*, which in Hebrew means *the man*, demonstrating that we are definitely talking about a human being. The passage, throughout Jewish history, was understood to refer, not to some monstrous metaphysical master of all evil, but rather to the rebellious antagonist of Genesis, Nimrod. Likewise, throughout Jewish history, the snake in the Garden of Eden, as well as the Satan in the books of Job and Zechariah, was understood allegorically—not as a literal being looking to infest your body and home with his minions.

The notion of the Devil, like eternal Hell, has served as an excellent tool for controlling the Third Estate.

208.

Again, in Matthew 5:17-18, Jesus creates trouble for himself.

"Think not that I am come to destroy the law, or the prophets: I am not come to destroy, but to fulfill. For verily I say unto you, till heaven and earth pass, one jot or one tittle shall in no wise pass from the law, till all be fulfilled."

Evangelicals interpret this to mean that Jesus came to fulfill the Law of Moses in its entirety. Unfortunately there were a large number of commandments that he either did not perform, or transgressed completely. As they would be too numerous to mention, let me proceed simply, and note that Jesus failed to perform, what was at that time, and is even today, considered by Jews the very first commandment of the Torah, which, listed in Genesis 1:28, is the commandment to procreate. Jesus, so far as I know, failed to procreate.

A sneaky apologist will claim that this command was given specifically and only to Adam and Eve. However, as they represented the totality of humanity at the time the command was given, it was universally recognized by the Jews that this was a commandment incumbent on all Jewish males. So did Jesus fulfill the Torah? No. He did not even fulfill its first commandment.

And not to completely embarrass the Christians, but the Apostle Paul grossly complicates the matter in Ephesians 2:15, when he eructs with the rather surprising statement that Jesus *did* completely abolish the Law, along with all of its commandments and ordinances.

Oops!

209.

Luke 2:2 says that Jesus was born during the census taken while Quirinius was governor of Syria. We know from a variety of historical documents that this occurred in 6 CE. Matthew 2:1 says that Jesus was born during the reign of Herod the Great, who died, ten years before, in 4 BCE. This leaves at least a decade discrepancy between the two *inerrant* Gospel writers as to when Jesus was born.

Oops!

210.

In Luke 2:1 the *inerrant* Gospel writer claims that the census which took place under Quirinius (in 6 CE) was ordered by Caesar Augustus, and that this was part of a larger census of the entire Roman Empire. However, we know, from a variety of historical sources, that Augustus only ordered a general census in 28 BCE, 8 BCE, and 14 CE.

Oops!

211.

Both Matthew and Luke misinterpret Micah 5:1-3, which states that the Messiah will come out of *Beit-Lechem-Ephrata*. In the contemporary world these are the two neighboring Judean West Bank towns of Bethlehem and Efrat. It seems that both Matthew and Luke had trouble reading Hebrew, for the verse seems to plainly assert no more than that the Messiah would be a descendent of the clan of the tribe of Judah from which King David emerged, a clan originating in the villages of Bethlehem and Efrat. Micah, using the common ancient literary device of referring to a family or clan by their area of geographical origin, meant nothing more than that the Messiah must be a descendent of King David. Micah does not in any way say that the Messiah must be literally born in Bethlehem.

However, because the Gospel writers had such poor Hebrew (or worse, they were reading the Old Testament in Greek translation) they assumed that the Messiah must literally be born within the confines of Bethlehem proper, so they had to invent a convoluted story in which Joseph, a resident of Nazareth, which is in the far north of Israel, had to travel to Bethlehem, which is in southern Israel, for a worldwide census that never took place.

Even had Augustus Caesar ordered a worldwide census at this time (which he didn't), there is no historical record of *any* census of the entire Roman Empire in which there was a requirement forcing people to travel to the location of their ancestral heritage—and even had there been, that requirement certainly wouldn't have included the man's very pregnant fiancée.

The very notion of a census travel requirement is bizarre, as it would have mandated the movement of millions of people over an inadequate public transportation infrastructure, and would have massively disrupted the entire Roman economy for many months. Anyone with even the slightest common sense or historical acumen would know that a massive shuffling of the population of the world's largest Empire could never possibly have occurred. The whole *no room in the inn* bit is no more than a complete fiction based on a poor understanding of Hebrew.

Oops!

212.

The Gospel of Matthew lists forty generations from Abraham the Patriarch to Joseph, the man who adopted Jesus. The Gospel of Luke lists fifty-five generations from Abraham to Joseph, leaving a fifteen generation, or well more than hundred year, discrepancy between the genealogies in the two *inerrant* Gospels.

Moreover, the genealogies diverge wildly after King David. Inerrant Matthew says that Jesus was descended from Solomon the son of David. Inerrant Luke says that Jesus was descended from Nathan the son of David. Since Luke throws in more than a dozen extra generations, you get a queer situation in which Matthew claims Jesus was the adopted son of Joseph, who was the son of a man named Jacob. Luke claims that Jesus was (apparently a couple hundred years later) the adopted son of Joseph, who was son of a man named Heli.

Oops!

213.

Many apologists attempt to explain this eyesore of a genealogical fiasco by stating that Matthew is giving the genealogy for Joseph, while Luke was giving the genealogy for Mary.

That is nonsense.

First, Luke himself does not claim to be doing this. Second, even if Luke was listing the female line, then that would still be entirely erroneous, and pointless. There has never been a single accepted case in the history of Judaism or Jewish Law, now or then, for someone to be able to inherit either the Davidic Kingship, or the Aaronic Priesthood, unless it be through the male line.

Oops!

214.

Luke's bizarre genealogy seems to come out of nowhere. Matthew's genealogy makes some sense, as he is following the list of King David's descendents listed in 1 Chronicles 3:4-19. However, Matthew, for no apparent reason, omits four kings from the genealogical record. Ahaziah, Joash, Amaziah, and Jehoiakim disappear for no clear reason whatsoever. While their addition would help to bridge the generational discrepancy between Matthew and Luke's genealogies, there would still be an enormous number of years separating the two versions of Jesus' ancestry.

Matthew also diverges wildly from the genealogy of David's descendents given in 1 Chronicles when he claims that Jesus is descended from Abihud, the son of Zerubbabel. The problem is that 1 Chronicles says that Zerubbabel had sons named Meshullam and Hananiah, as well as a daughter named Shelomith—however there is no mention of any child or descendent named Abihud. Therefore Matthew too seems to have invented a poor genealogy for Jesus.

Oops!

215.

Apologists sometimes try to gloss over this ridiculous series of outright fabrications by saying that ancient scribes were sometimes known to skip generations when giving genealogies. I would point out to those wily apologists that there is absolutely no reason that anyone should be skipping anything at all when giving what is ostensibly the single most important genealogy that could ever be recorded—moreover one that is supposedly recorded under direct divine inspiration.

However this notion that skipped generations is the solution makes no sense in the case of inerrant Luke, who already has far more listed generations than does Matthew. The case for inerrant Matthew is far worse.

In Matthew 1:17 the Gospel writer makes it clear that he is *not* skipping generations, as he seems to find divine meaning in the fact that there were fourteen generations from David to Jeconiah (when the Jewish nation went into captivity in Babylon), and fourteen generations from Jeconiah to Jesus. Poor Matthew! The man could not even count correctly. He lists only *thirteen* generations from Jeconiah to Jesus.

Further, Matthew fails to mention (because he likely had no idea) that the divine Lord of Hosts, in Jeremiah 22, absolutely and eternally bars any descendent of Jeconiah from assuming the Kingship, providing an additional, unnecessary (but noteworthy) flaw in Matthew's genealogy.

Oops!

216.

Both Matthew and Luke are very keen to have you know that Jesus was born of a virgin named Mary. This has become an integral facet of Christian doctrine. Indeed, with Catholics one might say the focus on Mary's intact hymen has become something of an obsession.

But Matthew and Luke fabricate this story of a virgin birth, and do so for one very important reason. Neither could likely read Hebrew, and they believed, based on Isaiah 7:14, that the messiah *must* be born of a virgin—hence the need for a virgin birth. However, had they been able to read Hebrew, they would have known that Isaiah 7:14, in Hebrew, says that the messiah will be born of an *almah*, which mean nothing more than a young woman, a word that has no connotation of virginity whatsoever. The Hebrew word for virgin, *besulah*, is not used at all.

But Matthew and Luke likely could not read Hebrew, or at least not read it well, and so they were undoubtedly reading Isaiah in the Greek translation known as the Septuagint. The authors of the Septuagint translated *almah* into the Greek word *parthenos*, which *does* have a strong connotation of virginity. Therefore the entire doctrine of the virgin birth is based on nothing more than the ignorance of two Gospel writers who could not read their own Bible in the original language.

It is worth noting that a great many early Christians did not accept the notion of the virgin birth (or the divinity of Jesus), and that neither the Gospel of Mark, the Gospel of John, nor any of the epistles of Paul ever once mention the virgin birth.

Oops!

217.

But I am needlessly giving you argument after argument. In truth, if the fundamentalist Evangelical Christians are correct, and the Bible is the inerrant, divinely inspired, literal word of God Almighty, you would need only a single incontrovertible proof against its authenticity. So now I will share the single proof, which, as that boy still reeling from the trauma of incarceration, permanently cured me of the notion that Christianity could possibly be true. The beauty of the proof is that it is incredibly short and simple, and can be comprehended by even the very young. Here you go:

Christians (and Jews) maintain that it is an absolute necessity that the Messiah be descended from King David through the patrilineal line.

Christians also maintain that Jesus was born of a virgin (and therefore possessed neither father nor patrilineal line).

So the choice is clear. Either Jesus was descended from David in the male line, making him eligible to be the Messiah, or he was born of a virgin. But it is absolutely impossible that both can be true—and therefore one of the two major doctrines of Christianity is necessarily false.

Oops!

218.

I have, from time to time, either from boredom, or simply to remove the sticky emollient of a pernicious Evangelical determined to drown me in the truth of Christ, mentioned the above, thirty-second proof. When I do this a most curious thing occurs.

First, the fundamentalist grows quiet, and perhaps their eyes become a bit crossed. Then they look up at me with a blank look that gradually morphs into a sheepish smile.

"I see you have a good point. I see that quite well," their eyes seem to say. "I know that it's a good point because I am very nearly a genius, and yet even with all my brilliance I can see no way around it. I know that I don't have the answer. But I do know that there are theologians out there, and they must certainly have the answer. So even though I don't know how to respond to you right now, I am quite sure that a perfectly reasonable rejoinder exists—even though I'm aware that what you've said makes perfect sense."

As someone who is descended from those very top theologians, and who had to swallow this metaphysical tripe since before I could walk, let me save you the time (and perhaps the hernia you may suffer the next time you ponder this paradox on the toilet), and tell you that *there is no answer*. I am sorry, but Jesus was a very mortal Jewish carpenter who has been dead some two millennia.

But no, I could tell you this, and I could show you that, and, as the sun set on our lives, none of it would matter. For you Christians do not believe this foolishness because it is *true*. You believe it because you need it, because you cannot imagine life without it, and most importantly, because you simply have nothing with which to replace it. Jesus is comforting. Jesus is soothing. Jesus is a drug. And you are all addicts.

219.

The Episcopal Church, despite falling under the label *Protestant*, might be a different religion than the Southern Baptist Convention, Evangelical Christianity in general, or even the Charismatic *Episcopalian* Christianity I had known in Orlando.

The Episcopalian congregation in Wichita Falls was ecstatic to see me. The denomination is in steep decline in America, and the sight of a youthful newcomer seemed nearly a miracle to the congregants.

The Terrible Beauty of the Evil Man

I found that I was initially enthralled by the liturgy, which, when intoned in solemn unity, seemed a thing of great beauty and power. As Stendhal wrote, let the peasants have a *Te Deum* and a whiff of incense, and the effect will obliterate the reason of hundreds of Liberal editorials.

I went for several months, wondering if everyone I had known really did have it all wrong—if the Bible was never meant to be taken literally, but was rather a text full of symbolic and universal truths.

I pondered this during my trips to that church, and as I stood, and kneeled, and recited prayers in unison with the aged congregants, I realized that I would be forced to confront an obvious question. If the Christian Bible were *in some way* divinely inspired, even if not literally, and was indeed possessed of universal truths, then what exactly were those truth-claims, and, even if I discovered them, would I agree with them?

220.

What I discovered, during my time in the Episcopalian Church, was that Christianity had little to do with Jesus, the Bible, or the metaphysical nature of reality. It seemed that, due to radical epistemological uncertainty, the hierarchy of the church was willing to make few unequivocal metaphysical truth-claims. A good number of the congregants were not even theists, in the sense that I had traditionally understood the word.

However, this is not to say that the Episcopalian Church was completely unwilling to make absolute truth-claims. They were. Those claims simply had nothing to do with metaphysics or theology. What became apparent to me in time was that Episcopalians don't really need the Bible, or even Christianity. But it is the Bible and Christianity that form the garment which magnificently clothes the truth-claims they do wish to make—truth-claims which are not theological, but rather which concern *values*. I cannot say what they taught in their seminaries. I only report what I saw in practice.

So far as I understand what it means to be a proper Episcopalian, a good Christian is simply a compassionate Egalitarian, an active proponent of *Social Justice*. You don't need to believe in God.

221.

We exist in a state of confusion. We want power. We desire control. The more we dominate our surroundings *the less we feel fear.*

When we fail to achieve power, whether over ourselves or our surroundings, we experience a loss of life—death begins to claim us. Fear brings the slow death.

We achieve power. We establish control. We experience domination over ourselves, the exhilaration of power over others.

We realize this euphoria at great cost. Power creates hunger. Certain lusts are insatiable.

A man eats continually, only to find himself malnourished, starving.

Fear returns, its tendrils creeping into and corrupting the sturdy brick of our minds. Everything won can be lost. Those subject to us resent us. *Ressentiment* is the ever present swell; the shoreline diminishes. Health declines.

Love mediates between Fear and the Will to Power. It is the only thing which can. Love is not lust. True ardor learns to relinquish furious lust. Lambent desire pleasures, then scalds. It is sacrifice which binds, tendresse that instructs. To love is to grant grace and light.

There is always danger that Love may be corrupted by Fear or the Will to Power. I love him; he may leave me. I love her; I must dominate her to guarantee the continuity of our love. How impossibly delicate to walk the perfect line authentic love requires!

Fear keeps us alive when danger may bring death. The Will to Power prevents stagnation, forces Life ever upward—family becomes tribe, tribe village, village civilization. Civilization permits the radical upward shift in awareness for all men.

We stumble daily in the rough boskage of men. Fear is on our right, the craving for power to our left. Love mediates.

He who never learned to love was never alive. He who forgets, dies.

222.

I have seen those who operate through Power, though in our democratic Age they do so clandestinely—we have forgotten hierarchy. Guilt saw to that.

No, *now* they work through Fear. I have watched them. I have catalogued their tricks. The traditional Christians are blatant, primitive, boring. Hell is coming; are you prepared? The Devil stalks you; have you called on Jesus? I yawn.

Others are more cunning. The lie containing the greatest degree of truth is most effective, most perverse.

There are terrors in the world—great terrors! Men starve. Children are abused. Women are raped. If you have no concern then you have no love in your heart! It is imperative that you commit to action on behalf of the wrongs in the world. It is necessary that, to be a *good* human, you participate in Social Justice.

Indeed, great wrongs do exist in the world. Men do starve. Children are regularly abused. Women, most unfortunately, are raped. In all of these cases energetic action should be taken. When the crooked is made straight Justice is established.

However, the establishment of Justice is not synonymous with *Social Justice*. No humane person on the planet wishes, in even the slightest way, to prevent the establishment of Justice. When we provide Justice we do two things. We show Love, and we ameliorate our Fear that such terrors could occur to us, to ours.

Social Justice, conversely, is concerned neither with Love nor the abolition of Fear. The aim of Social Justice, as the term is used today, is to invert the balance of power in a specific community or Civilization—and as such it is a direct manifestation of the Will to Power. He has hurt me, and has taken what was mine. I hate him. I will take his power. Through a combination of the use of Fear and an appeal to Love, I can create a situation in which *others* will satisfy my Will to Power. How clever!

Certainly Social Justice, in most cases, originally developed from an authentic drive to bring about true Justice—to alleviate reasonable fear, or to show love, that is, to give. How impossibly delicate to walk the line Love requires!

There are two churches in the world today. Beware the righteous, both religious and secular, who admonish you to love by teaching you fear or the hunger for power.

I have seen their tricks.

223.

I left Christianity completely. I became an agnostic. I saw no reason to maintain the pretense of religious belief. I saw no need for the trappings and forms of universal moral truths derived from a book that was flawed, based on illogical premises. If those moral values were worthwhile they could be just as easily derived from common sense and reason, without recourse to metaphysical claptrap.

I still attended the Episcopalian Church occasionally, to prevent my uncle from kicking me out of the house, but more frequently I did not go, skipped and went to a coffee shop, and he turned away, unwilling to risk a grand conflict with his wife, provided I maintained a pretense of belief.

But I was an agnostic. I did not know if there was a God, but I also did not know that there was not. Frankly, I was exhausted by the entire metaphysical marathon I had run over the course of my short life, and was glad to make the attempt to ignore the entire notion of God, angels, and the afterlife.

And, like any young man determined to give no thought to metaphysics or moral truths, I did the one thing I had always really wanted to do free of guilt.

I began to party.

224.

What is a party? There are many types, but when I say "I began to party," I refer to gatherings of decadent American youths doing their best to disable the pre-frontal cortex through the imbibing of a variety of substances, with alcohol the most quotidian, and with sexual congress their most productive ambition.

We shut down our executive functions, and why? For some it is an attempt to *feel*, after a painfully numb adolescence in which a youth's parents and clergy helped to successfully depress every desire to feel any stirring emotion that did not smack of religious devotion or scholastic achievement.

For others, particularly males, it is a prayer for courage. "With this beer my decision-making skills may weaken so greatly that I will attain the bravery necessary to do as my body has always commanded—namely to *fuck*."

Some party to gain a nebulous social acceptance. Adults in ill-fitting pleated khakis refer to this as *peer pressure*. Some of these minivan-drivers are so disingenuous as to suggest that this is the only reason youths party. Bosh. Regardless, I have never spent any significant amount of time with the low self-esteem young people requiring this type of psychological bulwark, and so have nothing useful to say regarding them.

There are many types of partiers, though I will comment on only one more. There are those who go to paralyze, for a few hours, the traumas of their lives. One was touched by a creepy uncle. One has lost a father. One has a verbally abusive mother. One lives in poverty, and will share a single old mattress on a wooden floor with two of his eight siblings after the party.

Here too, I would make a division. One goes to *forget* pain that is ongoing, or perhaps a pain from the past that has penetrated the consciousness so thoroughly that it affects their ability to function efficiently in society. Another goes to derail the continuity of the *vigilant focus* on the pain, so that even though it has not been (because it never can be) forgotten, reality can be experienced for several hours with complete knowledge of the trauma, and yet simultaneously with a dual stream of awareness which both moderately ameliorates the pain, and also provides a gate of perception that allows the conscious mind to target and analyze the trauma from a more primitive place in the psyche. You get Cro-Magnon on your pain.

This is, of course, most dangerous, and likely to lead to violence, particularly among young males, but, if it does not lead to crime, it allows for a relaxation of the vigilant focus, hyperawareness, unceasing analysis—and so provides a catharsis. The computer reboots.

I do not claim that partying is a sound method for approaching these varied issues, but there are several millennia of anecdotal evidence that demonstrate that the repetition of this behavior is doing something worthwhile for young people everywhere. Except Utah. They don't party in Utah.

225.

I remember when, as a small boy, I would beg my grandfather to allow me to accompany him and my grandmother on their daily jogs over the campus in New Orleans. He would occasionally consent, and off we would go. I would keep up for perhaps an eighth or quarter of a mile, and then would collapse, hands on my knees, panting. At that point my grandfather would give me an expression somewhere between a smile and a grimace, and would continue his jog without looking back. It was then that my grandmother would lose her jog for the day, and would sacrifice and walk with me for perhaps another half-mile, so that I might feel as though I had done a "real workout."

I don't believe it crossed my grandfather's mind to cancel his jog, not even once, to spend a half-hour walking and chatting with his eldest grandchild. In fact, the only time in my entire life I recall spending even ten minutes alone with him was when I was fifteen, during our family reunion in Oxford, Mississippi. He told me that my mother had asked him to determine whether I was taking drugs. I wasn't using drugs, so I sat down, curious as to how the interview would proceed.

"Son," he drawled, and then paused, staring at me uncertainly, obviously reticent. "Are you on *the dope?*"

"The *what?*" I nearly shouted, trying to stifle laughter.

"Your mother tells me you might be on the dope. So tell me, son… are you on the dope?"

"No sir, I don't do drugs. I never have."

"Let me tell you," he said, leaning in, his icy blue eyes staring into me, "substances cannot replace the Gospel. When I was a young man I was in a fraternity—Kappa Alpha—but never once in my life have I tasted a drop of liquor, beer, or wine."

"Weren't the others in the fraternity drinking?" I asked, mystified.

"Of course they were!" he snorted with something that, in a normal human being, might have been a chuckle. "But if you have Jesus you don't need a drink. You never will. There's a lot of temptation at your age. The flesh is powerful. You may also be tempted by women."

My thoughts at that moment jumped to the events of the previous evening, when my cousin Sarah Beth, a student at the University of Florida, had kept guard while I had done my best to take the clothes off her sorority sister—a young woman of delectable features who lived with her family in Oxford when not attending the University of Florida. We did not have sex, but I was, so far as I knew, the first fifteen-year-old to ever have a drunken make-out session with a hot sorority starlet. I blushed at the previous night's memory, and my grandfather saw the flush in my cheeks.

"You know, Beau, the lusts of the flesh are perhaps the most serious of all. Both your grandmother and I were virgins on the day of our marriage, and neither of us has ever regretted it. It has contributed tremendously to the stability of our lives."

"I'm sure that's… very rewarding," I mumbled.

At this point, my grandfather, convinced that I was not on drugs, and having successfully delivered a mini-sermon, was ready to be away from me. He briefly asked if I had any thoughts about my future, and, when I told him that many of my teachers thought that I was Ivy League material, he delivered a short homily on the dangers of both the Ivies as well as schools in California. His work done, he departed. That brief interrogation was the longest we would ever spend conversing alone together.

It was only years later, when he scrawled a few short lines to me on the back of my grandmother's monthly family update—his first message to me in the initial eight months of my incarceration—letting me know that he understood what I was going through, that I realized that he would never come to me. I would have to go to him.

So I did. I wrote back to him, from that rehab in Orlando, and told him how I felt about him—something I doubt anyone had done in decades. The grand theme of my letter was that he had simply never spent any time with me, even when I was staying in his home, and he could have used a companion for activities he truly enjoyed, such as golfing or hunting.

His meager response (and at least he did bother to write back) was that golfing and hunting were things that a father, rather than a grandfather, should teach their son, even though he knew my father, a tennis fanatic, detested both. Throughout his life he never once took me golfing, hunting, fishing, or threw a ball around the yard with me. No, we never once even played checkers or a card game together.

The truth is that he simply had no use for me, his eldest grandchild. And I was not the only one. I lived half a week in his home as a child, while my father completed his doctorate at the seminary in New Orleans, and then I was in close proximity to him at all holidays and major family gatherings. Though he was fond of the occasional wry joke, I cannot recall him ever demonstrating any manifest love to anyone other than my grandmother. He was an intensely cold, private man—a Christian without love. I once heard him described, by a Southern Baptist psychologist who knew him, as one of the most emotionally constipated men he had ever known.

But I do not believe that psychologist understood my grandfather at all. I think my grandfather was intensely self-aware. I'm just not sure he liked people very much. He certainly didn't care for noisy children. Love, as he saw it, was not love as I, or I daresay most people, understand it. Love for him was a form a duty—and that is exactly why he could live a life of the most rigid discipline without complaint. Had he been born a millennium earlier he could easily have been an ascetic hermit. He didn't need a drink, any interference whatsoever with a daily jog, an outside sexual liaison, or even a few moments alone with a grandchild. He wanted, and needed, and truly believed in nothing more than the duty of bearing the cross of Christ. I would not venture to guess whether he was ever happy, apart from his time alone with my grandmother (for it was clear that they were deeply in love), though I am certain he felt fulfilled. He was a soldier, in the truest sense—a cold, efficient commando of Christ.

It is helpful to understand him as a rather more affluent and less intelligent Kant—duty before all.

226.

But as I renounced Christ completely, and learned to party, I began to suspect why my grandfather, and the other members of my family (which formed a significant portion of the small coterie of Evangelicals who are intelligent, sophisticated theists) were so willing to serve, with their energy, talent, and brains, the rednecks and haute bourgeoisie of the Deep South.

I could never have known, had I not renounced all forms of Christianity, including variants such as Satanism, what lay beyond the wall of belief. But it was in the parties that I learned what a man has left after God, and I understood why so many of the highest men sacrificed themselves to what they must surely have suspected was false. It is clear that the commoners require their Jesus-drug, but it is in nowise obvious why the brilliant should seek the same high. Partying taught me what I should have guessed.

The walls of Christianity, shaken by many historical phenomena, began to truly collapse with Descartes, and that collapse only gained momentum with Voltaire, the Tübingen School, von Harnack, Darwin, and Thomas Henry Huxley, among others. Then there were those whom we suspect certainly knew Christianity was false, but prudently kept their mouths shut. Perhaps Goethe was such a one.

227.

The most interesting historical cases are those highest men who ought to have known better, and probably did, and yet fought until their deaths to keep from acknowledging what they suspected. Of all such men I can think of none greater, none higher, none more worthy than Pascal—a truly profound man. His *oeuvre*, a product of the distant seventeenth century, pierces me even today. And it is precisely the Pascals (the Plantingas) who will go to the greatest lengths, and develop the most prescient arguments, to avoid having to look beyond the protective *Wall* of Christianity. We need only the *Pensées*.

"What shall man do in this state? Shall he doubt everything? Shall he doubt whether he is awake, whether he is being pinched, or whether he is being burned? Shall he doubt whether he doubts? Shall he doubt whether he exists?"

How beautiful! He understands every consequence implied in Descartes as it is mouthed, and anticipates much in Kant. I cannot help but continue to drink from this perfect cask of Christianity. I am drunk on him. He has seen the Wall (demarcating the phenomenal and the noumenal), and, in an inability to face what may lie beyond (particularly if nothing lies beyond), forces you to admit that if you move from revelation and Tradition you may well find that you know *nothing at all.*

Aldous Huxley described Pascal perfectly in saying that "all his writings are invitations to the world to come and commit suicide. It is the triumph of principle and consistency." But what did Huxley mean? He understood that Pascal's Christianity is full of Fear, and that fear was appropriate, for Pascal truly understood the consequences of *awareness beyond the rule.*

He knew exactly what lay beyond the rivers of submission, the catalysts allowing one to gracefully admit an absence of control (for to submit is but to follow a rule), and it was that knowledge that mandated fear. His fear provoked anger at those who would finger the breaches in the Wall. "It will be one of the confusions of the damned to see that they are condemned by their own reason, by which they claimed to condemn the Christian religion."

But I believe Blaise knew the truth. He, very much as an aside, admitted the true *psychological* problem. "Without Jesus Christ the world would not exist; for it should needs be either that it would be destroyed or be a hell."

I know Pascal. I know everything he says. I *know* what he means. I lived in his horror and nausea and emerged from it only with fear and trembling. I know, painfully, too well, dear friends, that to leave the Garden of Christ is terrifying. The problem is not one of Truth. The problem is psychological.

Beyond the Walls of the Garden lies nihilism.

228.

There is a strange argument at play: If someone did not create me, then my existence cannot have meaning. Subconsciously: I strongly *desire* to have meaning. Consciously: Someone must have created me.

229.

The Agnostic says, "I cannot *know* a deity created me—therefore my life is lived as though no deity has created me."

We admit that the last two thousand years have been lived in the darkness, that we have pretended the sun shone. Now we light a candle, though that candle sheds no light.

Humanity begins to fumble, to attempt to create alternate meaning. Alas, every attempt at alternate meaning has simply been an attempt to recreate the exact moral commands of the deity we discarded!

230.

For success we must look to our Past. We must *remember* existence before Christ, before the morality of the carpenter. There are two roads—one leads to Athens, the other to Jerusalem.

231.

My new uncle had a son from a previous marriage. He was an unintelligent nobody steadily travelling nowhere, but had the positive characteristic of applying great focus to his physical development. He lifted weights daily, and imbibed such a plethora of supplements and pills that I became concerned for his liver and kidneys. At some point his weightlifting took on such an extraordinary proportion of his life that, even though he was shorter than me, and of a smaller frame, he began to carry considerably more muscle. Persons who have spent significant amounts of time in weight rooms know the type I am describing—poor bone structure, sallow skin, discolored veins running across bulging muscles. In short, he would have made an excellent advert for the ill effects of dysgenic breeding and excessive chemical consumption.

I have always found it worrisome when forced to exist in close proximity to those who are both witless and freakishly strong, but, nevertheless, he had moved in with us, and was living in the next room, so I attempted to befriend him. I asked him out to play billiards.

The Terrible Beauty of the Evil Man

We went to the pool hall, where we found that we were easily the two largest men. We racked the balls and began to play. We didn't have much to say, so we sipped our beers and turned toward our own thoughts. I thought about an essay I was reading by Camus; he thought deeply about whether he should leave an additional shirt button open.

After some moments a young woman entered the establishment, and was, as evidenced by her state of dress, and the manner in which she scanned the room, in urgent need of a sperm donor. She quickly migrated to our table, and attempted to engage us.

Her conversation was light, humorous, and coherent. I remained reserved, and kept my comments brief and witty. My new uncle's son, by contrast, was barely able to speak. What gurgling that did emerge was difficult to decipher. Yet I noticed something terribly interesting. This woman wasn't listening to anything we were saying. She was observing us as physical specimens. And she did not have the desire to gauge anything other than (what she saw as) raw masculinity. He was a physiognomic nightmare, with reddish acne and beady eyes. But none of that mattered. I was, through the sliver of material posing as her top, able to watch her nipples harden as her eyes ingurgitated his swollen biceps and the impenetrable torso shifting under a shirt that had far too few buttons closed.

"Ah!" I thought. "*This* is what it will be now. This will be life after Christianity! We will all drink. We will all fuck. And we will all be animals. The only thing that will matter is which of us is most brutish. Everything will be instinct."

232.

My brother Andrew came to live with me, with my aunt and uncle. He and my mother no longer got on very well. I believe there were a number of incidents, though I rarely spoke to my mother, so I know of only one specifically.

It occurred on a trip back from visiting her parents in Wichita Falls, Texas, to where she still lived in the Deep South. After leaving Wichita Falls she simply decided that she had had enough of my brother, and dumped him, with his luggage, on the side of the road. He was at that point, I assume, meant to somehow find his way, perhaps by hitchhiking, the hundreds of miles back home to the Deep South. I believe he was eighteen years old.

I was shocked when I learned that my mother had abandoned my brother. Formerly, when I was in high school at Morgan, she would occasionally dump me on the side of the road and force me to hitchhike home, but then we lived less than a dozen miles from Selma. This new abandonment made sense to me, according to the logic of her madness, but it was still a radical escalation. Regardless, I soon had a brother, and was no longer the only abandoned child.

One positive event occurred as a result of that travesty. I had saved several thousands from work since my release from prison, but was still a couple thousand short of what I would need to buy a reliable automobile. No relative was willing to help me financially, nor even willing to cosign on a small loan for me. With my brother there, and soon employed, I had a cosigner, and was able to get a loan for the last couple thousand I needed for my first truck. I quickly paid back the loan, and was the proud owner of a Ford F-150.

233.

With the loss of Christianity, and it was a *loss*, not something lightly shrugged from the shoulder, came the dissolution of the entire structure that composed my understanding of reality. This loss was superimposed over the collapse of my family and the trauma of reemergence into society. I had attempted to lose Christianity earlier in adolescence, due to terrible pain, but there was nothing to resemble the finality that came with the total break that was complete by the time I was nineteen. That loss formed an entirely different type of pain, and I was wholly unprepared for it.

I have but thirty years, and may still be too young, as I write these words, to have married, but it seems that my loss was not unlike the accounts of those who have divorced after marriages lasting many years. You would think the divorce a relief after the years of struggle and fight. But no. It is a tearing away, a devastation. Truly, you no longer engage in constant warfare and misery, but in the absence of conflict there is only a mortifying amputation.

But what could I have done? Could I have answered as did Thetis? In the *Iliad* Iris calls to Thetis.

"Rise, Thetis. Zeus, whose purposes are infinite, calls you."

"What does He, the great God, want with me?" Thetis asks. "I am ashamed to mingle with the immortals, and my heart is confused with sorrow. But I will go. There can be no vain word if He says it."

No, I could not have replied as did Thetis. I had no such faith. I would have spoken as did her son, Achilles, in his reply to the entreaty of Odysseus.

"The man who has done nothing dies just as does the one who has done much. *I have won nothing*, despite the many afflictions of my heart for setting it eternally on battle."

And I, Finis Leavell Beauchamp, for all my battles, had won nothing.

234.

The serpent said to take the fruit. The fruit was Truth. The Truth led to death. Today there are no truths but those manifold anaesthetizing comforts founded upon money and *contracts*. Who will die for Truth in the Age of Capitalism? That would be… unprofitable. We all decay, die in this Age, but we do not like to think of it, for we are numb, and our Spirits have atrophied.

Allan Bloom once remarked, in a critique of Rawls, how myopic it is to dismiss the notion that there will not again be men willing to die, and to kill, for Truth, as they were in the Age of the Wars of Religion. Bloom, in this matter, sees as does the eagle—that which is yet at a distance. Rawls saw nothing. Bloom rightly suspected that Nietzsche would have suggested a more appropriate title for Rawls' work—*A First Philosophy for the Last Man*. Today the anesthesia mediates between the untruths we suspect and the instincts we fear.

This state of affairs will end.

235.

The Blessed John of Ruysbroeck spoke of the movement of God much as we speak of the motion of the tides, saying that, "God is a Sea that ebbs and flows, pouring without ceasing into all His beloved according to the need and merits of each, and ebbing back again…."

For a long time I sensed truth in that, for it seemed that the presence, or sensation, of *Jesus*, would ebb and flow—though there was no rhythm to the movement, and the painful untruths that smothered me alternated absurdly and unpredictably with the inevitable return of the flow of goodness and structure and inexplicable comfort that I also called *Jesus*.

But for me, the Sea had gone eternally dry, and I felt that I was slowly dying.

236.

I lost the ability to function. I did not understand why at the time. I thought I was simply exhausted. In truth, I was attempting to run a brutal course. I would rise at 9 p.m. and endeavor to exercise. Two hours later my shift had started at the hospital, and it did not conclude until 7 a.m. An hour after work I was sitting in a classroom at the University. I finished classes by noon or shortly thereafter, and spent the next few hours attempting to do homework, though on most days that was a wasted attempt. I usually fell asleep at five o'clock in the afternoon, and rose again after four hours for a pathetic attempt at exercise before the start of my shift.

I quickly realized several things. If I intended to become a psychiatrist or neurosurgeon, I could anticipate a schedule like this well into my thirties, as well as a state of relative poverty until that time. I also realized that I didn't enjoy the pre-med curriculum, and found it difficult to imagine trudging through an additional few years of courses I didn't enjoy.

I decided that I did not want to be a doctor. I quit my job at the hospital. I ceased to regularly attend classes at the University. I quit studying. My partying grew reckless. Again, I had lost the ability to function. I thought it was exhaustion. In retrospect, I was but a couple of years from my last day of class at Morgan Academy, and though I would never, could never, have admitted it, I had in no way healed from the torments I had endured since that time.

237.

Time and Fate will force from you the truths you will not face. In that you have no choice. The wounded man may pretend he can run, but will only be able to do so briefly. The realization that I was not wounded, but totally broken, came abruptly.

I was coming home from a party. It wasn't a terribly exciting party, or I wouldn't have left sober enough to think I could drive. But I did think I could drive, and left the party with a young woman (a non-minor) in the passenger seat next to me.

I drove slowly and carefully through the streets of Wichita Falls, making my way to the young woman's residence, where, I assumed, we would engage in sexual pyrotechnics.

She didn't intend to wait that long.

The Terrible Beauty of the Evil Man

As I was driving she unzipped my pants. This excited me, and I unconsciously pressed down on the accelerator. She pulled forth my erect penis and lowered her mouth onto it. I closed my eyes and winced with pleasure. I opened my eyes and realized that a traffic light fifty meters in the distance was already yellow. I figured I could make it, and did. Sirens suddenly sounded behind me.

I was in the municipal limits, and was not speeding, so the police unit was behind me almost immediately—fast enough to notice a young woman appear in the passenger seat.

The sight of policemen coming towards me, to this day, provokes trepidation, though at that time, so soon after my incarceration, those feelings were far stronger. I took several deep breaths to still my trembling hands. The officer stepped out of his car and walked toward mine. I rolled down the window. The officer peered into the window, a grin on his face, attempting to see the face of the girl.

"Looks like you rolled through that light, bud."

"I'm sorry, officer. I thought I had the yellow light."

The officer sniffed loudly.

"Son, have you had anything to drink tonight?"

"No, sir. The young lady has, but I haven't been drinking. Just driving her home."

"Well I'm going to need you to hand me your ID, and step out of the car."

I stepped out of the car, trembling, face down, in a state well beyond any normal sense of what is meant by the word *panic*. I was certain that at any moment he would realize that I needed to be taken back to prison in Hale County, Alabama. I kept my face down as the officer looked at my driver's license.

"I don't know if the girl's been drinking, but you smell like alcohol. I'm going to have to call in a breathalyzer."

"I told you I haven't been drinking," I said in a steely voice. I knew that if the officer gave me a breathalyzer I would fail, even with any alcohol in my bloodstream at all, as I was not yet twenty-one.

"Let me see your eyes, son."

I slowly raised my gaze and met his eyes. Hatred poured out from me, and I have no doubt that it was palpable and shocking to him. Briefly, very briefly, I thought seriously that I might take him to the ground and begin choking him.

"Turn around!" he suddenly shouted. "Turn around and put your hands on the car!"

I stared at him and did not move. He grabbed my shoulder, spun me around, and wrenched one of my arms behind me. He grabbed his cuffs with his other hand. Using the arm he had twisted behind me, he tried to push me onto my automobile. I was six foot two and two hundred and thirty-five pounds. I did not move. He pushed harder, and slammed me into the metal.

With my face in the metal of the auto, and my other arm twisted behind me and cuffed, I let out a primal scream. I felt him jerk away, as though in fear, though, to his credit, he recovered in a fraction of a second and bounced me back into the metal of the auto.

I did not scream from pain. I screamed because, though I did not realize it, I had very nearly broken with reality. I do not know how to describe my sensations at that time other than to compare them to what I have read is experienced by some Vietnam combat veterans who are suddenly shifted into an alternate state of awareness by the sound of an unexpected loud explosion. In just that way the feel of the metal cuffs and metal of the automobile against my face pushed me into a reality in which I really believed that I was going to be taken to jail for the rest of my life. I felt not as though I were in Wichita Falls, but as though I were in Hale County, and that the officer behind me was intent on taking me back to that sky-blue cell, to my view of the catfish pond and lonely tree. I screamed again, and kept screaming.

My very nightmares had come true.

238.

They took me into the lockup and put me in a special room where several officers watched me carefully. Slowly, as though I were on a couch viewing a character on television, I watched myself slip back into reality. I asked the nearest officer why I was being held in a room rather than a cell, and was told that they were waiting on a nurse. When I asked why they needed a nurse he responded that it was because I had threatened to kill myself, and a nurse was needed to assess my risk for self-harm.

I truly have no memory of threatening to kill myself that night, though I may have said, "I'd rather be dead than get locked up," which, in fairness, I can understand an officer interpreting as a suicide threat.

The nurse arrived shortly and asked me if I wished to harm myself. I responded in the negative. She stared deeply into my eyes. The officers surrounding us were tense. She grabbed my cuffed hands and looked closely at my wrists. She saw the scar on my left wrist, still there from the self-cutting quasi-suicidal misery of my sophomore year of high school in Selma. She took her index finger and rubbed it into the scar.

"How'd you get this?"

"I got it when I was fifteen or sixteen," I replied.

"I didn't ask when you got it. I asked how you got it."

When I remained silent she nodded to the police officers and exited the room. The largest officer stepped in front of me and leaned down. I sat in the chair, cuffed, and bordering on a second departure from reality.

"We're going to have to keep you in a suicide cell tonight," he said. "There's a special uniform for those. We're going to need you to take off your clothes."

I looked around the room. There were male and female guards and they were ready to take me down. I wasn't sure, but I thought I might be able to take them. I have observed that, generally, police who have served more than one year seem to have developed an inexplicable sense that alerts them when they are in the presence of prisoners who have these types of thoughts.

"If you think you want to fight we're going to take you down."

I looked up, met his eyes, felt the hatred pouring from me.

"Then what?" I asked.

As soon as I mouthed that question a couple of the officers unsheathed their clubs, and I knew that I had asked the one question that guaranteed I would lose any possible fight. I slowly nodded my cooperation, stood, and was uncuffed. I blinked back a tear, and took off my clothes in front of the male and female officers. One of the men asked me if I had been arrested before. I told him I had been arrested when I was ten for stealing baseball cards. He wanted to know if I had gotten a Nolan Ryan. I stood there naked, and they all laughed.

239.

They put me in a bizarre garment constructed of a single piece of material, which fastened around the torso and genitalia using only Velcro. Apparently it is impossible to hang oneself with such a garment. They then put me in one of the two suicide cells. Once more, at the age of twenty, I was in solitary confinement. There was nothing in the cell.

I sat on the floor and listened to the screaming coming from the other suicide cell. There was someone in the other cell, separated from me by only a single layer of concrete, and he would not stop screaming. They told me that it was a patient from the North Texas State Hospital, the mental hospital where I had quit work only a month or two before. They had taken him from the intake unit, my old unit, earlier that night, after he had murdered one of the other patients.

So I sat on the floor of that cell all night, unable to sleep, listening to the screams of a murderous madman who, a mere month before, I might have been personally assigned to guard. I had not told the arresting officer I wanted to kill myself, but I had been understood that way. Sitting on the hard floor of that cell in a piece of padded Velcro I realized that I did, in fact, want to die. My thoughts returned to Dorit. Like her, I had no idea who I was, or why I should not choose to die. I knew no meaningful reason to remain in Life, and no good use to make of it should I stay.

I too was Broken.

240.

Which of you, my dear friends, has sat awake through the night, a prisoner terrified of confinement, an unbeliever desperately longing for Belief, listening to the unending cries of a murderer? I could only stagger, deformed and febriculose, the lost man.

241.

Bail was posted, I was released, and I was again before a judge. This time things worked in my favor. I pled guilty to reckless driving, and suffered no greater penalty than a fine.

As I stumbled through the next few weeks I found that I kept searching for something that wasn't there, as does the amputee after the operation, never realizing that what is missing is no wallet or watch, but a limb of the body.

I had wanted, very much, in those first months of agnosticism, in those first hours free of the carpenter's wood block, to simply enjoy *Being*, to relax and release all metaphysical worries. I never thought I would find myself so ill, so broken, that a single triggering of the memory of my life's greatest nightmare would bring me to complete paralysis.

So I stumbled, wandered, searching for something that wasn't there, or lost in the blindness of amnesia, struggling to remember. It took some time, but I realized that I now lacked one of the few things Christianity had truly provided. I no longer had the consolation of any grand meaning, any divine purpose. I had wanted only to engage in *Being*, but found Partying an utterly insufficient reason to *Be* at all.

I had read Camus' *Le Mythe de Sisyphe*, in which, in the first line of the book, he notes that the only real philosophical problem remaining is that of suicide. After the death of God, I had to attempt, as did Camus, to find some way to justify continued daily existence. To go on living because it is expected, is what everyone else is doing, is what your instinct tells you to do, can be no sufficient reason for a man disgusted by even the thought of active self-deception.

In my first turn, after Christianity, I read the Existentialists, who seemed to understand my sudden drowning in the absurd meaninglessness of existence, the nausea that evoked. However, once that nihilism was fully conceptualized and accepted, then continued meditation on the writings exploring the psychological sensations inside that anarchic vacuum became morbid, the stuff of decay, and I recognized the need to turn to a very different type of philosopher. I needed to understand the architecture of reality. Without blueprints accurately mapping time, space, consciousness, meaning, and truth, it would never become possible to pursue existential meaning, and I might very well perish of merely *Being*.

242.

I began to search through stacks of musty tomes, from the Midwestern State University library, that I believed had not been opened, in many cases, for some decades. I needed to try, first, to discover such very basic things as how the world had come to be, if it was not, as the young-earth creationists claim, created some six thousand years ago, in six days flat.

I needed, therefore, to reconcile competing truth-claims, such as those of the atheists who referred to the Big Bang and the various mechanical principles of physics, and left it at that, and those more sophisticated theists, who, in varied forms of the Cosmological Argument, claimed that the Big Bang couldn't be all there was, that there must have been an original cause, or creator.

I was still only a boy, not even old enough to buy a beer, but I figured, with gross arrogance, that I was the smartest person I had ever known, and that both the earlier contrasting claims, as well as the derivative arguments and truth-claims to which I would be led in time, were no more than so many pieces of the greatest of all puzzles. I was certain that I could discover Truth from an armchair. And I smiled, for I knew that Reason would see me through where Faith and Revelation had failed. My great nausea dissipated, and I felt that measure of energetic solace experienced by all who believe they labor toward an august and noble end. And this went on for some time.

But then I came to Kant.

243.

In *The Critique of Pure Reason* Kant, in pages of dense argument composed in arid prose, presents a series of four pairs of propositions, each pair comprised of two mutually contradictory, but yet seemingly true, assertions. These four pairs are known as Kant's antinomies.

What do you do when a diminutive Prussian bachelor both proves and disproves that you have free will? How do you respond if it can be shown that there is no valid proof for the existence of God, and yet it can be shown that it is impossible to disprove the existence of God?

Kant wished to demonstrate the futility of attempting to reason one's way to the truth of matters that cannot be known beyond the world of personal sensory experience, the realm he referred to as the world of phenomena. Kant contrasted this realm of experiential phenomena to all those matters concerning which pastors declaim regularly from their pulpits each week, but which cannot be *known*, or arrived at through pure reason, for they lie beyond the realm of phenomena, or sensory experience. Those matters lie in what Kant called the world of noumena, that which is beyond what one can reason or speak about, for one can have no possible sensory experience of them.

When I came to Kant, to his antinomy concerning the existence of God, one thing became clear: I would likely never be able to prove the existence of God, and yet it also seemed that it would be impossible to ever disprove God's existence. This meant that whether I relapsed to theism, or moved further away, to a position of outright atheism, I would in either case be forced to rely on faith.

Initially, this would seem to have locked me into a permanent agnosticism.

244.

Perhaps Kant was another, less passionate, more boring, Pascal. He does not experience the terror of Pascal, but the concern is similar. He does not wish to keep Christ, but needs to retain Christianity without the carpenter. He, too, saw what lay behind the Wall of Christianity, the impossibility of the (undoubtedly ever-present) nausea disbelief would cause, particularly when trying to arrive at any notion of *moral duty*—an intensely important concern to a proper Prussian.

The point is raised in the First Critique, when noting the interest of reason in this philosophical conflict, when compelled to adjudicate between the outcomes that must arise when forced, in practice, to choose to believe one or the other of the contradictory propositions of the antinomy.

"If there is no primordial being distinct from the world, if the world is without beginning and consequently without an Author, if our will is not free, if the soul is divisible and perishable like matter, the ideas and principles of morality lose all validity."

Kant will lead you into a jungle in which nothing beyond experience can be *known* to be true, but yet much beyond experience *must* be true, for without the belief in something beyond the Wall of Christianity we wouldn't know that we have a *moral duty* to avoid masturbation. Bosh!

I had traversed a maze of philosophical argumentation, and at every step in that maze I found signs pointing the other way, telling me to go back, to return to Christianity, even if it was only Christianity without Christ. But I could not do that, for I knew Christianity was a lie, and that I would rather die of withdrawal than return to the drug.

245.

Yet, I reasoned, I could not remain an agnostic, for to live as an agnostic, in my day-to-day life, was to live, practically, as though I had *faith* that there was no God, or, in fine, as though I were a strong atheist. Each day, over the remainder of my life, would practically play out as would the life of any hardened atheist. But Kant had shown me the atheist required just as much faith as did the theist. I had a problem.

I realized that, since either path required a measure of faith, if I continued on as an agnostic, hoping to avoid all faith, I would, by default, have made the decision to place faith in atheism. There was no way to avoid a life of Faith.

Philosophy and Reason had led me to a dead end.

I had come to one essential question. Would I, as a young man, certain of little more than that it would take faith to believe that there was a God, and equal faith to disbelieve, choose to continue my life as a faithless agnostic (which undoubtedly implied a leap of Faith into atheism—insofar as my day-to-day lifestyle would inevitably unfold), or would I choose to believe in the existence of a deity? The decision's radical implications for my everyday life mandated that (as I took the ramifications of the decision seriously) this could be no trivial abstract musing.

Bereft of even the possibility of epistemological certainty, the question became existential. I could have no certain knowledge of the truth, but yet had to make a choice—and that choice would need to provide existential meaning and hope and purpose, a reason to go on living and getting out of the bed each morning. Perhaps I was an accidental and random collection of molecules, floating on a green rock in the black void of space—and nothing I would ever do or say, even theoretically, would attain greater meaning. Clearly, it could never be shown, without recourse to metaphysics, that I was anything more than a temporary reticulation of elemental atoms, and that therefore each of my actions, whether free or pre-determined, was naught but a series of infinitely diverging meaningless possibilities in that grand cosmic accident we know as the garden of consciousness.

If there was no God, and if I was a temporary juxtaposition of atoms aligned at time *t*, then what possible difference could it make if I lived a long and virtuous life filled with hard work and loving acts, or if I rather chose to sell my truck, take the money to Vegas, get smashed on cocaine with whores, and then jump from the top of the Pyramid? Really, can anyone say that there could possibly be any metaphysical difference between those two lives for a convinced atheist? I have yet to see *that* argument in rigorous logical form.

Alternatively I might choose another existential path, also requiring faith, but one in which I chose to exercise belief in the existence of a deity. And if there was a God, in the traditional sense of the omnipotent, perfectly good and benevolent God, then, following from that proposition, I might conclude that I was no accidental collision of sperm and egg, but rather a unique metaphysical entity with a soul beloved of the Lord Almighty, and that I did have hope, and meaning, and purpose, and perhaps the promise of eternal life.

Which of those two paths do you suppose seemed more attractive to a battered twenty-year-old boy?

247.

I knew that Christianity was not true, that the carpenter was neither God nor God's son. However I had chosen to have faith that there *was* a God—to believe that Life held meaning and purpose independent of anything I might choose to make of it, beyond any purely mechanical explanation for reality and existence. But that presented an entirely new problem, one I had never before considered. If there was a God, and said God did not have a son named Jesus, then who exactly was the true deity? There were so many competing claims for the title!

248.

Some religions and gods were easy to discard. I saw no reason to take the pantheon of Hinduism any more seriously than the trove of Olympic gods and goddesses—granted even an awareness of the more sophisticated theological explanations for that glittering assemblage of divinity. Ditto for all forms of polytheism and animism.

Mohammed, Joseph Smith, and Bahá'u'lláh all built upon and multiplied the complex of fallacies first distributed by Jesus and Paul. Sikhism and Jainism struck me as absurd. Buddhism seemed more a philosophy than a Faith, and one that advocated a great turning away from virile Life at that.

Zoroastrianism, of all religions, required more consideration than you might initially suspect. It is an ancient and rational faith, and has far fewer logical problems than the aforementioned religions. It seems inconceivable or unserious to we moderns primarily due to its contemporary obscurity. However, after some consideration I found that I could not accept its core premise of cosmological dualism. I could not accept a religion that posited the existence of an independent metaphysical wellspring of evil and pain that operated at cross-purposes to an omnipotent and perfectly good deity. That would apply whether the being in question was named Shaytan, Lucifer, the Devil, or Ahriman.

My path through the world's religions was wearying, and time-consuming. Moreover it brought me no closer to the unknown deity in whom I had chosen to have faith. I wanted to know God, but I felt sure that none of the world's many religions knew anything of him at all.

249.

It happened in one hour, on a simple, quiet, weekend afternoon. I was sitting in a chair, relaxing, reading the Christian Bible in a rare effluence of nostalgia. I was submerged in the passage where David is chosen by Samuel, under divine inspiration, to become the anointed King of Israel. David would eventually receive a promise from God that his descendants would eternally inherit the monarchy of Israel, and it was from this promise that the messianic ideal, and later the cult of Jesus, took root.

Suddenly, sitting quietly, the afternoon sun streaming through the window and playing on my hair, I was struck by simple inspiration. I realized that *just because Jesus wasn't the Messiah didn't mean that there couldn't still be a Davidic Messiah.* That because the New Testament was riddled with internal contradictions didn't mean the Old Testament was as well. That the New Testament and Old Testament were mutually contradictory on numerous fronts didn't mean the Old Testament couldn't stand alone as its own Bible. Jesus and Paul and the other disciples may have been frauds or charlatans or simply ignorant fisherman caught up in a cult, but that didn't mean that Samuel or Saul or Solomon were anything but men engaged in a divine storyline. Virtually all of the numerous logical problems that had so troubled me with Christianity were eliminated if the New Testament was abandoned. Suddenly I was possessed of a complete monotheism with no Devil, no Hell, no Trinity, no Virgin Birth, no god-man, nothing that I found impossible to believe.

I realized that if I could believe anything at all it would be the Old Testament, and only the Old Testament. My next thought was to wonder if I was the only person in the world who believed that.

250.

Almost as soon as I experienced this initial inspiration I came to a second realization. I remembered that there were other people who believed in nothing more than the Old Testament. They were called *Jews*. And then I recalled that the Jews did have a religion, and that it was called Judaism.

The Terrible Beauty of the Evil Man

It may seem incredible that a young man who had plowed through everything from Sartre to Schopenhauer to Sikhism in a quest to get at some type of metaphysical truth after Christianity would have neglected to investigate Judaism or the Jews. In order to fully explicate this curiosity I must provide context.

First, as a former Evangelical Christian, I had been indoctrinated since infancy with the notion that Judaism *used* to be a religion—but was no longer. Judaism was a *Broken Covenant* that had been firmly supplanted, or repaired, by Christ. I had never once read the Old Testament without seeing it through the lens of the New Testament. It would have been akin to reading the American Constitution without mentally interjecting the Bill of Rights at every stage. It was inconceivable to me that there could still be persons roaming the earth, two millennia after Christ, who believed in the Law of Moses, *and nothing more.*

Second, while it had never been explicitly taught, I had simply imbibed, perhaps in the very air of the South, that the Jews remaining on earth were not members of a religion, but were rather a distinct racial group—similar to Africans or Asians. Though I did not know it at the time, there was sound reason for the assumption that Jews were not properly defined solely as adherents of the religion of Judaism, for the majority of Jews alive today are irreligious, are members of other faiths, or are only marginally attached, and primarily for cultural reasons, to any form of Judaism.

I had never knowingly met a Jew. I still assumed, incorrectly, that Dorit was an Israeli, not a Jew, and that those were distinct categories. One was a nationality, and the other a race. This would be similar to the assumption that any random South African I might meet could be a Zulu, Afrikaner, or a member of any other number of racial or ethnic groups. I did not know that Dorit was a Hebrew name, nor did I know anything of contemporary Israel beyond their half-century of military exploits.

What Jews I *had* seen were those Jews prominent in the American media or entertainment industry. And those persons *did* seem to be of an entirely different race, not in any way connected to Samuel, Saul, or Solomon, and were most certainly unconcerned with anything to do with the Law of Moses.

I wondered if there were any Jews left who still believed their own Bible. I remembered vaguely having heard that there were still rabbis in the world, but I had assumed that they were fringe gurus involved in a cult. I realized that I had no idea what these rabbis might believe about the Bible. I knew nothing of the tenets of Judaism. I did not know what Yom Kippur was, or Rosh Hashanah. I did not know *aleph* or *beis*. The only thing I knew about Judaism, a rumor I heard as a boy, was that Jews didn't eat pork.

I went to the school library. I had to figure out what the Jews believed.

251.

I went to the Midwestern State University library, and found myself in a quagmire. There were many shelves with hundreds of books on all things Jewish. I did not know where I should begin. I walked to the section that dealt with Judaism proper, and even that section contained more volumes than I would be able to read in a year.

I looked up at the ceiling, and then lowered my head and closed my eyes. I prayed the first earnest prayer I had offered up in many months.

"God, if you exist... I mean if you really, truly exist, and if you're the God of the Jews, then please show me which of these books I should read. I don't know what I'm doing."

I pulled a book at random from the shelf before me and walked to the check out. I got home and took a closer look at the slim volume.

I had arrived home with *This Is My God*, an introduction to Judaism by the Pulitzer Prize-winning author, Herman Wouk.

252.

In the short book Wouk does many things. He explains that there are three major streams of Judaism today—Reform, Conservative, and Orthodox. Orthodox Judaism is the Judaism that has existed for thousands of years, the Judaism that strictly adheres to the Torah. Reform and Conservative Judaism are denominations of Judaism that arose out of the challenges to traditional Orthodox Judaism posed by the Enlightenment.

Wouk wrote shortly after World War II, when modernity and the Holocaust had all but destroyed Orthodox Judaism, that is to say, any rigorous devotion to the notion that the Torah is the divinely inspired word of God. At the time the work was published, most observers expected Orthodox Judaism would disappear within a generation.

Wouk wrote both to explicate the religion, as well as to serve as a type of lay-apologist—demonstrating how an intelligent sophisticate can, in the West today, maintain believe in a literal God, inspired Scripture, and absolute moral values. It was almost as an aside that he described the festivals, rituals, and obligations of Orthodox Judaism. His sketch of Jewish history after the time of Jesus was new to me. I knew little of the last two millennia of Jewish history beyond the slaughter of the Holocaust, and the establishment of Israel as a refuge. I had been taught that anything that happened to the Jews after their rejection of Jesus was meant to serve as both a punishment and a warning to those who rejected Christ.

Wouk's urbane take on religion was radical to me. I had never read such a book. I was deeply affected. I remember turning the last page and sitting in silence for perhaps five minutes.

I then decided that I would become an Orthodox Jew.

253.

If we remember our existence before Jesus, who some call the Christ, we see the two roads. One leads to Athens, and the other to Jerusalem. I had attempted to return to Athens, and had fallen, bruised and cut, paralyzed and blind. I had to turn to the other road, an ancient road, well trod even when Rome was young. In order to remember how to *exist* before Christ I turned to Jerusalem.

Book VI

254.

"So I have died," the man mouthed slowly. He looked up at the figure before him, stared into the molten blue eyes. He felt that no matter how long he sat, the stranger before him would neither confirm nor deny that judgment he had passed on his own existence.

The man slipped away, lost in his thoughts, and forgot the motionless stranger before him, forgot the evening garden that enveloped them both. He thought of his wife, or the rivulets of details that ran together to evoke the image of his wife, though he could not remember her name, or what she looked like, or even the very word *wife*. He remembered nothing of the wedding, or the continual rise and fall and resuscitation that is part of every normal marriage. Perhaps then, it is strange to say that he thought of his wife, for in the nothingness he had forgotten all but one thing about her.

He remembered those shivering violet orbs that he could not have named eyes, but which he remembered as the portals to *her*, that other part of him that had been cut away. Those two trembling flames, the eyes of his wife, were only gateways by which they came and went to each other, into each other, into the other halves of themselves.

It was that fragment of remembrance which opened his soul, and the man smiled, for he found that even in nothingness he had retained one thing, one immutable and perfect possession.

He *knew* what it was to cleave to another with all of his heart and mind.

"I have loved!" he said, and sat up straight on the marble bench. He looked, and saw the stranger frowning.

"Have you?"

"Yes, I have! I loved her. I don't remember… it's all dim. But I know it! I know that I loved her. She was like me. We were one."

"So you loved yourself?"

"No, no. Nothing like that. I loved her *in spite* of myself."

"How is that possible?" the stranger asked. "God loves you, and does so without condition, for He is good and perfect, and asks only that you leave this vale of illusion and the pain that comes of your endless striving for Self."

"No," the man replied, standing and staring into the stranger's eyes. "I thought that I was a prisoner here, in this nothingness. But I am not. All of my life may have been reducible to uselessness and frivolity but for this one thing I've acquired. I have acquired Love, and on that I can build a world."

"None truly love but God alone. How can you, Son of Mud, imagine that you know what it is to give in so profound a fashion?"

"I know," the man replied, "that it is not through Fear, nor through Power." The wanderer suddenly laughed aloud. "I know that this is true. I had it. I, we, she and I… acquired it through sacrifice and toil and it became mine—it was ours, hers and mine. We will share it forever. A man may die, but what he has truly acquired cannot."

"Fool!" the stranger hissed. "What can you build in this void? What can you create? You are but animate earth and water! You think one truth, one love, enough to build a world? Do you think yourself God?"

"I am no deity," the man replied, "but I have become God-like." He stared into the stranger's eyes, and for the first time since he had entered the succession of nightmares and illusions he felt free of fear.

"You will fail!" the stranger shrieked, and as he did so the blue of his eyes began to fade, his beard whitened and grew wispy, his powerful frame withered.

"I may," the man admitted. He looked down into the darkness of the maze in which he stood. "The phoenix lives and dies and is reborn, endlessly and forever, from its own ashes."

"A myth!" the stranger croaked.

"All of it was a myth. All was untrue. But if I can take only this one Truth from the life I lived and lost, that will be enough for rebirth."

The man looked up, but the stranger was already gone, and the man knew that he would never return. The man sat down once more on the cool marble bench in that garden which was a maze, and he rubbed his chin thoughtfully, and then, for the first time in his existence, everything seemed very clear.

255.

All die. Few *will* rebirth. The pain is too great. A phoenix must rise from the ash of its own immolation. "No," says the Last Man, "let me die quietly, in my sleep, unaware, numb."

256.

Tear down the house you cannot repair. Tear it down quickly!

257.

"The greatest happiness for the greatest number!" he whispered to me in the darkness. He said that to me, and I struck him in the face and walked away, for I knew that he was riddled with disease, preaching degeneration, the death that comes slowly.

258.

As destructive is the notion that men should regulate their actions by the principle that the greatest good is that which produces the most happiness for the largest number of human mammals, the travesty of thought which proclaims happiness *the* good becomes far more perverse when applied to the individual. If we live in order to be happy, to feel happiness, then we begin to resemble nothing so much as hair— useless, unfeeling, perhaps lustrous, but truly dead.

"I will do what makes me happy!" he declares, only to find that too soon every filament of his being has atrophied from chasing nothing more than *comfort*.

"I shall do what will make me happy in the long run, even if it hurts now," says the more sophisticated degenerate. This is a man who diets all week to binge on the weekend. He spends life as a peasant to make partner, as a slave carting blocks for the pyramid of another. Then, at the end of his life, when he battles arthritis on the coveted private golf course, when his heirs falsely angle for his love in a bid for his estate, does he not look back and know that *happiness* killed him long before death ever could?

259.

Follow the rule, submit, and learn decay. Seek only happiness and find the slow death. Seek greatness and find pain. Die from that pain and choose rebirth. In rebirth there is more pain, but there may be joy everlasting.

260.

I had chosen to end my old life as a Christian, and even my much shorter life as a non-believer. I had chosen to once more take up a life of faith. I had chosen to be reborn a Jew.

But I had a serious problem. I did know a single Jew, and had not, so far as I knew, ever even met one. I opened the Wichita Falls' phonebook, and found one listing for a synagogue. I quickly called the number, but no one answered, and there was no voicemail. I called again, and again, for many days, but never received an answer. I drove by the synagogue many times, but could not find a business hour when somebody was there. It seemed clear that the building was neither derelict nor for sale, so I was unsure how to proceed.

I read more books on Orthodox Judaism, and did research online. I had become aware that Orthodox Jewish males customarily wore what I had always thought of as a *Jew-hat*, a hat I had only seen donned for Jewish weddings in movies. This unusual head covering, known to Jews as a yarmulke, and to Christian prelates as a zucchetto, was apparently meant to be worn by Jewish men not only at weddings, but during all waking hours. And it was through the casual sighting of this strange head covering that I had my first conscious meeting with a Jew.

The Terrible Beauty of the Evil Man

I was sitting on a bench under a tree on the university campus, quietly reading a book about Jews, when I first spotted this rare ethnic bird flying across the lawn. He was wearing a big black yarmulke, sported a beard, and closely resembled the pictures of Orthodox Jews I had seen on the Internet.

"Hey! Hey there!" I yelled, blushing as the knots of students near me turned and stared. However my quarry didn't hear me, so I pursued him quickly over the lawn.

"Hey, hello!" I called again, drawing up next to him. He drew back from me, as though afraid I might hit him, and asked if he could help me.

"I'm sorry if this is a weird question," I began, "but are you a *Jew?*"

"Yes," he replied with a wary nod.

"I'm sorry, but are there more of you? I mean more of you in Wichita Falls," I quickly added, blushing again.

"Are you asking me if there are Jews in Wichita Falls?"

"Yes. I'm sorry. This must seem very strange. I've been calling the synagogue that's listed in the phonebook, and I've driven by the place several times, but can never find anyone there."

"They only meet twice a month—every other Friday night. They won't meet again until the Friday night after next."

"Oh," I said, my face falling. "Well it's just that I really want to learn all that I can about Judaism. I'm going to become Jewish, you see."

"Really?" he asked, eyeing me dubiously.

"Well I want to. I believe in it. I've been reading some books. I want to become Jewish. I'd like to learn everything I can."

"Oh, I see," he said, brightening. "Well in that case maybe I can help you. Would you like to meet up for coffee this week? I may be able to help guide you through some of the basics, and can try to answer any questions you have."

"Would you? That would be amazing!"

We exchanged numbers and set up a time to sit down over coffee and discuss Judaism. I went home to study for the meeting, and to compose a list of my most pressing questions. I was certain that I wanted to be Jewish, but there was so much I did not know, particularly those things that cannot be gleaned from books, such as what Jews are really like in person. I was excited.

261.

We met for coffee and I pummeled him with a flurry of questions. He did seem knowledgeable, at least to a neophyte, and I was able to refine my inchoate ideas about Jewish practice and daily life. After some time, and several cups of coffee, I excused myself in order to use the restroom.

I had just ambled up to the urinal at the far left of a row of standing urinals, my mind humming with the trove of new information, when my new friend entered the bathroom. But then he, unexpectedly, chose the standing urinal next to mine, from among the several others that were unoccupied, and kept up the chatter of our conversation as though we were still at the table.

Every man knows the unspoken code of the restroom. You do not take the standing urinal immediately next to another man, even if that man is your best friend, unless it is the only unoccupied urinal in the bathroom.

I glanced at this Jew with my peripheral vision and noticed that his face was fully turned towards me as he urinated. I gulped, finished, and quickly returned to the table. When he returned I quickly directed the conversation in a way that might relieve my apprehensions.

"So, from everything I've read on Judaism, the Jewish family is pretty important."

"Yes, that's absolutely true," he agreed.

"So Jews don't believe in marrying non-Jews, right?"

"It's strongly discouraged."

"If you don't mind me asking, how can you hope to get married and start a family if you're living in Wichita Falls? There aren't very many Jews here, and certainly not many young, single Jewish girls."

"Oh that," he said with a chuckle. "That's not something I worry about. You see," he said, leaning forward and looking at me warmly, "I'm gay, so I don't suspect the issue will come up any time soon."

I leaned back in my chair, blushing furiously. In my rush to embrace Orthodox Judaism and learn everything I could about the Faith, I had unwittingly ended up on a gay coffee date.

262.

I was nearing the end of my second semester at Midwestern State University, in the spring of 2003, and was working assiduously to learn as much about Judaism as possible. Initial research on the Internet led me to a cluster of websites designed to serve as introductions to Judaism, the vast majority of which were operated by the Chasidic group known as Chabad, an acronym for the Hebrew words *chochmah*, *binah*, and *daas*, mystical terms that roughly translate as wisdom, understanding, and knowledge.

I felt comfortable learning about Judaism from these Chabad websites, as Herman Wouk had cited the group approvingly in his book, noting that his grandfather had been an adherent of the sect, while also presenting his grandfather as perhaps the most pious and devout Jew he had ever known.

Perhaps the first thing the casual observer will notice when viewing a male member of Chabad is that they do not shave. No, they do not even trim. As theirs was the primary example of Orthodox Judaism I uncovered in my initial research, I assumed that it was forbidden by the Torah for men to shave or trim their facial hair in any way. And so I stopped shaving.

This brought me into immediate conflict with my drill sergeant uncle, who demanded that I shave if I wanted to stay under his roof. I faced a crisis of conscience. Either I could shave, and continue to have a place to live, or I could refuse, and find myself on the streets.

263.

Determining whether or not to shave became the catalyst for telling my family that I was no longer a Christian, and also that I was going to become Jewish. I had moved far down the road of research on Judaism without telling anyone in my family that I was no longer a Christian. I knew that if I told I would be homeless, and that no family member would take me in. I decided to proceed in stages.

First, I had already hinted to my parents, as well as my aunt and uncle, that I had doubts about whether the Bible was literal and inerrant. I later told them that I believed that it probably wasn't literally true. After some time I told them that I thought Christianity probably wasn't even symbolically true. Days later I told them that I did not believe that the doctrines of Christianity were true in any way.

I was gambling, at that point, that none of them would break off contact with me, and that my aunt and uncle wouldn't throw me out, because they would believe that they could simply re-convert me through the efforts of their personal *testimony* and prayer. I was correct about all of them except my mother. Once she learned that I no longer believed in Christianity she broke off all contact with me.

This did not sadden me, as it had been a great many years since I had any emotional relationship with her that did not involve pain or fear. However, she had relocated from Selma, Alabama, to Jackson, Mississippi, after her separation from my father, and I had hoped to maintain a relationship with my youngest brother and sister, who still lived with her. When she broke off with me, she cut me off from them as well. That did sadden me greatly.

However, my aunt and uncle let me stay, and it was only as the battle over my lengthening facial hair escalated that I told them that I was letting it grow because I thought that Judaism might be true. This sent them into a state of shock. My uncle demanded that I recant. I responded by telling him that I was certain that Judaism was true, and moreover, that I intended to convert to Judaism. He demanded that I leave his home. I pled with my aunt, who is a merciful woman—and who was the owner of the house. We worked out a deal that allowed me to stay until the end of the spring semester, at which point I would be forced to find a new place to live. I had no job, and no significant savings. I had nothing but a truck, a few books, and my clothes. I did not know what I was going to do.

264.

My mother had moved from Selma, Alabama, to Jackson, Mississippi, after my parents separated. For the first time since her marriage she was forced to find a job, and no one in Selma would hire her. As she hadn't worked in more than two decades, she was unable to secure employment from anyone but her brother, who owned a successful investment firm in Jackson. The firm specialized in the large-scale financing of church construction.

After my mother moved, my father decided he would also move to Jackson, taking a teaching position there, in order to be close to his other children. But he was alone in Jackson, and did not have a great deal of contact with my siblings even after moving.

So when I asked if I could stay with him for the summer, once my uncle had thrown me out of the house, my father, in a fit of territorialism, and as a means of showing my mother that he had at least one of the children on his side, agreed to let me move in.

I told my father that I was only coming for the summer, and that I would enroll in a new university for the fall, somewhere that I could convert to Judaism, but my father merely rolled his eyes. He didn't take me seriously. He was quite sure I was *going through a phase.*

265.

I spent that summer in Jackson working for the apartment complex where my father lived, painting and repairing the apartments as needed. It reminded me of the summer after my junior year of high school, three years earlier, the brief summer weeks before prison, when I had done the same job in the run-down housing projects of Selma. Those project complexes were overseen by the mayor's son—the same mayor still in office all those decades after he taken part in the destruction of that infamous Selma Civil Rights march.

266.

I decided that I would transfer to the University of Texas at Austin. I still had residency in the state of Texas, and so I would have in-state tuition. I looked online, and saw that the university had a Chabad rabbi, so I knew there would be someone who could perform the conversion. I saved money and got rid of any possessions that wouldn't fit in the bed of my pickup truck.

I did not know what I would find in Austin, but I knew that there were Orthodox Jews and the chance to finish my last three years of college. I drew inspiration from the story of Abraham, who also had no idea what he would find when he left home for the land of Canaan, but believed that he was called to do so, taking the irrevocable step of faith.

I recall the day I left, the day my father finally realized that what I was doing was no joke, no phase, no twenty-year-old's flippancy. I remember the look of disgust in his eyes when he saw the seriousness in mine.

I got into the truck that held everything I owned, with nothing more than a tank of gas, the scant money I had saved over the summer, and a prayer. I left in the morning, and made for Austin.

I looked up and he was staring into me and I do not remember how I came to be in that place. I wished to turn, to stop the inevitable progression of nudity as he removed every layer of artifice with those golden cat eyes, but I was paralyzed.

"I know your name," I mumbled.

"You know my name," he agreed, laughing happily. "We've spoken many times," he added, and as he said it I knew it was true, and that knowledge allowed me to look away from him.

"Fear," I said. "Your name is Fear."

"You remember."

"I remember," I agreed, new terror flowing through me.

"You will not do this," he commanded, jerking my eyes back to his face.

"I have to. I *must* do what I feel is right."

"And what will they say?"

"I can't think about that," I replied, looking away in shame.

"They will say you are an evil man."

"They have said it before. Let them say it again. I will do what I believe to be right. In Austin I will find rebirth."

"Austin?" he asked, laughing loudly, and with horror I realized that Time had become incoherent, the unwoven cords of a rope, poorly spliced, so that I heard myself speaking the words I had just mouthed, as well as the sentences to come, and all of the conversations I would ever have with him interwoven in a great net of impressions.

"How many times have we had this conversation?" I asked, swallowing my nausea.

"We have always been speaking. This conversation will never cease."

"That is a lie," I said.

He looked away from me, and I was able to breathe, and I heard what sounded like the patter of rain against glass in another room. There was an oil lamp on a table between us, and I looked behind him, to his shadow as it played on the wall.

"I will do it. I must do what I believe to be right," I said, reoriented, responding in context, aligned at the axis of conversation and meaning and year in time.

"They will say you are an evil man."

"Do they not already say this?"

"Tell them what you are, and they will know you. They will discover and they will revile. You too lightly place and play with words on page."

"Is it they who say this, or you?" I replied, and as I did I felt him retreat.

"How many times can you blindly leap? How many times will the gods favor you?"

"Is this a tale of favor?"

"Is it not?" he asked, turning back to me.

"How can I know until I have died?"

"You have died before. Did you learn? No. You leap again for the thrill of the fall."

"You are right," I agreed, turning from him. "I have died before. I can die again. I am a fallen man."

"Do you believe this whimsy?"

"Do I jest? Does the man who has died so easily mock death?"

"Zeus, who grants man thought, has decreed that wisdom comes only in suffering. In our sleep, pain we cannot forget drips endlessly against the heart. Against our will, the Gods, by their grace, teach us."

"Do not quote the poets at me!"

"You will listen to nothing else," he said.

"You would save me from catastrophe to die the small death daily," I replied, turning from him.

"We have had this conversation before, and will have it again. It will never cease."

After some moments I turned back, to question him, but he was gone.

268.

I arrived in Austin, and a couple who had been friends with my parents for many years agreed to let me stay with them for a couple of days while I enrolled and secured housing. However, as soon as I arrived I encountered a series of problems.

First, the University of Texas would not let me enroll as a transfer student because I did not have thirty credit hours—one could not qualify as a transfer student unless one entered as a sophomore. I had dropped a four-credit Chemistry course during my first semester of partying and agnosticism and pre-med self-doubt at Midwestern State, and did not have the requisite number of college credits to transfer. I would have to take a semester of courses at the local community college in order to complete the missing credits that would allow me to enter the University of Texas. Undaunted, I made my way to the community college, figuring that a one-semester delay was insignificant when weighed against a task that would forever change my life.

The community college reviewed the Federal financial aid paperwork I had filled out in Jackson, the papers which would allow me to get the Federal funding to pay for the semester's tuition, housing, and food. When I told them that, since the time that I had filled out the paperwork, my younger brother Andrew had unexpectedly decided to begin college that semester, they told me that I would receive more funding if I re-filed the paperwork, noting that I had a sibling also attending college. So I again filled out the forms, only to discover that the new submission would not be processed until after the semester began. I would therefore be forced to find and pay for my own accommodations for at least the first month of school.

I looked diligently, but could not find affordable accommodations close to the campus. I had never before rented an apartment, and was unprepared for the multiple months' rent that all of the landlords demanded up front.

Resolute, I figured I could find an inexpensive hostel or shared apartment room until my funding came in. I needed only faith. I knew that I was there to finish college, but more importantly I was there to become a Jew. I went to the local Chabad house on campus to explain the situation to the rabbi.

I went to the Chabad house several times, but there was never anyone there. I had not wanted to initially explain my situation over the phone, but I finally called the listed Chabad phone number until I reached someone who gave me the rabbi's personal number.

He listened quietly as I explained my abandonment of Christianity, my philosophical search, my decision to become a Jew, my current financial situation. When he had heard all he sighed deeply and informed me that he was sorry for my trouble, but that he did not perform conversions, and if I wanted to convert to Judaism through Chabad I would have to move to New York City. It seemed that performing conversions was a rarified rabbinic specialty, akin to the lawyer who specializes in arcane tax law as opposed to a legal commonality, such as divorce, or the drafting of wills.

I was without housing, without the ability to enroll in school, and most importantly, without a rabbi to convert me. I was lost and broke, and had overstayed my welcome with my parents' old friends. And I had nowhere to go.

269.

I left the home where I was a guest, telling that extremely kind couple that I was fine and had a place to stay—lying to them. I got back into the truck that contained all my worldly goods, and drove aimlessly for several miles. Soon I found myself outside Austin's city limits, alone, and I pulled over on the side of the road. I did not know where to go.

I knew that my uncle would not take me back in Wichita Falls, that my mother wanted nothing to do with me, and that no extended family member would take in an avowed non-Christian. The only person I could hope to call was my father, though as I dialed his number I could think only of the disgust in his eyes as I had driven away.

I explained the situation, begged him to take me back into the apartment I had left only a week before. Almost before I had mouthed the request he began screaming incoherently. It had been years since I had heard him sound so deranged. He was yelling words, but they were nothing I could understand. I began to cry.

"Please!" I shouted, trying to be heard over his screaming. "I don't have anywhere to go. I don't have the money to live anywhere. I just need a little time, a little help!"

And then my father did make sense, for his next two lines were coherent, and are forever burned into my soul.

"I don't care what happens to you!" he screamed. "If you want help go join the Air Force!"

He hung up the phone, and all I could hear was the sound of a dial tone, and the sound of my own sobbing. And I will always remember that moment, for it was the very moment I stopped loving my father, that my love for him was forever destroyed. That was the day my father died to me.

270.

I slowly stopped crying, dried my eyes, and looked up at the empty highway before me. I had to figure out where I was going to spend the night, and, more importantly, where I was going to live. I thought for several moments, and realized that the essential issue was to find someone willing to let me live with them, or even rent me a room, despite my open attempt to become a Jew. Given the people I had known in my two brief decades, that would be no easy task.

I settled on the only close non-Protestant friend I had. My Roman Catholic friend Brian, who I had known since my first move to Wichita Falls as a twelve-year-old, was the only person who likely wouldn't judge me for choosing to leave Christianity. I didn't know what he would say if I called him, but he had been a good friend.

I decided to ask Brian if I could live with him while I enrolled for the new semester in Wichita Falls, got a job, saved money, and looked to move to another location with a university and an Orthodox rabbi who would perform a conversion.

I called Brian and asked if he thought his parents would mind if I moved in with them for a few weeks until I could find more permanent housing back in Wichita Falls. He told me that he was sorry, but he had recently moved out of his parents' home, and into a three-bedroom house with two of his friends.

I felt crushed. I really didn't have anywhere to go. I hung up the phone, and rested my head on the steering wheel of my truck. I took a deep, ragged breath, the kind of breath you have between a good, long cry you've just had, and another you feel approaching.

Two minutes after I had hung up Brian called me back. He had spoken to his two roommates. They had agreed that I could come and live in their garage for a nominal fee.

I smiled, wiped my eyes, and started the ignition. I pulled off the shoulder of the highway and began the long drive back to Wichita Falls. I didn't doubt the God of Israel. I assumed there was simply a better place for me to become Jewish. And I knew that I would keep going, no matter how long it took.

271.

I pulled into my new home near sunset, hungry and tired. I knocked on the door and met my two new roommates. Brian wasn't home. I was shown to the garage. I quickly realized that the garage wasn't insulated. This was a problem, for the temperatures were above one hundred degrees Fahrenheit nearly every day during a Wichita Falls' August. It appeared that the garage was also the home's laundry room and communal storage. I grimaced, and told myself I would survive until I could find something better.

Brian worked for a beer distribution company, as did one of the other roommates. The third roommate worked for a liquor store. When I reentered the home I opened the refrigerator, hoping I could find something with which to make a sandwich. The refrigerator was filled with nothing but beer and a lonely container of mustard. The freezer was stuffed with bottles of hard liquor. I went back out to the garage, my new bedroom, where I had noticed two other refrigerators. I opened them both. They were packed with cases of beer. Between the two refrigerators lay a beer keg.

I suddenly realized that in my spiritual journey I had managed to move into the garage of what might well serve as a frat house.

272.

I signed up for fall classes at Midwestern State, and began to look for a job. Since by then I had a rather ragged beard, and I told all potential employers that I would be unable to work on Saturdays, I found myself groveling for one menial position after another. Employers in the Bible Belt seem to view scraggly bearded young men who won't work on Saturdays with more than mild suspicion.

I finally found employment as a cashier with 7-Eleven—a massive convenience store franchise very comfortable employing bearded non-Christians. Unfortunately the store paid me so little that I was forced to work full-time to pay for my living expenses, and even then was still living from paycheck to paycheck. I realized that I was stuck in the garage, as my new job wouldn't allow me the funds to move to an apartment, or even a room, anywhere else.

As the fall semester wore on, and I spent forty or more hours per week on my feet mindlessly pushing the buttons of a cash register, I realized that I was too tired to both work and study full-time. I dropped down to half-time studies for the semester.

273.

Full-time work alone would not have been sufficient to force me from full-time university attendance. Three other factors significantly depleted my time and energy.

The first was my attempt to learn Hebrew. I knew, based on my Internet research, that to convert to Orthodox Judaism I would be required to fluently read, even if I could not fluently translate, random passages of ancient Hebrew taken from the Bible or the liturgy. I therefore sat down and made flashcards of the Hebrew letters and tried to teach myself to read an ancient Semitic language.

I felt like a fool, or a first-grader, during those early days with my Hebrew flashcards. Those of you who read Hebrew may perhaps understand how dizzy I became while squinting, trying to determine the difference between a *zayin*, a *nun*, and a *vav*, or between a *dalet* and a *raysh*. They looked like nothing so much as tiny squiggles on a page, and the differences between them were infinitesimally small to the eye that had not been trained to their nuance from childhood. Additionally, reading Hebrew is disorienting for the neophyte, as it is not read from left to right, as is English, but rather is read in the opposite direction, from right to left.

Moreover, Hebrew has no vowels, and beginners and children are taught to read the language and pronounce the words using a running series of tiny dot-patterns placed beneath the letters. The little patterns of dots look similar to the raised bumps of Braille. So not only did I have to learn to pronounce and quickly read the squiggles and bars of the all-consonant letters, I had to read an underlying text of dots that told me when and where to insert an invisible vowel, and how that vowel would be pronounced. Essentially you read two lines of text simultaneously.

Compounding the challenge, a number of letters greatly alter their pronunciation due to a second series of dots placed *inside* them. Not to confuse the Hebraically illiterate further, but only some of the letters with that tricky secondary series of dots buried inside their shape changed pronunciation—you had to learn which letters changed pronunciation with a dot inside them and which did not.

Finally, several Hebrew letters change shape completely if they are the last letter of a word. In those early days it could take me the better part of an hour to correctly mouth even a single Hebrew paragraph. It felt as though all my spare time was invested in learning classical Chinese or Vedic Sanskrit.

The second thing that served to drain my time and energy during that fall semester in the sweltering garage was the changing nature of the house in which I lived. A friend of my three roommates decided that he would drop out of Texas Tech University to join the two roommates who worked for the beer distribution company. Suddenly we had three men living in bedrooms, one in the garage, and another on the living room couch. Soon after the fifth man moved in, all three of the guys with bedrooms decided they would have their girlfriends move in with them.

Shortly after my move into the garage I found that I was living in a three-bedroom, one-bathroom home with four other men and three women. Eight people were doing laundry at all hours in my "bedroom," and, once the women moved in, finding a time when the bathroom was unoccupied became tricky.

The third thing that decimated my daily energy level was the simple exhaustion accrued from sleeping without air conditioning during those scorching summer nights. Each night at least one of my seven roommates would have forgotten to do necessary laundry until late at night, and the washer and dryer cycles made the garage even warmer. Entering my room during the daytime for more than a brief moment was impossible, as the temperature in the garage usually exceeded one hundred and ten degrees Fahrenheit. If I was home during the day, or was trying to study my flashcards at night, I was stuck in the living room, with seven other people moving about and conversing.

274.

But when I say that there were seven other people in the home each night I am lying. In truth, there were frequently at least a dozen people in the home each evening. We lived in a cul-de-sac, and each evening, from roughly seven o'clock until at least midnight, that street filled with the pickup trucks of the men and their girlfriends who came to party at our home. Often there were thirty or more people in the house, the backyard, and even my garage, which was opened up, and from which the house speaker system blasted country music and southern rock.

Because each of my male roommates worked in alcohol distribution, our home was always flush with copious amounts of booze, and everyone familiar with our crowd knew it. Further, since there were already eight people in the home, if each of the roommates invited only one friend to hang out for the evening, the entire cul-de-sac would quickly fill with trucks, music, and flowing alcohol. Generally, visitors also brought friends.

I quickly realized that I was in an environment where it would be extremely difficult to become the kind of man I assumed an Orthodox Jew was expected to be.

275.

The most difficult task facing me in preparation for what I was sure was my inevitable conversion to Judaism was not learning Hebrew, but was rather due to my realization, after browsing a number of books and online articles, that Judaism absolutely prohibits men (though strangely not women) from masturbating—ever.

You may have read that last line with a chuckle, but I can assure you, dear friends, that it is almost impossible for a virile twenty-year-old male accustomed to years of regular masturbation to quit the practice entirely. Masturbation produces a significant effect on the movement of dopamine in the brain, and quitting brings withdrawal, which I imagine varies significantly from person to person, but was for me severe.

I could not quit masturbating the first time I tried, or even the fifth, but I kept trying. Each time I tried to quit I quickly became tense and anxious. Within a few days it seemed as though every thought I had was sexual. By the end of a week I was hyper-sensitive to all tactile stimuli—as though my entire epidermis were covered in a light blister. By the end of two weeks I felt as though I was physically trembling all the time, as weak as a baby. In the third week I began to feel nauseous, as though I were going to vomit at any moment, particularly in the night. And during the nights this incredible discomfort was so powerful that I would suffer insomnia.

As difficult as quitting masturbation was, it was made far more painful by three matters of circumstance which were unavoidable. The first was that there were constantly women in the house. My bedroom was the jukebox during the nightly parties, and I could not sleep until the party was over and the garage door closed. Young, lightly-clothed, glistening, inebriated coeds flitted over the property each night under the late summer moon. Even with my unappealing wild-man beard, it was almost impossible to avoid the onslaught of flirtation and sexuality that enveloped us all each night.

Second, my roommates were all great fans of pornography—and their girlfriends seemed to care not at all. There were pornographic magazines all over the house, from the bathroom reading material to the living room magazine rack to the kitchen table. It was my first living experience where I was with neither highly religious family members nor prison guards, and I didn't know how to handle the barrage of carnality. My only previous experiences with porn had been fleeting encounters in the homes of adolescent friends. Moreover, the material these young men had around the home was no soft-core porn, but intensely graphic material.

The Terrible Beauty of the Evil Man

Finally, one of my roommates acquired a live-in girlfriend who had received breast enlargement surgery just before her arrival. This young woman was (politely described) a whore who worked for free. She kept "accidentally" walking out of the shower or bedroom with her towel falling off, or just totally topless. She loved it whenever anyone complimented her new breasts, and would frequently whip them out in front of men in the apartment and ask if they wanted to touch them and compare them to natural breasts. Of course her boyfriend, my roommate, was none too fond of this, and often stormed drunkenly into his room for the night, though he never broke up with her, or kicked her out, for in truth, this histrionic young girl was extremely attractive.

Eventually this young woman found that charming new men with her silicone sensations was no longer stimulating. She turned to finding additional lovers in the home. As the only single men in the apartment were me and the roommate dwelling in the living room, she came after us first. I turned her away easily. Sleeping with a roommate's girlfriend seemed a gross sin, even without Judaism, and, additionally, I had sworn off dating gentiles. My roommate in the living room was not as strong. He succumbed, and in time that action led to the dissolution of the entire home. My other roommate, the cuckold, was devastated when he learned what his girlfriend had done, and she was booted from our house.

I was told that she bought those breasts on credit, and that she eventually defaulted on the payments. I do not believe they were repossessed.

276.

As that late summer turned into early autumn I realized that to control my desire to masturbate, particularly given the environment in which I was submerged, I would need to somehow learn to completely subdue the spontaneous impulses of my central nervous system. Jewish mystics often refer to the sexual instinct as the *yesod*, or *foundation*, and there is much truth in this, for when a man can regulate his sexual desire as easily as he regulates his breathing it is certain that he has achieved a foundational mastery of his Spirit. In order to achieve control in that most basic of my instinctual drives, I understood that I would have to take drastic action.

I arrived independently at a conclusion I would later discover was the common solution for hermits, monks, gurus, and saints of all persuasions who, in ages past, attempted to channel their sexual energy towards spiritual purpose. I began to fast.

The slow starvation of the body provokes an emaciation of the biological drives. Fasting is not synonymous with starvation. Fasting is targeted periods of withdrawal from that which is necessary to sustain Life. When the body is not truly dying, but is only intentionally weakened for finite periods, the less cerebral instinctual rhythms of the body are crippled, and the mind and will must compensate, grow in strength and power. It is in that time of sharpened focus and raw will and physical asthenia that a man may achieve mastery over those passions that had formerly seemed as untameable as a pride of lions.

In short, I began to lose a lot of weight, especially muscle—but I was also able to cease to masturbate.

277.

One of the first things I had to decide, upon moving into that home of girls and porn and inebriation, was where I planned to move so that I could both finish university and convert to Judaism. Further, I had become aware that there was a great debate within Orthodox Judaism as to who was qualified to perform an *authentic* conversion. I knew that I wanted to convert in the most true and authentic manner possible, as I never wanted anyone to be able to question the sincerity of my conversion in years to come.

I found that the vast majority of rabbis listed as able and willing to lead a candidate through the conversion process, and whose conversions were considered above reproach, were living in or near New York City. This gave me pause, as I had never been to the North. I called one of the rabbis on the phone, a man in Queens, and he made it clear that not only would I have to move to a Jewish community to convert, I would have to live within walking distance of the synagogue that I would attend, for on the Jewish Sabbath, no transportation is permissible other than walking. Subways, automobiles, and even bicycles and skateboards, are all prohibited means of travel on the Jewish Sabbath.

I researched housing costs in those Jewish neighborhoods in the North and was astonished at the rental prices for a one-bedroom or even a studio apartment. At my current rate of saving, working at a convenience store, it would take me the better part of a decade to save enough money to move into an Orthodox Jewish neighborhood in any major metropolitan area.

I thought for some time on this problem, as it did represent the most serious obstacle in my attempt to become a Jew. After several days I arrived at a potential solution. There was one rabbi on the list affiliated with a synagogue in Memphis, Tennessee. Memphis was directly on the state line of Mississippi. Both of my parents had relocated to Jackson, Mississippi, and I had lived there the previous summer. The University of Mississippi, in northern Mississippi, was roughly an hour's drive from Memphis. I realized that it might be possible to transfer to the University of Mississippi (Ole Miss) using either of my parents' addresses to get in-state tuition, and then to schedule my classes in such a way that I would be free to drive to Memphis prior to each Sabbath. Once involved in the community there, I was sure I could make the connections necessary to allow me to find accommodations each Sabbath, thereby allowing me to begin the process of conversion.

I called the rabbi in Memphis and explained the situation. He said that in order for him to consider working with me toward conversion he would have to meet and interview me. He invited me to come to Memphis for a Sabbath so that he could evaluate my potential for conversion.

I was excited. Or at least I was excited until I realized that it would take at least two weeks' pay to afford the cost of a single night in a Memphis motel, as well as the round-trip gasoline the pilot trip would necessitate. Saving the salary of even two full weeks' pay, in my impoverished state, would take several months of extremely frugal living. I figured that, since I had cut back on my food intake, I had made a solid start.

278.

In that autumn the heat waned and my spirit waxed, and despite my poverty I was wealthy, for every penny I saved would carry me to Memphis, toward my first meeting with a Jew who had the knowledge and authority to make me Jewish, to give me the power to walk the road back to Jerusalem.

In that autumn it appeared that I was motionless, stuck in place until I could accumulate the funds to move. But that stasis was deceptive, for it is in the still hours that we most frequently traverse the great distances of the soul. As I studied the ancient Hebrew characters and tamed my body and walked alone in that perpetual crowd I found a great calm, a peaceful solitude. With great purpose many burdens weigh little.

With that autumn I began my twenty-first year of life.

279.

Toward autumn's end, when I finally had the money for the trip, I called the rabbi, who told me to be at the synagogue in Memphis for the Sabbath service the following Saturday morning at 8:30. I loaded a small bag with toiletries and my nicest clothes, and drove out into the night, intending to arrive in Memphis in time to change clothes in my truck and go directly to the service.

I drove that entire Friday night, and with each mile my excitement grew, for I knew that in only a few hours I would, for the first time in my life, meet an Orthodox Jew, and not only one, but an entire community. I would attend the service that morning, and then check into a nearby but inexpensive hotel. Saturday night the rabbi would interview me. Sunday I would drive back to Wichita Falls.

I drove for some time around the neighborhood where the synagogue was located without finding it. The building was buried in an extensive residential neighborhood, and everyone I stopped to ask for directions tried to direct me to a larger, better known synagogue about a mile away. I began to panic, thinking that I would be late, that I would be forced to enter the sanctuary after the service had begun, turning heads and creating a negative impression before I had even gotten the chance to interview. I did, however, finally find the synagogue, and hurriedly changed, running up to the door at 8:35.

I entered the synagogue and saw a man standing in the alcove outside the sanctuary adjusting a large, striped, tasseled quilt he was wearing. I approached him and asked if the service had already started, and if not, if he knew where I might find the rabbi. It turned out that the tall, gaunt, middle-aged man I had addressed was the rabbi I had traveled to meet. He introduced himself kindly, said that he was glad to meet me, handed me a prayer book and a Bible, and then entered the sanctuary.

My eyes lit up when I entered. The interior of the synagogue was painted in a palette of bright magenta and blue and purple that shocked the eye and immediately caused one to think that the interior designer had drawn inspiration from a rich mescaline experience. As soon as my eyes adjusted to the wild color I realized that the sanctuary was very large—the size of an auditorium—and that it was empty.

I found a seat in the back and looked around in consternation. The rabbi had descended the steps of the sanctuary, which was constructed in the shape of a shallow bowl, and he had taken a seat at the front. There was a podium in the center of the bowl, and near it were two or three wizened old men.

After a few moments several additional men of aged visage entered the hallucinogenic sanctuary, and began to don the large, tasseled quilts. I realized that I didn't have one of the quilts and wondered where I could get one. Around 8:45 one of the men approached the podium in the center and began chanting. I grew excited at this, as I had never before heard the melody of a Semitic tongue sung. However after only a moment he stopped. He then, every moment or so, barked out a single line of Hebrew. I wondered if the man at the podium was daft, and why the other men hadn't stopped him, and if perhaps the rabbi had meant the service was to start at 9:30.

I had finally arrived at an Orthodox service, and I had no idea what was going on.

280.

As the service progressed people trickled into the sanctuary. After an hour they took out a Torah scroll and began to chant from it, which I found enthralling. Midway through the reading of the scroll two women entered the sanctuary and proceeded to opposite sides of the auditorium. It was then that I noticed the sanctuary seating was trifurcated, and that while the center section had filled up with men, the two side sections, separated by low walls from the center, were for women.

More time passed, and whole families began to arrive. Children ran in the aisles as the chanting continued uninterrupted, and no one seemed to notice. At two points during the service the people stood and swayed back and forth during a strange silent prayer. There was a man seated in my row, and I felt that he must be mentally ill, for while the other men in the congregation swayed back and forth in a slow, slight rhythm, this man was dipping, weaving, and bobbing as though he were a boxer backed into a corner of the ring by a powerful opponent. Moreover, he occasionally let out loud sighs and moans that did not sound entirely asexual.

I began to feel dizzy. The experience was radically unlike an Evangelical Christian service. First, the Jews seemed quite comfortable entering the service at any point they wished. There were, in fact, people arriving more than two hours after the service had begun. Second, children were running amok in the sanctuary, and no adults were taking them outside for corporal punishment. Third, dozens of people were having loud conversations about mundane matters, and none of those who were praying or focused on the service appeared to view this as unusual. Fourth, the traditional Southern Baptist service is, from beginning to end, over in one hour flat—and if it goes on much longer the congregants become disgruntled. This Jewish service had been going on for nearly three hours, and showed no signs of slowing. I kept wondering if it would end, for I had not eaten since a snack in the truck at 4 a.m., and it was drawing close to 11:30.

At 11:45 the service ended, and I was pleased to find that there was snack food, which they called *kiddush*, served after the service. I spoke to the rabbi once more, to confirm that I would meet him for the interview that night, and then drove hastily to the cheap motel. I had not slept in some thirty hours.

281.

I met with the rabbi in his home that night, and he began with a number of arguments about how difficult it was to be a Jew, why I would not enjoy it, how many obligations it would entail, and how the remainder of my life would change radically and forever. Not to be dissuaded, I countered each of his points with a firm assertion of my conviction in the truth of what I had until then referred to as the Old Testament. I told him something of my family background, and my theological struggles and searching.

After some time he told me that he would begin to work with me if I carried out my plan of transferring to Ole Miss and coming to Memphis each Sabbath and Jewish holiday for study and counseling. He would, in effect, function as my sponsor, training me in all things Jewish until I was ready to appear before a Jewish rabbinical court for a conversion hearing. He wanted to know if I would begin at Ole Miss in the coming spring semester. I told him that I currently lacked the funds to do that, but that I would certainly begin by the next fall, and that in the intervening time I would study and learn as much of the material needed to convert as possible.

The Terrible Beauty of the Evil Man

A final matter I raised before leaving, as I knew that it would trouble me eternally if I did not ask, was whether I could be converted even if I had sinned in my previous life, even if those sins were grievous. And it was here that I was thinking about my time as a juvenile felon, as an outcast of my former society. He replied that when one became a Jew, one gained a new soul, and all former matters were forgiven. I smiled wryly. That sounded a lot like being Born Again.

282.

With my return to Wichita Falls I decided that it was important to begin to learn the traditional liturgy and prayers of the Hebrew faith. I knew, from my gay coffee date, that the synagogue in Wichita Falls was not Orthodox, and did not follow the traditional order of prayers. But I felt certain that through a few visits I might pick up enough of the basics to avoid feeling so disoriented when I returned to Memphis.

I began attending the synagogue in Wichita Falls, which met twice a month, and found that while half of the regular attendees weren't Jewish, and the half that were primarily viewed the gatherings as a chance to schmooze over bagels and lox, there was one man, formerly Orthodox, who led the services, and who was able to help tutor me in the basics of the prayer service.

The community was miniscule, and the congregants tended to see it as a cultural venue rather than a house of worship, yet it did, for a time, fill a valuable niche for me.

283.

As that autumn evolved into winter I found that the yarmulke I wore to work was becoming a problem. My specific 7-Eleven was on a major highway that ran through Wichita Falls, and the store was something of a lounge for a number of white supremacist bikers in the area. While I didn't mind dirty looks or the occasional slur, I did worry when a number of them began to make violent threats. Perhaps, though, I can be so honest as to admit that the threats may have been my fault.

There was one day at the store where I had endured the comments of a number of American citizens rather disenchanted with the Jewish grip on both the media and the international banking sector. Why motorcycle-riding neo-Nazis were interested in the intricacies of international finance puzzled me, but I ignored them and continued the mind-numbing punching of the plastic buttons of the cash register.

However, later in that shift a young family, of the upper-middle class yuppie vintage, entered the store to stock up on snacks in what was clearly a cross-country vacation. As I was delivering the change to the head of the home, he took the opportunity to kindly let me know that the Jews could go fuck themselves.

It was at that point in the shift that I detected in myself a certain lassitude. I was not yet even Jewish, the Jews themselves seemed determined to discourage me from conversion, and I was forced to listen to the logorrhea of every passing anti-Semite. I had had enough. I decided to act.

When the next Nazi biker entered the store, perhaps an hour later, I began quizzing him in detailed fashion about each of the (tacky) patches on his worn leather vest. He answered my questions easily enough, and then asked what kind of hat I was wearing.

"Oh, it's just a funny hat," I responded, exceedingly amused to have run into a neo-Nazi who had never seen a yarmulke.

"It's weird," he mumbled.

"That it is," I agreed amiably. "Listen, I like your vest a lot. I think your club sounds pretty cool. Do you think it might be ok if I came out with you guys one time? Maybe I could get a bike and join your gang."

This aristophrenic partisan of National Socialism stared at me, noted my long, untrimmed beard, my broad frame, and decided that I might indeed be the recruit his biker gang needed. It was shortly after that conversation that the neo-Nazis in the area moved from the occasional slur to outright threats of violence. They didn't find me as amusing as I did.

Shortly after this incident I requested a transfer to a store in a different part of town, due to the repeated threats. I was randomly assigned to another 7-Eleven in Wichita Falls, coincidentally located only three blocks from my grandparents' luxury condo.

284.

Not since the final conversation with my father at the beginning of the summer had I spoken to anyone in my immediate or extended family. It was now the beginning of winter, my fall semester at Midwestern State was over, and I was working each day at a location three blocks from where my grandparents lived. I decided that the situation was silly, that my rejection of Christianity shouldn't mean the permanent dissolution of all familial bonds. I determined to pay my grandparents a visit.

My grandparents' condominium, while very nice, was in a poor section of Wichita Falls, and was therefore probably the most secure residential building in town. I was buzzed in the front doors by the security guard who then asked for my name and identification. I found this strange, as I had been a guest many times over the years, and I knew the guard by sight.

"Finis Leavell Beauchamp?"

"Yes?"

"The Leavells have given me instructions not to admit you."

I felt as though I had been punched in the stomach. The guard looked up at me sheepishly and handed back my identification.

"But I'm their oldest grandchild," I mumbled softly, to no one in particular. I turned away quickly, blinking back tears, and rushed from the building.

I could have borne the fact that my grandparents no longer wished to see me, but I was crippled by the shame that came of having to learn of the ban from a stranger. I realized that I no longer had a family. I had been completely cut off.

285.

As that winter wore on my situation became dire. I had extended myself financially with the trip to Memphis, and the store position was insufficient to pay the rent on the garage-room, gasoline, truck insurance, food, and all the host of incidentals that normative life requires. The only area where I could effectively cut back was food. In time, the leftover hot dogs that 7-Eleven failed to sell by the end of each of my shifts became about half of my daily caloric intake. Most nights I made do with a can of chili and a beer—the beer helping my joints to come down from the pleasures of an eight-hour stand at the register.

But hunger and poverty didn't worry me. The cold worried me. Wichita Falls isn't near the Arctic Circle, but it grows cold in the winter, and as I huddled under a pile of blankets in my uninsulated garage, I grew concerned that I would freeze to death one night.

Now, in truth, I wouldn't have frozen, but at that time, hungry and cold, it certainly felt like I might. I couldn't afford to live anywhere else, and could barely afford the nominal rent my roommates charged for the garage. I developed a sincere appreciation for my roommates' need to unexpectedly do loads of laundry late at night. The machines that had been the source of such annoying midnight noise became the only natural heaters in my frigid quarters. I would lie under the blankets each night, and pretend that I was a glorious young cadet, following Napoleon into the Russian winter. Such fantasies ease many difficult hours.

286.

On one of my days off that winter I went to a coffee shop that was conjoined to a bookstore. The pleasures of a book, a journal, and a good cup of coffee have proved one of the great tonics of my life, and have, fortunately, been a pleasure I have never been unable to afford, even in one of my many periods of desperate poverty. Paper and coffee and ink are cheap, and most bookstores are notoriously lax about loitering when young people hang about, reading books for free.

On that particular day I made one of the more unforgettable acquaintances of my youth. I was in line for coffee, and noticed that two spots ahead of me was a short, portly, old man I had seen before at the local synagogue. I had previously failed to draw close to anyone at the Wichita Falls synagogue, perhaps because I felt that I had no future in a non-Orthodox milieu, or because the only congregant my age was a young man who had seen fit to inspect my genitalia at the urinal. Regardless, I decided that I would take the opportunity to approach the aged gentleman and begin a conversation.

He sat down at a table in the café, and I approached him, introduced myself, and asked if I could sit. He smiled and motioned me to the other seat. We began to converse and I quickly learned that he was no native denizen of Wichita Falls, but was rather a New Englander in Texas on a contract work assignment. He was something of an artist, having done some interesting work in film, and that piqued my interest, as I had, during my life in the South, encountered few artistic types of any sort.

I told him that I was not Jewish, but that I planned to begin the conversion process to Orthodox Judaism the following autumn in Memphis. When I continued with a brief sketch of my family history his eyes grew wide, and he appeared both amused and shocked. He asked how my family had taken the news, and I described my current living situation. The news upset him, and he grew thoughtful. He told me that he was only in Wichita Falls for a few more months, but that the period overlapped with the remaining time I planned to be there. He told me that he had a large one-bedroom apartment, but that he only used the actual bedroom, and that the living room was empty. He said that, if I wanted, I was welcome to it. He was willing to let me live there rent-free. I would only need to pay half the utilities.

I couldn't believe my luck. I had found an elderly Jewish man willing to let me live with him rent-free. I wouldn't have to freeze in the night. I would also, as a side benefit, have the opportunity to pick the mind of someone who had been living as a Jew in America since the 1930s. And as I stared at him I was struck by the deep sense that God was watching out for me, that an accidental meeting with an old Jew in a coffee shop had saved me from the torments of winter. He had nothing to offer but the corner of a living room, but that would be enough, for I had few possessions.

I looked into his eyes. I could see that he was a very kind man.

287.

As that winter passed I mourned the loss of my first Christmas, and then soon mourned the loss of university studies, for with my continual poverty I could not afford even the marginal costs, such as textbooks and supplies, needed to begin the new semester. I took solace in my private study of Judaism, which was progressing rapidly. I had an insatiable desire to learn and grow in the knowledge of Torah, Jewish customs, Jewish history, and Jewish law.

And as that winter progressed, slowly becoming spring, I became closer to my new roommate. He was a secular Jew, and had been irreligious since his bar mitzvah in the 1940s, however he agreed to have traditional Friday night Sabbath dinners with me, and even taught me how to make matzo ball soup.

During those Friday night dinners, which were the primary time that I saw him each week, he would regale me with wild tales of his debauched youth. I was astounded at this, as one doesn't expect to hear degenerate tales from a man half a century one's senior, but I assumed that he was merely, through me, attempting to recapture some sense of youth, and so I smiled, humoring him.

As time passed his stories became more perverse, and I began to wonder, as weeks became months, if there was something wrong with him. I couldn't be sure, but it seemed as if *I* was personally triggering something dark and nefarious in his personality. Because of the preponderance of explicit sexual content in his conversation I felt he must be sexually frustrated, and he did mention that he greatly missed the girlfriend he had left back in New England. Indeed, he was lonely on many counts, as he not only missed his girlfriend, but also his children, and even an ex-wife that all lived in the North. Though I felt that the situation was becoming strange, I tried to empathize with the crush of loneliness an older person must feel when cut off from loved ones in a foreign section of the country.

However, this new explicit conversation did create tension, and it did so in conjunction with another matter. This man had done some work in documentary film, though it had been some time since he had completed a major work of documentary art. His fixation on me reached a new level of intensity when he told me that he had chosen me as the subject for his next documentary—specifically focusing on the process of conversion to Orthodox Judaism.

I didn't know how to respond. For me, the decision to convert to Orthodox Judaism was intensely personal and private—a decision reached after much painful reflection and the reevaluation of many deeply held beliefs. I certainly didn't think my private religious journey was the province of a frequently obscene elderly man with a yearning to relive his glory days of documentary film work.

As spring unfolded he grew insistent about this new documentary idea, and nearly demanded that I comply, insisting that I owed him for the accommodations he was providing. Several times he got out his video camera, and was on the verge of turning it on and trying to film without my consent. At those times I simply walked out of the apartment and went for a drive. As time passed I began to return to the apartment only to sleep.

It was as this situation was growing untenable that he decided to take an extended trip to the Northeast to see his family and friends. I thought that this trip might allow him to satisfy his personal needs in such a way that his sexual outbursts would taper off, and his angst concerning his need to engage in an art where I was the only possible subject would be forgotten. The situation was unpleasant. I was partially resigned to it because I knew it would end at the conclusion of the summer, but mostly because I truly had nowhere else to go.

The Terrible Beauty of the Evil Man

288.

There is a time each of us knows well. It is an instant, or an hour, or a creepy slow-churned month spent in the presence of another, in which, without word or deed, that person manages to communicate that there is something irreparably damaged in the permanent makeup of their psyche. It is precisely the intangibility of the communication that often delays its reception. We begin to wonder if our imagination has become over-stimulated, finding patterns in clues that are no more than innocuous glances and gestures. We wonder if we are either very perceptive or suffering the first stroke of paranoia. The gulf between the decadence we suspect and the mere normalcy we can prove is so wide as to appear the shadow of hallucination. Perhaps such gulfs most frequently arise between lovers, as cases of simple jealousy metastasize into relationship-crushing cancers. However there are other cases that involve no simple overgrown jealousy, but indicate true degeneration in the mind of another.

I began to suspect that I was involved in just such a situation. I could not initially imagine how a chubby, old Jewish man could possibly pose any destabilizing effect on me, but as spring ground down winter I came to believe that there was something very wrong with him.

My initial suspicion was that he was sexually lonely, and was perhaps engaged in soliciting prostitutes. He had made a number of references to drugs. My suspicions wandered there next, and I wondered if he was suffering from an addiction. Eventually I assumed that it was I who was delusional. After all, he was already well into his sixties, had a girlfriend, children, a stable job, and numerous other indications that there could be no serious problem.

However when he went back home on his long vacation my suspicions, inflated to paranoia, took hold of me, and I felt I had no choice. I was concerned. I decided to investigate.

289.

By investigate, I mean that I decided to snoop. The anxiety aroused by his imminent return provoked me to action. I could not bear the thought of him hanging about, coughing up lewd chokes, bantering about drugs, thrusting at me with a video camera, without possessing some minimal assurance that he was not deranged.

I went into his room, and shuffled through several of the papers on his desk. I wasn't sure what I was looking for. There was nothing on the desk but mundane paperwork and bills. I looked under his bed. No corpses there. The only other place to look was his closet. I opened his closet and the smell of old man fell out of it and choked me. His clothes were normal. The upper shelves appeared to contain typical oddments and knick-knacks. There was nothing left to inspect but three large plastic cartons on the floor of the closet. I opened the first two and found only additional clothes. Feeling silly, blushing, I nearly got up and walked out. But at the last moment I decided to open the backmost crate. I was, after all, already there.

I opened the crate and found myself confronted with a large stack of magazines. Pornography was not unexpected, but it was the type of porn I encountered that sent the blood to my head. I had found a trove of magazines devoted to the glorification of the young, nude, male form—youths who, in fact, looked creepily like me. I pulled several magazines from the crate, hoping that the youthful, gay porn was only the top magazine or two. But no, his entire pornographic collection consisted of nubile male youths.

I remember the horror of that moment. I pulled a magazine from the pile, wondering, in bewilderment, what could possibly prompt a man with tangible evidence of a lifetime of heterosexual behavior to spend his last erotic hours in the contemplation of naked men half a century his junior. I flipped through the pages of that magazine. It was a series of photos of nude young men doing push-ups and various other gymnastic poses. To this day the title of one of those magazines is chiseled onto my memory—*Hungry Youths: The Youths of Hungary*.

290.

When my elderly roommate returned I thought I was prepared to confront him. I was not, however, prepared for him to confront me. He had returned in a drug-induced whirl, a ball of perpetual motion. He was rapidly repeating his ideas for the documentary in which I would star. I couldn't speak to him about what I had found, or what it implied, or if it was the sole reason he had invited me to live with him, because he had, while in the Northeast, partaken in several weeks of "artistic" discussion in a milieu of badly aged Beatniks doing pot, cocaine, and hallucinogens. This intellectual foment may have worked well for him in the Village during the Fifties, but was doing very little for his mental stability in Wichita Falls, Texas, in the twenty-first century.

The Terrible Beauty of the Evil Man

I was finally able to extricate myself from the conversation, telling him I needed to shower, hoping that the hot water would calm me and give me a chance to think of how to slow him, converse with him rationally. When I was done showering I listened, waiting to hear him withdraw to his room. I opened the door and dashed across the common area in my towel, to dress behind my makeshift partition. However, as soon as I opened the door to the shower he opened his bedroom door, and then, camera in hand, filming away, he advanced. Still wet and wearing no more than a towel, I lost my rationale. I began shouting, grabbed the face of the camera and jerked it down, then blurted out what I had found in his closet. I told him that I knew that he had no interest in doing a documentary, that it was all a lie. He had lured me into his apartment with free rent to seduce me, to get me naked on film.

At this rash pronouncement he could only sputter. I seemed to have confounded him. I yelled at him to go into his room so that I could change. He meekly complied, and I quickly dressed and rushed from the apartment.

I drove recklessly, unsure of where I was heading. I called my Aunt Nena, the only family member I thought might still care about me, explaining that there was an old pervert who was trying to make nude movies of me under the guise of a documentary about my conversion. My aunt told me that she would talk to my uncle and father, and call me back in the morning. It seemed that, as much as my family loathed me, the thought of a deviant preying on their young family member filled them with even greater revulsion.

I slept in my truck that night.

291.

I have, in the years since, come across more of these scurrilous older men, who have, pretending friendship, offered me a variety of types of seemingly benign assistance. Similar scenarios may also be the bane of other attractive young men who regularly stare at poverty in the morning. I suspect beautiful girls learn of this phenomenon at much earlier ages. Regardless, since that time I have learned to more carefully distinguish the bud of desire germinating in the pupils of the perverse from offers of sincere help. There have been people who wished to help me for no other reason than that they were truly good people.

But in the world there are many deviants who see another's plight as an opportunity to take by stealth what they could never acquire by merit. This is not prostitution. True prostitution requires no deception.

292.

The next morning my aunt woke me with a phone call. She had spoken with my father, and he had agreed to let me live with him for the summer, until my transfer to the University of Mississippi that fall. She told me that she and my uncle were concerned that this Jewish man was going to try to take sexual advantage of me, and that they wanted to come to the apartment complex where we were staying while I packed my things.

I went to work in the morning and let them know that I was resigning. I emptied my meager checking account. I said goodbye to my few remaining friends in the early afternoon. In the late afternoon I returned to the apartment complex, but the old man was gone, out at work. My aunt and uncle arrived shortly after I did, and watched me pack my few belongings into the bed of my Ford F-150.

The old man arrived as I was loading the last of my things. He seemed shocked when I told him that I was driving to Mississippi that very night. He mumbled something about the fact that I hadn't paid my utility bill for the month, but a stern look from my enormous uncle caused that utterance to fall weakly from his lips.

I said goodbye once more to my aunt, ignored the old man and my uncle, and got into the truck. My aunt slipped me some money for gasoline, and I knew, as I got into the truck, that I might never see Wichita Falls again. Indeed, at the time of this writing it has been a decade, and I have not returned. I looked into the rearview mirror as I was driving away. I did not know if I would ever see my aunt again.

I drove throughout the evening and early night, pulling into a rest stop near Shreveport to sleep for a few hours. I woke with the dawn and was in Jackson by mid-morning. I rang the doorbell and saw my father for the first time in nearly a year. He looked at me and grunted, motioning me to the room I had occupied a year before.

I was right back where I had been the day I left on my ill-fated quest to Austin.

The Terrible Beauty of the Evil Man

293.

I expected my father to treat me rudely, to make regular querulous remarks about my religious convictions, or conversely, to hug me and weep, as he once more had a child in his home. But no, it was neither of those. My father ignored me that summer. I was a ghost floating through the apartment.

Between the time my father escorted me from Selma to our new life in Texas, and the time that I arrived back in Jackson for that second summer, my parents had progressed from separation to divorce. Shortly after, my father, still in middle-age, decided to begin dating. It had been at least two years since he had been on intimate terms with my mother.

He did not have to travel far to find a new girlfriend. There was one in the apartment complex where we lived. And when I moved back to Jackson that summer, it was to find that my father was in the midst of a heated romance, and that I might soon have a new stepmother.

294.

I was unable to regain the position I had held the summer before, as the maintenance man for the apartment complex. That position had been given to another before I arrived. I also knew that, given my year's growth of wild beard and my unwillingness to work on Saturdays, I would likely be unable to find even a menial summer job in Jackson, Mississippi. But my father told me that he wouldn't charge me rent, and the food was free, and so I found that even my very meager savings would likely provide me all I needed to get through the summer, which was no more than money for toiletries, and the gasoline money needed to get to and from the local library.

So as my father gyred his way through a summer romance that led to a late summer engagement, I sat quietly in the apartment, reading books, thinking deeply about the many ways life had bent and folded me into a new man, and how in turn I had twisted and pivoted against life. I continued my Judaic studies, determined to arrive in Memphis at the end of the summer with a head start on the curriculum for the potential convert. But I never completely eschewed my philosophical musings, and continued to think deeply about philosophical matters. And so even as I walked the road back to Jerusalem, I had, folded in my back pocket, the map of the road that led to Athens.

. 295.

It was that hint of philosophy that led me, over the course of that summer, to reevaluate many of the conclusions I had made about Judaism during the previous year. As I have mentioned, much of the introductory information about Orthodox Judaism online is dominated by Chabad—and their worldview is one of mystery, the Kabbalah, wonder-working rabbis, and many other things that you might find fantastical.

Philosophy led me to reread the original work that had convinced me that Judaism was the true and correct faith, Herman Wouk's *This Is My God*. As I once more turned the pages of that book I realized that I did not want to be part of a movement that lusted after a dead rabbi, or engaged in sober contemplation on the ineffable mysteries of mysticism—which to me meant indefinable, which meant unknowable, which meant there is literally nothing to talk about, if you will recall the last proposition in the *Tractatus Logico-Philosophicus*.

All of this thinking led me to reevaluate Modern Orthodoxy as a credible and sophisticated counterweight to the charisma and mysticism of Chabad. I researched the differences between the two, and realized that it was possible to live within the letter of Jewish law, according to the majority of Orthodox rabbinic legal opinions, without gallivanting about in a large, untrimmed, unsightly beard. As my time to begin at Ole Miss was quickly approaching, along with my course of studies at the synagogue in Memphis, I decided to shave the beard I had been certain would never again know a trim.

296.

It was time for the new semester at Ole Miss, and with it a final departure from my father's domain. It was then that I received fortuitous news. By coincidence, my father's pending nuptials worked in my favor.

My new stepmother-to-be, Gloria, had one child, Jack, from a previous marriage, who was also transferring to Ole Miss that fall. Gloria had spoken to my father of the need to make sure that "the boys got settled in good housing up at Ole Miss." Undoubtedly my father had not given my housing or finances at Ole Miss the slightest thought, but his fiancée's actions on behalf of her son left him looking quite shabby. He decided that he would assist me by cosigning on an apartment lease so that I could live with Jack. Gloria would sign for Jack, and my father would sign for me. We ended up in a very decent apartment.

The Terrible Beauty of the Evil Man

I met Jack late that summer in Jackson, dreading the moment, almost certain he would prove a degenerate or weakling. I was pleasantly surprised to find that my future stepbrother possessed deep integrity and character. He is austere, but just, and good. I owe him quite a lot. Had he not transferred to Ole Miss that semester, I would have ended up impoverished, living in a dorm with the freshmen.

297.

I pen these words from my thirtieth year. In that autumn, as I entered Ole Miss, I was twenty-one. I had seen little of the world, though I had learned much of the souls of men. The first thing I noticed, when I arrived in Oxford, was the physical beauty of the residents. Even now, years later, I have found no other location with a comparable distillation of pulchritude. I have heard it whispered that the most beautiful people in the world are found in the Germanic patches of Brazil, although that is a European beauty, infused with a hint of the tropic. I have seen pockets of people in Manhattan, whilst strolling through Tribeca, Soho, or the West Village, who are as attractive as any on earth. But for all that I will always remember Ole Miss as the place where I encountered the apex of Southern beauty—the belle.

To attract notice at Ole Miss a young flower must be absolutely flawless.

298.

In the sun's violet demise I sat in the quadrangle at the blue sonorous fountain amidst the autumnal russet and ocher and held my bookbag and watched with keen disbelief as America's last concentration of beautiful aristocratic sybarites gamboled with insouciant grace through the lanes and lawns and Greek Revival that ran together in such a riot as to leave the eyes insensate, so that the entirety of my awareness seemed to devolve on the ability of my mind to reestablish, from the rudiments of fragrance and tactile impression and the music of laughter, that is, from the perfume of flower and grass and oak, the polished stone of fountains warm in the last of the year's humidity, the ballade composed of the passing purl of conversations I would never know nor understand, the fact that I was but one picayune mote of *récueillement* ablaze with a jocularity provoked by the realization that

I had escaped prison, fled poverty, and evaded perversion, and in that ebullient reverie I perceived that I had become part of an archaic but rapaciously virile order, one speck in the helical twining of Tradition and unreconstructed Pride that was Ole Miss.

I did not realize it then, but I was no mere speck. I had returned home.

299.

Rash action, product of the conscious mind, is only a partner in the minuet danced with the psychically unavailable longings of the subconscious. Steps, movements, turns on the floor, are only a series of interlocking struggles between acknowledged and unacknowledged desires. I had chosen to convert to Judaism, and through a sequence of minor decisions and fortuitous occurrences had decided that simultaneous study at Anglo Ole Miss and Jewish Memphis was the most effective route to both conversion and a university degree.

But did my conscious mind really so easily suppress that of which my subconscious must surely have been aware? For, including even the seminary in New Orleans, there is no place so steeped in the aroma of my family as is Ole Miss. Was I willingly forgetful, or had I not known?

It became apparent immediately upon my initial investigation of the grounds. I soon passed a small building—the Leavell Building, named for Richard Marion Leavell, my great-great-grandfather's eldest brother, the first honors graduate of the university, later professor there of Philosophy and Political Economy in the late nineteenth and early twentieth centuries, a member of the state legislature, and a former captain in the Army of Northern Virginia. My great-great-grandfather's brother, and his nine nephews, including my great-grandfather, Leonard O. Leavell, were Ole Miss graduates, and all members of Sigma Chi. Indeed, filling out the legacy information on the official fraternity rush form required some time, and a few clarifying calls to relatives. Even the well known Square Books is owned by the couple who live in my great-grandfather's childhood home, and who use it as something of a bed-and-breakfast for itinerant literati.

So then, what was it I really wanted—to convert to Judaism, or to reestablish a sense of belonging in a family that had shunned me, even if only by burrowing into a Yoknapatawpha soil through which slithered the ghosts and memories of ancestors long dead?

The Terrible Beauty of the Evil Man

300.

It was on a recent trip to Oxford, Mississippi, to see my youngest brother, David, who I had not seen in some years, that we decided to revisit our ancestral home. We were greeted by the couple living there, who told us that if we were interested, there was a slim volume of vintage photographs of Oxford for sale in their bookstore. In that volume they told us we would find a photograph of our family that was more than a century old, the crystallization of a moment in time when my great-great-grandparents and their nine sons were gathered around the front porch of the very house where we stood speaking.

My brother and I went to the bookstore, and located the volume and photograph. There, in black and white, in a shot taken in the 1890s, was my family, adorned (in an age in which the vast majority of the denizens of Mississippi had only the rudiments of education) in sleek suits and bow ties and expressions of cold intelligence. They were in Oxford, but not of Oxford.

Or were they? For as I would come to learn, Oxford is no ordinary Southern college town, but is rather a repository for perhaps the last concentration of unreconstructed upper class WASPs in America. For a great many occasions, including even the football games, blazers and ties are not *passé*, they are *de rigueur*.

301.

It was fabulously surreal to move, in mere months, from a world of poverty, of scraping remainders from the grill at a convenience store in order to avoid starvation, to reinstatement in a world of wealth and grace and that inextricable, inexplicable combination of mildness of manner and the penchant for violence and honor, honor through violence, that so characterizes the white, aristocratic, Southern male.

But I understood that world. I am descended, on both sides of my family, from Southern landowners, men who fought in a war we never referred to as Civil, but deemed rather a War of Northern Aggression. I was born to that world, bred in it through generations of intellectual Southerners in both my mother and father's families (for the Beauchamps, too, are an old family), though had you asked me, even six months before, if I would ever again know anything of that life, I would have been amused at the question.

Perhaps you wonder how I acquired the resources to seamlessly move from impoverishment to mix in this well-heeled milieu. The answer is simple. For that first month, my father decided to help me. This was partially due to the example my new stepmother had set in the support of her son. It was also because he had come to believe that assisting me to thrive in an environment so steeped in family history might be the last, best way to prevent me from becoming Jewish.

For, at Ole Miss, there are the elite, and then there is everyone else.

302.

There is only one path to the ranks of the elite at Ole Miss, and that is through participation in the Greek system. At most non-Southern universities, particularly the liberal intellectual castles of the Northeast, the fraternal system is regarded with suspicion at best, and outright loathing at worst. Fraternities are, in the banalities common to the Egalitarians, nests of pompous vipers bent on exclusionary practices meant only to perpetuate outmoded and crude paradigms such as hierarchy, patriarchy, racism, and elitism.

Yawn.

While this may be the case at a small minority of fraternities, it was certainly not my experience, and indeed, my time in a fraternity was a very pleasant experience. Fraternities are accurately characterized neither by the caricature of *Animal House*, nor as secretive gatherings for proto-Fascist political activity.

However, some of you find troubling, *in quacunque quantitate*, the very notion of rank, any existence of human gradation, an exclusive social elite, and no anecdotes from my life will sway you from the belief that the youth of this nation are spiritually imperiled by fraternal activity. Take no trouble to explain. Your views are not mysterious. Egalitarianism is not a cabala.

But no, I grow embroiled in a tedious morass of cant. I am spiritual, not political, and I stagger, incondite.

303.

I looked into the mirror in my apartment and admitted that there was a war in my heart. I had fallen into a land of beauty and nectar and ambrosia, and yet, still yet, it was a world from which I was irrevocably divorced. Perhaps without the lacerations of incarceration, or the ineradicable expurgation of Christian faith, I might have been able to lull myself with that sweet, hypnotic rhythm of the perfect remnant of the South time had largely forgotten. So I looked into the mirror and realized that I faced a conflict. Did I continue on toward Orthodox Judaism—an act all who knew me considered a windmill-tilt worthy of Quixote—or did I relearn to live at home, forget the traumas of years past, lapse into the comfort of the known? I faced a choice.

304.

One: I face a choice.

Two: I have a *belief* that I face a choice.

Three: I am *aware* that I have a belief that I face a choice.

Four: Acknowledgement of my awareness that I believe I face a choice is itself a belief.

Five: I must *choose* whether I should believe that I am aware that I face a choice.

Six: Infinite regressions are for chalkboards. The choice is usually made before we are consciously aware of the question. Reason is limited. We are creatures of instinct.

305.

I joined the fall fraternity Greek Rush because that is what everyone who wanted to have a social life of any significance at Ole Miss did. I was told by the University's Office of Greek Affairs that Ole Miss had a higher percentage of its students in the Greek System than any other public university in the nation.

But no, that is a lie. I did not join Rush because it is what everyone else did. I joined because my great-grandfather and eight of his brothers had been members of Sigma Chi at Ole Miss, and I had heard that fact repeated with pride dozens of times throughout my childhood. It seemed inconceivable that there could be a Leavell on the Ole Miss campus who did not sign up for Rush, who did not pledge Sigma Chi. It would have been an abomination.

My family had cut me away like a malignant tumor, but I could not cut them from my heart.

306.

In Rush the hundreds of youths hoping to earn a spot at one of the dozen or so fraternities are broken up into mobs and herded from house to house where they have the opportunity to hear a brief discourse from a spokesman of that particular fraternity, and then to meet and converse with the members.

Each frat has its own feel, its own direction, its own sense of exclusivity. One fraternity catered to those interested in politics. Another pulled many of its members from those poised to inherit large agricultural estates in the Delta. Several were essentially generic, functioning primarily as exclusive country clubs, with services, amenities, private dining halls, friends, formal and semi-formal private parties, and a steady stream of surplus sex—all yours for the regular payment of several hundred dollars a month (an astounding amount of money to most Mississippians). Sigma Chi was just such a generic country club.

Rush was conducted in three rounds of social invitations, and the fraternity used each of these rounds to observe you, test you, determine whether to invite you to the succeeding, more intimate and exclusive round of Rush. The first round was the only round at which the hopefuls would have the chance to visit each fraternity mansion.

As I progressed from ornate mansion to ornate mansion one thing commanded my attention. The fraternities, other than perhaps two or three holdouts, had mushroomed in size to the point that some had in excess of two hundred members. I realized that by joining any of these groups I would not be joining a fraternity in the sense that I had always imagined the experience; I would join a private club the size of a small company, in which services and perks, rather than brotherhood and connection, would be the item for sale.

So as I pushed through the initial round of evaluation, my mind closed to all possibilities other than Sigma Chi, I was pleasantly surprised by a visit to a smaller fraternity, near the end of the day. Unlike the other fraternities, with their one hundred and fifty to two hundred members, this fraternity had a mere forty. And unlike the other fraternities, who, in side conversations after the spokesman's discourse, let you know how amazing were their parties, how beautiful the women that surrounded them, how powerful the connections they provided, this fraternity spoke only of brotherhood, and more, of the secrecy of their organization. Indeed, they would not even use the word *fraternity*, but preferred to refer to themselves as a secret order—one that presented itself to the world as a literary society.

That they purposely chose to remain small, on a campus where size meant prestige and power, that they spoke of secrecy and brotherhood when others spoke of glamorous parties and gorgeous, unprincipled women, was unique in that initial round of Rush. Their appeal unsettled me, for I felt, when I stepped on the Ole Miss campus, as though I were already a member of Sigma Chi, that there could be no Leavell on campus who was not a Sigma Chi. But this smaller group intrigued me, and I kept their name in mind as I went to bed that night. To some they are known as Delta Psi, but to others they are called St. Anthony Hall.

307.

As soon as I began Rush I encountered a serious problem. The second and third rounds of Rush were scheduled to fall out over Yom Kippur—the most sacred day in the Jewish calendar. I walked over to the Sigma Chi house, and told them that I had a personal obligation from which I was unable to extricate myself. I told them that I was the nine-time legacy they had heard about. They immediately took me to the chairman of their Rush committee.

"You're telling me that you can't make the second *or* third rounds?" he asked me frantically.

"Unfortunately, no. I have something I just can't get out of."

"Do you understand that maybe only a dozen of our members got to meet you in the first round, and that they won't remember you, because they met hundreds of other guys that day?"

"I'm a nine-time legacy."

"Do you understand that we've *never*, ever admitted someone as a pledge who skipped the second and third rounds of rush?"

"I'm a *nine-time legacy*," I repeated, staring him in the eye.

"You're really going to do this?" he asked. "You're putting me in an impossible position. I'm not the only one who makes this decision, and the other guys really like being able to have a say. If you do this, if you skip out on the last two rounds, I honestly can't guarantee that we can give you the bid. I'll do everything I can, but I can't guarantee anything."

I paused. I realized he was telling me that I would likely, despite my lineage, not get a pledge bid if I did not give the *serenissima signoria* the singular pleasure of checking my gums and lifting my hooves. I thought, in that moment, very seriously, about making up an excuse, any excuse, and telling the rabbi that I wouldn't, couldn't make it for the Yom Kippur services. There would be no way he could know that I didn't have food poisoning. Perhaps, had it not been for the impression made by the men of St. Anthony Hall, I might have wavered more. But their contrast with Sigma Chi was significant, and I felt that had the nine Leavell brothers passed through Ole Miss when I did, they would have been off-put by what Sigma Chi had become, would have been drawn to a group that was small, elite, literary, focused on brotherhood, and not to what had become a semi-corporate country club.

I shook my head. All of the concern about fraternities was silliness. A fraternity, or even a secret society, was an interesting diversion, but I had determined to give the rest of my life to the Jewish people. At the end, there was no choice for me. Rather than attend those parties I would drive to Memphis and would spend twenty-five hours without food and water, beating my chest, crying out to God, and repenting for the wrongs I had committed.

I had to choose between two worlds. One offered fasting, self-affliction, and atonement. The other offered lush hedonism and the cool rhythm of camaraderie. I chose the Jews.

308.

I went to Memphis for Yom Kippur in the Hebrew year 5765, three days after my twenty-second birthday, prepared to exchange greetings and smiles with the new friends I had made in the previous two months, particularly over the holiday of Rosh Hashanah. I had become so used to the (what I saw as) extremely deconstructed approach to punctual attendance, as well as attention on the service proper, that I was greatly taken aback by the gravitas with which the faithful approached the Day of Atonement.

Nobody was smiling. Children weren't running in the aisles. Everyone was as somber as though they were at a funeral—and perhaps in their minds they were, for it is on that day that Orthodox Jews believe that the separation between the physical and metaphysical planes is at its thinnest, and it is on that day they have the chance to truly repent and renew their service to God. It is the day on which they may receive absolution or strict justice.

On that day there is no food, there is no water, there is no bathing, there is no sex. No, you may not so much as even brush your teeth in the morning. It is a day of trembling, a day of dread. There was weeping, shudders of regret, and all of those intangible sensations that one expects only at a wake or in a courtroom as sentence is pronounced in a capital case. For that is what Yom Kippur is to the Jews, and as I stood there, praying for some eighteen of those twenty-five hours, struggling to keep up in the prayer book, but finding that my rudimentary reading skills were crystallizing under the pressure of the intense focus and emotion of the day, I realized that, though I was not yet a Jew, I was in a sense reborn, and nothing I would find back at Ole Miss, whether in the form of parties or brotherhood or debauchery, could ever compare to the shock of that day of total catharsis. I, who had wilted and decayed in so many ways, was slowly, despite the long absence of all spiritual nourishment, returning to life.

When the night fell and the feverish effluence of prayers had come to an end the community grew silent, and then the shriek of a ram's horn split both the air and my heart. A man who had prayed near me throughout the day walked over and slapped me on the back.

"Well, how was your first Yom Kippur?" he smiled. "Did you have enough? Ready to eat?"

"No," I said solemnly. "I could do it all again right now."

"Ha!" he exclaimed. "You really must have a *yiddishe neshama*."

He turned and walked away. I stood silently, dizzy from hunger, trembling from the blast of the horn that still rang in my ears.

309.

I returned to Ole Miss a different person, unsure of how to handle a bid from Sigma Chi even if they gave me one. I went on the appointed day, to the place where they handed out the pledge bids. There was one envelope, one bid, for me. I looked at the letter, and nearly dropped it in shock. Sigma Chi had refused to extend me a bid. The letter I was holding was not from them. The letter I was holding was both wholly unexpected and wholly welcome.

I had been invited to join the newest pledge class of Delta Psi.

310.

At Ole Miss the fraternities induct their pledge classes on the same night, and the mood is as solemn as any evening on campus all year. Each fraternity attempts to ensure that the pledge induction is both mysterious and meaningful, and the ceremonies typically end in a private party that doesn't conclude until the next morning.

The gravity with which the students and alumni of Ole Miss approach this ceremony may be a source of both amusement and bewilderment to Northerners, but the evening often draws the wealthy and powerful from all over the state. Numerous classmates informed me that the recent majority leader of the United States Senate had flown in from Washington to oversee the pledge induction for Sigma Nu.

My induction as a pledge did not mean that I became a member of Delta Psi, but only that I was given the opportunity to work, with a select group of pledge brothers, for that honor. And while I did go on, in time, to become a full member of St. Anthony Hall, about the circumstances leading to that I can say no more, for the most distinctive characteristic of the Hall is the secrecy that surrounds us, our traditions, and our practices. We are a literary society, and proceed in silence.

311.

I was sitting with Big Dave one day on a break from Ole Miss. Yes, it was that same Big Dave who had watched out for me in prison. I had kept in touch with him in the months after my release. He was someone that I had known, even while incarcerated, would ever after be a friend. I knew it because all of the people I had thought were my friends, my teammates and classmates from Morgan Academy, everyone, in short, that I had known, had abandoned me in my dark hour. Big Dave had no interest in helping me, yet he did. He was a friend when I was as low as I could possibly go. That's exactly when friendship is defined and qualified—it is forged in the furnaces of life, not the calms.

Big Dave wasn't looking well. He was bald, morbidly obese, and leaning hard on a cane. Each time I was able to see him he looked worse. He had been sick a long time and was declining rapidly. However his health had in no way affected his jollity, and he was glad when I made the drive from Ole Miss to Greensboro, Alabama, to tell him about the start of my conversion, my fraternity pledge, and those other daily quirks of life which are conveyed so much better in person. At some point the conversation turned to my family.

"So your folks aren't happy," he said. It wasn't a question.

"Nope. Don't want to talk to me. Haven't spoken a word to mom in over a year."

"Damn shame."

"Yep."

"Dad?"

"He was coming around a bit, back when I started at Ole Miss. Figured it would set me straight, get me off this Jewish kick. He got me set up in an apartment with my new stepbrother, helped me get into Rush."

"So?"

"He's not talking to me again. I didn't go to his wedding."

"Why the hell not?"

"It was in a church. Jews are prohibited from entering churches for any reason."

"No shit?"

"Yep. Told him I would go if he would have it anywhere but a church, but he was adamant. Now we're not talking again."

"Shit. I'm sorry to hear. What else then?"

"Got a part-time job tutoring disadvantaged kids in the public schools. Working twenty hours a week. Taking a full-time load this fall semester, and it looks like I'll have straight A's. I get five hours sleep on a good night, but closer to three most nights. I decided to major in Philosophy—they didn't have that major at Midwestern. Guess I got used to thinking in prison. Then I got to thinking about thinking. Prison does that to you. Figured I would keep it up."

"Damn straight you did. I told you to sleep through the whole thing, but you just wanted books."

"Well, Big Dave, there's only so many hours the body will sleep."

"I reckon. Another shot?" he asked, pouring the good bourbon, the Maker's Mark, which he brought out when I came over, because he knew I liked it. "Well," he continued, "what else?"

"Let's see. I got the job. Classes are good. Family is shit. I'm pledging the frat, which is fun, takes about forty hours a week with all they got me doing. I started playing for the Ole Miss rugby team, but had to quit 'cause the games were always falling out on the Sabbath. And that's where I'm really focused. Each weekend I'm in Memphis learning all things Jewish."

"The hell the Jews got you learning? How to snip your pecker the right way?"

"Naw. But they got complicated rules for just about every damn thing under the sun. I learned most of what they want from a convert before I got there. The rest I picked up in the first month or two. I'm not really sure what's going on now. They have a curriculum that's supposed to take a year or two. But I think I got it down, so I guess they don't know how to fill up the rest of the year. Rabbi says now I'm in an 'observation phase.'"

"The hell is an *observation phase*?"

"Damned if I know. Guess they want to make sure I'm not crazy. He says becoming Jewish isn't just accepting the theology and joining a religion—it's joining a family. He says the people have to like me."

"Well do they like you?"

"Sure they do. They're real sweet folks. I gotta keep a calendar just to keep track of all my Sabbath meal invitations. I'm booked a month in advance."

"Well... so what else?"

"Ain't that enough?"

"Well, hell, it's good to see you."

"Stop talking, Big Dave. Pour."

And then he poured, and I got drunk with a man I could be sure would always be my friend.

312.

I would step into the rabbi's home each Sabbath, and he would take my coat and lead me into his living room for a study session. During those first weekends in Memphis I quickly learned to follow the prayer services (which can change in substantial ways from day to day), and the intricacies of what one must and mustn't do on the Jewish Sabbath. I created no small amusement in the home of my first Sabbath host when I asked if I was allowed to flush the toilets or use the sink. He couldn't imagine why I would ask such an inane question. I didn't know why he thought it strange to ask if you could run water when flipping a light switch was *verboten*.

Regardless, my lessons with the rabbi proceeded efficiently in the first several months. He was particularly helpful in taking me through the labyrinth of Jewish blessings. Orthodox Jews make blessings both before and after they eat and drink. The blessing can change depending on what you ate or drank, in what order you ate or drank, whether you changed location during your snack or meal, how much time has elapsed since you've imbibed, or in the event that you forgot to make the original blessing.

It is therefore necessary that a potential convert, as someone who, naturally, will need to eat and drink after becoming Jewish, master this maze of convoluted sanctifications prior to conversion. Two weeks after my initial lesson on blessings I was able to correctly identify *ho'adomoh*, and not *ha'etz*, as the correct pre-blessing for the banana, and to name *borei nefashos* as the correct after-blessing. The banana represents something of a trick question in this field of law, and the rabbi was surprised that I had managed to so quickly demonstrate competence, though he was perhaps more surprised that I had arrived in Memphis capable of pronouncing the blessings in halting, though quite correct, Hebrew.

Early on then, the rabbi was forced to bypass the traditional pre-conversion curriculum, and to instead take me through several of the trickier problems in fundamental Jewish law. For example, there are thirty-nine primary categories of prohibited Jewish labor on the Sabbath, and those combined categories contain hundreds of prohibited activities, covering everything from flipping a light switch to building a house. In addition, there are many objects, collectively known as *muktzah*, that are often directly unrelated to labor, but which one may not even touch, or, if one must touch them for some outstanding reason, may only be handled in ways that are composed of a further system of rules so recondite that it would not be unreasonable to compare the matter to the nightmare of the US tax code.

The rabbi might ask if it were permissible, on the Sabbath, to pour water from a hot-water urn into a teacup, and then to place a teabag into that teacup. Was that considered the prohibition of cooking (*bishul*) on the Sabbath or not? If so, must two or three cups be used to transfer the water from the urn to the teacup before the teabag is inserted, and why? Once the tea has seeped into the water, is it permissible to remove the teabag, or does this constitute the prohibition of *borer*, or separating that which is unwanted from that which is desired? If it is *borer*, can the prohibition be overcome by using a spoon to remove some of the (desired) tea with the (undesired) teabag? If the case involves neither cooking (*bishul*) nor forbidden separation (*borer*) then perhaps one has performed the prohibited act of dyeing (*tzovayah*), as the tea, when it seeps out, dyes the water.

By mid-spring I had realized three things. First, I was covering material that many of the congregants in that Modern Orthodox synagogue weren't even aware constituted legal questions—placing me, the non-Jewish *goy*, in the frequently awkward position of deciding whether I wanted to accept tea that had been made by the hostess in a prohibited manner. Second, I realized that this material was far more advanced than the curriculum a convert typically covered before being presented to the rabbinical court. I have since come across many young Orthodox Jews, possessed of twelve years of all-day Jewish schooling, who would not have been able to answer those legal questions with that degree of nuance. And finally, I grew aware that if I were to progress to any type of deeply authentic proficiency in the world of Jewish learning, I would have to move soon after my conversion.

I would need to do what most serious young Orthodox men my age were doing. The corpus of Jewish Law is too vast, too complex, for even a very brilliant person to gain true fluency through only part-time study. Moreover one needs mastery of both ancient Hebrew and Aramaic—two dead Semitic languages not easily acquired. I would need to study in a Jewish seminary, known as a *yeshiva*. I would have to drop out of Ole Miss. I would have to move to Israel.

313.

With the progression of time and meetings this rabbi came to accept that I was serious, committed, undeterred by the linguistic and legal rigors of study on which so many potential converts to Orthodox Judaism falter. His acceptance of the seriousness of my purpose made him aware that he had almost total control over the future of my life. I had given up an entire world, a family, a culture, and, as I expressed to him repeatedly, had so thoroughly repudiated my former beliefs that I would truly rather have died than gone back to Christianity or agnosticism.

314.

Prior to the very recent past, conversion to Judaism, even where it was not illegal and a capital crime, was still exceptionally rare, and the persons who persisted in the effort to become Jewish, knowing the suffering they would surely face, were considered righteous individuals, even if, in the grand scale of Jewish learning, they might never approach the basic level of scholarship expected of a Jewish adult. This attitude towards converts and conversion has changed greatly since the Enlightenment, which the Jews refer to as the *Haskalah*, and with each passing year the attitudinal change grows. Where there is no criminal penalty for becoming Jewish, where there is no true chance of capital punishment, the respect and honor given the convert decreases proportionally. Perhaps this is understandable. Honor wanes as risk decreases. That is the way of man.

315.

Though the Torah repeatedly iterates the command for each Jew to love the convert, something the Torah does not even command a child vis-à-vis their parents, the Five Books of Moses say little of the person who has declared a sincere intention to become a Jew, but who has not yet formally converted.

In our Age, the duration of time elapsing between the declaration of intent to convert (persisting in that intention despite repeated rabbinic attempts to discourage the declarant), and the actual moment of conversion, has become a period of grave potential abuse.

Conversion today typically requires a solitary rabbi, knowledgeable in the laws of conversion, to sponsor the potential convert, training them in the basics of Judaism, teaching them greater and lesser laws that they will find necessary in their life as a Jew, and helping them to integrate into the larger tribe of Jewry.

For most potential converts, this process, assuming they are reasonably intelligent, and have no substantial prior knowledge of Judaism, takes a minimum of two years, though the period of time may be longer or shorter, depending on their tenacity, as well as their scholastic aptitude. Cases where the process takes much longer occur when the candidate has significant trouble learning to read Hebrew. At the end of this inculcation in the foundations of Judaic law, custom, and worldview, the sponsoring rabbi will take the sincere candidate before a rabbinic legal court for the conversion proper.

A twofold travesty has occurred. First, there is a bitter political war within Orthodox Judaism over who is *kosher enough* to serve on a rabbinical court that performs conversions. In brief, the more strict community accuses the moderates of converting persons of dubious sincerity, who have no genuine intention of fully adhering to Jewish law after the conversion. The moderates accuse the more stringent Orthodox community of demanding standards of adherence that are beyond the requirements of Jewish law, and are but onerous strictures (*chumras*) adopted as safeguards against violations of the Law itself.

Anyone approaching the issue in good faith and with an honest desire to arrive at the truth (as opposed to a preferred political outcome) can see the merits of both sides. One does not wish to make people Jewish who have no intention of fulfilling Jewish Law, and yet one does not wish to cast aspersions on the valid conversion of someone who converts in a community that, while abiding by the Law, does not adopt the myriad extra-legal stringencies of a more rigorous community.

As an example, in all Orthodox communities it is expected that women will dress modestly, and the custom is for women to wear skirts that will cover the knees when the woman is standing. Mini-skirts and décolletage are not permitted. However, some communities have adopted the additional requirement that women should also, for the sake of modesty, wear pantyhose or stockings under their skirts. If one lived in such a community, the fact that it had become a community-wide standard would necessitate the adoption of that custom. Yet the wearing of pantyhose is not technically required by Jewish Law.

Examples of debated stringencies such as this, for both men and women, could be multiplied *ad nauseum*, and have become the source of conflicts between communities where the persons most hurt and degraded are the potential converts, who, rather than being treated as persons that may have given up life, culture, and even family to become Jewish, end up as pawns in a larger ideological war.

The potential convert, with only the rudiments of Jewish knowledge, is not capable of grasping the scope of the larger debate, and feels only the hurt and rejection when, for reasons they cannot understand, their conversion is repeatedly delayed, or entirely invalidated *post facto*, or they are forced to undergo multiple Orthodox conversions, due to factional agendas beyond their control.

The second problem lies in the nature of control that the sponsoring rabbi has over the would-be convert. A person who gives up, in many cases, *everything* significant about their past life, in order to engage in what may be a multi-year program of study, which, if the rabbinic court rejects their candidacy, will negate the totality of that enormous sacrifice, is a person who, by the very nature of the situation, is lonely, uncertain, and is at times perhaps even quite emotionally desperate.

The sponsoring rabbi has absolute control over the candidate, and can, at any time the candidate displeases him, simply refuse to continue sponsorship, and further, may even smear the potential convert's credibility with the few other rabbis who specialize in this type of work. Moreover, the sponsoring rabbi need never tell you if he intends to bring you before the rabbinical court in three months or three years, or even if he never intends to bring you before the court at all. The candidate is truly under the psychological control of the sponsor.

316.

Working with a convert may be rewarding for a genuinely kind rabbi. But it is often an arduous, multi-year process, akin, in most cases, to teaching a first-grader, and further, it is one that may have no benefit whatsoever for the Jewish people, for the drop-out rate during this lengthy program of study is understandably high. It is little wonder that few rabbis wish to devote the time and emotional energy needed to undertake the sponsorship of even a single potential convert, much less to repeatedly engage in this task.

So one obvious question concerns just what sort of person is willing to engage in this laborious but often futile task. Judaism is not evangelical. There is no mandate to convert anyone to Judaism at all—indeed, one is required to discourage a potential convert several times before agreeing to teach them.

The answer generally lies along one of two paths. Either the sponsoring rabbi is a truly good person, and desires to bring those who are deeply dedicated into the Jewish fold, or the rabbi is a person who finds (even if subconsciously) the possibility of having near absolute control over another's life, often for years at a time, a pleasant proposition.

In 2009 these conversion perversions came together. A highly regarded ultra-Orthodox rabbi in Monsey, New York, was set up, with millions of dollars in financial backing, as the leader of a watchdog group dedicated to making sure that no one got into the tribe without the strictest of supervision and standards. In the process he maligned the conversions and standards of more moderate communities with whom he disagreed. This rabbi, so terribly concerned about the purity of converts and the conversion process, was recorded on the phone, by an attractive woman he was personally sponsoring, demanding a variety of outlandish sexual favors (including attempts to pimp her out to his buddies) in return for allowing her to become Jewish.

When you take people who are powerless within the framework of this religious legal code, who only wish to follow their convictions, and put them in the middle of an ideological war that they have no ability to grasp, when you place them under the sponsorship of a single man who has no oversight and no checks on his authority, then you create a tremendous rift between communities that might be in harmony, and also devastate the lives of people who are Jewish infants waiting to be born. It is troubling to consider just how irresponsible it is to place an adult male in a position of unchecked power over another human being. These rabbis *may* function as angels, but they may also function as tyrants.

317.

But who was this rabbi sponsoring *me*? I could tell you that he was tall, thin, even gaunt, with a short brown beard coating a narrow face on which rested spectacles, but to tell you what a man looks like, in this case, would tell you very little of the man.

He was originally from New York, and had come down to the South to minister, after his rabbinic ordination, to an area that is (in the minds of most New York Jews) the outer wilderness. He had in tow an Ivy League educated wife—or perhaps she had him in tow—I am uncertain, as she appeared the more strong-willed, possessing both a sharp mind and an assertiveness I found startling.

This rabbi had studied at Yeshiva University, where I suspect that as a young man, earnestly applying his mind to pages of dense talmudic argumentation, he had never thought that he would live out his life as anything but a rabbinic scholar, or perhaps as both a rabbi and a historian, as that walking synthesis of Judaism and academia which so characterizes the Modern Orthodox ideal. I cannot imagine that he thought he would spend the bulk of his working life as the caretaker for what was (and is) a slowly dying synagogue comprised primarily of elderly Jews.

In the Orthodox Jewish world, the epitome of religious life for the male is the acquisition of religious scholarship, gained in painstaking labor over the course of decades, primarily through mastery of the Talmud and its commentaries. It is in this attachment and adherence to the Law that the Jewish male achieves communion with the Divine. Logic is paramount. Feelings and impulses are subordinate to obligation and schedule. Men are separate from women, both physically, and in religious code and observance. Cleaving to God and study of the Law are the two most important activities for a Jewish man, surpassing (and this debate in the Talmud is itself widely studied) even the realm of Action, of performing the commandments one is studying.

It should be no surprise that a young man raised in a culture such as this is more logical, cool, rational, organized, regular—and perhaps I may venture to say that those who are predisposed to the greatest success in this subculture, that is, those who can sit and study dry legal texts for twelve to eighteen or even more hours per day, may possess an advantage if they have a touch of Asperger's.

318.

I see him in my memory now, much as I have seen him in the eight years that have since elapsed. He was dry, technical—our conversations, our lessons, rarely diverged from the strictly technical aspects of the Law. He was everything that a Southern Baptist pastor was not. I had always thought that would feel cathartic, and in some ways the continual probing intellectual analysis was. I had always felt unclean when exposed for too long to the cloying saccharine Evangelical need to *feel* as an act of worship.

Yet it was only as those Spring study sessions wore on that I became consciously aware that I was, and had been for some time, subconsciously trying to express to him that I needed more than mere instruction in the Law. I had been through so much, in such a short number of years, and though I believed that the Torah was divinely inspired, I knew that from religion, from my rabbi, my spiritual nourishment would need to be emotional as well as intellectual.

319.

Much of the emotional content of Judaism flows through the family. The activities and holidays are observed with intellectual precision and rigor, but are undergirded with an emotional love that emanates from the Jewish home. And as much as the Jews of Memphis had welcomed me into their homes with love and graciousness—and the Orthodox community of Memphis is composed of many of the kindest, warmest, most generous and giving people I will ever meet—I still felt that I needed that warmth, that emotional bond, with the man who was guiding me through the most important decision of my life. I needed him to understand how vulnerable I felt, how completely alone. I needed more than an instructor in technical legal matters. I needed a mentor, and that implies an emotional bond. If not to him, then to whom could I speak of the anguish I felt at the abandonment of my family, all for what I believed to be divine truth?

320.

There are times when we attempt to communicate with another in a thousand broken ways—broken because we cannot explicitly tell them of matters we need them to know, matters which are unspeakable as we are unaware that we are even trying to communicate, for we cannot perceive that we *need*.

The sensitive, delicate soul, the authentic psychologist, can look into the other person, discern what is needed without exchange of words, and then provide necessary succor or advice. Even the commoner will, given enough time, gradually come to realize that there is an unspoken need in another, or that support is required, even in cases where that other individual is unaware of their own struggle.

When a person fails to read, recognize, register any of the many unspoken forms of communication whereby another attempts to express a need, we say that perhaps the person lacks emotional intelligence, is unresponsive to unspoken cues, to all the sinuous trills by which our eyes and face and posture speak so much more clearly and articulately than does our voice.

But who is it then, really, that lacks intelligence? Is it the one who cannot hear even blaring unspoken speech, or is it the one who, lacking either all insight or courage, is unable to express with plain language what they have repeatedly attempted to say without words?

This rabbi was unable to hear anything I was saying. But it was I, so convinced that God and Truth would cure every ill of my fragile heart, who was unable to speak at all.

321.

It was an afternoon that spring, on one of the last full holiday days which make up the eight days of Passover, mere weeks prior to the end of the academic year at Ole Miss, when I finally realized, and then verbalized, what I had voicelessly told the rabbi many times in the previous months.

We were sitting in his living room, and each had a massive copy of the Talmud tractate of *Pesachim*, which deals with the laws and customs of the Passover holiday. I was staring at the long block of lines on the page, which seemed naught but so much Pali, listening as the rabbi chanted a few lines, translated them, and then asked me questions to ascertain whether I was following the argument.

My Hebrew, which was rudimentary at best, was useless in this new game the rabbi had introduced, for the Talmud is written in the Babylonian dialect of Aramaic, a tongue once the *lingua franca* of the Middle East, but now dead for hundreds of years. I had no trouble following the line of argument, and was easily able to hold the different streams of rabbinic discussion in my head, for the legal question was not complex, but the words on the page, the very language, were for me an insurmountable barrier, and I began to wonder why the rabbi was using our personal learning time, meant to prepare me for conversion, in just this way.

322.

Jewish law requires that on the Passover holiday no leavened bread, indeed, no products containing even the fermentation of yeast (for instance, beer), may be consumed or even owned by a Jew. Intertwined with these negative prohibitions is the positive commandment that one must consume, at least at certain times, a specific quantity of unleavened bread, which the Jews call *matzoh*.

While it may be a matter of traditional study for a pious Jew to learn at what times, and in what amount they should eat *matzoh* on the Passover holiday, the various historical rabbinic opinions on these matters are rarely studied by anyone other than advanced students of Judaism. But no, I jest. That topic would be commonplace for an educated Orthodox layman who learns on a daily basis. A better example of an obscure debate would be a thorough analysis of the major and minor legal opinions listed in the Talmud over how long the dough may have contact with water before the bread is leavened (eighteen minutes), what shapes the *matzoh* may have, whether it may used for various purposes if broken or cracked, and whether ingredients such as first fruits (*bikkurim*), or secondary tithes (*maaser sheni*) may be used in its composition.

The rabbi and I were nearing the end of the eighth day of the holiday, and he had been jumping from arcanum to arcanum in our daily private lessons, leaving me wondering why I could possibly need to know such material in order to become a Jew. Even though I was aware that I knew but a miniscule portion of the vast corpus of Judaic learning, I was also aware that it was unlikely that there were even five men in the synagogue who had ever learned those sections of the Talmud, and further, I knew that there was no requirement that a potential convert be able to learn Talmud at all. As recently as two centuries ago, it is doubtful if even a quarter of fully Orthodox men could independently read a page of the dense Aramaic in which the Talmud is composed.

At some point I looked up from the euphemisms, acronyms, and missing premises of the Talmud and asked the rabbi if we could take a break.

"Rabbi, I was wondering... *why* do I need to know this before I become Jewish? This is a point of recondite legal theory. These questions were decided more than a thousand years ago. This has no effect on what I will or won't need to know in day-to-day practice as a Jew."

"Finis, I've told you many times that one of the most essential activities a Jew can undertake is learning for learning's sake, *Torah lishmah.*"

"I understand, and we've done that on many occasions, but there are so many things I need to know for day-to-day practice that we could study. And frankly, for me to become a student of the *Gemara* (the analytical sections of the Talmud), I will need to learn Aramaic, and not just how to pronounce it, but how to read it well, grammar and all."

"You will, you will. You'll learn a few words at a time. I've been assigning you small numbers of words to memorize."

"Forgive me for saying so, Rabbi, but this is an impossible language. For me to learn to read the page in front of me I'll need to devote at least a year, probably more, to full-time learning in a yeshiva. We both know it won't happen through private study lessons in your living room."

"What are you saying, Finis?"

"I guess I'm saying that for me to grow further I need to be in a place where I really can grow further—a place where I can learn full-time. I don't need to be here. I need to be in a yeshiva. But I can't do that until I'm a Jew."

"I've told you that you will not be converted until you actually live here in the Jewish community. And how will you go to yeshiva? How will you pay for it?"

"You know the Gordons have asked me to house-sit for them this entire summer while they're in Israel. I'll be full-time in the community in a few weeks. The school year at Ole Miss is nearly up. I'll be fully immersed in the Memphis community. And several people in the community have expressed interest in helping me study in Israel. There are many scholarships available."

"How will you finish college? What are your plans?"

"I think God wishes me to go to Israel both to learn and to live. I can finish college there. My intention is to purchase a one-way ticket. I do not think I will return to America. I have nothing here. My family and I are irrevocably split. My former friends believe I will burn in hellfire for eternity."

The rabbi leaned back in his chair, stroked his beard, and then sighed and sat back up.

"Well this is all very theoretical. Let's get back to the *Gemara*."

"Wait!"

"Yes?" the rabbi asked, surprised that I had interrupted him once he had indicated that the conversation about my future was at an end.

"I need... *more*."

"More?"

"Yes. I don't know how to say it. This is all very difficult for me," I mumbled. "I don't mean the way you must guard the flour used to make *matzoh*," I added quickly, certain that without clarification he would interpret me literally, as referring to the textual question on the page in my lap. "I need to feel like you understand what I'm going through here."

"In what sense?"

"I mean I've given up everything to be here. I've learned everything you've asked me to and more. I'm moving into the community in weeks. I just... feel this great sense of uncertainty about my entire future... due to not knowing what's going to happen, what's on your mind about my conversion. And every time I try to talk to you it's as though you don't hear or feel what I'm saying. I've given up *everything*, and everything to come is so uncertain! Do you understand?" I asked, my eyes pleading with him.

"Well," he paused, stroking his beard once more, "others have converted here before you. The conversion process is not supposed to be easy. Being Jewish isn't easy. To an extent it helps me, observing how you respond to this process, in determining whether you will make a successful Jew."

It was then that I tried to blink back the tear which had formed in my eye, lest he see it, and interpret it as a weakness, or some other factor by which I might be disqualified from becoming Jewish. I had been told that I already knew what was needed for conversion, and that I was simply in a *period of observation*, though I did not know what he was hoping to observe.

"Rabbi, I just… I just want to be able to talk to you about things, you know? Not only Torah matters or the *Gemara*. I feel very alone in all of this."

"Well, Finis, I don't understand. We're *talking* right now. And you can talk to me whenever you wish. But right now we need to delve back into this *sugya* (talmudic argument), because when you do become Jewish, and go to yeshiva, which is your desire, this is exactly what you will spend your time doing."

And with that the rabbi leaned back over the page and began to chant the lines in a melody that had been handed down in the ghettoes of Poland and Lithuania for hundreds of years. And I blinked back the tears that were welling up within me, though one fell to the page, but that did not matter, for the rabbi didn't see it.

323.

I finished the year at Ole Miss studying for finals, preparing to move my stuff to Memphis, and continually feeling as though I were on the brink of a shutdown, for the body and mind, even in those humans possessed of the greatest natural vigor, are capable of absorbing only so much of the residue of toil and trauma, hope and anxiety.

I remember well that last day in Oxford. My lease ended only a couple of days after my last final, but my last final was on a Friday, and I would have to make it to the synagogue by sundown, so I was frantic in that last week. I took my series of finals, for which I had not, due to my Judaic studies, adequately prepared. I stayed up all night before my last final, cramming in the semester of work I had neglected, and took the test near noon.

I then had to pack all of my belongings into my truck, tie them down, and get to Memphis in time to shower and shave before the Sabbath. Unfortunately, it was a particularly hot and humid day for May, and it rained heavily throughout the afternoon. It is difficult to pack all you own in one day, even if it is not a great deal of property—one tends to look over everything one packs. This is more difficult when you have not slept the night before.

It is a great change, and a hurt, to leave behind a place you have loved, where you have been happy, even if to do so is a necessary step in what you believe to be the grand quest of your life. Attempting to move the entirety of my earthly possessions in a state of exhaustion under the watch and care of a near-monsoon was no calming thing.

I arrived in Memphis mere moments before the setting of the sun. I was still wet, reeking of sweat and the moldy smell of clothing that had begun to dry. I hobbled out of the truck and went up to the door of the Felt family, with whom I would spend that Sabbath. Mrs. Felt, as kind and generous a woman as I have ever known (she paid for my textbooks my second semester at Ole Miss, without being asked, because I had expressed uncertainty as to how I would afford them), took one look at me and rushed me indoors. I stepped into the shower in the last minutes before the Sabbath, the *eighteen*, and showered in ninety seconds, as I had done in the days of the Mt. Meigs boot camp.

I stepped out of the shower and tried to put on my suit and tie. I couldn't seem to knot the tie. I was shaking. I fell back onto the bed in the room where I was staying and lay there shaking. I was having a seizure, and it is the first one I distinctly remember. For some years I had forgotten the seizure I had years earlier in Orlando, and I remembered it only when rereading the detailed entries I had made in my mandatory journal.

Mrs. Felt knocked on the door, and came in. I had stopped shaking, but I was disoriented and confused. She asked me what was wrong. I told her I had been up all night cramming for a final and was exhausted. She assumed, as would any Jewish mother, that I had gotten sick after having been in the rain. She insisted that I stay home from the synagogue, pray in solitude, *daven b'yechidus*, and spend the night resting.

I had finally made it. After years of hardship I was living in an Orthodox Jewish community. But the cost had been great, and my central nervous system was shutting down from the strain.

324.

I recovered from my seizure and moved in, after the Sabbath, to the house I would occupy for the summer. The home belonged to Alvin and Elaine Gordon, a prominent elderly couple in the community. He was the chief partner of a respected law firm in Memphis, though, by that time semi-retired, he spent half the year at a second home in Jerusalem. They left for several months in Israel at the time the academic year ended at Ole Miss, and asked if I would house-sit for them until the end of the summer. They offered me lodging and food, as well as a nominal stipend for the service, and that, combined with a tutoring position I found with a local tutoring company, provided me financial stability over the course of the summer, ameliorating the ongoing embarrassment of penury.

The Gordons' offer was made solely from kindness. They could easily have arranged for a neighbor or friend to care for their home while I was gone, but they knew I needed a place to live in the community, and could not afford to rent in upscale East Memphis. It was not the first of their kindnesses to me, and would not be the last. They are the most generous couple I have ever known. They gave to me simply from goodness, and not because they wanted anything of me whatsoever. There were times when they stood between me and destitution, keeping me from having to choose between food and medicine when sick, and many of the other horrors of poverty.

The rabbis call such people *baalei chesed*, and *baalei tzedakah*, and claim that their reward in the afterlife will be great.

325.

That summer I had little to do but tutor, and go to the thrice-daily prayers, and run to and from the rabbi's home for study sessions whenever he beckoned. This gave me more free time than I had known in many years, as tutoring, which pays well by the hour, does not require a significant outlay of time.

I had time to deepen and enrich the many friendships with members of the community that I had made the previous year, when I had only been able to visit from a distance. Orthodox Jews all live in walking distance of their synagogue (as one may use no locomotion other than one's legs on the Sabbath), so I found that I was now in walking distance of many friends. I quickly integrated.

Most importantly, I was living a mere ten-minute walk from one of the most renowned rabbis in the world. His name was Ephraim Greenblatt, and he was a short, frail man with pink cheeks, and a very long, untrimmed white beard. He wore a black hat and a long, black, frock coat on even the hottest days of that Memphis summer. Despite the black felt hat, the long, woolen, black frock coat, the long-sleeve white dress shirt, or even the woolen undershirt (*tzitzit*) worn by all rigorously Orthodox males, I never once saw him perspire while walking to and from the synagogue. It is those minor but unusual details which so impress themselves on our mind, and aid in our memory of another, even when many years have gone.

He was a fairly recent widower, his wife having passed in a tragic accident, hit by a car while crossing a busy intersection. He was alone in his home, with nothing but his twenty or thirty thousand volumes of scholarly Jewish works. Despite his advanced age and frail health, he spent roughly eighteen hours a day learning Torah, writing scholarly works on the Law, and answering questions on complex jurisprudential matters.

He received so many questions and letters each day, from advanced scholars all over the world, that the Post Office installed an industrial-size business mailbox outside his home.

326.

I had met Rabbi Greenblatt almost as soon as I arrived in Memphis the previous fall. He was quickly pointed out to me, for he was the pride of the community, though his mastery of the corpus of Jewish learning was so far beyond even the most learned there (including my rabbinic sponsor) that it would be fair to describe the distance between him and that of even the educated elite of the synagogue as comparable to the distance between H.L.A. Hart or Learned Hand and the typical first year law-student at a middling law school.

When I first arrived in Memphis I would sit in the back of the synagogue, as I was timid, and often felt confused, alone, and conspicuous. But the din of mundane business and social conversation at the rear of the synagogue was so great that I found it almost impossible to focus on the prayers. In my case, following the speed of the Hebrew as it was read by the congregation required full concentration. So I gambled boldly. One Sabbath I walked straight up to the front and sat directly behind Rabbi Greenblatt.

I did this for two reasons. I noticed that in his vicinity no one would speak casually. It would have struck them as sacrilegious. Second, I felt, though I had no rational way of expressing this, that there was a near-tangible aura of holiness surrounding him, and I thought, though I didn't know *how*, that if I could pray in physical proximity to him, perhaps that holiness would refract onto me, and I would find my own prayers made more efficacious.

That first week, and for several after, I felt that it was an impudence for me, a gentile, a *goy*, to sit so close to a man that many intelligent Jews regarded as one of the greatest men alive. But I had to dare. I was determined to become not only a Jew, but a good Jew, even a great Jew. I couldn't do that from the back of the synagogue. If Rabbi Greenblatt had told me to leave, I would have instantly returned to the back. But he didn't. He shook my hand, and then returned to the supplementary mystical meditations on the prayers that are practiced only by a coterie of the most knowledgeable living Jews in each generation, and, so far as I knew, he noticed me no longer.

Sitting in the same seat each week is a Jewish custom, and the seat behind Rabbi Greenblatt was unfilled (for few wished the onerous burden of being unable to converse each Saturday morning for three-and-a-half hours), so I quickly found that I had gained right to the seat. Installed in a position behind Rabbi Greenblatt, I was soon able to anticipate many things he might need or want.

He refrained from participating in the post-service snack (*kiddush*) with the rest of the congregation for fear that an unlearned woman or female guest might walk up to him and hug him—a not unthinkable proposition in the friendly South—or that he would have to hear uncouth or slanderous conversation from a congregant who knew no better. And so each week I would bring a plate of food from the *kiddush* to the small office off the sanctuary where he retired. There we would exchange a few words of conversation—he might gently quiz me on my progress in my studies, and then I would retire before the stream of men who entered seeking guidance.

That year allowed me to found a relationship with Rabbi Greenblatt. So when I found myself, the summer after Ole Miss, living a short walk from his home, I decided to pay him a visit.

327.

The first time I entered his home I was frightened. I didn't know if it would be a gross breach of protocol to simply knock on his door in the middle of the day, if I would interrupt his studies or religious meditation. But he smiled, and welcomed me in, padding away slowly before me. I closed the door and followed him into the dim interior.

The Terrible Beauty of the Evil Man

Anyone who loves the smell of old books, as I do, would have been enthralled by his home. It was dusty, and musty, and reeked of the smell of the tens of thousands of ancient, cracked volumes that lined every wall. In various niches, where there was a small space between bookshelves, were lodged photographs of the most eminent rabbis of generations past. Nothing else decorated the home. He took me into what, in a normal home, would have been the living room, but was his study. There was a desk and a couple of chairs, and he motioned for me to sit.

I sat down, and was quiet, bashful—most unlike me. I didn't know what to say. Rabbi Greenblatt chatted merrily, seemingly glad of the company, and told me stories of all sorts, jumping between decades and continents with the fluidity of a trapeze artist dancing from bar to bar. He told me of his personal teacher, Rabbi Moshe Feinstein—considered by many the single most important rabbi in the world in his lifetime. He told me of his youth in Israel. His accent was thick. I asked him if Hebrew was his first language. "Yiddish," he replied, "but I picked up Modern Hebrew." He told me of his time in the militant Jewish underground in the years prior to the independence of Israel.

"All day I stood at the *shtender* (book podium) without rest, and by night I would go out to fight the British," he chuckled.

He made this remark casually, as an aside in a free-flowing stream of consciousness that had taken me across much of the Jewish twentieth century, and as he did so I realized that I was in the presence of a modern David—a man who was both a scholar of the Law of Moses as well as the only significant decisor of Jewish Law (*posek*) in the world who had very likely killed a number of men.

(Years later I would hear similar fascinating tales in the home of his uncle, the equally esteemed Rabbi Nuta Greenblatt. The most poignant concerned the night he walked home alone through a hostile Arab neighborhood, returning from the last Friday night Sabbath service held in Jerusalem's Old City, before Eastern Jerusalem was overrun by the Jordanian army, the synagogues destroyed, and many of those same rabbis and students he had prayed with were killed.)

I was shocked that Rabbi Greenblatt was chatting about anything but the Torah, or quizzing me on my learning, for that was all I had come to associate with what a rabbi was, due to the personal style of my rabbinic sponsor. But Rabbi Greenblatt, though he affected great simplicity in his style and manner, knew, without being told, that I was frightened in his presence, and his stories and cheerfulness were a way of calming me and showing me kindness.

328.

I cannot think of Rabbi Greenblatt without attributing to him the virtue of loving-kindness, which the Kabbalists call *chesed*. We often find that, when peering into the heart and mind of another, one specific characteristic rises to define that individual's development as a human.

In the great masses of humanity few achieve a disentangling of pain and confusion and foolishness to the extent necessary to truly personify a virtue. In Jewish tradition, particularly in the lore of the Kabbalists, there are identifications of singular virtues associated with specific biblical figures.

For example, Abraham is considered the personification of *chesed*. Isaac is the personification of *gevurah*, which may best be described as an austere strength, a sense of restraint, the unflinching commitment to strict justice, a profound sense of awe in the presence of the Divine. Jacob is the personification of *tiferes*, which literally means splendor, but which is better understood as the perfect synthesis of *chesed* and *gevurah* (compassion and restraint)—as in the case of a man who is deeply merciful, but yet not so merciful as to pervert justice or the upholding of Truth. Joseph is the personification of *yesod*, which literally means foundation, but is best understood as the characteristic of sexual purity, for the rabbis believed, millennia before Freud, that the sexual impulse is of foundational motivational importance in behavior, that the ability to control the passions, as well as the central nervous system, best personified in the sexual drive, is the platform on which every higher achievement of the spirit rests. Without the ability to regulate the passions, without the ability to control the body, all else is fragile construction.

But to return, it was loving-kindness, more than any other virtue, that radiated from Rabbi Greenblatt, though he cloaked it in gentle simplicity and humor. That was, for me, an important lesson. I had not realized that wise, long-bearded rabbis can (and should) also be possessed of cheerfulness and the ability to laugh.

There are far too many men of the middle ground—rabbis who have much learning, but who have not attained the totality of the Torah, of personhood, but who are, to the public, giants of the Law, and it is some of these who have damaged Judaism for the marginally affiliated, through their projection of the synonymy of legal expertise with radical and unpleasant gravitas. Perhaps such men feel that without this morbid aura they cannot sufficiently impress their learning on the masses, but when in the presence of a rabbi who casts a chill in any room he enters, then, my friends, beware.

The greatest rabbis I have known, while possessed of all the virtues which compose the fully-formed spiritual man, choose, from among those other virtues, to project humility and kindness and joy—not their achievement, zealotry, or any baleful fixation on sin.

329.

I was sitting in Rabbi Greenblatt's home one summer day, a month after I had moved to Memphis, and we were conversing about Torah sages of the previous generation, many of whom he had known or met. I was particularly interested in hearing stories of his master, Rabbi Moshe Feinstein, the Yoda of twentieth-century Jewish law.

At some point Rabbi Greenblatt changed the subject and asked about my conversion, casually remarking that he was surprised it was taking so long.

"I don't know, Rebbe. He said months ago that I knew what was needed in order to convert, but that he wouldn't convert me until I moved here. But I've been here a month and he's said nothing about when or if I'm to be converted."

"Hmmm," the rabbi sighed, settling into his chair, frowning as he stroked his beard.

"You have also been learning with my *talmid?*" he asked, referring to one of his close students, my friend Yosi Eisen, a young rabbi in the community.

"Yes, we've been spending a lot of time together."

"Hmmm," he sighed again, continuing to stroke his beard.

"We're learning *Gemara* now mostly, the rabbi and I," I continued. "He's got me learning a few words in Aramaic each week. It's a slow process though. I don't understand the grammar. I'm just memorizing basic nuclear words. Really I need to spend more time with Hebrew than Aramaic at this time. I feel like I'm in a Calculus class before I've mastered Algebra. I told him I want to go to Israel to learn in yeshiva. I want to learn full-time and move to Israel permanently."

"You want to go to yeshiva in *Eretz Yisroel?*"

"Yes, Rebbe. I plan to leave as soon as I'm converted. Some members of the community have told me they'll help me purchase a plane ticket. I only plan to buy a one-way ticket. I don't have anything to come back to in America. I don't have a relationship with my family or the friends of my old life."

"Have you asked him when he is going to convert you?"

"He said it would be sometime after I moved into the community here, as long as I passed the observation period."

"I observe you right now," he said quickly. "You are ready."

"Rebbe, I want very much to be Jewish. I think that my ability to keep growing is stunted here. I don't just want to be Jewish. I want to be a Jew in Israel who learns day and night."

"Yes!" Rabbi Greenblatt thundered, emoting with a remarkable degree of force from his frail frame.

"Well, Rebbe, when do you think he will bring me to *beis din* (the rabbinical court)?"

"You should ask him."

"I should ask him *if* he will convert me, or I should ask him *when* he will convert me?"

"Tell him that you are ready, and you want to go *Eretz Yisroel* to become a *ben Torah.*"

"I can do that?" I asked incredulously. At that point the psychological control that my sponsoring rabbi had over me was so all-encompassing that I had never imagined that I could simply walk up to him and tell him that, in my opinion, I should be converted.

"Yes. You can ask, you can ask. The rabbi said you must learn certain things. Now he says you know them. My *talmid* has told me you know them. He said you need to live here in the *eiruv* (the lines demarcating the boundaries of the Jewish neighborhood). Now you live here. He says he has to observe you. I observe you, and I see that your heart is fully turned toward *Talmud Torah* (Torah study). There is no reason you can't ask him to bring you to *beis din.*"

And with that a great joy flowed in me, and as I left Rabbi Greenblatt I felt certain that in only a few days I would be called before the rabbinical court.

I requested a meeting with my sponsoring rabbi, and he summoned me to his home.

"I… I don't know how to say this. I guess… I was wondering if you could let me know, tell me that is, when you were planning to, when you were thinking of bringing me to *beis din*… now that I live here, of course."

"The decision to bring you to *beis din* is mine alone," he said, looking at me sternly.

"Well yes, I understand that, Rabbi. I was only wondering if you could give me some idea of your thoughts on the matter."

"Finis, we generally do not convert people who have not lived in the community for at least a year," he said, averting his eyes.

"Rabbi, I…." I stuttered, suddenly forlorn, realizing that the rabbi meant to keep me in Memphis far longer than he had earlier implied.

"Rabbi, when we talked before you told me that I knew what was needed for conversion candidates, and have for some time. You made it seem like I would be converted shortly after I moved here."

"I don't know what you understood, but I don't generally perform conversions when I haven't been able to observe the candidate for a year."

"I've been here for every Sabbath and holiday since last fall, have been adhering to Jewish Law completely, studying so much that it was detrimental to my university studies, and have done everything you've asked of me."

"That is true, but like I said, we require an observational period."

"I thought you said the last few months have been the observational period," I objected.

"It has been, but now I am able to observe you far more closely, as you are in the community, and I hear feedback about you from many residents."

"What?" I asked, unsettled by the thought that everyone with whom I conversed might be a potential informer.

"Yes, Finis. Your ability to meld well with the community is significant during this observational process."

"But Rabbi, the community loves me. I've made many good friends. You've observed me for months. We've spent many, many hours alone together. You've never complained about anything I've done."

"You are well liked, it is true," he said, and as he spoke, I felt that no matter what I said, he had decided that I would not be converted for a very long time. I realized that the Gordons would be back long before that time, and I would have to vacate their home. I would have to find new housing in that very expensive neighborhood, and, if I wished to continue my college education over the coming year, to transfer to the University of Memphis.

"Rabbi, may I be frank?" I asked, summoning courage.

"Please do."

"I'm not growing here. I mean… I *am* growing, but I'm running in sand. I need to be in a yeshiva full time. I'm ready for it. I need to move to the next level, and I can't do that here. I know more than many members of this synagogue. This is not a community where I will achieve a high level of scholarship."

"Even if I were to send you to *beis din* tomorrow, we have a policy of keeping new converts under observation for some time after the conversion, in order to insure that they are sincere in their observance of the Torah."

"*What?*" I asked, my voice rising. "Rabbi, I've told you on numerous occasions that I planned to go to Israel as soon as I was converted. I've told you that several members of the community have offered to buy me a plane ticket to Israel. Arrangements have been made to give me a year's full-tuition scholarship, including room and board, to a yeshiva in Jerusalem. You've known this for months, and you've let me believe that all I needed to do was move here. You never mentioned a post-conversion observation requirement."

"What would you do when that year ran out? What is your plan?"

"I've been told that outstanding students receive funding indefinitely. I will work hard. I hope to secure that funding as long as God wills me to learn. If not, I still wish to remain in Israel. I'm sure that in one year I can acquire at least conversational Hebrew. I should be able to stay and work my way through the remainder of college as a transfer student. I've already completed two years of university. I should be able to remain in Israel indefinitely. Find a wife. Start a life."

"Look, I'm not sure what you thought, but the conversion, and how it is carried out, *if* it is carried out, is my decision alone."

"If I go to yeshiva I can learn full-time and grow in ways that would be impossible for me here. If I stay here I will have to move out of the Gordons' house in a couple of months, and will live in poverty to pay the rent in this neighborhood. How does me staying here learning *Gemara* with you for a couple of hours a week justify me not going to Israel for full-time study?"

"Finis, the post-conversion observation is a requirement."

"Rabbi, this doesn't make sense. If I'm in yeshiva I will live in the dorms, in a completely kosher, all-male environment, supervised at all times by an entire rabbinic staff, learning Torah all day. How can you possibly give a more thorough post-conversion observation?"

At this the rabbi sighed, and leaned back in his chair. He sat silently for several moments. I waited, terrified and upset.

"Finis, you are a qualified candidate. You have learned the material with remarkable speed. I am not debating that," he said, a note of humanity finally apparent in his voice. "This is just not the way things are done. I am confident in my method, and I am the decisor of the Law in this matter. I have years of experience. This is not my first conversion. I know a great deal more about this than you, and I have to ask you to trust me."

"Rabbi Greenblatt said I was ready. He said he had observed me, and that I was ready for conversion, and that I should go to Israel to learn full-time as soon as possible. He is a world-renowned expert in the Law."

As soon as I mouthed those words, played my trump card, the rabbi evinced palpable shock, and he sat up, rigid. I was still, and willed my hands to stop trembling.

"Rabbi Greenblatt told you that?"

"Yes, sir. This week. In his home. It was he who suggested I meet with you about this."

The rabbi leaned back in his chair once more, and his thin frame seemed to deflate. Several moments passed in silence.

"Finis, I will have to call my personal rabbi to ask for guidance in this matter. I will call you to me when I have conferred with *my* rabbi. We will speak later."

And I was shown the door, and stepped out into the Memphis summer night, full of anxiety, and the fear that I had ruined my conversion. It is a mark of the total psychological domination he had over me that I felt such fear after simply asking for a timeframe.

331.

My answer came a week later. The rabbi informed me, with all due respect to the world-renowned Ephraim Greenblatt, that he would do as he saw fit, and would not bring me before the *beis din* until he was ready, though he could not say when that might be. I was devastated, and felt I had no one I could talk to other than Rabbi Greenblatt. I asked Rabbi Greenblatt's student, my friend Yosi, to meet me at the rebbe's house, and then trudged there under the blazing Memphis summer sun.

When I arrived Rabbi Greenblatt ushered me in, but told me I would have to wait. He was giving a private lesson to Ethan, Yosi's younger brother. Ethan chanted the *Gemara* with a speed I found incredible, though Rabbi Greenblatt persistently interrupted, asking him to reconcile an argument in the Talmud with a legal question raised centuries later in one of the early major commentaries on the Talmud (a *Rishonic* work), commentaries Ethan was to have mastered prior to the lesson. Or, trickily, Rabbi Greenblatt threw in a question in which contradictions between the *Rishonim* received the tertiary analysis of later sages, the *Acharonim*— and here he was testing Ethan's ability to think creatively through the problem in the Law, for he had not assigned those tertiary commentaries as homework. These latter problems were highly abstract. One had to retain and manipulate the varied legal arguments of a dozen centuries simultaneously, wrestling to find the fine point of logical or conceptual material which required definition or resolution.

I understood very little—including what was translated into English. I felt I was listening to a conversation underwater. I was jealous. Ethan was my age, and as I sat and stared, he seemed the paradigm of everything I wanted to be. The rabbi was no longer the genial old man, but grandmaster in a skirmish where two minds moved pawns, rooks, and knights in a sequence of dizzying feints, traps, and opaque reticulations. I could not follow, with my fumbling maneuvers, the movements over the board, and so I lapsed into a daydream in which I was in Israel, a land I could only roughly imagine, engrossed in just such a debate, star pupil of an esteemed expert in the Law.

Shortly after I began to daydream, Yosi arrived. He alternated between the occasional interjection into his younger brother's lesson, and the whispered explanation to me. Soon after Ethan's lesson ended he excused himself, and Yosi and I were alone with the grandmaster.

Rabbi Greenblatt, as though by thaumaturgical transformation, shifted from a being recognizable only as an overpowering analytical mind merely cloaked in flesh, to the smiling, gentle old man who seemed perpetually caught between slumber and a quiet chuckle.

"So, *nu*, Yosi?"

"How is Rebbe?

"*Gut.*"

"And you, Finis? How are you?"

"Not so good, Rebbe. That's why I've come. I need to speak. I took your advice and went to the rabbi to ask if he would convert me. He wasn't happy. Not happy at all. He called his rabbi, and thought about it for a few days. He says he won't convert me now, and won't give me a timeframe for when he will convert me."

"Hmmm…." Rabbi Greenblatt mused as he stroked his beard. "This is not right. My *talmid*," he said, motioning to Yosi, "says you are ready. I see you. I hear you *daven* (pray) behind me. You are ready."

I smiled. I had not known that he took any notice of me when I sat behind him in the synagogue.

"So, Yosi, you are learning with him regularly as well? You are spending time together?"

"Yes, Rebbe. Finis is a great guy. I feel like he's a brother. We've been together all summer. He's learned a lot. He's holding."

The three of us sat in silence for some moments as the rabbi thought. Yosi interrupted the quiet.

"Will Rebbe assemble a *beis din* and convert Finis himself?"

"No, no," Rabbi Greenblatt quickly shook his head. "I cannot do this. His rabbi and I are in the same town. It would cause problems for the *kehillah* (community). How long did he say it would be before he converted you?" he asked, looking at me again.

"He didn't say exactly, but he seemed to imply that he would want me to live here for at least another year. I will have to find new housing when the Gordons come back. I don't know how I will afford that. I will have to transfer to the University of Memphis."

"*Meshugas!* You don't need to be in university, you need to learn Torah."

"What will Rebbe do?" Yosi asked.

"I think…." Rabbi Greenblatt was silent for a moment. "I can call the *beis din* in Baltimore. We will send you there this week. I will recommend you to them. When you come back you will be a Jew. You can leave for Israel when the Gordons come back, and you have completed your obligations to them."

"Rebbe will send Finis to Baltimore?" Yosi asked. The thought surprised him almost as much as me.

"Why not? It is a *gut yeshivishe beis din*. They will test him thoroughly. He knows the learning."

"When will I go?" I asked, still in shock.

"I will have to call them. We will find out when next they meet," he answered. "Go and prepare."

And with that, Yosi and I left the house, reeling from the news that my multi-year journey was suddenly over, and that I would be Jewish in mere days. I felt more human, as though I were a slave, and had been told of my release.

333.

Word of this arrangement emerged (not from me), and the next night, late at night, I received a phone call from my rabbinic sponsor. He was irate. Absolute power over me had been taken from him without his consent.

He called me a "time-manipulator," and accused me of having gone behind his back. (I did not point out that he could not be truly concerned about his personal time if he desired to give private lessons into the undefined future.)

I told my sponsor that the suggestion to ask him to convert me, as well as the decision to proceed in Baltimore, had come from Rabbi Greenblatt, who had said that he was morally uncomfortable with the delay in my case. My sponsor responded that it wasn't up to Rabbi Greenblatt. I said that I could not respond to the differing judgments of two men who possessed far more knowledge than me. Still angry, he hung up, letting me know that he would have words with Rabbi Greenblatt.

That was the only time, during that year, or in the many years since, that I have seen or heard that man evince a strong emotion of any kind.

The Terrible Beauty of the Evil Man

334.

A compromise was reached, behind closed doors. My future was again determined by backroom legal wrangling. In order to avoid creating dissension in the community, Rabbi Greenblatt agreed not to send me to Baltimore for an immediate conversion. My sponsor agreed to defer to Rabbi Greenblatt, to accede to the request that I be allowed to convert soon, in Memphis, and then proceed immediately to Israel to learn full-time in yeshiva.

I was disappointed that I would not be converted immediately, but would have to wait until the end of the summer. I would be converted at the end of August, when the Gordons returned, when I would evacuate their home for a new life in Israel.

My rabbinic sponsor had refused to relinquish his right to continue to *observe* me for the remainder of the summer. So the next morning of that summer marked the start of an anxiety-riddled series of weeks, as I knew he would use any pretext to prevent my conversion. No matter what I said, I knew he felt I had deliberately attempted to undercut his authority over me.

He did not in any way dispute that I knew the material necessary for conversion. What, then, did he want? I have reflected on this in years gone. Surely he knew what a painful, lonely state I was in, competent to become a Jew, but held back for nebulous observation.

It is only after the passage of time, the perfection of hindsight, that I feel I have any insight into what must have motivated him. He was a New Yorker transplanted to a South with which he never identified. He wished to learn, to achieve scholarship, but led an aging congregation that was largely disinterested in the recondite disputes of the Talmud. He had, over the years, retreated into himself, so that whoever he had been, years before in New York, was no longer visible, but was buried far beneath, in a place that perhaps even he could no longer go.

For him, I (as well as the converts who came before and after me) must have represented a possibility to shape and form a soul into someone with whom he could begin to emerge from that self-constructed cocoon. I didn't represent someone who could be formed into another him. That was impossible. Rather, I could be commanded to give my time, my attention, to what most deeply interested that buried facet of his personality—the young, hopeful scholar.

But to turn me into a private study-partner-on-demand, was, from a psychological perspective, to turn me into a type of *toy*, an imaginary friend. To prolong this, even when numerous members of the community asked him to end it, when other rabbis wished him to end it, including one of the most renowned sages in the world, to the point that it had to be threatened to be taken away from him, was to demonstrate how deep was the loneliness, not in me, but in him.

335.

How strange a thing, to tell a young man that he will not be allowed to convert unless he bonds strongly with the community, implying that he must befriend them, be pleasant, learn the stories of their lives, and in return share such details about himself—and yet make the young man aware that each of those he must befriend, bond with, open up to, are sources that may be asked for private, incriminating information.

What an impossible position! Failure to become part of the tribe, to *open up*, is grounds for failure—simultaneously everything you say in private conversation can be used to disqualify you.

336.

I lived the next two months in a state of paranoia. My sponsoring rabbi, along with Rabbi Greenblatt, had determined that I could be *observed*, and my conversion discontinued if that observation proved illuminative of any problems in me. As my sponsor had known and interacted with me for more than a year, and for many dozens of hours in an intimate setting, it was unclear what he hoped to detect through further observation.

Throughout the school year at Ole Miss I had felt happiness and gratitude. I believed I was nearing the end of a multi-year project, nay, a profound quest in search of truth travelled from the earliest catechisms of my father. Yet the closer I drew to my goal, the more I began to *fear* the rabbi who had the power (and, I believed, the motivation) to end it all.

So as we sank into that endless summer, the hotter Memphis broiled, the more my former equilibrium was upset. By the time we reached August, I would appear breathless and trembling if I arrived five minutes late to any of the thrice-daily prayer services. I grew vigilant in every conversation, in even off-hand remarks, aware my sponsor was regularly interviewing members of the community about their interactions with me.

All of the observation, with the (supposed) intent of determining whether I was psychologically sound and able to adjust well to the Jewish people, served only to cause me to feel *less* psychologically sound and less willing to integrate into the community. It had not been so during my year at Ole Miss, but I remember that summer as the summer of paranoia, and it is sad that it should have been so. Nevertheless, it could have been nothing else. I had been threatened with the dissolution of all that I had sacrificed for, and worked toward. How shameful that the lead-in to my entry before the rabbinic court should have been a time of such terror. It should have been a time a joy.

337.

The Gordons returned at the end of August, and my case was called for the following week. The rabbis gave no indication that my case would fail when it reached the rabbinic court, and so I purchased a one-way plane ticket to Israel.

338.

It was a Thursday night in late August, in the week immediately following *Tisha b'Av*, the ninth day of the Hebrew month of *Av*, the Hebrew Day of Sorrows, the only day other than Yom Kippur in which a person must refrain from eating, drinking, and bathing of any kind for twenty-five hours. My conversion, I had been told, would be the very next day. I was scribbling thoughts in a journal, sitting at a table on the balcony patio which overlooked the Gordons' backyard.

Old Mr. Gordon, shuffling slowly, came out to join me under the starlight and pregnant moon. I set aside my journal and looked at him. We sat for some moments in silence.

"Well," he said, looking over at me, "now you've seen it."

"Seen what?" I asked.

"The whole of the Jewish year. You came in August of last year. August is now nearly finished this year."

"I suppose that's so," I mused. "I hadn't thought of it that way."

"It is interesting that the last of our days of observance you have witnessed is the day of our greatest tragedy."

"You mean that both the First and the Second Temple were destroyed on *Tisha b'Av*, though they were destroyed centuries apart?"

"*Tisha b'Av* is the day on which we lost both Temples, yes," he said quietly, "but it is also the day on which our tribe has endured many more sufferings, exiles, and pogroms. Even now, even this year, the Jews are being cast out of their own land on *Tisha b'Av*. The unthinkable is occurring as we speak. Jews are making a part of Israel *Judenrein*."

"I know how severely the Jews have suffered."

"Do you?" he asked, staring into my eyes in the dim light that reached from the house behind us. Fireflies lit the sky, glowing lackadaisically, dancing endlessly in a waltz that led nowhere. Perhaps it was the starlight, or the warm air, or the fireflies, but suddenly my sense of time and space was altered, and I felt as though Mr. Gordon and I were no longer in Memphis, no longer anywhere, but yet at the same time located everywhere, and at all times, spread out over distances and ages as vast as Jewish history itself.

"We have suffered thousands of years for our sins. Everyone who would become a Jew must accept this. You cannot become a Jew unless you understand that you may be forced someday to choose between what is right and painful, or what is wrong and easy. When the Jews were expelled from Spain—this happened on *Tisha b'Av*—many of the Jews chose to stay behind, convert to Christianity, remain in the ease of the lives they had lived in Spain for hundreds of years. Their children and grandchildren were lost to us, lost to the Jewish people. Only those who left with nothing survived. But the Jewish people went on."

"I would have left," I asserted quietly. "I would have gone with nothing. I have lived with nothing just to be here."

"Yes," Mr. Gordon nodded in the near darkness, "you have. But a Jew may be called on to give up more than his possessions and home. He may be forced to give his life for being Jewish. Such is not uncommon in our history."

"Mr. Gordon," I said, my chest suddenly tightening, unexpected tears forming at the corners of my eyes, "I... I would," I faltered, unable to express the emotion I felt. A tear slid from my eye and I sighed.

"Mr. Gordon," I began again, "I have no desire to die, but I would walk straight into Auschwitz tomorrow if that was what it took to become a Jew. That is how strongly I believe."

"Then," he said, slowly raising his bulk from the chair, "you will truly become a Jew."

And he walked toward the door behind us, over the hardwood planks that formed the floor of the balcony, and yet I seemed to remain outside of time and space, stretched out, like the starlight, over years past and years to come, and as I remained in that trance I forgot that Mr. Gordon had even risen, until he called to me, one last time, before heading inside.

"Remember," he said, "that the month of *Av* does not only bring pain. In *Av* there is also comfort."

I did not know then, what he meant, but I would learn, in time.

339.

For females a conversion to Judaism consists of two parts. The first is a hearing before a rabbinic court. At this hearing they may ask you whatever they wish. They test your knowledge, determine that you possess no heretical beliefs, ascertain whether you are attempting to convert for some dubious purpose, and inform you of the obligations, both major and minor, of what will be your new life as a Jew.

The single most important component of the court hearing is a declaration by the candidate that they accept and submit to the entirety of the commandments of the Torah, both Written and Oral, and that they will adhere to Jewish Law without reservation for the remainder of their life. If the candidate does not swear this, or swears this with no intention of fulfilling the oath, it invalidates the entire conversion, and the candidate does not become a Jew. This makes the most important element of the court hearing a determination of whether the candidate is sincere when they vow to abide by and uphold the Law for the remainder of their life.

The second part of the conversion, for the Jewish female, is ritual immersion in a specially built pool of water, called a *mikveh*. (This custom in Judaism is ancient, mentioned in the Torah itself. It formed the motive for John the Baptist giving Jesus a dunk in the Jordan, and from that act arose the entire notion of Christian baptism.) When the woman rises from the waters of the *mikveh* she is no longer a gentile, but is as Jewish as the oldest, most revered rabbi in the world.

For males conversion to Judaism requires an additional step that falls between the court hearing and immersion in the waters of the *mikveh*. That requirement is the circumcision of the foreskin of the penis.

Fortunately, I had been circumcised as a baby, so there was no skin removal in my case. In cases where the candidate has been previously circumcised, there is a requirement to take a symbolic drop of blood from the penis. This is known as the *dam ha'bris*, or blood of the covenant.

As I entered the office in which sat the rabbinic court that would make me a Jew or leave me a forlorn gentile, I confess that I was very distracted by the thought that someone might soon pierce my penis.

340.

The three rabbis who comprised the rabbinical court for my hearing were Rabbi Joel Finklestein, senior rabbi of the Orthodox congregation Anshei Sphard Beth El Emeth of Memphis, Rabbi Shai Finklestein, (no relation to Joel), senior rabbi of the Orthodox congregation Baron Hirsch of Memphis, and Rabbi Ephraim Greenblatt, who served as the *av beis din*, or lead judge, of the rabbinical court.

Rabbi Joel Finkelstein had received ordination *Yoreh Yoreh* from Rabbi Yosef Ber Soloveitchik, of blessed memory.

Rabbi Shai Finkelstein, a native of Israel, had received ordination *Yoreh Yoreh* from Rabbi Yisrael Meir Lau, *shlita*, the former chief rabbi of Israel. He later received advanced ordination *Yadin Yadin* from the chief rabbinate of Israel.

HaGaon Rabbi Ephraim Greenblatt, of blessed memory, author of the multi-volume *Revivos Ephraim* as well as other noted works, received ordination from his master, the *Posek HaDor*, *HaGaon* Rabbi Moshe Feinstein, of blessed memory, as well as from *HaGaon* Rabbi Isser Zalman Meltzer, of blessed memory.

My hearing took place in the waning hours of *Erev Shabbos, yud dalet Av*, 5765, which was Friday afternoon, August, 19, 2005.

341.

I walked into the office. The three rabbis were seated close together. Rabbi Greenblatt was in the center, with Rabbi Shai on his right and Rabbi Joel on his left. The room was cramped, as we were in an actual office, which was not large. There was a desk in the room behind the rabbis, and the walls were covered with book-stuffed bookshelves from floor to ceiling.

The door on my right, I sat in a small chair, three feet from the rabbis, with nothing between us. They briefly exchanged small talk related to mundane matters of communal governance, and then they turned to me as one. I gulped.

"Let's begin," Rabbi Greenblatt said.

"Finis Beauchamp," Rabbi Joel solemnly intoned, "do you understand that you are here for us to determine if you are fit to convert to Judaism, knowledgeable in matters of the Law, and possessed of the appropriate beliefs, character traits, and worldview befitting a Jew?"

"I do," I responded timidly.

"Then let us begin. First, are you here of your own free will? Has anyone asked you to convert to Judaism? Has anyone offered you an incentive to become a Jew? Are you here under coercion?" Rabbi Joel asked.

"No. Absolutely not. I decided to become a Jew more than two years ago. It was my own decision, and it cost me my relationship with my family, and virtually every friend I had. Everyone from my past life thinks I am going to burn in hell forever. I had never known any Jews at the time I made the decision. The choice was, and is, my own."

"Do you understand," Rabbi Shai interjected, his strong Israeli accent making it difficult to understand him, "that just because you have come this far in the conversion process, does not mean that you need to continue? You can quit right now! Do you understand that you are free to end the process, to freely live the life of a righteous gentile— without the yoke of the Torah?"

"I understand that, but I wish to continue with the conversion."

"But why?" Rabbi Shai pressed. "Don't you realize that there is a place in the World-to-Come for the righteous of all nations? We Jews do not believe in this *eternal Hell*. You choose to place yourself under a tremendous burden. The Law is vast, it is an ocean, and there is punishment in the World-to-Come for failure to keep it. As a non-Jew you will not suffer punishment of any kind, provided you do not violate one of the seven laws binding on all the sons of Noah. Seven commandments are much easier than the six hundred and thirteen laws of the Torah."

"Well, Rabbi," I said, pausing momentarily as I strove to quickly balance the many reasons why I did not wish to live out the remainder of my life as one of the righteous gentiles, or *b'nai Noach*. "There are many reasons why I prefer to convert rather than live as a *ben Noach*. There are very few people in the world who believe that Judaism is true, but yet are not Jewish. Even most Jews do not believe in Judaism. It would not be easy for me to find a community with which to associate. It would be extremely difficult to find a non-Jewish wife who shares belief in the truth of the Torah with no additional Testaments or perverse doctrines. Assuming I did find such a woman, where would we educate our children? There are no schools or communities where one can live and raise children in this belief system."

"That is a valid point," Rabbi Shai acceded.

"Wait," I interrupted. "Those are reasons, but they are not *the* reason. I made a choice more than two years ago to have faith that there exists a deity. Before that I was an agnostic. I did not know which of the various religions was true, but through research and reason came to believe in Judaism, the original monotheism, a religion free of the many logical problems that had bothered me in the religion of my birth. I knew early that I did not have to become a Jew simply because I believed that Judaism was true, just as I don't have to become a mathematician because I believe that the Pythagorean Theorem truly describes the relationship between the sides of a right triangle. I choose to become a Jew because my every instinct pushes me to become the best, do the most, reach for the highest. If the Torah is true, that implies that God has chosen the Jews as his special people... to be a light unto the nations. I could not, in good conscience, accept this as truth and not attempt to become a part of that people. If God has chosen the Jews to bring Goodness and Light into the world, I would go through life filled with regret if I knew that Truth and yet failed to become a member of the sacred covenant."

I could see that this answer pleased the rabbis. There was silence in the room for a moment after my proclamation, and I waited expectantly, nervous, wondering in which direction the rabbis would next take the interrogation.

342.

"The world is not an easy place to be a Jew," Rabbi Joel said abruptly. "Nearly every country Jews have ever lived has thrown them out. Today, in the United States, Jews are treated equally and fairly, but this is a historical anomaly. The Jews who live in Israel, which is where you say you want to go, rarely go more than five consecutive years without being forced to engage in a war for their very existence. It is war after war after war, and they can't afford to lose a single one. If they did it would be another Holocaust. If the American or global economy goes bad, if there is ever another Great Depression, we know from history that Jews are likely to be blamed. If Jews become too successful, then too they will be hated. We will be hated for failure and hated for success. You may be blamed for the evils of Capitalism at the same time as you are blamed for the evils of Communism. I can guarantee that there will be persons who will hate you simply for being a Jew. Some will wish to hurt or kill you. Some may even try."

"It is known from the Torah," Rabbi Shai added, "*amar Rebbi Shimon bar Yochai, 'Halachah hee—b'yaduah sh'Eisav sonei le'Yaakov!'*" (The ancient Sage, Rabbi Shimon, the son of Yochai, said, "It is a *law* that Esau hates Jacob!") "It is certain," Rabbi Shai continued, "that if you become a Jew you will face hatred. The Torah itself says this. If you don't convert, you will avoid all of this. Why should you face hatred when you have no need to? There are many cases in history of righteous *b'nai Noach*, and their reward in the afterlife will be great indeed. You can walk away from this. You don't need to do this."

"I spoke of this matter last night," I answered quickly, then paused, aware of the gravitas lining the faces of all three rabbis. "I was with Mr. Alvin Gordon last night, who you all know and respect. I was on his porch balcony... the moon was very bright. I was thinking ahead to today's hearing. He came out to speak to me, and this was the topic he broached. I don't have a simple answer for you, just as I didn't have one for him. There isn't one. I know the Jews suffer. Even now, as we speak, Jews are evicting other Jews from Gaza, a part of the Land of Israel. This situation would have been unthinkable to Jews of previous generations. I can only tell you what I told Mr. Gordon. I have no desire to die, but if I had been forced to walk into Auschwitz itself to meet with you today, and *knew*... if I was absolutely certain, that I would be stuffed into an oven an hour after the conversion... I would still do it. I would walk into Auschwitz itself, knowing I would die, if I could become Jewish for even a day."

The two Rabbis Finkelstein sat back in their chairs, taken aback by the extreme zealotry of my answer, but Rabbi Greenblatt leaned forward, almost unblinking, and for a fragment of a second he was no longer that kind, gentle, old man, but rather the frightening embodiment of raw intellectual and spiritual power, merely cloaked in flesh, that I had seen but once before, as he learned with my friend, Ethan Eisen. But then, as quickly as I saw that spark leap forth from his eyes it was gone, hidden once more behind the smoky haze of aged irises.

I felt that the force of my answer had unsettled them. I wasn't sure if my answer made me sound mentally unstable—and if they would then disqualify me. I struggled to explain my declaration.

"I cannot imagine that there is a Truth one can believe, and spend a *lifetime* living with rigor, that he would not also be willing to die for. To live a lifetime in the service of a belief *is* to die to every other life one might have lived had he not embraced that ideal! To assent unconditionally to one possible life is to die to all others. And if a man believes so strongly that something is deserving of the labor of his entire life, and more, it is so abundantly clear that he would even die for that Truth… then what difference if he might die for that Truth at an undefined time in the future, or if he will definitely die for that Truth in an hour? If it is *true*, then it is true. I have no desire to die, but if it is worth dying for, it is worth dying for a decade from now, or an hour from now. The *when* of it makes no difference at all. Time is irrelevant when one serves an eternal God."

"He is right!" Rabbi Greenblatt exclaimed, and the other rabbis nodded with him. They paused, and I could see that they were pleased with my answer. They were ready to move to the next portion of the hearing.

343.

"Finis, what religion did you practice before you decided to embrace Judaism?" Rabbi Joel asked quietly.

"I was an agnostic for some time prior to my choice to become Jewish," I responded, "but before that, from birth until my eighteenth year, I was a Christian—a Southern Baptist."

"And do you still believe in the principles of that religion?" Rabbi Joel continued.

"No, absolutely not."

"Do you believe God has a son?"

"No. I find the concept absurd."

"Do you believe that the man the Christians revere is divine?"

"No."

"Do you believe that he rose from the dead?"

"No."

"Do you believe, even if you do not think that he is divine, or the son of God, that he is in fact the *Moshiach* (Messiah) for whom we wait daily?"

"No. I do not believe that he was the *Moshiach*. I do not believe, for a variety of reasons, that he was even eligible to be the *Moshiach*."

"Do you believe the *Moshiach* is someone else, some other person who has already come?" Rabbi Shai asked.

"No, Rabbi. I do not believe that the *Moshiach* has revealed himself. I await his coming each day."

"As do we all," Rabbi Shai agreed, before continuing. "Do you think that you know who the *Moshiach* is, or that you are the *Moshiach*?"

"No," I replied with a chuckle, but then quickly sobered when I realized his question was serious. "I have no idea who the *Moshiach* is. I only believe that he has not been revealed at this time. As for me, I'm not even eligible to be the *Moshiach*, as the Law says he must be a direct descendent of King David in the patrilineal line, and I am descended from gentiles, with no Jewish ancestry whatsoever."

"Do you believe there are any prophets greater than Moshe (Moses), such as Mohammed, or even other holy Jewish prophets, such as Shmuel (Samuel)?" Rabbi Shai asked.

"I do not believe Mohammed was divinely inspired in any way. There have been other holy prophets in our faith, but there is no prophet greater than Moshe, nor can there be."

"Do you believe the *Moshiach*, when he comes, will be a human, or the son of God—a deity?" Rabbi Joel asked.

"I believe he will be human. There is only one God. That is the central thesis of Judaism. There cannot be a God that is divine and also a man who is divine. This is a core belief."

"Hmmm," Rabbi Greenblatt grunted, signaling that I was correct, and that the other two rabbis should move the hearing forward.

344.

"Finis, do you understand that, should you become Jewish today, you face punishment for the violation of any of the Laws, even those you consider minor?" Rabbi Joel asked.

"I understand."

"Do you understand that there are punishments which may be carried out in the World-to-Come, and that there are punishments that God inflicts on the sinner in this world?"

"I understand."

"Do you understand that God gave authority to Moshe to impose judgments on the people, and that Moshe passed that authority on to the rabbis, and that authority exists in our own Age? For example, you are called here before us today, because we have the authority to decide on the case of your conversion."

"I understand."

"Do you accept the absolute authority of the Torah, both Written and Oral?"

"I do."

"Do you belief that Moses was divinely inspired by God when he wrote the Torah?"

"I do."

"Do you agree to follow all the commandments of the Torah?"

"I do," I said, realizing that I had responded to the central, essential question of the court hearing.

"Is there even one *halachah* (law) you are aware of that you do not intend to fulfill?"

"No," I replied. "I don't know every *halachah* that there is, or even the majority, though I've learned much of what is required for daily life. Nevertheless, there is no law I know of that I intend to disobey, or fail to fulfill, and I will certainly live and abide by any laws that I should come to learn in the future."

"Do you accept the absolute authority of *Chazal?*" he asked, referring to the greatest sages of each generation, extending in a line back to Moses.

"I do."

"Do you accept the authority of the Talmud and *Shulchan Aruch?* Do you accept the authority of the leaders of our generation to rule on matters of the Law, both old and new, that may arise?"

"I do."

"Do you understand that, should you be converted today, when the *Beit HaMikdash* (Third Temple) is rebuilt, you will be required by the Law to bring a *korban* (offering), which is required of all who convert?"

"I understand, and agree to bring the *korban.*"

"Do you understand that if and when you marry a Jewish woman, and have children, you are responsible for making sure that those children attend Jewish schools, and receive a thorough education in the principles and learning of our faith?"

"I understand, and wish for that very much."

"Do you understand that you could be summoned before a *beis din*, like this one, for cases related to violations of the Law? If that *beis din* is a legitimate *beis din*, you would be required to attend the summons, and to abide by their judgments."

"I understand, and accept that."

"Now," Rabbi Joel said, leaning forward, and looking at me seriously, "do you understand that at the current time there is no *Sanhedrin?*" (The seventy-one-member Supreme Court of Judaism—extinct for two millennia.)

"Yes. I am aware that the *Sanhedrin* no longer exists."

"Do you understand that if the *Sanhedrin* is reconvened, which could certainly occur in your lifetime, they will have the authority to impose the death penalty for certain crimes?"

"I understand," I said with a gulp, for the two Rabbis Finkelstein had taken on a morbid air. Rabbi Greenblatt looked at me expressionlessly.

"If it is the Sabbath, and you are starting a fire, and two people come to you, and tell you to stop, you must stop. If you refuse, you could be put to death by the *Sanhedrin*," Rabbi Shai added. "Again, why do you wish to take this burden on yourself? If you do not become a Jew, you can light fires, cook, travel, or do whatever you wish on the Sabbath. You are not committing a capital crime."

"I understand the Law on this matter," I said with a sigh. "I understand that, under certain circumstances, if a *Sanhedrin* is reconvened, they could put me to death for various violations of the Law."

"Do you understand that even without a *Sanhedrin*, a legitimate *beis din* has the power to punish you, perhaps by monetary fine, or by other means, and that this can occur as soon as you become a Jew? Even another Jew, if he feels you have offended or wronged him, can bring a complaint to *beis din*, and, if they choose, they can summon you," Rabbi Joel said.

"Yes. I understand. I have no intention of violating the Law, but understand that there are punishments and ramifications if I do."

"Then it is time to find out if you know the Law," Rabbi Shai said. I realized that the quiz was about to begin.

345.

"What does a Jew do as soon as he awakens?" Rabbi Joel asked.

"He says *Modeh Ani*, and he washes *negel vasser.*"

"How does he wash?"

I explained the convoluted ritual by which Jews ritually wash their hands in the morning.

"How many times a day does a Jew say the *Shema*?" Rabbi Joel asked.

"Three."

"Three. I see. So we say it at *Shacharis*, *Minchah*, and *Maariv*?" he asked. (The three daily prayer services.)

"No. We say it at *Shacharis*, and *Maariv*. We do not say it at *Minchah*. The third time is at night, just before sleep. Some have the custom to say it a fourth time if they recite *Akeidah* in the morning, but our synagogue doesn't recite that aloud."

"Ha!" Rabbi Greenblatt laughed, looking at Rabbi Joel with a twinkle in his eye.

"When the Jew puts on the *tefillin* (phylacteries), which does he put on first?" Rabbi Shai asked.

"He puts on the arm first, then the head."

"He puts the arm on all the way?"

"No. He puts on the *shel yad* (arm) and says *l'haniach*, and winds it around his arm, but does not wrap it around his hand and fingers until after he has put on the *shel rosh* (head) and said *al mitzvas tefillin*."

"I see. Have you put on *tefillin* before?" Rabbi Shai asked me.

"No."

"So which arm will you put your *tefillin* on?"

"My left arm."

"Why?"

"Because I'm right-handed. And the prayer box goes next to your heart."

"Ok," Rabbi Shai agreed. "What will you do if someone gives you an apple and you want to eat it?"

"I make the blessing *borei pri ha'etz* before I eat, and I make the blessing *al ha'etz* after."

"Please recite the blessings," Rabbi Joel interrupted.

I recited the two blessings from memory, modifying the name of God in the prescribed manner, so as not to take the name in vain.

"And you say them the same way if you take only a small bite, and then discard the apple because you feel full?" Rabbi Joel asked.

"No. You say *borei pri ha'etz* before, but not the *al ha'etz* after. You didn't eat enough of it."

"How much of it is enough?"

"A *shiur*."

"How much is a *shiur*?" Rabbi Shai asked.

"It depends on what you're eating or drinking. A *k'zayis* or a *revi'is*. I don't know for everything. I would either ask a rabbi, or keep eating until I was sure. A *shiur* for most foods isn't that big, and I'm a big guy. I would really have to hate the food to put it away without finishing a *k'zayis*."

"What if you're talking with friends, and it takes you a long time to eat the apple?" Rabbi Shai asked.

"You have a limited amount of time to eat a *shiur*."

"How long?"

"As I understand it, there are varying legal opinions. I would try to eat a *shiur* in three minutes, then I could eat the rest slowly."

"How long do you have to consume a *revi'is* of a drink?" Rabbi Joel asked.

"You should drink the *revi'is* at once without delay."

"How much is a *revi'is*?"

"Hmmm… not a lot," I said, holding up my fingers as if to indicate an amount in a cup.

"How much is not a lot?" Rabbi Joel asked.

"Like three or four ounces, I guess."

"What if you are drinking coffee?" he continued. "You can't drink a *revi'is* of coffee without delay if it is boiling hot. Do you still make a blessing after?"

"You can make a *sh'hakol* on water, and have in mind that it should also cover the coffee, then drink a *revi'is* of water. You can then drink the coffee normally, and say *borei nefashos* on both."

"If you want to eat a granola bar, then an apple, and have it with a glass of water, in what order do you eat these and make the *brachot*?" Rabbi Joel asked.

"You say *borei minei mezonos*, eat some granola, say *borei pri ha'etz* and bite the apple, then say *sh'hakol* and drink the water. When you're finished you combine the blessings for *mezonos* and *ha'etz*, then say *borei nefashos*."

"Please recite the blessing you say after you go to the bathroom," Rabbi Shai requested.

I then launched quickly into this paragraph-long blessing.

(Incidentally, if you, the disinterested observer, ever see a religious Jew outside a bathroom mumbling to themselves with their head down, they are not speaking on a phone you can't see, they are thanking God for the successful evacuation of their bladder and intestines. The prayer is literally a paragraph long, and was undoubtedly composed by a geriatric rabbi who knew true gratitude after a successful bowel movement.)

Rabbi Greenblatt coughed again, signaling a need to move the proceedings along.

"Which holiday do we eat outdoors?" Rabbi Joel asked.

"*Sukkos.* We eat in the *sukkah.*"

"And what type of roof does a *sukkah* have?"

"It's *schach*—it's made of sticks or bamboo or something like that."

"And what is the legally appropriate way to get the bamboo, or *schach*, to completely cover the roof?"

"You don't. It's not supposed to. There have to be gaps in the roof so you can see the sky and stars."

"Ha!" Rabbi Greenblatt chuckled again.

"How would you make an oven kosher for Passover?" Rabbi Joel asked.

"Honestly, I would not try to *kasher* a kitchen by myself for my first Passover or two, or even three. The rules are too complex. I would get help from a rabbi. Anyway, if I'm converted today, my next Passover will be in a yeshiva, and there the rabbis will supervise the *kashering* of the yeshiva kitchen, and I will be able to observe and ask questions."

"Still, if you were to try to make the oven kosher for Passover, how would you do it?" he persisted.

"Well, I don't really know. If it's a new oven, it probably has a self-cleaning cycle. You clean the oven, run the cycle, and I think that's it. If it's an old oven, I'm not sure. I think you have to use a blowtorch. Like I said, I wouldn't try to do this on my own for several years. Even if I knew how to do it I probably wouldn't use a blowtorch. Seems like a good way to burn your house down. I'd just go without an oven for a week."

"This was Rebbe's opinion," Rabbi Greenblatt noted, referring to both the blowtorch, and his master, Rabbi Feinstein. "He knows, he knows," Rabbi Greenblatt continued, sighing as though flustered, ready to move on. "What else is needed?" he asked, glancing at the rabbis on either side of him.

"We'd like to have you read several passages of Hebrew from the *siddur* to demonstrate your reading skills," Rabbi Joel said, handing me a prayer book. "Please flip to *Ashrei*, and begin reading. Then please turn to *Aleinu.*"

I began quickly reading through the *Ashrei*, (Psalms 145, with a few additions), a page-length prayer, and got about halfway through before Rabbi Greenblatt clapped twice, and began laughing. I looked up, startled.

"He reads like a scholar. *Like a scholar!*" he said, still laughing. "I hear him behind me on *Shabbos*. He sings the *Kel Adon* very well!"

I blushed, knowing that even if I read correctly, I certainly didn't read like a scholar, and glad that the rabbis had asked me to read familiar prayers, and not an obscure piece of ancient Hebrew.

Rabbi Greenblatt looked at Rabbi Shai, then to Rabbi Joel.

"So *nu*, is there more you need to ask? He *knows*."

The two Rabbis Finkelstein looked at each other and shook their heads.

"Would the Rabbi like to ask Finis anything?" Rabbi Joel asked Rabbi Greenblatt.

And it was then that I passed through one of the most fascinating and unusual experiences of my life.

346.

Rabbi Greenblatt shifted in his chair, as though he were making himself more comfortable, though I noticed that he had inched forward slightly. His head was down as he resettled, and when he looked up he smiled.

"So you want to be a Jew?" he asked me kindly.

"Yes, very much," I said, a touch of gratefulness in my voice. I felt a tangible sense of relief, as though I had passed from the hands of two very thorough interlocutors into the embrace of a warm grandfather.

"And you want to go to Israel? To learn in yeshiva?"

"If the Rabbis make me a Jew today, I will leave for Israel right after *Shabbos*."

"It is not easy," he said, "to sit and learn all day. It is not like learning after work, or in your spare time. You wake very early and you learn. And in the middle of the day you learn. At the end of the day you learn. You take a little supper. Then you go back to learn at night. You stay awake and you learn more. You sleep a little. You wake up, wake up like a lion, and do it again. You do this every day. You take no day off. Even you learn on vacation. Even you learn on *Shabbos*. You never stop."

"I understand, Rebbe. I want to do this. I have been poor a long time. I haven't had the chance to devote myself to learning like that.

I've had to work, and to work very hard. The learning I've picked up has been from the scraps of time I had, when I was already tired at the end of long days. I just want the chance... even if I could only have a year, just one year, free from any other worries... just to learn. If the Rabbis decide to make me a Jew, I have a scholarship to learn in yeshiva for a year. I want it very much."

Rabbi Greenblatt nodded, looking at me closely. He then looked down, as though considering the position of his hands in his lap. He closed his eyes, and as he did so he seemed to shrivel into himself. He was already small in the chair, sitting in his long black frock coat between the two larger rabbis on either side of him, but at that moment he seemed to grow even smaller. His head was almost completely covered in a large black yarmulke that stretched to his hair-sprouting ears. Thin spectacles rested on his nose, and his beard grew wild below his pink cheeks, wild and untrimmed except at the mustache.

He was breathing slowly with his head bowed, and for the briefest moment I felt that he might have fallen asleep—but that suspicion had no more than a fraction of a second to form as a complete thought before I knew that it was impossible, and that Rabbi Greenblatt was certainly not asleep, but was changing, and changing in a way that, despite the number of times that I have reflected on what followed, and the number of years I have had to consider it, I still struggle to describe.

347.

He looked up, looked up and our eyes met, and as they did I felt a tangible shift in the spacetime in which I existed. His eyes did not merely meet mine, they locked onto me, as though one ship had commandeered another with grappling hooks. My peripheral vision involuntarily disappeared. I could still see the two Rabbis Finkelstein on either side of him, but they appeared to have faded, or were somehow less present, as though Rabbi Greenblatt had jerked me from the movement of time as they were experiencing it, pulling me into a distorted time in which he and I alone existed, and could have been alone together for dozens of years, whilst only seconds would pass for the other two men in the room.

No longer was he the gentle, frail, old man who smiled and nodded and chuckled quietly. No longer was he the presence who seemed to move gingerly in the background of any room he entered, never seeming to project any sense of personhood in the way that all humans project something of their selves into the arena of whatever domain they occupy.

It was this negation of any projection of self that had always confused me in the year that I had known him. It was so subtle that one never consciously noticed it when with him. I recognized the absence of persona only when engaged in private reflection outside his physical proximity. The attempt to continue such contemplation in his presence invariably collapsed, as though by clandestine deployment of an invisible soporific he caused amnesia to drown the memory of those reflections.

I had no notion of how someone could have achieved such international renown, receiving queries for judgments on matters requiring a profound breadth of knowledge, wisdom, and the finesse of twinned psychological understanding and discretion so honed as to manifest particularly in the elegance of their simplicity—all the while projecting nothing of the manifold brilliance such jurisprudential erudition necessarily requires. I had seen flashes of some other person inhabiting that same body, who I knew to be the real Ephraim Greenblatt, but who, through steady, quiet waves of amnesia I would forget ever existed, remembering only the kindness and gentleness of a soft-spoken elderly man who seemed to emanate (though the very expression invokes paradox) non-Being.

But his eyes were locked onto mine, and as he looked into me, I realized that all of that which the world saw when they looked at him was artifice, a supreme *act*, the most perfect example of intentional self-restraint and constraint I had ever seen and am ever likely to see in my lifetime.

348.

Each of us knows well, though there is no scientific terminology that provides rigorous empirical language by which we may describe it, that there are persons possessed of far more *life-force* than others—some to such an extent that it noticeably impacts us, impresses itself on us, when we interact with them. It is unknown whether the characteristic arises primarily from genetics, from environmental and psychological factors, or from chance admixture of all three. The dearth of such life-force is a quality of those persons we term dull, phlegmatic, listless.

And I wish to say that this life-force is not synonymous with what we refer to as the *charismatic personality*, for many in possession of great life-force are not typically charismatic, but are rather introverted, while many charismatic persons are shallow, or simply histrionic, and lack this vital force. But again, persons possessed in significant measure of this *force* (for that strikes me as the best word to express this undefined concept) of personhood do exist, even if we cannot, at this time, describe the mechanism by which that force is generated, or why it varies in kind and degree and range to such an extent in the human population.

Nevertheless, each of us has had experiences where we feel that the raw vitality of another has overflowed from them into us, and that others notice this same characteristic in the person, and though it is not rigorously quantifiable, or verifiable, or testable, it does seem to exist non-subjectively. At times, it seems this force is so concentrated in an individual that they not only douse others with whom they come into contact, but that this dynamism inundates entire cities, nations, Ages.

As we know this from personal experience and common anecdote we know it too from history. The life-force of Napoleon, though encapsulated in a small frame, was so great as to overflow into all of Europe, moving millions. The historical record is instarred with persons who seemed to exercise such an effect on those who came into contact with them—even prior to or without an accession to political power. I refer you to examples as distant in space and time as Alcibiades, Hannibal, either Cato, Aurelian, da Vinci, Cesare Borgia, Swedenborg, Byron, Wagner, T. Roosevelt, Hamsun, Gandhi, and Wittgenstein.

Charles XII and Peter the Great provide perhaps the greatest historical example of a case in which there simultaneously existed two persons possessed of both absolute political power and that supreme dynamic life-force, and who were given the rare opportunity to use those gifts to dance in competition with a true peer—a dance that ended one empire and established another, rerouting European geopolitics for centuries and permanently altering the development of the West.

And as the eyes of Ephraim Greenblatt, the *true* Ephraim Greenblatt, locked onto me, jerking my consciousness into a different realm of perception, I realized that all that had passed before had been, as a matter of form, a test of the intellect, but that now I would be tested on entirely different grounds, and by a person of blindingly forceful Being, so that before I realized it, I felt he was viewing me from inside my own mind.

349.

"If you become Jewish you will live in a Jewish community always?" he asked me.

"Yes," I responded slowly, struggling to retain my view of the room, the chair beneath me, the other rabbis.

"If you become Jewish you will marry a Jewish person? You must never marry a non-Jew."

"I will only marry a Jewish person," I answered, though speaking verbally seemed strange, redundant, for I felt certain that he was with me in my mind, and that though we were speaking with words, the words existed as mere forms, and that those forms were crude, crumbling models that approximated our true conversation as a schoolboy's woodshop project resembles a cathedral.

"Do you want to become Jewish because of a woman, because there is someone you want to marry?"

"No," I answered. "I decided to become a Jew before I ever knew any Jews," I said, struggling to continue to see him, for by that point, not only had the use of words and sound begun to seem superfluous, but even my ability to visually see was rapidly fading. "I want to become a Jew because I believe it is right," I said, looking directly at Rabbi Greenblatt, whose face and eyes were the last things I could still *see*. The rest of the room, including the rabbis on either side of him, were not only no longer visible, I was no longer even aware of the existence of anything other than myself and the rabbi.

"Do you believe the words of the Torah with all of your heart and soul?" he asked me, though by that point I could not distinguish whether I had heard him audibly, or whether I had simply understood his question from within my mind.

"I do," I responded, and again, I no longer knew if I was speaking, for by then I had lost the ability to see Rabbi Greenblatt completely. I had completely broken with all normative, scientific, explicable sensory perception, and I knew that he still had one question left.

350.

Rabbi Greenblatt, it was rumored (and he once confirmed this to me verbally), was well-versed in the arcane mysticism known to the world as the Kabbalah, though what the bulk of humanity understands as the Kabbalah, through the frivolous pronouncements of non-Jewish celebrities, bears no resemblance to Kabbalah as it is practiced in Orthodox Judaism, where its serious study is heavily restricted, taught at most to a few dozens or hundreds of the most advanced and pious scholars in the world. This kabbalistic study has little or nothing to do with supernatural action, but is a complex system of theological postulates combined with a series of meditations that correlate to Jewish liturgy and the performance of various legal commandments. I easily admit that I cannot have knowledge of whether those esoteric studies and meditative exercises granted Rabbi Greenblatt awareness of, or direct access to, my mental states during that interview.

I have always been, since my break from fundamentalist Christianity, possessed of a tenacious skepticism when confronted with truth-claims for the supernatural, or for most categories of metaphysical claims. I give no credence to the ramblings of alleged wonder-workers. I discount entirely tales of anecdotal miracles, both current and historical.

Concerning the miracles in the Jewish tradition, such as Moses parting the sea, I realize that I can have no certain *knowledge* of the veracity of the claims concerning those events; in such matters one must rely on an unbroken chain of testimony, much as one relies on an unbroken chain of testimony for belief in the proposition that Constantinople fell in 1453. (Of course, *why* one would accept testimony-chains concerning supernatural events [miracles] *solely* in the case of Judaism or the Jewish scriptures rests on a prior set of arguments for the truth of the central tenets of Judaism, namely that there exists a deity, that he chose the Jews for a specific function on Earth, and that through Moses he revealed the Torah as the legal code whereby this function was to be effected.)

I am reasonably well-versed in the development of epistemological discussion since Descartes' original formulation of the problem of how one may possess certain knowledge of anything at all. I understand what is meant by *justified true belief*. I understand the distinction between knowledge *a priori* and empirical, experiential, sense-based knowledge. I understand Hume's crippling critique of induction. I can explicate the Gettier problem. I understand the nature of the serious skeptical problem conceived by Wittgenstein, and elucidated by Kripke, concerning what it means to *follow a rule*. I understand why it is different to say that something is *necessarily* true, or to say that it is necessarily true *in all possible worlds*, rather than to simply say that it is *true*.

I can articulate why there is a difference in kind between unverifiable claims made by a physicist who posits the probable position of an electron orbiting the nucleus of an atom, the declaration of an idealist who asserts that, "The Absolute enters into, but is itself incapable of, evolution and progress," or the fustian of a charlatan who says "the Nothing is prior to the Not and the Negation...."

In short, I find it very uncomfortable to state that I had an experience which I cannot explain purely through reference to normative sense-reception or the truths of science and formal logic. I suspect that most people, even those well versed in epistemology and logic (including atheists and agnostics), have had at least one personal experience that they simply cannot explain—experiences that, granting the incredible power of imagination, or worse, hallucination, do not seem, on sober reflection, to appear to have been the product of either imagination or hallucination, events which remain inexplicable. I can count on one hand the number of such experiences I have had in this life.

One of them occurred in that chair across from Rabbi Greenblatt.

351.

By the time Rabbi Greenblatt reached his last question, and I knew, though I don't know how I knew, that it was his last question, I had lost the ability to see or hear. I retained sensation, but what I felt was not the touch of the chair beneath me, the ground at my feet, or the temperature of the air.

I could no longer see, in the normative sense of the word, the office I was in, the three rabbis before me, or my own body. Rather than three people and a room, what I saw may best be described through the analogy of lightning. We imagine lightning moving from a cloud to the earth in the form of a jagged bolt. What I saw resembled electric current existing, not as a bolt, but as a spherical or elliptical semi-solid mass that was simultaneously spinning, rotating, collapsing, and reforming at speeds so fast the energy-ellipse maintained roughly constant shape and consistency.

There were three separate masses of this energy, where the three rabbis were seated, although the outer two seemed like pale, single sparks, and less like the solid sphere of energy that I recognized as Rabbi Greenblatt.

What had happened (or, depending on your view, what I merely believe I experienced) was that somehow (I could not begin to know how) Rabbi Greenblatt had, during his questioning, progressively pulled me from the world of normative sensation. I lost the ability to structure the sensation of reality my brain automatically generates as it interprets the electrical signals my senses involuntarily gather. I was still in the office, but, as I understood it, I perceived the office in such a way that my eyes, ears, nose, and other nerves were useless, but in which I continued to receive sensations.

Rabbi Greenblatt was conducting a radically different rabbinical hearing. He was not testing my knowledge or trying to determine if I possessed heretical beliefs. He was examining me from the inside, in the realm of the Spirit. A philosopher might say that he had gotten directly at the noumenal thing-in-itself.

So when he posed his last question, I did not feel that I had been verbally asked, but rather as though his awareness was burning into my brain, or as though that searing consciousness was not purely him, but that he was a funnel, a conduit by which the divine effluence moved.

"Will you love God, as it says in the Torah, with all of your heart, and soul, and resources?" he asked, and as he asked, I felt that he truly wanted to know, to know me, but also there still, inseparable from him, was that radiant loving-kindness, so that the question, and the strangeness of the experience, did not frighten me, any more than a child is frightened when a father asks his son for love.

And I do not know if I physically said yes, if there had been an audible question, or if the question and answer took place in my mind, but once I answered I felt him withdraw, and my vision returned. I was disoriented, as though I had suddenly stood after not eating for some time, but then I lapsed back into the normative cerebral functioning I had possessed only moments before, when questioned by the other two rabbis.

Rabbi Greenblatt leaned back in his chair, and once again I felt him, tangibly this time, draw back under the artifice of non-Being, to that illusion, to the role of the quiet, simple, kind, old man. And his immediate reorientation shocked me almost as much as did his ability to wade at will into my mind. The level of power, humility, and self-control required to cloak that capability frightened me. Many times in the years since I have reflected on how few people possessed of such power would have the desire, much less the ability, to hide it.

352.

However we may define humanity (even if one is a materialist and an atheist) we must surely assent to several propositions. There are important facets of *homo sapiens* not quantifiable or empirically describable with current scientific knowledge and technology. There has been no final resolution of the mind-body problem, nor do we possess more than a rudimentary understanding of the workings and micro-architecture of the human brain. Much about our genome remains unknown, and there are many other unanswered questions related to the biochemical workings of the human body.

We do not have a thorough understanding of normative consciousness, and certainly not of alternate forms of consciousness, such as the varied forms of seizure and hallucination, or of consciousness influenced by hallucinogens. We do not even understand much of simple sleep and dreams.

I do not doubt that Theresa de Ávila experienced a truth. I cannot know that what was captured in that perfection of Bernini was an authentic reception of the divine afflatus. I remain convinced that Christianity is certainly a crude parcel of dogma. Yet I do not believe that Spanish woman was in any way engaged in the production of fictions. I believe her. She experienced *something*.

I can have no knowledge of what occurred to me in that chair. I have considered the matter with a skeptical eye. It is obviously possible that I either hallucinated or experienced some sort of seizure. It is unlikely that I engaged in an extended daydream before three attentive judges. Likewise, had I suffered a hallucination or seizure it is most unlikely that they would not have commented on it, or stopped the interview.

The most probable materialist explanation is that I was so focused on the interview, and so emotionally invested in it, that when the final set of questions came, my attention increased to such an extent that all extraneous sensory information was voided, and my mind achieved extraordinary efficiency of focus on Rabbi Greenblatt's questions.

However, I cannot exclude the possibility that I did have an unusual experience. I cannot explain what happened in that chair any more than I can explain the incredibly improbable timing of the kiss that saved my life in my freshman year of high school. Concerning those rare occasions which appear inexplicable to even the most skeptical of us, I leave the final judgment to you, my reader.

353.

The rabbis asked me to exit the room, and I waited outside the office for several of the longest moments of my life. However, they quickly emerged, and congratulated me, for they had decided to convert me to Judaism.

At this point an additional rabbi was called to join us, and my earlier anxiety returned, for I realized this new rabbi was the *mohel*, the man who would take the ritual drop of blood from my penis.

The five of us then proceeded to the building outside the synagogue which functioned as the *mikveh*, and which housed not only the ritual pool of water, but also showers, changing rooms, and the balcony from which the rabbis would observe my immersion in the pool.

354.

When we got to the *mikveh* the three rabbis forming the court once more asked if I was certain I wanted to proceed. The first essential condition of the conversion, my acceptance of the authority of the Torah and the commandments, could have been repudiated, and I would have remained a gentile.

However, I assured them, despite my anxiety concerning what was about to happen, that I still very much wanted to convert. I then turned toward the *mohel*, who opened a small kit which I assumed contained knives and scissors.

I gulped.

355.

My *mohel*, the Chabad emissary to Tennessee, Rabbi Levi Klein, looked up at me and chuckled.

"Don't worry," he said, "this isn't the full operation. I'm only taking a drop."

"I know," I said, still nervous. "Have you ever done a full circumcision on an adult?" I asked, trying to distract myself from what was about to happen, waiting as he washed his hands and readied his equipment.

"No," he said. "We don't do that here in Memphis. The convert would have to go to New York for that."

"That's funny," I said. "I once intended to convert through Chabad, and they told me I would have had to go to New York."

"The emissaries of Chabad are like field agents," he replied. "Conversion is a specialty practice. Their concern lies more along the line of trying to help those already Jewish, but whose connection to *Yiddishkeit* has weakened."

"Yes, that's what I… learned," I said, faltering, for the rabbi had dropped to eye-level with my genitalia.

And while I cannot be certain of the exact locution, I believe I do accurately remember what next emerged from the rabbi's mouth.

"Please produce the *bris*," he intoned solemnly.

I began giggling uncontrollably. He looked up at me, startled.

"Are you sure you want to do this?" he asked. "This is your last chance to say no."

"No, no. I want to do it! I want to do it. I'm just nervous, that's all," I said, attempting to stifle the laughter provoked both by my extreme nervousness, and by the fact that in asking me to pull out my penis he had told me to *produce the bris*.

I can only ask you to imagine how you would have reacted if a man with a massive, untrimmed beard, dressed in a crisp suit, was at eye-level with your midsection, asking to see your penis with the intention of piercing it with a needle.

I unbuckled my pants and dropped my drawers, and, ladies and gentlemen, I am confident that my penis could not have been more tiny and shriveled had I, at that moment, suddenly emerged dripping from the waters of the Arctic. Nevertheless, the rabbi set to work.

He gripped my penis and quickly injected my manhood with a needle a millimeter in length, similar to the needle a diabetic uses to draw a drop of blood for a blood sugar test. The experience felt like the pinch one might experience from a minor zipper accident.

A drop or two of blood emerged from my penis, which he caught on a cloth. He placed an antiseptic pad over the spot and told me to hold it down and apply pressure. He then spoke with the rabbinical court, though I heard nothing, for I was concerned with the nature of the incision that had been made.

356.

Rabbi Joel told me I should undress completely, shower thoroughly in the *mikveh* building, remove my contact lenses, and then go through the door behind me, which was the door to the pool of the *mikveh* itself. I asked Rabbi Klein, as he was leaving, if my penis was alright. He assured me that it was already perfectly healed and sterile, wished me luck, and then left.

I showered quickly, and removed my contact lenses. I am essentially blind without corrective vision, so once my contact lenses were removed I found myself cold, damp, nude, and unable to see the door I was meant to walk through. It was a blur before me. I walked forward and felt for the doorknob.

I opened the door, and a smell, like the smell of a swimming pool, rose to my nostrils. I reached forward, and felt a banister guiding me down a series of steps into the waters of the *mikveh*. The water was surprisingly warm. I walked down into the middle of the pool. The water reached to the lower part of my chest.

"Do you understand what you are about to do?" Rabbi Joel called out from above me. I squinted, looking up, seeing three blurry shapes standing at the balcony above me. I could distinguish two dark shapes which were the suits of the two Rabbis Finklestein. Of Rabbi Greenblatt I could see nothing more than the puff of white that must have been his beard, but which, in my blindness, resembled a great cotton ball.

"Yes," I called up to him.

"Then we will ask you once again. Will you uphold the Torah of Moses, both the Written and the Oral Torah, and keep the commandments for the rest of your life?"

"I will."

"Please immerse yourself now. Make certain that you are completely submerged."

Then, with a great surge of emotion, I immersed myself in the waters for several seconds, and then rushed upwards to the air and light. I looked toward the rabbis, waiting for them to say something to me, to declare me a Jew, but they were busily chattering amongst themselves. I waited for a moment in total confusion.

"You must immerse again," Rabbi Joel called down. "You must make certain that you are completely immersed, including all of your hair. The water must completely surround your body."

"I should go now?" I called up uncertainly.

"Yes. Immerse now."

I expelled most of the air from my lungs, so as to drop further in the water, and then immersed in the waters, pulling my legs up away from the floor, and turning so as to be sure that I was fully submerged—and as I did so I noticed that I was in the fetal position, surrounded by fluid, and

I realized that I was a fetus in a womb, and that in the next second, an eternal second, when I rose from the waters, I would not be rising from a pool, but emerging from a womb, a newborn.

I rose from the waters, and as I did I heard all three rabbis shout, "Mazal Tov!"

357.

I had become a Jew. I have not a drop of Jewish ancestry, but I was suddenly a full, true member of the tribe, with a conversion that would be accepted in even the most stringent ultra-Orthodox communities in the world. When I had awoken that morning I was, despite my knowledge and theological beliefs, as much a gentile as anyone could be. When I emerged from the waters of that *mikveh* I was as Jewish as Moses.

I had pursued God with all of the faith and devotion of which I had been capable. The path had been difficult. But I had been found worthy. I had become one of the chosen people.

358.

The moments following my immersion were harried. I rose from the waters, dried, and quickly dressed. The rabbis needed me to make a *brocha*. I made the blessing as requested. I put on *tzitzit* for the first time, the ritual undershirt worn by all Jewish men, and made a blessing over that action as well. We returned from the *mikveh* to the synagogue, for the rabbis needed to write the *shtar* (legal document) declaring me a Jew, which would require all three of their signatures.

As we walked from the *mikveh* back to the synagogue I had the immediate, powerful sensation that my vision had radically changed. I have said that I can count on one hand the number of times in my life I have had a personal experience that I cannot adequately explain through reference to truths deducible from science or logic. On that one day I had two of those experiences.

The first was in that chair across from Rabbi Greenblatt. The second was the change in my vision. Everything I saw when I stepped out of that *mikveh* appeared more vivid. The greens of the trees were far more green. The condominiums that bordered that side of the synagogue appeared in incredible detail, and the colors were so much more rich as to provide an intense, but pleasant, impact on my central nervous system. I can best compare the experience to a case when one sees the split-frame comparison of a classic movie that has been restored, where, side-by-side, you simultaneously see the film pre-and-post restoration.

I have no explanation for how or why my vision appeared to change in this way. I immediately blinked several times, wondering if my imagination was overactive. I did not, on reflection, sense that this was due to imagination. I was emotional at the moment, but the emotion was one of solemnity and sanctity as opposed to wild euphoria. The fact that I immediately sought to explain the shift through logical reflection suggests that I was rational and oriented at the time.

But it was impossible to pretend that it wasn't happening. The only materialist explanations I can proffer are that I was overcome by emotion, or that I was hallucinating. Yet I have never hallucinated, and I have experienced many types of sudden trauma and unexpected bursts of euphoria in my life without experiencing any correlating alterations in sensory perception. Moreover this optical intensification continued indefinitely. I remember it continuing throughout that day and night, and the next, and the next, until I forgot what my previous vision had been like.

Did my corneas and retinas shift in form and structure? That seems impossible. I do not believe that occurred. I was never the theist who gave credence to quotidian miracles. I do not have an explanation for the cause of the experience.

As with any other occasion, and I believe there are only three in this book, in which I cannot explain, in any rational way, something that I have experienced, I leave the final judgment as to what truly occurred to you, the reader.

359.

In order to write out the *shtar* (contract) it was necessary that I choose a new Jewish name.

"Yosef Menachem," I said. "That is my new name."

"Yosef Menachem ben Avraham Avinu," Rabbi Ephraim corrected. "You are Yosef Menachem the son of Abraham our Father, and the son of Sarah our Mother. They are your parents now, your true parents. At times as a *ger* (convert) you may feel alone, but you must remember this... that your parents are the parents of us all. Your father Abraham was the first *ger*. Your father and mother provide you, the *ger*, with the greatest *yichus* (prestigious lineage) of any Jew."

"Did you know, when you chose your name, that *Menachem* would be on your *shtar* twice?" Rabbi Shai asked.

"Huh?"

"Your name is Yosef Menachem—it literally means, 'He (God) will add comfort.' And now it is *Menachem Av*, the time of comfort, and in only hours it will be *Shabbat Nachamu*, the Sabbath of Comfort."

"No, I didn't think about it," I said, confused, striving to cope with the disorienting blur of thoughts and emotions I was feeling, as well as the new vivid vision. I had chosen the name Yosef secretly, long before. I closely identified with the biblical character of Joseph due to the parallels in our early lives, and also because he had recognized his brothers long before they had recognized him.

"*Yosef* I knew," I said to Rabbi Shai, "but *Menachem* just came to me, from nowhere. I had been thinking of different possible second names for months. None of them felt comfortable. I hadn't considered Menachem at all—I don't know why. But when it came to me it felt right. I wasn't thinking about the time of the year. If anything I was thinking about the time of sorrow, about *Tisha b'Av*."

The rabbis exchanged strange looks, but then the document was written and signed and they handed it to me, with strict warnings never to lose it. Then they left, for the Sabbath would arrive in mere hours, and they had preparations to make.

My sponsoring rabbi then had me put on *tefillin*, and say several blessings for which he maintained that there were legal opinions for me to recite, even late in the day, long after the time they are normally recited. That was the first time I had put on the leather straps and prayer boxes, and, together with the *tzitzit* I felt a tremendous wave of validation. I knew that I would no longer feel so out of place in the morning prayers whenever guests came to our synagogue, staring at me strangely, asking if I needed to borrow their *tefillin*.

Then my rabbinic sponsor disappeared as well, and I was left with a new undershirt, *tefillin* bag, and a piece of paper that served as receipt of my permanently altered identity.

But I didn't have time to pause and reflect. I had to go back to the Gordons, where I would spend my last Sabbath in Memphis, and the sundown was quickly approaching. The Jewish day extends from sundown to sundown, and so though I was brought into the world as a Jew in the last hours of the fourteenth of *Av*, my first full day as a Jew was the Sabbath, *Parshas Va'eschanan, Shabbos Nachamu, Tu B'Av*, 5765.

360.

I dressed carefully, in my best clothes, aware that when I said blessings over things as trivial as taking a sip of water or using the restroom those blessing now counted, mattered, and that I was no longer trapped by the inescapable sense that I was riding coach on a theological flight that could crash any day.

I took a pre-Sabbath *l'chaim*, a shot of single-malt whiskey, with Mr. Gordon, and a certain Dr. Deanston, and did so for the first time not only man to man, but Jew to Jew. I drove to the synagogue for the first prayer service where I would count in the quorum of ten men that in Judaism is required to say many sections of the liturgy.

I arrived at the synagogue, and walked up to *every person there*, and introduced myself as though I had never seen them in my life.

"Hello, my name is Yosef Menachem. I'm pleased to meet you. What's your name?"

And this rather startled some of them, but others laughed, and introduced themselves, and everyone hugged me, for that congregation had shown me great love, looking with anticipation to the day that I would be one of them.

I prayed *Minchah* then, which is the afternoon prayer service. This was my first prayer service as a Jew. The sun began to set, marking the beginning of the Sabbath, and I prayed *Kabbolos Shabbos*, which is a series of mystical prayers and psalms containing an intricately interwoven layering of both simple and esoteric meanings; it is a means of welcoming the Sabbath, of preparing the heart and mind for the radical temporal shift in spirituality that Orthodox Jews believe occurs through multiple dimensions of the Jew's Being over the course of the Sabbath.

Finally, I prayed *Maariv*, the evening prayer, and then walked, still in something of a dream, to my evening meal. I had been invited to a celebratory dinner given in my honor. The hosts had asked if I desired any special dish. I told them there was no particular food I wanted, but specifically requested that the only wine available be a certain type of wine which, when opened, is rendered non-kosher if touched by gentiles. I had been through so many awkward instances in the previous year, asking people not to pass me the wine, that I took to inspecting each bottle prior to the meal. At meals attended by none but very uneducated Orthodox Jewish laymen this was necessary, as they not only would not have known that law, they may not even have known how to read the Hebrew disclaimer.

I think I may have become somewhat tipsy, as everyone wanted to make a *l'chaim* with me, but as I walked back to the Gordons' house I walked beneath a full moon, with a full heart and belly, thanking God with each step.

361.

I woke up the next morning and went to the synagogue to pray *Shacharis*, the morning service. It was the first morning I had awakened and put on *tzitzit* like every other Jewish man. I still didn't put on (and don't even today) the large woolen quilt I had seen the first time I walked into the synagogue, for that garment, the *tallis*, is worn, amongst the majority of Jews of European background, only after marriage.

I wondered, as we drew near the end of *Shacharis*, if I would get an *aliyah*, a call to read the Torah during the weekly communal reading. It is a great honor to receive an *aliyah*, and though I had never before been eligible, I wasn't sure that I would receive one, for though it was my first day as a Jew, I was now the most junior Jew in the world. Only eight *aliyos* are given each Sabbath. Five had passed, and I was growing nervous.

But then I heard my name, my new name, Yosef Menachem ben Avraham Avinu, called loudly from the front, at the podium in the center of synagogue, and I made my way forward, trembling. It was the section of the Torah known as *Va'eschanan*, which is divided into seven sections. I had been given the sixth *aliyah*, *shishi*, which contains the *Shema*, the most important line in the Torah, or in all of Judaism. That verse is the first prayer that any Jew is taught in life, and there are many Jews who have lived and died knowing nothing more of Judaism than that one line.

And so my first call to the Torah, on my very first day as a Jew, allowed me to receive the *aliyah* containing the foundation of all Judaism. I made a blessing, and then the *baal koreh*, the man responsible for chanting the scripture, began. It was the first time I had ever seen the inside of a Torah scroll, for though I had seen them held open each week in the synagogue, I had been too far away to see the Hebrew letters in any detail.

So as the *baal koreh* chanted the lines in a melody that has been handed down for centuries, or even millennia, the thing I noticed, as I followed the reading, was the tremendous physical beauty of the letters. The letters in a Torah scroll look nothing like Hebrew letters in a prayer book, or in any Israeli newspaper. The letters of a Torah scroll are written in an exquisite calligraphy, and certain letters are decorated with resplendent crowns. The effect was so overpowering that I felt my eyes water, and I struggled to control my emotions, for I did not want to shed tears on the parchment.

And then my *aliyah* was over. I made the concluding blessing, and as I finished I was struck in the back of the head, and the men standing near the podium ducked and ran. I turned to see what had struck me, and was buried under a hail of flying candy. All the Jews, both the men in their section and the women from theirs, had stood and were throwing all types of hard candies at me. They were laughing and cheering, and I began to laugh. And then the men came down from their section, and two of them grabbed my hands, and I was at the center of a quickly moving mass of men, hands joined, dancing around the podium in a flying circle.

It was then that I did cry, though I have never revealed that, for I was embarrassed of it at the time. But I choked back what I could, for I was closer to an outright bawling than I'd like to admit.

362.

After the Torah scroll was put away the *haftorah* was read—a scriptural portion from one of the books of the prophets. That Sabbath was *Shabbos Nachamu*, which refers to the *haftorah*, taken from Isaiah 40, which begins with the words "*Nachamu, nachamu!*" or "Comfort, comfort!" This section from the prophets is always read on the Sabbath following *Tisha b'Av*, making that Sabbath a tangible symbol of God's attribute of mercy overcoming his attribute of strict justice. It is true comfort following great sorrow.

That particular Sabbath was also *Tu b'Av*, or the fifteenth of the month of *Av*, which is a mysterious day in Judaism. It is known as a day of Love, a propitious day for finding a bride, and is mentioned in the Talmud tractate *Ta'anis*, which says that there are no days so joyous for the Jews as *Tu b'Av* and *Yom Kippur*—a strange declaration. In tractate *Bava Basra* the *Gemara* provides many reasons for this joy. *Tu b'Av* is the absolute antithesis of *Tisha b'Av*, providing joy in equal measure to the sorrow recently experienced.

Tu b'Av and *Shabbos Nachamu* do not always fall on the same day each year. I could not have picked, had I tried, a more perfect first day as a Jew.

363.

The Sabbath ended. I would have been content to rest in it forever, but soon, too soon, I stood with the congregation for the ceremony of *havdalah*, which marks the conclusion of the day.

After *havdalah* I said goodbye to everyone, and hugged them all. I was leaving Memphis, and had only a one-way ticket. I told them I never intended to leave Israel, and that if they were to see me again, it would be in Jerusalem.

That was a difficult parting, but there was adrenaline in it. I was fulfilling the second meaning of the word *aliyah*. It can mean a call up to read from the Torah scroll, but its higher meaning is to go up to live, permanently, in the Land of Israel, the dream of Jews scattered over the world in millennia past.

364.

That Saturday night I packed. I had sold what possessions I could. My truck had gone to my brother the week before. I had a full scholarship for one year, including room and board, to a yeshiva in Jerusalem, but the funds from the sale of the pickup truck were intended to purchase incidentals, and to assist me in the event of an emergency.

I finished packing late in the night. Everything I owned I would carry in two rolling suitcases. All other worldly wealth would be strapped to my body under my shirt in a money-vest.

I was leaving, with a one-way ticket, for a country to which I had never been, whose language I did not speak, whose culture I knew not at all. I had a new legal name, a new religion, and not an inkling of what I would find when I arrived.

I was petrified, but excited. Going to Zion is so powerful an idea it has become a cliché. But I was literally engaged in that grand metaphor. I would be gone in hours.

365.

I was on the plane, my bags stuffed in cargo, my *tefillin* in my carry-on, with some Jewish learning material to study on the connecting flight to New York. My entire life-savings was strapped beneath my shirt. I would land in New York, with a layover of several days, and would stay in the apartment of my friend Yosi, who had, at summer's end, moved from Memphis to Manhattan. I knew that a layover of a few days would be interesting, and would allow me to explore the greatest city of the West. I never intended to return, and knew I would never have another chance to visit that grand city.

I was leaving both Memphis, and everything and everyone I had ever known. I had never lived outside the South. Next was New York for a few days, and then Zion Eternal. The plane's engine started, and we began to taxi on the runway.

366.

It was as the plane began to lift off that I realized I had done the impossible. I write now from my thirtieth year, and even today view with disbelief the concatenation of near constant convolutions my life had taken by the time that plane left the ground in my twenty-second year. In only a few years I had emerged from the wreckage of my former life, the horrors of solitary confinement, potent first world poverty, traumas unnumbered and unbearable. I was a new man, with a new name, religion, and homeland. I had taken a life that was but ash, and had rebuilt myself anew, on more logical foundations than anything I had known in the South. It was not the plane that ascended. It was I, first Finis Leavell Beauchamp, then Yosef Menachem, rising like the phoenix.

367.

From the time that plane and my life arose, bearing me in an entirely new direction, a great many more strange adventures befell me. I should very much like to tell you of my life as a Jew, of my time in Jerusalem, of my travels throughout Israel and the Jewish world, of the varied Jewish communities with which I have interacted.

I assimilated quickly, and so in most cases I had the unique property of passing, chameleon-like, through those divers locations and dissimilar Jewish sub-cultures without anyone suspecting that I had already lived an entire life as a non-Jew, as one who had, for decades, never even met a Jew, and that in turn granted me access to many facets of Jewish culture and Judaism that are never discussed before gentiles.

Surely you must understand how strange is the story I have yet to tell. Unfortunately, for that I require an entirely new volume, as this meager history, of the man called Finis Leavell Beauchamp, is already far too long. There are too many new truths I will need to *show* you, but of course the most important of those is the Truth about the Jews.

368.

But all of these words are only susurrations in the interior maze and world of *saudade*. And we know too well how to translate that word. *Saudade* is the seeds of our most desired future spread out over the soil of our past.

369.

FINIS—FINIS NON EST

Book VII

Saudade

I searched for you
In Morning's wood.
Light, golden and
Soft as your hair,
Fell through the trees
Onto my face
In warm tresses.

Ambidextrous,
Light is supple,
Quite capable
Of deceiving,
Rendering blind
When clarity
Is most desired.

So through darkness
I learned of the
True violent
Catharsis that,
Trembling, is found
When, in its folds,
Bodies are bound.

Yet Darkness, louche,
Invidious,
Hides you fast with
Lithophanic
Duplicity.
Lachrymose blush—
Night's shameful trick.

Both Light and Dark
Have conspired to
Render our hearts
Twain. Desperate,
I will now search
In delicate
Shades of twilight.

❖

I pray now for
Amnesia.
To fall into
The hypnotic
Slumber, numbness,
Wisdom bought of
Forgetfulness.

Each plangent click
Deafens the ear
As the clock's hands
Incessantly
March to nowhere,
Tracking bits of
Infinity.

I lay on the
Bed, focusing
On the rhythm
Of my breathing,
Sleepless, silent,
Suffering your
Absence alone.

Calculations
Designed to thrust
Consciousness from
Me prove fruitless,
And I turn on
My side to ease
The ceaseless pain.

The Terrible Beauty of the Evil Man

I stagger by
Night, incondite,
Febriculose,
Noting the host
Of vagaries,
Susurrations,
Smoke of the moon.

Deliberate,
And then tell me
I was secure.
I did not know
I was merely
Dreaming, playing
The last lost man.

I should destroy
The hot fabric
Of dreams, the night's
Combat, silly
Misadventures,
All that kept me
From your caress.

Erotic plans
Come to nothing
If not grounded
In Love that gives.
True ardor learns
To relinquish
Furious lust.

Stark paradox
Suffuses Love.
Lambent desire
Pleasures, then scalds.
Sacrifice binds,
Tendresse instructs.
Two become one.

I search for you,
Though I stumble,
Bruised in the rough
Boskage of men.
Truth is oblique;
Many wrong paths
Narrow the way.

I search for you.

Finis Coronat Opus

Made in the USA
Lexington, KY
14 July 2014